# Paralegal Advanced Competency Exam

# PACE®

## Study Manual

**Seventh Edition - Revised**


Published by the National Federation of Paralegal Associations, Inc.
400 S. 4th St, Ste 754E
Minneapolis, MN 55415
(317) 454-8312
certifications@paralegals.org

AF703648

We are grateful for the opportunity to give examples from the following:

*Corpus Juris Secundum*, published by The West Group, St. Paul, Minnesota.

*Am. Jur. 2d*, published by The Lawyers Co-operative Publishing Company, Rochester, New York and Bancroft-Whitney Company, San Francisco, California.

*California Digest*, published by the West Group, St. Paul, Minnesota.



Distributed in the United States by the National
Federation of Paralegal Associations, Inc.
400 S. 4th St, Ste 754E
Minneapolis, MN 55415
(317)-454-8312
www.paralegals.org
certifications@paralegals.org

ISBN-13: 978-0-13-515078-8

**TABLE OF CONTENTS**

# Contents

CONTRIBUTORS ..... A

AN INTRODUCTION TO PACE® ..... i

10.00 EXECUTION OF CLIENT LEGAL MATTERS ..... 1

20.00 DEVELOPMENT OF CLIENT LEGAL MATTERS ..... 22

30.00 LEGAL RESEARCH AND WRITING ..... 88

40.00 OFFICE ADMINISTRATION ..... 169

50.00 BANKRUPTCY ..... 195

60.00 BUSINESS LAW ..... 209

70.00 AGREEMENTS AND CONTRACTS ..... 223

80.00 ETHICS ..... 233

90.00 FAMILY LAW ..... 256

100.00 INTELLECTUAL PROPERTY ..... 265

120.00 TECHNOLOGY IN THE LAW ..... 302

BIBLIOGRAPHY FOR FURTHER RESEARCH AND STUDY ..... B-1

GLOSSARY ..... G-1

APPENDIX ..... X-1

## CONTRIBUTORS

### Introduction

NFPA extends a thank you to each of the contributors of this updated PACE Review Manual, with a special acknowledgment to the hard work and dedication of the following contributors for the tireless and thankless job of coordinating all of the authors, proofing, editing and formatting of this final document.

*Kristen Baker, CRP®, OCP; Thersa Prater, RP®; Linda Odermott, RP®, OCP; Erin Ramil, CRP®, and Juanita "Nita" Serrano, RP®*

### 10.00 Execution of Client Legal Matters

**LORETTA NESBITT, RP®** is a graduate of Louisiana State University and received her paralegal certificate from the National Center for Paralegal Training. She is an RP® and a board-certified paralegal in civil trial law through the Texas Board of Legal Specialization. She is a past president of the Dallas Area Paralegal Association and has taught the online PACE® Review Course through AIPS for a number of years. Ms. Nesbitt has more than 20 years of experience as a litigation paralegal and is employed by Van Osselaer & Buchanan in Austin, TX.

**THOMAS C. HOLMES, RP®** has worked as a paralegal since 1983. He currently works for the law firm of Dunn Carney in Portland Oregon, concentrating on Land Use and Real Estate matters, Business Law and Administrative Law. Mr. Holmes served as president of the Oregon Paralegal Association (OPA) from 1995-1998 and previously served as OPA"s Primary Representative to the National Federation of Paralegal Associations and currently sits on OPA's Board of Directors as the NFPA Secondary Representative. Mr. Holmes previously sat on the NFPA Ethics Board and has presented several CLE programs. He graduated in 1979 from Vassar College with a B.S. in Psychology.

### 20.00 Development of Client Legal Matters

**LORETTA NESBITT, RP®,** previously described.

**THOMAS C. HOLMES, RP®,** previously described.

*With special thanks to Maggie Haase, RP® for updating the Intellectual Property portion of this Section.

**MARGARET HAASE, RP®** began her legal career in 1968 in Los Angeles at Paul, Hastings, Janofsky & Walker, working for Robert P. Hastings in the corporate department. In 1972, she moved to Hahn, Cazier, Hoegh & Leff, where she worked for Robert R. Thornton and was introduced to the intellectual property field. In 1975, she married Dennis B. Haase, a partner in the Hahn firm. In 1996, they relocated from California to Arkansas, where Ms. Haase obtained a certificate for attending University of Arkansas paralegal classes. In 2000, she passed the NFPA PACE® exam. In 2005, Ms. Haase completed a certification course for patent paralegals (based on the United States Patent and Trademark Office Manual of Examining Procedure) from IPLegalEd of Cupertino, CA, with an overall score of 99%.

Ms. Haase is a member of the Arkansas Paralegal Association, currently serving as the Treasurer and Primary Representative. She participated in the 2007 PACE® update and served as the co-host coordinator for the 2008 NFPA national convention.

## 30.00 Legal Research and Writing

**DORA J. L. DYE** has over 15 years of experience as a senior real estate and corporate paralegal in the San Francisco Bay area and 19 years of experience as a paralegal educator. She is currently the program coordinator and an instructor in the Paralegal/Legal Studies Program at City College of San Francisco. She holds a Bachelor of Arts in Spanish with distinction in general scholarship and a Master of Arts in Spanish from the University of California, Berkeley. She also holds and has a Master of Business Administration in international business with distinction from Armstrong University. Ms. Dye served as president of the San Francisco Paralegal Association in 1993 and 1994. She has been the listserv manager for the American Association for Paralegal Education since 1999 and serves currently as their Director of Associate Programs. Ms. Dye just completed a two-year term as a member of NFPA's Advisory Council.

**DAVID A. DYE** is Director of a character education program, Learning for Life. He has been involved in paralegal education for more than 25 years and is a founding member and past president of the American Association for Paralegal Education. He graduated from the University of Missouri at Kansas City School of Law and also holds an undergraduate degree from UMKC. The material presented in this chapter is adapted from the instructional notes and student workbooks that the authors have written for the courses that they teach. It has been reproduced here for the sole use of this PACE® Study Manual.

**CELIA C. ELWELL, RP®** has been a paralegal since 1984. She is a member of the Kansas Paralegal Association (KPA) and the National Federation of Paralegal Associations, Inc. (NFPA). Ms. Elwell passed PACE® in July 1999. She taught paralegal classes at the University of Oklahoma's Department of Legal Assistant Education for fifteen years. She is a co-author of *Practical Legal Writing for Legal Assistants* (West 1996) and was the legal research and writing columnist for *Legal Assistant Today* from 2002 to 2004. She has also published paralegal articles in the *National Paralegal Reporter®* and various paralegal newsletters. Ms. Elwell acknowledges with grateful thanks the permission of her co-author, Robert Barr Smith, Esquire, to include excerpts from their book in this presentation. Mr. Smith is the former Assistant Dean and Director of Legal Research and Writing of the University of Oklahoma College of Law in Oklahoma City, Oklahoma. Mr. Smith is currently an emeritus Professor of Law at UOCL, having retired from full-time teaching in 2008.

The National Federation of Paralegal Associations, Inc. acknowledges, with thanks, permission from Delmar Publishing to reproduce excerpts from *Practical Legal Writing for Legal Assistants* by Elwell and Smith. Delmar offers high-quality, practical and comprehensive, specific texts and resources for on-the-job reference. For further information on their publications, please write to West Publishing, College Division/Paralegal Series, 620 Opperman Drive, St. Paul, MN 55164-0779.

### 40.00 Office Administration

**LAURIE ROSELLE**, a graduate of Purdue University, holds a Master of Business Administration. Ms. Roselle is the President and CEO of Liniger's in Indianapolis. From 1986 – 2007, she was the director of legal services for Clifford Chance Rogers & Wells in New York City. She is a past president of the Legal Assistant Management Association. Her paralegal certificate was earned at the Institute for Paralegal Training.

**MARY McKAY, RP®, CP** has worked in the legal field for nearly 27 years, with extensive experience in commercial and civil litigation. She is employed as a paralegal coordinator and senior litigation paralegal at Glenn Rasmussen Fogarty & Hooker, P.A. in Tampa, Florida. Ms. McKay completed her paralegal studies at the University of Miami. For nine years following graduation, she taught paralegal studies at the University of Miami and at Miami-Dade Community College. She is a frequent seminar speaker both locally and nationally. In 2005, Ms. McKay was runner-up of *Legal Assistant Today's* Paralegal of the Year award. In 2007, she received *Legal Assistant Today's* Paralegal of the Year award. She is a member of the National Federation of Paralegal Associations and the National Association of Legal Assistants. Ms. McKay has served locally as Tampa Bay Paralegal Association's President, President-Elect, and First Vice President and as the NFPA liaison for TBPA. She presently serves as TBPA's PACE® Ambassador. From 2006 through 2009, Ms. McKay served on the national paralegal board as NFPA's Director of Region III.

### 50.00 Bankruptcy

**EDNA M. WALLACE, RP®** is a paralegal at Whitham, Hebenstreit & Zubek, LLP, Indianapolis, Indiana, where she works exclusively for Michael J. Hebenstreit, Chapter 7 Bankruptcy Panel Trustee. She holds a certificate from the American Institute of Paralegal Studies, where she was awarded highest honors for outstanding scholarship and academic excellence. Ms. Wallace has over 27 years of experience in the legal field. She is the NFPA Primary for the Indiana Paralegal Association, Inc. and is their Regulation Section Chair. Has also served as NFPA's Ethics and Professional Responsibility Coordinator.

### 60.00 Business Law

**DIANNA L. NOYES, RP®** graduated from California State University, Sacramento with a Bachelor of Arts in Criminal Justice. She received her paralegal certificate in 1992 through the University of California, Davis Legal Assistant Certificate program; and completed her M.S. degree in Legal Studies and Public Policy from California University, Pennsylvania in 2006. Ms. Noyes has worked for 19 years as a paralegal in the areas of family law, probate and estate planning, business and social security. In 2002, Ms. Noyes sat for and passed the Paralegal Advanced Competency Exam. She has served in numerous capacities on the Board of the Sacramento Valley Paralegal Association, as their Representative to NFPA for several terms, and is a lifetime member of SVPA. She served two terms on the NFPA Board as President and as Director – Region I. Ms. Noyes is a member of the Research Triangle

Park Paralegal Association, the American Association for Paralegal Education and the California Alliance of Paralegal Associations. She authored *The California Family Law Paralegal*, fourth edition presently under revision 2008; *The California Probate Paralegal* second edition in 2014; and two versions of the *Legal Research Scavenger Hunt Workbook* in 2009. She has been teaching Family Law for 21 years at MTI College in Sacramento, California; various courses for Kaplan University's online paralegal program; and Elder Law and Estates & Probate for California University, Pennsylvania. Ms. Noyes has been involved in curricula development, has written and taught CLE courses for Duke University, AIPS and other continuing education providers, and has been a frequent speaker on numerous topics.

**70.00 Agreements and Contracts**

**BETH MAGEE, RP®** is a Contract Administrator with Convex Group, Inc. in Atlanta, Georgia. In her current position, she reviews a variety of contracts in the media, investment and financing, corporate and mergers and acquisitions fields, among others. Ms. Magee is a member of the Georgia Association of Paralegals and received the GAP 2001 PACE Scholarship. In 2002, she took and passed the Paralegal Advanced Competency Exam. She volunteered on the PACE® Item Writing Committee in 2007. A GAP member since 1987, Ms. Magee has served as NFPA Primary and Secondary Representative, Newsletter Editor, PACE Ambassador, President and Public Relations Coordinator for the 1999 NFPA Mid-Year Convention. She has also served as NFPA's UPL Coordinator. Ms. Magee graduated from the University of North Carolina at Chapel Hill with a B.A. in Journalism and has a Certificate, with Honors, from the National Center for Paralegal Training, formerly in Atlanta.

**80.00 Ethics**

**SYBIL TAYLOR AYTCH, RP®, M.ED.** is a first-generation American and a native of New York City. She has extensive experience in complex litigation, antitrust law, commercial bankruptcy law, and trial preparation, specializing in litigation support, discovery management (including e-Discovery), trial technology, and project administration. Since 2000, Sybil has been the Senior Paralegal in the Commercial Bankruptcy, Restructuring and Creditors' Rights group at Quarles & Brady LLP in Phoenix, Arizona. Prior to moving to Phoenix, she was the Senior Specialist and Coordinator in the Corporate Restructuring group at Skadden, Arps, Slate, Meagher & Flom LLP in New York for 8 years.

Sybil holds a double bachelor's degree (B.A.) in French and English from Smith College in Northampton, Massachusetts and a master's degree (M.Ed.) in Educational Psychology from Northern Arizona University in Flagstaff, Arizona. She was also educated in Paris, France and earned a *Certificat en Littérature* in French Literature from l'Université de Paris- La Sorbonne and a *Certificat en Sciences Politiques* in International Law from l'Institut d'Études Politiques. She obtained the PACE Registered Paralegal credential in 1999.

Sybil has an extensive background in ethics. Since 2001, she has been an Adjunct Professor in the ABA-approved Paralegal Studies Program at Phoenix College where she teaches Ethics and Professional Practice, among other course; served on the NFPA Ethics Board from 2007-2010; co-author (with Therese A. Cannon) of *Ethics And Professional Responsibility For Paralegals* (8th ed. 2017) and *Concise Guide To Paralegal Ethics* (5th ed. 2018); served as a member of the ABA's Standing Commission on Paralegals Approval Commission 2004-2008 and continued as a Specially Designated Chair from 2008-2010.

She is a founding member of the Manhattan Paralegal Association (now the New York City Paralegal Association); an Item Writer and Exam Developer for the original PACE Exam and subsequently served on the PACE Standards Committee for 6 years. Sybil was the recipient of NFPA's *Outstanding Local Leadership Award* in 2002. She currently serves as the first Coordinator of NFPA's Diversity and Inclusion Committee. She is also a founding member of the Paralegal Division of the Maricopa County Bar Association in Phoenix, Arizona and served as its first President. In addition to two textbooks, she has authored numerous articles for various professional publications, including the *National Paralegal Reporter.*

* NFPA wishes to extend special thanks and acknowledgment for edits provided by the 2019 NFPA Ethics Committee chaired by Pamela Starr, CBA, J.S.M, MATD.

**90.00 Family Law**

**Cindy Welch, RP®** is the author of many articles for *The National Paralegal Reporter* and has written for the *Texas Paralegal Journal*. Over the years, Cindy has served her local association, the Dallas Area Paralegal Association (DAPA) in several elected and appointed positions as well as serving on the National Federation of Paralegal Associations (NFPA) Board. In addition to membership in NFPA and DAPA, Cindy has been a member of the Paralegal Division of the State Bar of Texas for many years.

After graduating from the University of Texas at Dallas with a B.S. in Business Administration, Cindy attended El Centro Community College for her paralegal certificate. Previously Cindy worked for a group of trial consultants as well as a national mediation and arbitration firm and at the time of publication she worked for the Law Office of Rhonda Cates in the areas of family law and labor and employment. She also spent 10 years as an instructor for paralegal students. Cindy became a PACE Registered Paralegal® in 2001.

**100.00 Intellectual Property**

**MARGARET (Maggie) HAASE, RP®**, previously described.

**110.00 Probate and Estate Planning**

**DIANNA L. NOYES, RP®**, previously described.

**120.00 Technology in the Law**

**Angela R. Hopson, RP®, IRP** is a Corporate Paralegal, with 21 years of experience, at Cummins Inc. in Indianapolis, Indiana, where she works in the Litigation and Labor and Employment Legal Functions. Mrs. Hopson graduated from the University of Indianapolis and earned an Associate's of Science degree in Legal Assistant (Paralegal Studies) and a

Bachelor of Arts degree in Political Science. She has a Human Resource Management Certificate from Indiana University-Purdue University at Indianapolis. She served the Indianapolis Law Librarians' Association as Secretary and Database Manager. Mrs. Hopson is a member of the Indianapolis Bar Association Paralegal Executive Committee and has served as Secretary, Committee Chair, Law Day Chairperson, and as an Ask-A-Lawyer Coordinator. She has been a member of the Indiana Paralegal Association ("IPA") since 1997 and is currently the Regulation Section Chair. She has served IPA as the Ethics Director, Database Manager, Job Bank Director, and IPA's National Federation of Paralegal Associations (NFPA) Primary and Secondary Representative Delegate. She has also assisted the NFPA as the Bar Association Coordinator and the Website Content Coordinator. Mrs. Hopson is an Indiana Registered Paralegal through the Indiana State Bar Association's Affiliate Membership Committee. She is a Certified Paralegal Trial Specialist and was a presenter at the Institute for Paralegal Education's (IPE) Trial Preparation from Start to Finish Seminar and spoke on Successful Techniques for Using Evidence and Exhibits in November of 2007 and again in October 2012. Mrs. Hopson was the Course Writer for Technology in the Law Office course, presented by Pearson Education in 2009. She was the co-recipient of the Paralegal of the Year award from the Indianapolis Bar Association in 2008, was named Paralegal of the Year from the Indiana Paralegal Association in 2011 and selected as an Indianapolis Bar Foundation's Distinguished Fellow in 2012. She is a Certified TrialDirector™ 6 Trainer and sat for and passed the Paralegal Advanced Competency Exam

## AN INTRODUCTION TO PACE®

### *The Paralegal Advanced Competency Exam History*

As an active and vital part of the legal service industry, the paralegal profession continues to evolve through regulation and voluntary certification, licensing of legal practitioners, and other means.

As a member-driven organization, the National Federation of Paralegal Associations (NFPA) is governed by its membership with each member association having one vote on issues impacting the organization and the profession through their delegate representatives. In 1994, the membership voted to develop an examination to test the competency level of experienced paralegals. Since that time, the delegates have approved a number of resolutions to ensure the certification remains relevant, current, and viable.

The decision to develop the Paralegal Advanced Competency Examination (PACE® or exam) was an effort to help guide the future of the paralegal profession by acknowledging the vital role paralegals play within the legal service industry; it was created in direct response to states considering regulating the paralegal profession and a method to measure paralegal competency. NFPA firmly believes in the eligibility criteria to take PACE®, but NFPA also recognizes that any state or governing agency may choose to use the exam and modify the criteria.

PACE® contains domains of general paralegal practice, ethics, and technology questions. Eligibility requirements for a paralegal to sit for PACE® include both work experience and education. In addition, there was a need for global grandfathering to allow experienced paralegals who did not initially meet the education requirements to sit for the exam. As a result, the eligibility requirements for PACE® include a grandfathering clause for paralegals who had four years of substantive paralegal experience on or before December 31, 2000. All other paralegals must meet the education and experience requirements outlined at https://www.paralegals.org/page/pace-pcce to be eligible to sit for PACE®.

The paralegal profession is, in general, bolstered when paralegals choose to take the exam for a number of reasons, including:

- The fair evaluation of the competencies of paralegals across a myriad of practice areas;
- A professional level of expertise by which all paralegals can be evaluated; and
- The paralegals who receive the PACE® Registered Paralegal (RP®) credentials after passing PACE® help to validate and add a level of professionalism to an industry that currently does not require industry standards or mandatory regulations.

While all eligible paralegals are encouraged to take PACE®, successful completion of the exam is not currently required by any state or bar association to be employed as a paralegal.

**TIP:** *If your application is approved after processing by NFPA, you will be designated as a "**candidate**." NFPA will then send you an Authorization to Test letter stating that you may now contact Prometric to schedule an appointment to take the exam.*

### Independent and Fair

Since the beginning, NFPA has consistently sought certification experts and psychometricians to validate and update PACE® to ensure the exam produces valid and verifiable results, while consistently issuing credentials to paralegals who demonstrate advanced problem solving and critical thinking skills, a measurable level of experience and knowledge, and paralegal competency.

PACE® was originally developed with the assistance of an independent examination development firm, Professional Examination Service Inc. (PES). PES was selected from a panel of submissions due to its more than 50 years of experience developing professional examinations for groups such as the Federal Reserve System, the National Association of Securities Dealers, Inc., the Environmental Protection Agency, and Emergency Medical Technicians and Paramedics.

PES developed PACE in conjunction with an independent task force of paralegals, paralegal educators, attorneys, and members of the public who assisted in every step, from the preparation of the initial job analysis for paralegals, to the creation of the exam and the ongoing revisions.

In 2017, NFPA began revising and updating PACE® in partnership with Prometric, a "Trusted Provider of Market Leading Test Development and Delivery Solutions." Because of Prometric's industry expertise, technology, testing systems, and networks, it brought convenience, security, and consistency to NFPA's exam process. Prometric has a proven, world-renowned track record in consistently providing Test Development and Delivery Solutions to global organizations and to millions of test takers, "making it easier for employers to hire the most qualified candidates; provide better opportunities for workforce populations; and foster a business environment of accountability." Again, NFPA brought in an independent task force of paralegals, paralegal educators, attorneys, and members of the public to assist with the review of the amended job analysis, question item writing and evaluation, and ongoing revisions.

To ensure the exam results remain valid and verifiable, the exam is administered independently by Prometric through its secure network of 8,000 test centers in more than 160 countries.

For more details about the processes and procedures related to the administration of the PACE®, see the NFPA *Policies and Procedure Section 11 – Paralegal Certification* found at www.paralegals.org.

**Requirements**

To satisfy the eligibility requirements, the applicant must meet one of the eligibility pathways through education and/or work experience. To avoid rejection of the Application to take PACE®, the applicant must be eligible according to the following criteria at the time the Application is submitted:

Experience and Education Criteria

- A minimum of four years of substantive paralegal experience obtained on or before December 31, 2000; OR
- An associate's (2-year) degree in paralegal studies obtained from an institutionally accredited **and/or** American Bar Association (ABA)-approved paralegal education program **and** at least 6 years of substantive paralegal experience; OR
- An associate's degree in any course of study obtained from an institutionally accredited school **or** ABA-approved program **and** at least 7 years of substantive paralegal experience; OR
- An associate's degree in any course of study obtained from an institutionally accredited school **or** ABA-approved program, successful completion of the PCCE, **and** 2 consecutive renewals of the CRP® credential; OR

- A bachelor's degree in any course of study from an institutionally accredited **or** ABA-approved school **and** at least 3 years of substantive paralegal experience; OR

- A bachelor's degree in paralegal studies from an institutionally accredited **or** ABA-approved school **and** at least 2 years of substantive paralegal experience; OR

- A member of the active duty, retired, former military, or the reserve component of any branch of the US Armed Forces, qualified in a military operation specialty with the rank of at least an E6 in a paralegal rate as a Staff Sergeant (Army and Marines), Petty Officer First Class (Navy), Technical Sergeant (Air Force), or higher as a supervisory paralegal within that branch of service **and** 12 hours of continuing legal education (CLE), including 1 CLE hour of ethics, within 2 years preceding the Application.

Degrees obtained outside the United States must be evaluated by a professional evaluation service for their equivalence to United States degrees. It is the responsibility of the applicant to pay any fees related to this type of review. Paralegal certificates obtained outside the United States must be evaluated by the Certification Standards Committee (Standards Committee).

A summary of education and substantive paralegal work experience criteria can be found at https://www.paralegals.org/page/pace-pcce. To determine if an educational program is ABA-approved, NFPA relies on the list of approved programs maintained on the ABA's website.

Documenting the Substantive Paralegal Work Experience Requirement

Before completing the Affidavit of Work Experience, the applicant should confirm their work experience meets one of the criteria described previously.

Minimum work experience is defined as full-time employment performing the duties of a paralegal at least 80% of the time. "Duties of a paralegal" is defined as the performance of substantive legal work that requires knowledge of legal concepts and is customarily, but not exclusively, performed by a lawyer. The paralegal may be contracted with or employed by a lawyer, law office, governmental agency, or other entity, or may be authorized by administrative, statutory, or court authority to perform this work. The required time period is calculated using the number of hours worked per week times the number of weeks, as verified by the employer.

A Sample Affidavit of Work Experience is included in the Application and Affidavit of Work Experience Section. The Affidavit must indicate the number of years worked, whether part time or full time (or the average number of hours worked each week), the specific dates of employment, the employer's name, and the name of the supervisor. Detailed instructions for completion of this Affidavit are included at https://www.paralegals.org/page/certification-applications.

**Substantive paralegal work experience must be verified by each employer (or previous employers, if necessary) by letter from the employer.** Each employer must verify the applicant's substantive paralegal experience (as defined above) and the time during which the work was performed. The "experience confirmation letters" must be on the employer's letterhead and specify dates, capacity of employment, and confirm the substantive paralegal experience. The individual or combined experience confirmation letters must equal the total experience required for the applicant's selected eligibility pathway.

The applicant must also submit a "letter of reference" from a member of the legal community, defined as a lawyer, judge, or RP® The letter must be on the individual's stationery and verify his/her knowledge of the applicant's substantive paralegal experience. The letter must state the number of years the individual has been familiar with the substantive paralegal work and detail the type of work the applicant performed.

The letter of reference and employer's letter verifying substantive paralegal work experience can be submitted as one letter, provided all of the required information is included. The letter should state that it is responding to both required eligibility requirements. A sample combined experience confirmation letter and letter of reference is included at https://www.paralegals.org/page/certification-applications.

Character and Fitness Requirements

Applicants applying to take PACE® may be disqualified based on character and fitness requirements for any one of the following reasons:

1. Conviction of a felony or comparable crime as defined by an individual state that does not have a felony designation; OR

2. Currently under suspension, termination, or revocation of a certificate, registration, or license to practice by a professional organization, court, disciplinary board, or agency in any jurisdiction; OR

3. Knowingly making a false statement or misrepresentation deemed material to the Application or Affidavit statement.

If an Application is denied for any of the reasons noted above, the applicant has the right to appeal.

Application Procedures

To submit an Application, applicants must submit the application through the Submittable Review Portal found on the NFPA website, www.paralegals.org, by following the link to apply for PACE®.

To access the Application, the applicant will need to create a login and password to log into the system by providing an email address (username) and password. If an applicant does not have an email address, once can be obtained via sites such as gmail.com, yahoo.com, hotmail.com, etc.

**TIP:** *If you are a member of NFPA or a member of a state or local paralegal association that is a member of NFPA, you should log into the NFPA website prior to starting the Application in Submittable.*

Applicants will create a user profile that includes their personal and contact information.

**TIP:** *The Submittable Review Portal is a separate portal from the NFPA website. You will need to create a unique login and password for use in the Submittable Review Portal. We recommend using a generic email address such as a Gmail account or yahoo, as some applicants have experienced access issues when they have used a work email address and then* *changed jobs suddenly, making access to the emails or notifications from Submittable inaccessible. This may also require the full deletion of an applicant's profile in order to recreate their account, causing delays in reviews or access to information. The name you use on your application* ***must*** *match the name that appears on the ID you will use as proof of identity to take the exam. You may only have one open application at any given time.*

Examination Content Outline, Development, and Composition

The NFPA website contains the exam specifications for PACE®. The specifications are the result of surveys of advanced level paralegals across the United States, initially verified by PES and later Prometric. These core activities cut across practice lines and are not state-specific. The skills were further verified by practicing paralegals, attorneys, and paralegal educators with guidance from the testing specialists at Prometric. Examination questions for PACE® were developed by practicing paralegals and other content specialists under the guidance of testing specialists from Prometric. **PACE® consists of 200 multiple-choice questions lasting no more than 4 hours.** PACE® sample questions can be found in this study manual. Each question has been vetted, verified, and the correct answer can be traced back to a widely available, reputable and verifiable source.

Scoring

PACE® is scored on a scale score. The scale is an arithmetic conversion of the raw score. Because PACE® has multiple exam forms, and the exam forms may vary slightly in their level of difficulty, the scale score is used to ensure the different forms have the same meaning.

The scale for PACE® ranges from 300 points to 700 points. **The passing score is 550 points.**

While the passing score of 550 does not change, the number of questions answered correctly to achieve a score of 550 can change. If the exam form contains questions assigned a lower point value, the candidate will be required to answer more questions correctly to achieve the 550 score. Conversely, if the exam form is more difficult, the candidate will be required to answer fewer questions correctly to achieve the 550 score. Candidates are not unfairly rewarded or penalized because the exam form was less challenging or more difficult.

The exams are periodically updated and the passing score and weighting of the questions is set with each new exam form. As previously stated, candidates are provided "instant results" of their examination at the Prometric Testing Center upon completion of the exam.

Passing the Exam

After a candidate has successfully passed PACE®, the candidate will receive a certificate from NFPA authorizing the use of the credential "PACE® Registered Paralegal" and the credentials "RP®" behind the candidate's name, in addition to the title of paralegal, legal assistant, etc.

Retaking PACE®

If the candidate fails the exam, the candidate is eligible to submit a new Application together with the fee no earlier than 6 months after the date of the failed examination. The applicant may also apply to waive the 6 month waiting period and retest at applicant's own risk, no earlier than 4 weeks after the original exam date, and before the next scheduled scoring run. The *Application to Waive the Six Month Waiting Period* is available at www.paralegals.org. The additional testing fees would be submitted at the applicant's own risk and no fees will be refunded.

If an applicant reapplies within 2 years of the date of the exam, there is no need to resubmit copies of the supporting documentation, however (effective October 2018), there is a limit of 3 attempts in any 2-year period to take the exam (*i.e.*, the initial attempt plus 2 retakes).

When completing and submitting a new Application, applicant must indicate they are retaking PACE® and must include the number of previous attempts and the dates thereof.

Maintenance of RP® Credential

To maintain the RP® credential, the RP® must complete 12 hours of NFPA-approved CLE in a legal or specialty field every 2 years from the date the exam was taken and successfully passed. At least 1 hour of the 12 required CLE hours must be in legal ethics. Dual credentialed paralegals in good standing, holding both the CRP® and the RP® credentials, may use the same CLE hours required in both renewal processes, so long as the hours are completed within the 2-year time period, according to their renewal date. *See* the RP®'s CLE requirements at www.paralegals.org (click on Renewing Your Credentials under Paralegal Certification). CLEs that exceed the 2 year time frame or are not NFPA-approved will not be accepted as part of the renewal.

**TIP:** *The deadline for submitting proof of completion of the required CLE credits is the 2-year anniversary from the date the exam was taken and passed – not the date the official results were received from NFPA.*

RP®s should plan to submit their renewal Application, statement, and CLE evidence approximately 60 days prior to the renewal deadline, but no more than 6 month in advance of the renewal date. NFPA will send a reminder to the email address on file from the RP® database prior to the renewal deadline. RP®s have an obligation to notify NFPA if RP®'s contact information (including e-mail address) changes to ensure that accurate information is maintained. Any changes can be sent by e-mail to certifications@paralegals.org. Failure to receive a reminder email from NFPA is not an excuse – calendaring this important renewal date is the responsibility of every RP®.

**Failure to receive a reminder email from NFPA will not be considered a justifiable reason for NFPA to approve a Request for Extension, nor will it prevent possible temporary or permanent suspension of the credential.**

Evidence of meeting the continuing education requirements must be submitted using the online *PACE® Renewal Application.* Proof of the completed CLE hours must be submitted for all NFPA-approved CLEs used to support the renewal Application. The certificate of completion or attendance must state: (1) it is approved by NFPA, a Bar Association, or other NFPA-approved provider, (2) the number of CLE hours awarded, (3) the type of CLE, and (4) the date of completion. For more details about the CLE requirements, see the NFPA website for the NFPA CLE guidelines at www.paralegals.org.

**DO NOT submit a CLE approval request and Renewal Application at the same time. DO NOT submit a non-NFPA approved CLE as supporting documentation without first having it approved by the NFPA CLE Coordinator.**

CLEs not pre-approved by one of the NFPA-approved organizations must be submitted to the NFPA CLE Coordinator first, together with the appropriate review fee. Once approved, the CLE Coordinator will provide a CLE Approval Certificate (CLE Certificate) that should be submitted in conjunction with the corresponding CLE Certificate in support of a Renewal Application. (*See* NFPA CLE guidelines at www.paralegals.org for more information).

The completed *Renewal Application* containing the Affidavit, supporting documentation, and the CLE Certificate(s) must all be submitted at one time to NFPA with the appropriate renewal fee. CLE approval requests must be submitted to the NFPA CLE Coordinator at least 90 days prior to the RP®'s renewal deadline to allow adequate time for the CLE Coordinator to review, approve, and provide a letter approving the CLE hours listed as part of the renewal. The CLE approval process must be completed in advance of submitting a completed Renewal Application.

An administrative fee must accompany a *Request for Extension* or *Request for a Retroactive Extension* and must include an explanation for the request to be reviewed by the Vice President and Director of Paralegal Certification. The administrative fee will be assessed as a late fee if the Renewal Application is not received prior to the renewal deadline and requires a retroactive extension request to the date of the missed renewal. *Requests for Extensions* or *Retroactive Extensions* exceeding 60 days must be reviewed by the Standards Committee and the accompanying administrative fee must be submitted in advance of the review. Questions about renewal of the RP® status should be directed to the Vice President and Director of Paralegal Certification in an e-mail to Certifications@paralegals.org. No *Extension Requests* may exceed six months in length, allowing for exceptions for active duty military deployment, extreme crisis, or family emergencies; subject to the review and approval by the Vice President and Director of Paralegal Certification.

**Suspension and Revocation**

The Standards Committee or its designee shall revoke or suspend the RP® credentials as described below.

The RP® credential shall be **suspended** for a period not longer than 60 days based upon any of the following:

1. Failure to file a *Renewal Application* by the renewal deadline;

2. Failure to meet CLE requirements by the renewal deadline; or

3. Failure to provide the appropriate evidence of continuing education by the renewal deadline; or

4. Failure to pay the renewal fees by the renewal deadline.

The RP® credential shall be **revoked** based upon any of the following:

1. Failure to renew the credential, complete the extension process within 2 months of the renewal date, **or** complete the required CLEs during a pre-approved "inactive status";

2. Knowingly making a false statement or misrepresentation deemed material to the Application, registration statement, or status of credentials or renewals;

3. Knowingly and intentionally disclosing any or all exam questions;

4. Suspension, termination, or revocation of a certification, registration, or license to practice by a professional organization, court, disciplinary board, or agency in any jurisdiction;

5. Conviction of a felony or comparable crime as defined by an individual state that does not have a felony designation;

6. Becoming the subject of a second suspension pursuant to Section 6 of the

Paralegal Certification Policies and Procedures.

With the exception of Item 1 above, the RP® credential shall be permanently revoked based upon the above stated reasons.

The Standards Committee will usually respond to all Requests for Appeals with an approval or denial decision within 15 days of the date the appeal is submitted, unless stated otherwise or more information is requested (10 days for the Standards Committee to review and deliberate and 5 days for transmissions to and from the appellant). Individuals do not have the right to appear in person, bring witnesses, or be represented by counsel. The Standards Committee is under no obligation to provide an analysis with their decision, but they may, if they choose to do so.

Final decisions issued by the Standards Committee may be appealed to the NFPA Board of Directors no later than 30 days after a final decision is issued by the Standards Committee.

However, should an individual's revocation be due to a failure to timely renew their credential, the individual **may** apply for a retroactive extension after the credentials have expired, but no later than six months after the credential renewal deadline has passed, by submitting an *Appeal Request* in the Submittable Platform, or via email to Certifications@paralegals.org. The *Appeal Request* must be made no later than 30 days from the date of the *Notice of Revocation* and must set forth justification for such an extension. The retroactive extension will be reviewed by the Standards Committee. Additional information or documentation may be requested by the Standards Committee, or its designee, in support of the *Request for Extension* or *Retroactive Extension*. The individual shall provide the requested information or documents within 30 days of the written request or the request will be denied.

Should any individual holder of an RP® credential fail to submit the appropriate renewal documentation or complete the retroactive extension process within the stated deadlines; **and** the individual's credentials have been revoked; **and** an appeal or Request for Extension is denied by the Standards Committee, said individual will be required to reapply to determine eligibility, retake, and pass the exam in order to have the RP® credential reinstated.

Should the Board of Directors uphold a denial by the Standards Committee, the individual has the right to submit a request for binding arbitration within 60 days of the date of the notice of denial of appeal. Requests for arbitration must be filed with the American Arbitration Association pursuant to its Commercial Arbitration Rules, along with the appropriate fee:

American Arbitration Association
701 Pike Street, Suite 950
Seattle, WA 98101
Telephone (206) 622-6435
Website: www.adr.org

For more detailed information on suspension and revocation procedures, contact the Vice President and Director of Paralegal Certification at Certifications@paralegals.org.

**Requests for Exceptions and Appeals Process**

Requests for exceptions or appeals of any of NFPA®'s certification policies should be submitted in writing using the appropriate appeal form or via email to the Director of Paralegal Certification at certifications@paralegals.org.

If an individual with suspended or revoked credentials is communicating with the intent to request an official appeal, the communication, whether in writing or via e-mail, they must state as such in the written communication. At the time of appeal request, the requesting individual must also provide all evidence that the Standards Committee and or the NFPA Board should consider.

The following exceptions and appeals will be reviewed by the Vice President and Director of Paralegal Certification:

- Renewal or Retroactive Extensions under 60 days.
- ADA Test Accommodation Requests.
- Waiver of Six Month Waiting Period to Retake the Exam.

If the individual is dissatisfied with the decision of the Vice President and Director of Paralegal Certification, the individual may request a review of the decision by the Standards Committee within 30 days from the date the Vice President and Director of Paralegal Certification renders an opinion. The Standards Committee's decision may also be appealed to the Board of Directors of NFPA within 30 days from the date the Standards Committee renders a decision.

The Standards Committee will usually respond to all Requests for Appeals with an approval or denial decision within 15 days of the date the appeal is submitted unless stated otherwise or more information is requested (10 days for the Standards Committee to review and deliberate and 5 days for transmissions to and from the appellant). The Standards Committee is under no obligation to provide an analysis with their decision, but they may, if they choose to do so.

The following exceptions and appeals will be reviewed by the Standards Committee:

- Appeals from candidates whose Applications to sit for exams are denied.
- Appeals from individuals whose certification has been revoked.
- Denials of requests for extensions.
- Renewal or retroactive extensions exceeding 60 days.
- Appeals from individuals whose renewal extension was denied.
- Requests for an Eligibility Criterion Exception.
- Requests to approve "Inactive" status for an RP in good standing for a period of up to 4 years.
- Requests for reactivation of an "Inactive" RP.
- Requests to approve "Emeritus" status of a paralegal who meet specific the Emeritus criteria.

The NFPA Board shall review any appeal of a Standards Committee decision at the next regularly scheduled Board of Directors meeting and respond to individual, in writing, within 10 days of such meeting. Individuals do not have the right to appear in person, bring witnesses, or be represented by counsel. The NFPA Board is under no obligation to provide an analysis with their decision, but they may, if they choose to do so.

Should the Board of Directors uphold a denial by the Standards Committee, the individual has the right to submit a request for binding arbitration within 60 days of the date of the notice of denial of appeal. Requests for arbitration must be filed with the American Arbitration Association pursuant to its Commercial Arbitration Rules, along with the appropriate fee:

American Arbitration Association
701 Pike Street, Suite 950
Seattle, WA 98101
Telephone (206) 622-6435
Website: www.adr.org

Arbitration forms and rules may also be obtained at the above address.

**Arbitration Clause**

Any controversy or claim arising out of or relating to the Application shall be settled by arbitration administered by the American Arbitration Association in accordance with its Commercial Arbitration Rules. Judgment upon the award rendered by the arbitrator may be entered in any court having jurisdiction thereof. Any such arbitration shall be conducted in Seattle, Washington, unless another place is selected by mutual agreement of the individual and the NFPA President.

The arbitrator will be selected from a panel of persons having experience with and knowledge of the U.S. legal system.

The scope of arbitration shall be limited to whether the individual is eligible to take PACE®.

| **Tasks in Domain I.**<br>***Execution of Client Legal Matters* – 26 Statements** |
|---|
| **Task Statements** |

1. Prepare binders for interviews with clients and depositions
2. Stay current on legal technology
3. Manage databases
4. File legal documents using the federal court electronic filing system
5. Update and maintain stock record databases for clients
6. Prepare stock certificates and maintain stock records
7. Prepare and oversee closing checklists
8. Order certificates of existence (or equivalent) and copies of corporate documents from appropriate state authority
9. Assist lawyers in preparation of SEC filings with regard to securities offerings and other dealings
10. Prepare for and attend transaction closings
11. Create and maintain data rooms for client due diligence and corporate documents
12. Compile and assemble documents and prepare closing index for closing books
13. Perform conflict checks; obtain detailed information about client and all adverse parties
14. Docket deadlines and reminders
15. Create and balance trust account ledger
16. Preparation and/or organization of electronic files
17. Draft engagement letters
18. Create and implement legal hold for data preservation
19. Prepare minute books, maintain corporate databases and file annual reports with state authority
20. Set up and configure logistics for hearings, trials and other official proceedings (may include electronic testing and set up before proceeding, confirming availability of certain electronics at venue, confirming training of location specific equipment, maintaining a hearing toolkit containing extension cords, tape, chargers, etc.)
21. Timely record documents and UCCs in proper jurisdictions
22. Based on acquisition and loan closing statements, confirm all closing funds are wired to or transferred to attorney's appropriate escrow account, prepare all disbursements and wire transfers, reconcile and balance funds, and coordinate disbursements and wires
23. Research and update contact information
24. Conduct background and criminal record checks
25. Take notes during hearings, meetings and other case related events
26. Perform all duties according to ABA and NFPA's ethical guidelines

| **Tasks in Domain II.** *Development of Client Legal Matters* **– 29 Statements** |
|---|
| **Task Statements** |

1. Obtain information about who the client is and who the adverse parties are for a particular case
2. Collect, manage, and preserve electronically stored information (ESI)
3. Act as a liaison between clients, counsel, courts, and other parties to disseminate Information
4. Attend organizational meetings with clients and/or lawyers to take instructions, obtain information, report on status of matters and recommended course of action
5. Communicate with clients and arranges the execution of relevant documents (*i.e.*, merger, change of corporate structure)
6. Obtain and complete requisite applications and corporate consents for business and not-for-profit corporations
7. Prepare capitalization tables
8. Develop protocols for data classification, collection and searching
9. Order title and trio reports and review accuracy of same
10. Prepare, identify and record real property documents such as deeds, liens, record abstracts, construction liens, and post recording notices
11. Review, analyze, select, and compile/organize key documents for use by attorney (may be used as exhibits or supportive documents for a number of documents/arguments)
12. Determine legal names of the party entities, send out initial conflict check to firm, document responses, and review any conflicts with attorney
13. Open files based on research of legal party entities and results of conflict check
14. Assist attorney with various pleadings and legal documents, prepare and review documents, prepare and attach exhibits, prepare final accounting documents as necessary for final submittal
15. Coordinate preparation of new surveys and provide instructions to surveyors
16. Coordinate title searches and document requests with title agents, vendors, and attorneys
17. Determine proper jurisdictions and coordinate lien searches with title attorneys and search companies
18. Request payoffs and other information regarding the bank's borrowers
19. Retrieve lien releases, surveys and other necessary documents from court records, clients, other firms and parties
20. Liaison with clients: assist clients and third parties with inquiries and document requests
21. Receive and discuss with attorney inquiries from outside firms on closing files and firm's clients
22. Consult with attorney on client needs, closing and title issues and problems, and any other matters necessary to his evaluation and attention
23. Prepare, file, and arrange to serve subpoenas
24. Prepare witnesses for testimony
25. Prepare for arbitration and mediation

26. Provide experts with necessary documents
27. Prepare living wills, health care proxies, durable powers of attorney
28. Organize client financial records to initiate will/trust preparation
29. Calculate federal and local estate taxes

| **Tasks in Domain III.** |
|---|
| ***Factual Legal Research and Writing* – 32 Statements** |
| **Task Statements** |

1. Conduct legal research and investigation
2. Interview clients and witnesses
3. Locate and interview expert witnesses
4. Conduct jury research
5. Determine best authority, primary and secondary sources, validate research for accuracy, apply legal research to client's particular matter
6. Review and keep abreast of changes to the Federal Rules of Civil Procedure
7. Review and keep abreast of changes to the Federal Rules of Evidence
8. Review changes to charter documents and other corporate documents
9. Drafting pleadings, correspondence, motions, discovery responses, and specialty-related documents
10. Analysis and summarization of legal research in proper legal memorandum form
11. Prepare factual summaries
12. Prepare deposition summaries
13. Prepare declarations and affidavits for attorney fees and costs, cost bills, assignment of judgments or claims, and judgments
14. Process requests for disclosure under the Freedom of Information Act (FOIA)
15. Work with lawyers to prepare all documents required to form corporations (both profit and nonprofit), limited liability companies, and any other type of business entity in any state
16. Review, summarize, and analyze corporate records, compile information, and recommend course of action to correct deficiencies
17. Assist lawyers with corporate reorganizations, share or asset purchase transactions, or tax reorganizations including the coordination of closing documents, searching status, filings, reports and other matters, summarizing search results, preparation of documents and checklists, and assisting with corporate due diligence
18. Prepare draft responses to auditor's requests for information
19. Assist lawyers in the preparation and filing of UCCs (including review of security documents to ascertain collateral description) and perform and review UCC search requests
20. Assist attorney with due diligence searches, including litigation, UCC, and corporate status searches
21. Review, organize and prepare responses to audit inquiries from clients
22. Perform litigation, UCC, and lien searches and review and summarize results
23. Review security agreements and prepare UCC financing statements
24. Prepare Articles/Certificates of Incorporation/Organization/Registration to form entities and/or assume business registrations in domestic and foreign jurisdictions
25. Prepare bylaws or LLC Agreements
26. Prepare resolutions/actions for varying types of transactions
27. Prepare Officer/Secretary/Incumbency Certificates and Guarantees for transactions
28. Prepare stock certificates and appropriate transfer documents

29. Prepare correspondence, escrow letters, closing documents (*i.e.*, deeds, mortgages, assignments, agreements, affidavits, guaranties, UCC financing statements, exhibits, satisfactions, terminations, amendments, and legal descriptions), closing binders, title insurance commitments and owner, loan and leasehold title insurance policies
30. Factual research and review of contracts, property titles, tax records, liens and encumbrances, easements, surveys, documents and other information for clients and closings
31. Prepare cover letters and deliver closing documents, title documents, final recorded documents and title policies to proper parties by firm messenger, iCloud or disk
32. Conversant with the Uniform Probate Code and the Uniform Trust Code

| **Tasks in Domain IV.**<br>***Office Administration*** **– 18 Statements** |
|---|
| **Task Statements** |

1. Apply ethical rules and concepts to practical situations
2. Keep up-to-date on technology needed to perform job (firm document saving system, iCloud programs, saving and manipulation of Adobe/pdf files and data, e-filing documents with courts, scanners, OCR programs, and other office equipment)
3. Keep abreast of law related to attorney's practice or of relevance to firm by taking webinars, receiving updates by subscription, reading legal literature and journals, and educate attorneys and/or general public
4. Track and maintain hours, both billable and non-billable, in a timely manner in accordance with policies
5. Open and maintain electronic and physical case files
6. Use document management systems to store and retrieve electronic files
7. Monitor and comply with court deadlines
8. Coordinate workflow
9. Maintain confidentiality
10. General knowledge in computer applications
11. Identify trial technology tools and implement tools at trial
12. Keep comprehensive list of attorney's client matters
13. Maintain calendar, contract deadlines, due diligence dates, and tickler items
14. Keep both paper copy client file and digital file current and complete by copying, scanning and organizing documents, faxes and emails, retaining any attorney handwritten notes, and storing any email communications in digital files
15. Prioritize workload and set deadlines
16. Manage and enlist legal assistants and office assistants to assist with administrative tasks
17. Review file, complete any needed tasks, organize before closing the file and returning to file room
18. Review and process vendor invoices

# 10.00 EXECUTION OF CLIENT LEGAL MATTERS

## *10.1 Conduct a conflicts check by reviewing client database and identifying potential conflicts to adhere to professional responsibility standards.*

A *conflict of interest* exists when a member of a legal team holds information about a client that, were it revealed to other members of the legal team, may cause some harm, injury, unfair advantage or prejudice to the client. As legal professionals, we want to avoid even the appearance of a conflict.

There are two very basic types of conflicts of interest. The first occurs when an attorney or paralegal has a personal interest that suggests less than complete energy and loyalty in representing the client. Examples of this type of *personal conflict* include being related either by family, friendship or business with parties adverse to the interests of the firm's client. Another example of *personal conflict* would be if husband and wife attorneys represented parties on opposite sides of the litigation. This conflict would be especially troublesome if the plaintiff and his attorney (Attorney A) had entered into a contingency fee agreement. As is typical, the defendant's attorney (Attorney B) is paid by the hour. One might question how diligent Attorney B would be when his spouse stands to gain substantial income if his client loses the lawsuit. A conflict of interest may even exist when you know a person named to a panel of potential jurors. Is that juror more likely to agree with your client's position and not give the other side a fair hearing?

The second type of conflict of interest occurs when present or past representation conflicts with representing a new or current client. An example of a potential *concurrent conflict* may involve the following scenario: You worked on the plaintiff side of *Smith vs. Jones* for the Able firm. You transfer to the Baker firm and are asked to work on the defense side of the same case. While working for the Able firm, you may have been privy to information that could now be used against the client of the Able firm.

Yet another potential conflict exists when a firm represents client A against adverse party B in one matter and then is asked to represent party B against former client A in a different matter. Potentially, the firm could use confidential information obtained in its representation of client A against that client in the subsequent matter. This type of potential conflict is thought to be *successive* in that once an attorney has represented someone, that attorney cannot represent another client who wishes to sue the former client. A related type of conflict of interest is *vicarious representation.* Under this theory, if one lawyer represents the client, all lawyers in the firm are treated as though they represent the client.

### *Screens, Ethical Walls, Cones of Silence and Consent*

Avoiding a conflict of interest or a potential conflict of interest in representing clients is one of the most important ethical aspects of a law practice. If a conflict does occur, there are ways to remedy the situation by erecting what is called an "ethical wall." Sometimes called a "screen" or a "cone of silence," an ethical wall is an imaginary boundary around an individual with a potential conflict of interest. The wall is designed to bar all communications between the members of the legal team handling the matter and that person. The ethical wall is created to avoid even the appearance of impropriety. By erecting ethical walls, paralegals and attorneys are not limited in their ability to obtain other jobs. Once a potential conflict of interest is determined, the client must consent to the continued representation. Procedures are then put into place for the creation of the ethical wall.

In a situation where a conflict is determined to exist, the first level of conflict management may be to simply exclude a paralegal or attorney from working on the case in any manner, or it might require that a full-fledged ethical wall be put in place. NFPA's model of how to construct an ethical wall includes:

- Warning all employees in the office about the importance of not sharing information;
- Disallowing those with confidential information from discussing the case or client with others in the office;
- Restricting access to files;
- Separating those working on the file from those with the conflict; and
- Notifying the affected client of the potential conflict.

See NFPA's Web site at www.paralegals.org for additional information on conflicts of interest and creating ethical walls.

*Notify Your Attorney*

Whenever you are aware that a potential conflict may exist, you must advise the supervising attorney immediately. The attorney will evaluate the potential conflict of interest.

*ABA Model Guideline 7* provides that paralegals take reasonable steps to prevent conflicts as if it were that of a lawyer. Canon 1.6 of the *NFPA Model Code of Ethics and Professional Responsibility* instructs paralegals to avoid conflicts of interest and disclose any possible conflicts to the lawyer, employer or client, depending on the employment situation. For more information, review *Canon 1.6, NFPA Model Code of Ethics and Professional Responsibility*, available online at www.paralegals.org.

- Ethical Consideration EC-1.6(d) instructs paralegals to create and maintain an effective record-keeping system that identifies (1) clients; (2) matters; and (3) parties with which the paralegal has worked.
- Ethical Consideration EC-1.6(e) allows the paralegal to reveal sufficient non-confidential information about a client or former client to reasonably ascertain if an actual or potential conflict exits.

*Conducting Conflicts Checks*

On a larger scale, a law office must maintain a database of names of clients and adverse parties from which to check for conflicts of interest. Various database programs exist that enable an office to check easily and accurately for potential conflicts of interest. Office policies and procedures must be in effect to check accurately for potential conflicts of interest prior to new representation and with each new case opened.

Office policies and procedures vary among offices and, therefore, will not be tested. It is nonetheless incumbent upon you to know the procedures in your place of employment. You should also know:

- what a conflicts check is;
- how a conflicts check affects the firm, its lawyers, its clients, its witnesses, your family and personal contacts and your business relationships;
- why a conflicts check is necessary (*i.e.*, preserving the attorney/client privilege, avoiding disqualification);
- when a conflicts check should be conducted;
- the ethical considerations behind a conflicts check;
- the paralegal's responsibility in a conflicts check (*i.e.*, keeping a log of past and present assignments and contacts, what to do when a potential conflict is discovered);
- the consequences should a conflicts check not be thoroughly conducted; and
- how to conduct a conflicts check by accessing a client database.

***10.02 Develop, organize and maintain a client file by categorizing documents, exhibits, evidence and/or other information to ensure proper organization and preservation.***

A wise teacher once commented that a *client file* is the backbone of the office. There are many effective ways to organize and maintain client files. First, you must be familiar with the area of law that relates to the particular file. Litigation files are organized differently than corporate files. Tax audit files are set up differently than adoption files, and so on. Moreover, one litigation file may be set up differently from another litigation file because of the issues involved.

Second, you must be familiar with a particular office's procedures for creating and maintaining client files. Consistency is the key in being able to locate documents quickly.

Third, you must be familiar with the manner in which a particular attorney wishes the files to be organized. Some attorneys prefer a "put it somewhere so we can find it when we need it" approach while some prefer to establish the organizational approach themselves. The critical element in all files is that they start out and stay organized.

*Organizing Case Files*

A consistent system of matter organization (as opposed to a system for the organization of one matter) is essential to a well-run law office or legal department. The system of organization may depend on the specialty area. For example, employment law matters may be organized by the plaintiff's last name, while litigation matters may be organized by case name, case matter or opposing party name. Bankruptcy matters may be identified by debtor's name. Whichever system, matter documents should be organized consistently.

There are various methods of organizing physical documents. The most common methods include organizing documents by source (person who provided the documentation), subject matter, in chronological order, witness name or by production order (these documents are typically *Bates-numbered* or control-numbered).

Regardless of whether documents are maintained by source, source information should be catalogued. While the manner of organization may vary, it is essential that your system of organization is consistent and that you are able to locate documents using your system of organization.

Ideally, every matter in your office should encompass the same basic structure. For example, all litigation matters should contain the following basic files:

- Correspondence;
- Billing Information;
- Memoranda;
- Court Documents (*e.g.*, pleadings);
- Discovery;
- Exhibits;
- Witness Files (Expert and Fact);
- Client Documents - Documents Collected; and
- Documents Produced.

Specific cases may require organization of medical records and literature, manufacturing specifications information or contract documents. The larger the file becomes, the greater the need for indexing documents in some fashion.

There are several effective ways to index. Correspondence and pleadings may be organized in simple, reverse chronological order with appropriate tabbing. Pleadings should be indexed with tabs for each pleading. Some pleadings files may be better organized by topic; for example, pleadings dealing with a motion to dismiss or a motion *in limine* may be filed together rather than chronologically. Some offices separate pleadings from discovery-related pleadings. Some offices maintain all pleadings in the same file.

*Developing and Maintaining Case Files*

Paralegals spend many hours developing and maintaining case (physical or digital) files through investigation, factual and legal research and document control tasks. Most tasks performed will eventually go into the case file (either the physical file or an electronic database). In this section, we will discuss the key tasks and files associated with the development of a client's legal file. You will note some overlap with the skills required to complete these tasks and the tasks in Domain 20.00 – Development of Client Legal Matters.

*Client Documents and Document Control Techniques*

At the onset of the case, and often throughout the course of the case, the paralegal will be asked to collect and control documents received from the client. As documents are being collected, it is important to use document control or tracking techniques to maintain the integrity and admissibility of the documentation. The source of the document should be identified and maintained. Source logs and/or source information sheets should be paper-clipped to the document. The log may also include investigation notes related to the document. Original documents should not be altered with handwritten notes or highlighting, staples or hole-punching. Once original documents are copied or scanned, the copies can be arranged in file folders, notebooks or on CD-ROM disks.

In cases involving more than a couple of inches of documents, it is good practice to establish a control numbering convention or system to help you track all documents. The system will depend on the case and perhaps office procedures. There may be a universal numbering convention (CON 000001…), or you might want to include information regarding your party or client (BCON 000001…for client Bruce). You may even want your numbering convention (*Bates-stamping* is popular) to identify the source of the document. No matter the system, you need to be able to look at the document number and know whether it is a control document or a document produced. The *Bates*/control number prefixes should not be the same.

In today's legal environment, vendors serving the legal community scan or OCR (Optical Character Recognition) documents into an electronic format for little more than the cost of the first copy. The electronic versions of paper documents can then be control or *Bates-numbered* electronically at a more reduced cost to the client. Having your documents in an electronic format also enables you to perform searches for key terms, review documents at a much faster speed and reduces having to manually handle documents as often.

*Client Documents and Document Collection Techniques*

In some cases, clients will be bringing relevant documents to the law office. Beforehand, discuss the process they should employ to collect the documents. Remind them of all the sources of documents available: employees, spouse, accountant, etc. and not to overlook electronic evidence stored on computers, hard drives, CD-ROMs or memory sticks. In business disputes, it is recommended that you (at the lawyer's direction) go out to the client's place of business to collect documents and see the business environment firsthand, determine the key players and be thorough.

*Preserving Evidence*

Amendments to Fed. R. Civ. P. 16, 26, 33, 34, 37 and 45 (effective December 2006) address the discovery of electronically stored information. We will discuss the amended rules in greater detail in Domain 20.00. *Electronically stored documents* include e-mails, attachments, spreadsheets, word processing documents and even documents that have been deleted. Electronically stored documents all have *metadata*, which is data hidden in the documents regarding such details as authors, editing times and digital file formats, *e.g.*, .xls.

Companies and their legal counsel have a duty to preserve relevant documents, whether in physical or digital form. The duty to preserve all relevant data begins as soon as there is a *reasonable anticipation* of litigation on a particular subject. The company or its lawyers must communicate the instruction NOT TO DESTROY documents or data related to the subject matter to all employees likely to have data or documents.

The ordinary operation of computer systems creates a risk that a party may lose discoverable documents. Fed. R. Civ. P. 37(f) provides a safe harbor that unless specific exceptionable circumstances are absent, sanctions are not imposed for a loss of electronically stored information resulting from *good faith operation* of electronic information systems. However, good faith includes a party's intervention to modify or suspend certain features to prevent the loss of information when a party has a duty to preserve the information because of "pending or reasonably anticipated litigation."

<u>*Developing Case Files through Investigation*</u>

You are often the chief investigator in the legal matter at hand. As an investigator, you must have a working knowledge of external resources, many of which are available online. These include:

- Court records (old and current, criminal and civil);
- Other federal and state governmental agencies, such as Department of Motor Vehicles or the Internal Revenue Service;
- Professional organizations and unions;
- County or state tax offices;
- Secretary of State offices;
- Hospitals and doctors;
- Public library;
- Colleges and universities;
- Banks;
- The client's employer, co-workers, family and friends; and
- Web sites on the Internet.

Investigate the opposing counsel/opposing party or witnesses (if lawyers) by using *Martindale Hubbell*, a listing of all law firms and practitioners organized by state and then city. *Martindale Hubbell* is contained in most law firm or law libraries and often in city or county public libraries. Free, limited information is available at www.martindale.com.

Today, information is literally at your fingertips via the personal computer. Familiarize yourself with the resources offered internally via your firm's computer databases. The legal research jump station on NFPA's home page at www.paralegals.org provides terrific research tools for legal and factual investigation. In addition to the online information available in your office or a local law library, determine what, if any, databases are maintained by your firm. For example, many firms maintain databases of information related to expert witnesses. This information will be helpful in obtaining or investigating an expert witness. Both internal and external resources result in additional leads and witnesses, all of which lend themselves to further investigation and additional witness interviews.

There is no area of work in a law office setting that excludes the necessary basic knowledge and practice of the English language. You must be able to read and understand the file information to organize and categorize it accurately and effectively. This effective organization must be accurately communicated to all who may need to retrieve information from the file. Organization of the client's file must be understood by more than one member of the legal team.

***10.03 Develop and maintain a calendar or "tickler" system by reviewing relevant authorities and procedures to identify events and deadlines.***

With the many deadlines occurring daily in a law office, a firm must have a scheduling system that ensures nothing is overlooked. The method used to keep track of all-important dates relating to a case is commonly called *docket control*.

It is critical that a legal team keep apprised of deadlines that, if missed, could lead to malpractice claims, disciplinary proceedings or damage to a firm's reputation. A good docket control system is also essential in maintaining good client relations. Missed deadlines are key issues raised in legal malpractice cases today. In many instances, paralegals are responsible for the day-to-day maintenance of a case, so a good working knowledge of docket control systems is essential.

A docket control system contains all trial dates, court appearances, hearing dates, deposition dates and filing deadlines for current cases. The characteristics of a thorough litigation system, for example, would:

- Provide immediate and automatic calendaring;
- Provide a double check of entries;
- Allow sufficient lead time for completion of tasks;
- Provide for follow-up to ensure the actual performance of work; and
- Be easy to maintain and operate.

Docket control, which can be either manual or computerized, consists of a calendaring system and a tickler system. If a computerized program is used, attorneys and staff should be encouraged to maintain a manual system as a backup in case of a computer failure. This also serves as a method of double-checking entries. Regardless of type, a docket control system is useful only when the information is accurate and timely.

While docket control is chiefly connected with litigation matters, you may need to establish a date or docket control system for "drop dead" dates in practice areas such as tax and regulatory law. Many legal software programs have built-in docket control features.

*Calendars and Tickler Systems*

Use electronic and/or manual calendars to assist you in meeting case deadlines. Most firms maintain a *master calendar* that contains trial dates, hearing dates and deposition dates for every attorney in the office, as well as key case deadlines. Its purpose is location of any attorney in an emergency, as well as for future scheduling. Microsoft Office's calendaring software can be used to maintain a simple master calendar. Specialized calendar and deadline software is also available. Master calendars vary in size and format, but the following information is always included:

- Attorney identification;
- Case name;
- Type of event (hearing, deposition, trial);
- Time; and
- Location.

Every person in the law office (attorneys, paralegals, legal assistants and support staff) may be responsible for providing information for the Master Calendar. Typically, only a designated person or group of people input and edit the calendar deadlines. In some law offices, information is forwarded to a docketing clerk for input into the system. The docketing clerk is also responsible for generating and distributing docket reports at regular intervals.

Law office personnel may maintain a *secondary calendar* in addition to a master calendar. This secondary calendar contains dates and times of appointments, conferences and personal reminders. Primary and secondary calendars are often combined into one. Constant communication among the team members is essential to keep everyone informed of changes and to maintain up-to-date calendars.

A *tickler system* is a method of controlling deadlines by using reminders. A tickler system can also be utilized for tracking verbal commitments. A tickler might be requested to remind a member of the legal team that a client has agreed to provide information by a certain date or that a presentation is due to be given. An attorney's or paralegal's unexpected illness is not a cause for concern if a tickler system is in place and kept up-to-date. The reminders are simply given to other attorneys for review and resolution.

Where a calendar entry requires only that a particular activity be noted once on all calendars, an entry that requires reminders or "*ticklers*" must be handled differently. How many reminders or how often an attorney or member of the legal team is to receive reminders is discretionary. Any number of reminders may be requested, depending upon the project, time constraints and circumstances of each case. It is not necessary, for example, to have more than one reminder when alerting team members of an opposing party's due date -- the action is that of the opposing party, not your team.

There must be a method in place so the docket clerk can differentiate between due dates of clients and opposing parties. Reminders may be given to one or all members of the legal team, but it is suggested that a minimum of two members receive reminders.

In today's legal environment, tickler systems are primarily computerized. There are many software programs available that have been written specifically for calendaring applications.

In the old days, we used a manual tickler system that was easy to set up and is still used by some today. This requires:

- A file card box at least 3 inches deep;
- One set of 3x5-inch monthly divider cards;
- Three sets of 3x5-inch daily divider cards, numbered 1 through 31;
- Three 3x5-inch yearly divider cards; and
- Tickler slips or 3x5-inch cards.

The monthly divider cards are placed in the box in sequence. The three sets of daily reminder cards are placed behind the current and the two following, monthly dividers. The yearly divider cards are placed behind the monthly dividers. Tickler forms are then placed appropriately.

The box is checked daily, and the ticklers for that day are removed and distributed. No tickler cards should remain when the current month ends. At that time, the daily divider cards are transferred to the month immediately following the ending month. The yearly index cards can be used for long-range dates, such as statutes of limitations.

*Docketing Systems*

Docketing is typically performed on a daily basis as documents are received in the mail. A docket information sheet is used by many law firms to facilitate entry of information into both calendar and tickler systems. Forms may be purchased from companies specializing in legal supplies, or law firms may design their own forms. The following information is usually contained in a docket information sheet:

- Name of requesting party;
- Responsible attorney;

- Name of case and/or file number;
- Action to be taken;
- Date, time and place; and
- Date event was docketed.

*Docket Meetings*

No matter the system used to remind us of court deadlines, someone needs to make sure the work gets done and the deadlines are met. As we know from Legal Ethics, the attorney is ultimately responsible to the client for ensuring work is performed in a timely manner. Some law offices hold regular weekly or bimonthly docket meetings. In larger firms, specialty practice sections may meet to review upcoming deadlines.

*Calculating Deadlines*

- In determining due dates, it is necessary to consider the *trigger date*. This is the date that starts the clock running. When days are counted to determine the due date of a document, the first day after the trigger date is day 1.
- The date of the act, event or default from which the time begins shall not be counted. In other words, start counting on the next day.
- Deadlines are calculated from the service date, not the filing date. The trigger date is the service date.
- When a party is served by mail, three days are added to any deadlines that follow. Service by mail is considered complete when mailed.
- The last day of the period is included in the calculation, unless it is a Saturday, Sunday or legal holiday. If you are filing a document, this rule also applies to days in which weather or other conditions have made the courthouse inaccessible.
- When the time period is fewer than eleven days, intermediate Saturdays, Sundays and legal holidays are not counted.
- Legal holidays are considered to be New Year's Day; Martin Luther King, Jr. Day; Presidents' Day; Memorial Day; Independence Day; Labor Day; Columbus Day; Veterans Day; Thanksgiving Day and Christmas Day; as well as state holidays and holidays enacted by Congress or declared by the President. When calculating deadlines, be sure to review the calendar.
- Be aware that more and more courts allow filing by fax and electronic means.

Review procedural and local rules for deadline information, including federal court rules (Fed. R. Civ. P. 6). Fed. R. Civ. P. *12(a)(1)(A)* states that the defendant's answer is due 20 days after service upon the defendant. Fed. R. Civ. P. 34 also provides that discovery responses, such as a request for production and request for admissions, are due 30 days after service unless otherwise ordered by the court.

### *10.04 Develop and maintain a client database by organizing and/or inputting information into selected categories to permit easy access.*

A *database* is an organized collection of related information. In the law office, a database can be used for a variety of reasons, but one of the most popular is the organization of client data. A *client database* can be constructed using spreadsheet software, specialized database management programs, or even using a word processing program (though while searchable, lacks sorting capability). Regardless of the manner in which a database is created, it is used to store information in a form that allows easy and quick sorting, indexing and retrieval. Examples of types of client databases include case management, conflict of interest checking, calendaring and litigation support.

There are numerous computer programs that support database design and assembly. The key in choosing a method lies in first deciding what is to be accomplished.

There are two types of computerized databases:

- Summary, which contain selected bits of information or fields of information; and
- Full-text, which contain the entire text of documents.

In today's legal office, databases often contain both summary and full-text (or image retrieval) databases. With the cost of imaging or scanning (taking a digital picture) and OCR -- which allows you to search for words at less than 20 cents per page -- it is more economical and cost effective to image and OCR all documents rather than have a copy made.

Some thought must also be given to system and hardware constraints. A summary-only database does not usually require more than a standard personal computer. The software is relatively inexpensive and does not demand much for data storage. The huge disadvantage of a summary-only database is that once you perform your search, you then have to manually locate, pull and copy the appropriate documents. This is not taking advantage of the relatively inexpensive imaging and OCR technology that is available today.

A *database file* is the database that contains all of the information, consisting of records and fields. *Fields* are pieces of information that can be abstracted such as client last name, address or telephone number. *Records* are groupings of fields.

A client database is made up of confidential information. Any chosen system must provide security to maintain the integrity of the records. This can be accomplished by using passwords and restricting access in terms of inputting and updating data. It is also important to remember that any reports generated from the client database contain confidential information and should not be disseminated outside of the firm.

*Combining Summary and Full-text*

Basic-to-Complicated Summary Databases

Simplistic databases are a good choice for some cases. However, if the case has any volume and the paralegal is going to need to use the database for preparing witness files, a second layer of sophistication will be useful. Keep in mind that you can search a witness name using the simplest full-text format; however, there is no sorting function. Therefore, after you search and pull up all documents related to a witness or term, you will have to print the documents and then manually sort them.

**Simple Full-Text Databases**

The simplest form of full-text database begins with loading the images and OCR text for viewing into a document-viewing software program such as IPRO. A legal services vendor can create an IPRO load file for you when the documents are imaged and assign numbers to the images. This very simplistic software allows you to see the document numbers and do simple searches, which is ideal for reviewing documents either by the paralegal or attorney. It is faster and therefore much more cost effective to review documents in electronic form, as opposed to reading paper copies.

**Detailed Full-Text Databases**

A detailed, full-text database, on the other hand, is more storage intensive, requiring a large hard disk or optical disk drive. More sophisticated software, such as Summation® and Concordance®, allows for sorting. For example, by creating a date field, you would be able to sort in date order. These programs sort by fields including date and provide a more sophisticated reporting system. These types of document management programs allow you to combine summary and full-text retrieval functions into one database and provide a sophisticated reporting system. However, you are going to have to manually code the summary information. A legal services vendor may also provide services that automatically populate basic fields, including the DATE and DOCTYPE fields. Because this is leading edge technology, you will have to proof and edit these fields.

Examples of basic summary database fields are:

- BEGDOC – The beginning *Bates*/control number;
- ENDDOC – the ending *Bates*/control number;
- DATE;
- DOCTYPE – letter, email, report, etc.;
- TITLE – the document title, first line or regarding "Re:" line; and

- OCR – You are not to manually code this field, but always include it as a field so that you can search the OCR. This field, like the BEGDOC and ENDDOC fields, can be automatically populated into the database by a legal services vendor who images and performs the OCR.

Software such as Summation and Concordance allows you to create any fields you would like in the database and amend your database if you discover additional fields are needed. The complexity of the case, case document volume and specific attorneys working on the project will dictate the fields you will want to include in the database. The more fields you have, the more expensive coding will be if you outsource it, and the more time-consuming coding will be for you if you choose to code in-house. In most cases, limiting the fields to only basic fields is good practice, economical and all that you will use. The combination of limited, basic fields and relying on the OCR text as your catchall to pick up names and key words is adequate for most cases.

Once the database fields have been determined, data can be entered. It is important to remember that the database is only as useful as the information is correct. Written guidelines should be established to ensure that both original and updated information is entered accurately and consistently. If possible, only one or two persons should be responsible for entering data.

Report generation can occur as soon as data has been input. If the database was created in a word processing program, reports can be assembled by selecting certain fields of interest and designing a template using the key fields, which would then be merged with the original database. For example, it would be easy to produce a report displaying a list of all clients residing in a certain geographical area, including name and address.

Litigation-specialized database software programs have built-in report writers that eliminate the need for creation of an additional document and the merge process. If a formal written report is not necessary, on-screen word searches can be performed to obtain necessary information.

<u>Web-Based Summary and Full-Text Databases</u>

The database systems we have been talking about are typically maintained on an individual, personal computer or an office network so that more than one person can access the documents and database. If you travel outside the office for a deposition, hearing or trial, you will have to download the database and its applications to a laptop. There are also situations where co-counsel or attorneys working on the case reside in different office locations, cities or states.

Technology vendors can also provide software and service to create Web-based summary and full-text databases that are at your fingertips anywhere there is Internet access. Of course, Web-based databases are more expensive than computer-based software, not only in setup but throughout the course of the case. Web-based databases require more vendor technical support throughout the life of the case. The paralegal typically will have less control over the system and database maintenance functions than the non-Web-based programs allow. Look out for possible $100 per hour technician charges every time documents are added, as well as the cost of service.

### *10.05 Coordinate events, activities and services related to client matters by using available resources to advance the client's goals and interests.*

Coordination of events in a law office is no less important than coordination of actions on the parallel bars is to a gymnast. You will coordinate many cases, even many types of cases over many time periods, whether within one day or over multiple years. Coordination is essential for the smooth running of both the case and your career.

*Personal Calendar*

Many tools aid the coordination of events, activities and services, but few do as much as a personal calendar. A successful calendar is the accumulation of all important events (deadlines, hearings, trials, etc.) for all cases. (*See* Section 10.03 for a discussion of calendaring.)
The successful calendar will include dates the paralegal and attorneys will be in and out of the office and dates for federal and state holidays. When courts publish a calendar of set hearing dates, these dates should be added to the calendar.

The form of the calendar is a personal choice. Some paralegals prefer a standard paper daily/weekly/monthly calendar, while others prefer a computerized version. Most authorities suggest that a computerized calendar be backed up with a hard copy of some sort, whether it is a printed copy or a standard, paper calendar.

Remember that, quite often, an attorney, paralegal or other member of the legal team will need access to calendar information while away from the office. It will be more efficient if that information can be portable, perhaps maintained in a pen and ink day planner, or on a portable computing device such as a laptop, handheld computer/PDA or even smartphone. Again, it is always important to keep these calendars up-to-date and synchronized with the office calendars. With electronic calendars, synchronization is usually part of the function of the calendar software.

*Prioritizing Work*

The next logical step is prioritizing the work for the upcoming events. Few of us doubt that this is easier said than done. As Deanna Jean Brown questioned in *Time Management for Paralegals*:

> How can you manage time when your time is not your own, when other people haven't done their homework, the computer is down, the courthouse didn't deliver, the client forgot to, well, what was that again? How do you know which of the squeaky wheels really needs the grease and which wheel is stuck and not making a sound but will be the first to fall apart? What a challenge!

While to-do lists may be ideal ways to utilize time, they are important in prioritizing what *must* be done over what only *may* be done, or what *must* get filed over what would be nice to get off the desk.

A successful calendar will assist the paralegal in prioritizing the first tasks to be approached. Factors to be considered in prioritizing will include which project has the most pressing deadline, which case has the most exposure and, at times, which attorney has the most seniority.

The experienced paralegal has discovered the best ways to prioritize tasks for his/her particular office, attorney or caseload. Calendar reminders and/or to do lists are essential tools of our trade.

*Checklists*

All paralegals are responsible to their employers and clients for proper management of their time, whether or not their time is actually billed to clients. Some paralegals are so disciplined and have their work so deeply and mentally ingrained that they keep on task without the need for lists, but most of us benefit in managing our time by making lists. With written checklists, there is less chance of letting any deadline or missing document fall through the cracks.

Some of these lists will be procedural checklists, or systems, for the routine tasks: what is necessary to file amended articles of incorporation with the secretary of state; how to prepare and file a motion for relief in bankruptcy court; how to prepare a witness and exhibit list; or what documents are necessary for administration of a will. Again, the routine details could fall through the cracks without a written checklist as the experienced paralegal may be caught up in the detail of the larger, more important tasks. It is also easier to delegate from a written list than from memory.

There are books of commercially prepared checklists, but the checklists that come from personal experience and from your own office are most beneficial. These checklists need to be kept where they can be referred to and accessed without hunting, and they need to be kept up-to-date with all court, rule and statute changes.

The key to good time management is self-discipline and a commitment to knowing that your work is important. Handling interruptions, fielding telephone calls and coping with changes in the calendar may be irritations, but they are all part of working in an office. Time management includes finding stress-handling mechanisms that work for you.

*Elements of Communication*

The coordination of events in a law office cannot occur without excellent written and oral *communication* amongst clients, the in-house team of attorneys, paralegals and staff colleagues, as well as the outside team of court and agency personnel, vendors, witnesses, etc. There is no area of work in a law office setting that excludes the necessary, basic knowledge and practice of the English language.

An experienced paralegal will accurately read, interpret and employ statutes and court rules relating to deadlines, trials, hearings and pleadings to be filed. Achieving good communication – verbal, listening and written – with outside resource personnel mandates a command of English to accurately and effectively convey one's needs and wishes.

Meeting with the client or sitting in on conferences in which the legal issues are discussed are both invaluable aids to good communication during a case or project and allows for accurate forecasting and projection of needs for the client and the case. Effectively reading the documents in a case, whether they are a municipal bond offering statement or an expert report, will also aid in good communication.

Another element in good communication is to know where to go to find answers to questions. This involves knowing what sources are available. Asking intelligent questions is essential in gaining the information needed.

Learn the expertise of your colleagues in the office. Many questions can be answered and cleared up without leaving the office. Make use of colleagues in your professional associations; many are willing to assist in providing answers and information.

Become familiar with the personnel in the court clerk offices and agencies in which you practice; they are a wealth of information. Simple Internet searches can also provide needed information.

Frequently, the experienced paralegal will be a negotiator in a case or project. It is only through a clear understanding of the issues in the case and clear and honest communication with another party that the negotiations will be carried out successfully. Good communication with the supervising attorney will allow you the ethical comfort level and authority to negotiate with another party in a project. When negotiating involves a legal opinion, it is essential that you refer the other party to the attorney in charge.

Hand in hand with good verbal and written communication skills are good computational skills. Many areas of law require basic -- not advanced -- mathematical skills. It is incumbent on the advanced paralegal that these skills be used effectively and without error.

To coordinate the events in a case effectively, it is paramount that you be familiar with the areas of law involved in the case. The experienced paralegal will have come to a working familiarity with the legal terminology involved in the cases and projects on which he/she works. Experienced paralegals will educate themselves in the different legal systems, statutes, rules and regulations involved in their projects: federal litigation, immigration requirements, probate statutes, adoption statutes, corporate filing requirements, etc.

The experienced paralegal will be up-to-speed on ethics issues involving client confidentiality, and what *not* to communicate. It is imperative that a client be able to trust the law office representing him/her to protect the case information from unwarranted disclosures. Paralegals know their ethical responsibility to maintain all client information as confidential.

Finally, the coordination of events in a case may require the location and access of sources both inside and outside the office. Experienced paralegals work continually to develop and maintain a network of these sources.

Internal sources may include the expertise of other colleagues, including attorneys, paralegals, secretaries, managers and the office library. Outside sources will vary widely and may include litigation support specialists, expert witness databases or subscription services, Internet access, foreign language interpreters, suppliers of frequently used forms, a trusted copy service, delivery service, court reporters (both local and out-of-area) and investigators. Paralegals are often asked to identify and evaluate outside services to perform tasks as part of furthering the case. They should become familiar with the kind of contracts that may be used to secure those services and how to evaluate them.

The operative verb in developing a list of resources is "network." One resource leads to another, which leads to yet another, and so on. Clients may need services offered by a financial counseling service, community health service or emergency shelter. The experienced paralegal will maintain a reference list of these various resources in the community. They also understand that this information must be updated periodically as service providers change and new resources are developed. When the need for a service provider becomes apparent (through client interview, document review or attorney request), you will already have the research done and the telephone number and name of a contact ready.

## SAMPLE QUESTIONS FOR EXECUTION OF CLIENT LEGAL MATTERS

1. If an ethical wall is established for a paralegal, that paralegal:

   a. is prohibited from working on a particular file.
   b. may perform work on a particular file but may not have direct client contact.
   c. may perform work on a particular file only under the supervision of an attorney.
   d. may perform work on a particular file if authorized by an attorney.

2. One method for expanding research after locating a relevant case is to:

   a. cartwheel to access a digest topic.
   b. check the state's annotated statutes.
   c. locate an on-point law review article.
   d. use a headnote to access a digest topic.

3. A document database consists of dates, facts, figures, etc., placed in a support structure -- a set of electronic records containing specific elements of information arranged in a structured format. The steps involved in organizing materials and planning data fields in the database allow for greater efficiency. A well-designed database will allow a paralegal to:

   a. use and reuse the same elements of information.
   b. locate expert witnesses in various fields.
   c. track press coverage about the client.
   d. check company financial statements.

4. To calculate a due date:

   a. start counting on the date the relevant document was received.
   b. do not count weekends.
   c. check local rules and statutes to determine the method used.
   d. count weekends.

5. Use of the Internet or inter-office e-mail to keep the legal team and client informed about the status of a matter:

   a. should be employed carefully with regard to client confidentiality, as such correspondence may become discoverable.
   b. is an economical, paperless method to achieve effective communication by avoiding use of the tickler system.
   c. may be disallowed by the courts for violation of the best evidence rule requiring original documents.
   d. may be unacceptable to the client due to the high cost of installation and maintenance.

6. A paralegal's firm represents a worker who is suing the manufacturer of wood scaffold plank. The worker fell when the scaffold plank broke. The paralegal is asked to prepare subject matter files to organize documents to be received from the defendant manufacturer. Which of the following subject matter files is the paralegal most likely to use?

   a. industry standards.
   b. medical records.
   c. board of directors' minutes.
   d. telephone records.

7. As part of maintaining a tickler system, the paralegal must read all local legal publications to review them for:

   a. changes in local court rules.
   b. possible client conflicts.
   c. calendar information for the relevant courts.
   d. legal notices that might impact clients.

8. A client conflict of interest check is conducted:

   a. after the initial consultation with the attorney.
   b. prior to the initial consultation with the attorney.
   c. after the client signs the representation agreement.
   d. prior to the filing of the law suit.

9. A type of the internal network system developed and used by paralegals to advance the client's matter include:

   a. court reporters.
   b. law librarian.
   c. expert witness.
   d. courtroom clerks.

10. Tracking documents with a specific code for easy retrieval is often referred to as:

   a. Bates-stamped.
   b. Endorsed filed.
   c. Specialized filing.
   d. Date stamped.

*Answers:*

1–a. Only option (a) will avoid a potential conflict of interest. A properly erected ethical wall should effectively and completely prevent the conflicted paralegal from having any contact with the file in question. The paralegal should have no more contact with the file than if he/she were not working in that office, which rules out options (b), (c) and (d) as possible answers.

2–d. Option (d) is the best answer because the digest topic is an inclusive source. A headnote is a summary of a portion of the court's opinion added by the editors of the reporter to assist the reader/researcher. Using the headnote to reach a digest topic may well lead you to options (b) and (c) state law or an on-point digest article cited in the digest. Cartwheeling is a brainstorming technique to help you think of a variety of synonyms and antonyms. Exhaust the digest topic resources before you turn to cartwheeling.

3–a. The purpose of the database is to use and re-use the same elements of information, which might include fields such as names of expert witness, articles published about the client and financial data. The best answer is option (a), which is all-inclusive.

4–c. Date calculations vary from court to court. It is imperative to check the local rules and statues to determine the appropriate calculating method.

5–a. To answer this question correctly, you must be alert to the ethical concept of client confidentiality. Option (b) is clearly incorrect because one never wants to avoid using a tickler system. Option (c) is not relevant to the question. While option (d) may or may not be correct, depending entirely upon the client (and therefore not testable), choosing option (a) reflects your awareness of the ethical pitfalls of using e-mail indiscriminately.

6–a. Use your critical thinking ability to answer this question. The documents are to be produced by a manufacturer of scaffolding. How much weight is scaffolding reasonably expected to hold? Is the defendant manufacturer meeting acceptable industry standards with its product, or was the product defective? You can best organize the documents by ascertaining what the industry standards *are* and organizing your files on that basis. Option (a) will help you more than options (b), (c) or (d).

7–c. To select the correct answer to this question, you must know the purpose of a tickler system, which is to remind people of important dates. Of the four options, only option (c) deals with dates.

8–b. A conflict of interest check is done prior to the client's first meeting or consultation with the attorney. That way, appropriate waivers can be obtained if necessary.

9–b. Internal network generally refers to those working within the law firm's setting, such as other paralegals, secretaries, paralegal managers, attorneys and the law firm's librarian. External network refers to vendors and others whose services you use to support your client.

10–a. *Bates-stamping* refers to assigning a specific code or number to a particular set of documents for easier tracking. For example, documents produced at a deposition will be marked by the court reporter one way; documents produced by an expert witness will be marked by another way; usually using a combination of letters and numbers that will make identification of the document easier.

# 20.00 DEVELOPMENT OF CLIENT LEGAL MATTERS

## *20.01 Interview a prospective client by obtaining relevant facts and information to assist in the determination of whether to offer legal representation.*

*Considerations for the Interview*

The purpose of a prospective *client interview* is to determine the prospective client's needs and to obtain facts and information that will assist the lawyer in determining whether to offer legal representation. The general purposes of the client interview are:

- To determine and sort facts between personal knowledge;
- To identify physical evidence;
- To locate leads for additional information;
- To determine remedies;
- To assess damages; and
- To evaluate the client as a witness.

A client interview may have additional, specific purposes. Determine the purpose of the interview -- what do you want to know? Communicate that purpose both to the attorney before the interview and to the client during the interview. Once the goals are set, prepare to conduct the interview and accomplish those goals.

Your role in the client interview will depend on the practice area, your experience and skill level and the attorney's practice habits. You may be asked to conduct the interview alone or to assist the attorney in conducting the interview. Regardless of your role, having the ability to listen is essential to effective interviewing. Listening is not only hearing. Effective listeners work at listening, resist distractions and judge content -- not delivery. Effective listeners interpret, follow body language and paraphrase to check for understanding. They do not let past experiences, bias, attitude or expectations of what will be said distract them from listening.

To conduct an effective interview, you must immediately gain the trust of the client and understand the client. Although every interview is unique, all clients have problems and are probably worried or upset over the circumstances surrounding the lawyer's representation. Approach each interview with an understanding that the client is in a crisis or stressful situation.

Communication is a two-way street. You must understand the client and the client must understand you. Modify your vocabulary to match the educational background of the client. Use key words the client will understand. Avoid legal jargon. Be alert for signals that the client does not understand something. If you do not understand industry terminology, ask questions. For example, in the oil industry, the term "Christmas tree" has a different meaning than that of a traditional Christmas tree.

Eliminate any behavior that may be considered to pressure the client. For example, avoid the traditional seating arrangement in which the paralegal sits behind a desk with the client on the other side, reinforcing the authority image. Instead, arrange the seats "catty-corner," using an end table or smaller desk. Act relaxed, not nervous. Maintain eye contact. Watch for facial and body language. Maintain a sincere, interested attitude. Let the client know you are on his/her side. Be thorough, leaving the impression that no stone has been left unturned.

During the course of the interview, determine the client's needs. What does the client expect, want or need?

Determine the client's financial resources, including, but not limited to, the client's ability to pay for services. Also, determine the client's non-monetary resources, such as experts or factual and investigative resources. What types of documents in the client's possession or control relate to the matter at hand? How many documents are there? Where are the documents located? If the documents are voluminous, determine the personnel resources of the client. How can the documents be copied? Are there personnel to assist in the collection of documents? If applicable, determine your client's access to industry information and experts.

Your ability to communicate in the client's native language is essential to performing successfully as a paralegal, particularly during the client interview. Prepare to have an interpreter on hand, if necessary. Correct relaying of information from the client to your attorney is a critical part of a paralegal's job.

*Prepare for the Interview*

Research the facts and the law. Read the file, including correspondence and client documents. Prepare a chronology and/or cast of characters to assist you in grasping the facts of the case. Understand the legal aspects of the case. Review the appropriate statutes, case law, etc.

Prepare an outline of the interview. Do not write every question. Use key words and leave space for note taking.

Determine what types of documents you would like the client to bring to the interview. Communicate your document wish list to the client, along with confirmation of the time, date and location of the interview. If there is time, follow any verbal communication with written communication.

*Conduct the Interview*

Use ice-breaking techniques to put the client at ease and conduct an effective interview. Offer the client a beverage. Talk "small talk" on the way to the conference room or location of the interview. Do not discuss case matters in the hallway or restrooms. This gives the appearance of a lack of confidentiality.

Conduct the interview in a confidential environment, such as a conference room, without interruption. The atmosphere must be professional and confidential. If you conduct the interview in your office, hold all calls, close the door and make sure that materials related to other cases are not in this client's view. If you are not careful with another client's materials, this client will not believe that his/her materials are now in and will remain in a confidential environment.

Do not ask difficult questions at the beginning of the interview. Do not alienate the client with blunt, direct questions.

To get the client talking and more relaxed, begin the interview with preliminary data and routine information such as addresses, telephone numbers, employment and educational information. Then, state the purpose of the interview. Begin the body of the interview with a narrative. Ask open-ended questions to encourage the client to narrate his/her story. Narrative questions begin with "Tell me about…" Get details later. An interview may be more productive after the client has been allowed to say what he/she wants to say.

Listen and watch while you interview. How is the client reacting to your questions? Listen for hints or leads to other information. Be flexible, not tied to your outline.

To avoid suggesting answers, ask non-leading questions such as who, what, when, where and how. Follow up on details after the narrative has been told. To insure that the client remains at ease during the interview, ask "why" questions carefully. "Why" questions sometimes evoke defensiveness. Rather than beginning questions with "why," try asking "What were your reasons?"

Ask questions using simple words. Focus on only one issue per question. Paraphrase the client's responses from time to time to check for understanding.

Explore judgment questions, such as time and distance, so that judgment statements do not trap the client. Role-play time and distance to insure the accuracy of the statements.

*Following the Interview*

Immediately following the interview, prepare a detailed summary memorandum. This summary should be in standard memorandum format, well-written and organized by subject matter rather than as a chronology of questions asked during the interview. Check spelling and use proper grammar. Details are essential. You are the eyes and ears of the attorney during the interview.

The summary memorandum must reflect all relevant details, including the date and time of the interview, documents collected during the interview, witness names, addresses and telephone numbers. It must also contain information on damages, detailed information concerning the client's knowledge of the facts related to the matter, leads to additional information and a to-do list that describes documents to be collected and investigation to be sought.

Central to performing well as a paralegal is the ability to write in clear, concise and grammatically correct English. Documents written by the paralegal are a permanent record of the paralegal's work product. You will be judged in terms of performance by your writing. Further, well-written and concise memoranda are easy reference pieces on which attorneys rely in preparing client matters, not only at the very beginning of the case, but usually up through the time of trial.

Most client matters take years (or at least months) to conclude, at which time the paralegals and attorneys working on the matter will have assisted in many other matters. The facts of a particular case may not be as easy to recall from your memory alone.

The summary memorandum is your record of information gained through the client interview and will be referenced regularly during development of the client matter. Information contained in the summary memorandum should be organized by subject matter so that facts may be gleaned from the memorandum at a glance.

*Engagement Letter*

It is customary, and generally required by attorneys' ethical rules, to prepare a letter to the client establishing the ground rules of service to the client. This may be called a representation letter or an engagement letter. This letter should include fees, billing rates, retainer information and an outline of the work to be performed. The attorney should discuss this letter with the client and answer any questions. After the attorney has discussed the agreement with the client, the letter should be countersigned and dated by the client and a fully-executed copy should then be provided to the client.

*Trust Account*

Trust accounts are special bank accounts maintained by attorneys in which client monies are deposited. Client retainers must be deposited into trust accounts until those monies are billed; they cannot be transferred to the attorney's account until they have been earned. Settlement checks are often deposited into client trust accounts and then appropriate amounts (typically minus attorney fees and expenses) are delivered to the client. Monies from client trust accounts may not be used by the attorney as general operating expenses for the use of the attorney. Misuse of client trust account monies may result in criminal or disciplinary proceedings against the attorney. Attorneys are required to keep a careful accounting of the trust account.

The term *retainer* refers to compensation paid in advance to a lawyer for services to be performed in a specific representation. A retainer may represent the entire sum to be charged (plus expenses), but more often is in the nature of a deposit to the attorney as an advance on the fees to be earned and costs advanced. The attorney must present, from time to time or at the conclusion of the matter, a statement of amounts owed by the client for services rendered. The amount of the retainer should be specified in the engagement letter. Again, client retainers must be deposited into trust accounts until those monies are billed; they cannot be transferred to the attorney's account until they have been earned.

*Privileges*

All jurisdictions have enacted statutes that address privileged communications arising out of certain relationships. These privileges grant the right to a designated person not to testify about or disclose a confidential communication. Statutes give certain persons the right to prevent others from testifying about or disclosing any confidential communication between them during the course of the specified relationship. The most common privileges include:

Attorney-Client Privilege

Confidential communications between an attorney and client during the course of their relationship are privileged and protected from discovery. A communication is confidential if it is not intended to be disclosed to third persons, other than those to whom disclosure is in furtherance of the rendition of professional legal services to the client, or those reasonably necessary for the transmission of the communication. Only the client has the privilege.

This privilege extends to representatives, agents and employees of the attorney, including paralegals in an in-house legal department. A specific federal rule concerning this privilege, as well as the others mentioned below, failed to be enacted by Congress. Federal Rule of Evidence 501 is, therefore, the sole rule regarding privilege.

The attorney must obtain all relevant information related to the matter to best represent the client and the client must feel secure that information given to the attorney will remain confidential. Canon 4 of the ABA Model Code of Professional Responsibility states: "A Lawyer Should Preserve the Confidences and Secrets of a Client." NFPA's Model Code of Ethics and Professional Responsibility and Guidelines for Enforcement states: "A paralegal shall preserve client confidences and privileged communications." Attorneys and paralegals are under a continuing obligation to preserve client confidences, even after the client matter is concluded or the paralegal is no longer employed by a firm or client.

Physician-Patient Privilege

The patient has this privilege against disclosure of confidential communications with the physician necessary for treatment of a medical condition. Some jurisdictions have eroded this privilege for exceptions related to driving while intoxicated or commitment proceedings. Be sure to check the court rules and applicable statutes.

Attorney Work Product

This privilege prevents the attorney from being forced to disclose certain information that the attorney obtains while preparing for a lawsuit. Federal Rule of Civil Procedure (Fed. R. Civ. P.) 26(b)(3) allows a party to obtain discovery of a document that was prepared in anticipation of litigation or for trial "only upon a showing that the party seeking discovery has a substantial need of the materials in the preparation of his case and that he is unable without undue hardship to obtain the substantial equivalent of the materials by other means." In order to qualify as attorney work-product, the material to be protected must be something tangible: a written record, a compilation of data or information, a drawing or diagram. It must also have been created or compiled by or for a party or by that party's representative. The information must have been created or compiled in anticipation of litigation or trial.

*Authorizations and Releases*

To effectively conduct a client interview and begin the development of a client matter, you must understand legal terminology such as representation letter, trust account, retainer, authorization and release. Medical, tax and employment authorizations for the release of records may be essential for the development of a client matter and should be obtained during the client interview.

An *authorization* is a signed statement authorizing someone, such as a doctor or employer, to give the attorney information that would otherwise be treated as confidential. An authorization may be called a release, which authorizes the release of materials that might otherwise be confidential.

Check your office policies and procedures before you conduct a client interview. Is there a standard client information sheet, medical release, employment release or form representation letter? Determine the attorney's or firm's procedures for opening a client matter, starting a new case or representing a new client. It is important to note that it is inappropriate to seek releases if the attorney will not be accepting the case, so be sure to check with the attorney first.

### *20.02 Analyze facts and information gathered from the client by using critical thinking skills, knowledge of law and experience to propose a course of action.*

*Gathering Facts*

You must quickly gain expert knowledge of the facts and information gathered from the client, not only by reviewing documentation but also through a detailed analysis of facts and information. The use of two simple forms of analysis (chronologies and summary memoranda) is appropriate in most matters.

The form used will depend on the facts of the matter. No matter the form, the analysis must be memorialized in writing and key facts should be easy to locate. Consider all resources available in the law firm or the corporate/governmental setting, including the use of databases.

You must know the law to propose a course of action for the matter. Key concepts discussed below include the recoverability of damages, the elements of a cause of action, the right to sue, the capacity to sue and statute of limitations.

The client is an obvious source of information (facts) and documentation. Assist the client in collecting relevant documentation by providing a written list of broad (rather than specific) subject matters needed to further the client's case. You should quickly gain a working knowledge of the client's working environment, particularly that of a corporate client and the potential sources of documents. Requests for documents should always be in writing so you have a complete record of documents requested and when they are due. Requests for documents should further specify that any documents related to the matter must not be altered or destroyed.

Changes in the Federal Rules of Civil Procedure have been made to clarify how electronically-stored information will be handled through discovery. Attorneys must now make sure that electronically-stored information that will be relevant to the litigation be maintained and not altered or destroyed. Fed. R. Civ. P. 26 has been changed to put a greater emphasis on the discovery planning conference, and, in particular, obligating the parties to meet and discuss electronically-stored information and how it will be handled in the discovery of the case (*See* Fed. R. Civ. P. 26(f)(3)). (*See* Legal Technology and the law for more details on E-discovery.)

As documents are being collected, it will be necessary to use document control or tracking techniques to maintain the dignity and admissibility of all documents. Original documents should not be altered with handwritten notes or highlighting. To the extent working copies are altered with notes and highlights, the words "working copy" should be clearly marked on the document. The source of the document should be identified and maintained. This may be done through a source log or source information sheet attached (paper clipped) to the document. The log could include investigation notes related to the document.

Your law office or law library will provide further internal resources for case investigation. Review related case files in your law office, particularly client document files. Review legal research files or databases of researched material so that you do not recreate the wheel by performing unnecessary legal research. Your computer provides many resources in investigating facts and the law. A simple search using one or more of these computer database services will provide newspaper or periodical articles referencing an individual or company, assets and liabilities of an individual or company entity, judgments against an individual or entity, names and addresses of company officers and directors, the last known address, telephone number and neighbors of an individual, and much more.

You are often the matter's chief investigator. As an investigator, you must have a working knowledge of external resources, many of which are available online. These resources include:

- Court records (old and current, criminal and civil);
- Other federal and state governmental agencies, such as Department of Motor Vehicles or the Internal Revenue Service;
- Professional organizations and unions;
- County or state tax offices;
- Secretary of State offices;
- Hospitals and doctors;
- Public library;
- Colleges and universities;
- Banks;

- The client's employer, co-workers, family and friends; and
- Web sites on the Internet.

Investigate opposing counsel or opposing party or witnesses (if lawyers) by using *Martindale Hubbell*, a listing of all law firms and practitioners organized by state and then city. *Martindale Hubbell* is contained in most law firm or law libraries and often in city or county public libraries. Free, limited information is available at www.martindale.com.

*Analysis*

Once the facts and information are gathered, begin to analyze the information. Your analysis must be communicated in writing so that you maintain a record of the communication and the analysis. Memorializing your analysis in writing (even though it may be clear in your mind) is essential for the proper development of a client matter. The specific written communication obviously depends on the facts being analyzed. Be flexible and imaginative in creating these communications. Know your resources, such as secretarial or word processing support and presentation and word processing software options.

Two very simple forms of analysis communication are the *chronology* and *cast of characters:*

A *chronology* is the organization or analysis of facts or events in date order. A simple chronology in chart or column form that specifies the event date, event description and information source is adequate for most client matters.

A *cast of characters* is an organizational tool wherein individual players are listed with a summary of his/her role in the matter. Players are typically listed in alphabetical order. A voluminous or complex matter might dictate preparation of a cast of characters in addition to a chronology.

Today, information is literally at your fingertips via the personal computer. Familiarize yourself with the resources offered via your firm's computer databases and information resources. The legal research "jumpstation" on NFPA's home page at www.paralegals.org provides terrific research tools for legal and factual investigation. In addition to the online information available in your office or a local law library, determine any databases maintained by your firm. For example, many firms maintain databases of information related to expert witnesses. Additionally, if you are a member of NFPA and/or a local paralegal organization, then you already know the benefits of obtaining/sharing expert information from/with your peers.

Use your computer to organize and sort relevant facts and documents by creating a database. Databases may contain documents collected, documents produced, deposition or trial exhibits and/or privileged documents. Discuss creating a database with the attorney early in the development of the client matter. Creating a database may initially be an expensive and time-consuming process, but it will more than pay for itself. In many cases, databases can be used to sort dates, witness names and types of documents.

Legal Analysis

To propose a successful course of action for the client, you must use critical thinking skills to identify interrelationships among cases, statutes, regulations and other legal authority as they relate to the facts of the case. You must be able to apply legal authority to a specific, factual situation and recognize when and why certain factual situations make it appropriate to apply exceptions to general legal rules. You must also be able to determine which areas of the law are relevant to a particular factual situation. These tasks are generally referred to as *legal analysis*. A common method is nicknamed "IRAC": Issue + Rule + Analysis = Conclusion.

- Locate a specific rule and quote that language exactly;
- State the major facts;
- State the legal issue by summarizing the controversy in terms of specific language in the rule and specific facts that raise the controversy;
- Draw the connection between the specific language in the rule and specific facts in the analysis; and
- Reach a conclusion based upon the above-referenced steps. Phrase the conclusion in terms of a rule.

You must be prepared to analyze case law. *Case law* is the body of law created by decisions of court judges from which your judge will interpret the rules of law to a particular set of case facts.

- Analyze court opinions with a clear understanding of the facts of your matter;
- Apply your facts to the court ruling or holding; and
- Search court opinions for code or issue references that relate to your matter. (*See* Domain 30.00, Factual and Legal Research.).

When analyzing statutory law, first take the *literal approach*. This approach assumes that the words used reflect the true intention of the legislature and that the legislature intended that the words used be interpreted in light of their common or ordinary meaning.

Then, take the *intrinsic approach*, looking at the overall structure of the legislation or the entire legislation. This might include the study of transcripts of hearings and floor debates to determine the true intent of the legislation.

The rules of analyzing statutory law include:

- *Rules of Construction* -- rules that control the judicial interpretation of statutes.

- *Plain Meaning Rule* -- the court will interpret a statute that is clear on its face as it reads or the literal interpretation.

- *Previous judicial interpretation* -- statutory interpretation made by a higher court is binding.

- *Legislative Intent* -- use legislative history, committee reports and hearing records.

Factual Analysis

The size and complexity of the client matter determine the types of factual analysis needed. In addition to analyzing court cases and statutes, you must analyze all facts. The following are examples of factual analysis:

- The chronology is efficiently prepared while you review matter documents, facts and witness statements. Chronologies are not limited to factual information. You may want to include allegations.

- A voluminous or complex matter might dictate preparation of a *cast of characters* in addition to a chronology.

- Create a timeline for case information. The style and format will vary depending on the matter.

- Create a case profile for your client matter, particularly if your matter is voluminous. This case profile should contain a brief summary of the case or matter and claims made by the parties. You may want to include key factual information and perhaps personal client information such as date of birth, social security number, etc.

The time-consuming task of reviewing documentation is virtually a waste of time if an *analysis memorandum* or *chronology* is not prepared. Analysis documents should be concise, well-written and organized by subject matter or chronology as appropriate. Use proper grammar and spelling. Use the spell-check feature of your computer. Proofread your written work product and, if possible, have another person proofread your written work product.

A *timeline* or *chronology* is most efficiently prepared during the course of reviewing facts and information. A record of the information source should be maintained to audit or compare dates and events via different sources. The timeline should include references from client documentation as well as court papers (such as allegations in a complaint).

*Causes of Action*

In determining whether a cause of action exists, you must review both the law and the facts of the matter. Not all damages suffered by an individual are recoverable through a judicial process.

A *legal right to recover* or right to relief must exist. This legal right to relief is known as a *cause of action.*

In addition to having the right to sue, the client must have the *legal capacity to sue. Legal capacity to sue* refers to the requirement that a person be of sound mind, lawful age and under no restraint or legal disability. An incompetent or minor does not have the capacity to sue in his/her own name.

In most states, a corporation does not have the capacity to sue unless it is registered to do business in that state. The Secretary of State's office in each state usually maintains a registry of entities such as corporations, partnerships and limited liability companies. Before bringing an action on behalf of a corporation or limited liability company, determine if the entity has complied with all state regulations relating to authority to do business.

A partnership, on the other hand, may sue in the names of all general partners or in the partnership's name. If the partnership's name is a fictitious name, however, the name must have been registered or filed under the Fictitious Names Act in the state where it does business. Check the state statutes for registration requirements.

A governmental entity may use its own name or under certain statutes bring an action on behalf of another. When you bring an action against a governmental entity, consider the *doctrine of sovereign immunity*, which basically exempts federal, state and municipal agencies, as well as their political subdivisions, of liability resulting from injury or damages arising out of the exercise of governmental duties such as construction of public roads or responding to 911 emergency calls. Review state statutes to determine if consent statutes exist that set a procedure for filing an action against a governmental entity.

Determine the elements of the cause of action by legal research. Identification of the elements of the cause of action is essential in the development of a client matter. For example, determining the elements of the cause of action in a litigation matter is important in that each element must be satisfied to win the case. Once you determine the elements of the cause of action, use logic or analysis to compare the facts of your matter in accordance with the legal elements of the cause of action.

The same kind of analysis is done when defending a client against a claim. The elements of the cause of action will be compared with the facts alleged by the claiming party and then with the defendant client's version of the facts. The goal is to find a legally justifiable reason for the defendant's actions, to refute the alleged facts that are the basis for the claim or to develop the facts to show that the situation is not one in which a cause of action truly arises.

### Statutes of Limitation

Even though the elements of a cause of action may exist, the law imposes time limits in which to initiate actions. Paralegals must be aware of these time limits, known as statutes of limitation.

Unless a matter is filed or acted upon within a certain time limit, it will be dismissed regardless of the merits of the matter.

Paralegals must be able to determine and calculate the appropriate statute of limitation. For example, civil actions against the United States of America are barred (prohibited) unless filed within six years after the right of action first accrues pursuant to 28 U.S.C. § 2401(a), whereas a tort claim against the United States must be presented in writing to the appropriate federal agency within two years after the claim accrues. Statutes of limitation as to torts and most contract law are defined by state statute.

*Organization of Client Matters*

A consistent system of matter organization (as opposed to a system for the organization of one matter) is essential to a well-run law office or legal department. The system of organization may depend on specialty area. For example, employment law matters may be organized by the plaintiff's last name, while litigation matters may be organized by case style or opposing party's name. Bankruptcy matters may be organized by debtor's name. Within the system, matter documents should be organized consistently.

The method of physical organization of matter documentation may vary. The most common methods include:

- Organizing documents by source (person who provided the documentation);
- Subject matter;
- In chronological order;
- Witness name; or
- By production order.

Documents compiled for use in the matter are typically number-labeled sequentially so that they may be indexed and easily retrieved. *Bates-numbering* refers to an old method of marking documents using a number stamping machine and the term has survived.

Regardless of whether documents are maintained by source, source information should be catalogued. While the manner of organization may vary, it is essential that your system of organization is consistent and that you are able to locate documents using your system.

Ideally, every matter in your office should encompass the same basic structure. For example, all litigation matters should contain the following basic files:

- Correspondence;
- Billing Information;
- Memoranda;

- Court Documents (*e.g.*, pleadings);
- Discovery;
- Exhibits;
- Witnesses;
- Documents Collected; and
- Documents Produced.

*Information from the Client*

There are many ways to summarize information collected from the client. Your task is to organize and summarize this information in a user-friendly fashion. Choose a system of organization that allows you to easily and quickly locate documents relative to date, witness name and subject matter. As you are structuring your database, begin with the end in mind (*i.e.*, how you will use the database). Corel WordPerfect and Microsoft Word are word processing tools that offer limited sorting capabilities. Obtain input from the attorney regarding the database structure.

As you review documents, summarize them in the form of chronologies or cast of characters. Summarize documentation as simply as possible, and be consistent. Typically, date, witness name and subject matter are all that is needed in a summary.

Computers assist in synthesizing information by way of databases and less complicated word processing and sorting tools. Regardless of the size of the matter, you will need some type of computer software. Become familiar with all types of computer tools that are available to you. The Technology section of this Manual discusses several programs to assist you in various areas of practice.

Technology has made imaging -- or creating digital images of documents for storage -- commonplace in many law firms and corporate environments. Check with numerous vendors to stay current on the latest technology. Where imaging is concerned, be certain that your equipment can handle the software and that your printers are prepared to handle the volume of documents.

*Information to the Client*

Once your factual investigation is underway (and it is never really complete until the conclusion of the matter) and a good portion of the facts is gathered and organized, you and the attorney should begin to identify options and alternatives for the client. For example, the alternative to litigation is settlement or disposition of the matter. Alternative Dispute Resolution such as arbitration or mediation should be explored. If litigation is to occur, the client may have legal options such as where to file the lawsuit, including the location of the courthouse and in which court (federal/state). These options are determined through legal research and application of the information to the client's factual situation.

Check with the attorney before sending any work product to the client. The client is entitled to and should receive most of your work product. This is particularly true of organizational memoranda and chronologies. The client should be informed and understand all of the facts related to its matter.

Apply the same principles to written communications being sent to the client as used in written communications to attorneys. Use clear and concise language, correct grammar and correct spelling in your communications.

Be mindful of the level of communication. Do not give legal advice in a client communication. If you relay legal advice to a client, be sure that your communication indicates the advice is from the attorney. For example, "Lee Lawyer asked that I..."

A client, particularly a corporate client, may ask for budget forecasts. In other words, the client wants to know how much money they can expect to be charged in fees and expenses over a certain time period, typically a quarter. In determining budgetary forecasts, communicate with the attorney. Determine the events likely to occur during that time frame, the costs of those events in terms of time (for example, how long it will take the attorney and paralegal to prepare for, attend and participate in a deposition) and actual expenses (court reporter, travel, etc.).

### *20.03 Serve as a liaison among client, counsel and other resources by using communication skills and techniques to exchange information and foster the client relationship.*

*Liaisons*

You may be called upon to be the liaison between the client, expert witnesses and counsel. Strong communication skills are essential in fulfilling this role. As liaison, you must thoroughly understand the legal concepts of confidential communications and conflict of interest. You must further understand the danger of giving the client legal advice without clarification to the client that the attorney is actually providing the information (*i.e.*, giving the advice).

Acting as Liaison to Clients

To serve as a liaison between the client and counsel, you should be aware of the internal resources available in the law office, such as materials available in the law office library, firm databases (for expert witnesses, as an example) and forms library (either manually filed or online computer forms). You should also be aware of external resources available for legal or factual research of a client matter. These include materials available at public libraries, governmental agencies, Freedom of Information Act requests, specialty libraries such as medical school libraries, courthouse records, other public records and professional association materials. Inform the client of the resources available and solicit client resources as well.

Acting as Liaison to Witnesses

You should have a clear understanding of the federal or state rules that apply to experts to serve as liaison between counsel and expert witnesses. *Expert witnesses* are people who, by education or specialized experience, possess superior knowledge not acquired by ordinary persons. Experts are consultants, usually hired on an hourly basis.

If a witness is not testifying as an expert, the witness' testimony is limited to their personal recollection of a fact at issue. Of course, the witness may only testify as to what they heard/saw and cannot relay information from third parties, which is considered *hearsay*.

The obvious difference between expert and fact witnesses is that experts are allowed to give opinions and inferences based upon their specialized knowledge. The proper use of an expert witness can bring a matter to a successful conclusion. Special rules apply to expert witnesses. Determine and review the appropriate court rules concerning experts. For example, Federal Rules of Evidence 701-705 relate to expert witnesses, as do Federal Rules of Civil Procedure 26(b)(4) and 35(b).

Paralegals perform tasks related to experts including:

- Locating potential experts;
- Interviewing potential experts and narrowing the field of potentials;
- Evaluating experts;
- Locating background information on experts;
- Serving as a liaison with experts; and
- Preparing experts for legal proceedings.

The paralegal should consider using the following resources in locating potential experts:

- The client;
- In-house databases or expert witness files;
- Bar and trial association files and databases;
- Advertisements in law journals and other publications;
- Jury trial reporting services;
- The public library;

- The yellow pages;
- Local colleges and universities;
- Professional associations;
- NFPA's home page at www.paralegals.org;
- Expert witness locating services;
- Value-added online services, to which one subscribes and pays a fee; and
- Resources on the Internet beyond www.paralegals.org.

An expert witness can be one of your key legal resources. The paralegal often serves as liaison between the expert and the attorney by providing the expert with case documents and information, scheduling depositions, preparation sessions and maintaining regular contact with the expert with regard to progress reports and needs of the expert.

Use caution in communicating with the expert. Fed. R. Evid. 705 states that an expert may be required to disclose the underlying facts or data that form the basis of their conclusions. Communications with experts are, therefore, potentially open to discovery. The information you provide to the expert will be used by the expert in forming an opinion. Make certain that your facts are straight! Communication with the expert should be formal in nature regardless of your familiarity with the expert so as to maintain the appearance that the expert is a disinterested third party.

Maintain a clear record of all information and documents provided to the expert. The easiest way to manage information provided to the expert is to maintain a separate expert file containing copies of all documents, information and correspondence with the expert. In voluminous matters, consider maintaining a list of documents rather than the actual documents.

*Communication Skills*

Communication is the process by which information is exchanged through a common system of symbols, signs or behaviors. Communication may be formal or informal. Here are some rules of effective communication:

- Clarify your ideas before you communicate;
- Identify and examine the true purpose of each communication;
- Follow up your communication -- use some form of feedback;
- Be sure your actions mirror and support your communication;
- Be mindful of overtones; and

- Use your time wisely.

Use different methods as appropriate.

Lawyers are under an ethical duty to keep their client advised of work performed and events occurring in their client matter. At least in part, keeping a client advised of events pertaining to their matter may be the paralegal's responsibility as liaison. As a matter of course, the client should receive photocopies of all correspondence between attorneys and third parties, all pleadings, discovery (including deposition transcripts) and motions filed with the court. Further, the client should receive in memorandum or summary form the attorney's account of key events as they occur in the case. A well-informed client is usually a happy client and, if not happy, a realistic client.

Communications with the client should be so frequent that very few of the events that occur during the representation, particularly the outcome, should surprise the client. An easy method of keeping the client informed is to send them copies of all incoming and outgoing correspondence.

In addition to sending written communications, you may be the attorney's liaison and provide frequent verbal communications to the client. When verbally communicating to the client, clearly identify yourself and your position with your employer. Further communications should be clear and concise. You should be ready to answer procedural questions ("What will happen next?"), but avoid answering questions that require legal advice.

Never predict the outcome of the client matter to a client. One never knows how long a matter may take to reach conclusion. Forecasting the outcome or even the length of time of a matter leads to client dissatisfaction when those expectations are not met.

Communications to the client in written form should be clear and concise, written in grammatically correct English. Communicating with the client either in writing or verbally, regardless of how friendly or casual the client may seem, should always remain professional – no slang!

All communications between the client and paralegal (acting as client liaison for the attorney) are to be maintained as *confidential*. Clients must feel secure that the information given will remain confidential based on the attorney's need to have all information from the client. Keep in mind that you have a continuing obligation (past your employment with the firm or the firm's representation of the client) to maintain those communications as confidential.

As liaison, the paralegal's communications should be written in a way in which the attorney-client privilege is clearly preserved. Communications should be on law firm stationery or other stationery that indicates a legal source, such as a corporate legal department's stationery. It is advisable to indicate "Confidential Communications Subject to the Attorney-Client Privilege" at the beginning of the communication. The client should be advised to indicate clearly in its written correspondence that the information therein is intended to be privileged.

In all communications, you must avoid even the appearance of impropriety by maintaining the confidentiality of client communications of current as well as previous clients. In addition, maintain a confidential and secure working environment by clearing out any other client's materials from conference rooms, work rooms or offices to which the client has access.

Review your office policies and procedures as they relate to confidentiality and client communications. Written communications should be on firm letterhead and clearly indicate your title (paralegal, legal assistant). A lack of title suggests that the person signing the correspondence is an attorney. In addition, make sure your e-mail signature indicates your title clearly.

### *20.04 Collaborate with counsel, client, consultants and other resources on an ongoing basis by analyzing and discussing potential legal issues and facts related to the client's matter to develop and maintain an effective strategy.*

To develop and maintain an effective strategy and reach the desired resolution for a client matter, you must be able to apply general principles of law to specific facts of the matter. You must have a general understanding of the process of legal reasoning.

*Court decisions* are based on a specific set of facts and established rules that apply to a narrow set of similar circumstances.

*Statutes*, on the other hand, are written in a very broad or general format designed to apply to a broad range of circumstances that are future oriented. Statutes are very difficult to write and often ambiguous.

As stated earlier in Domain 20.02, one approach to legal analysis is the *literal* interpretation. Courts read statutes literally, assuming that the words used reflect the true intentions of the legislature and that the legislature intended that the words used be interpreted in light of their common meanings.

A second approach is to consider *intrinsic* factors, where the court will look beyond the literal interpretation to the context and to the overall structure of the legislation or the entire legislation. This might include the study of transcripts of hearings and floor debates to determine the true intent of the legislation.

The paralegal must understand basic legal concepts such as jurisdiction and venue, standing and capacity and the elements of a cause of action, contract and corporate structures. Knowledge gained from the factual analysis may be applied to the legal issues.

*Jurisdiction* is the power of the court to hear and determine a case. Federal courts have limited jurisdiction. In order for federal courts to hear a case, there must either be *diversity of citizenship* (the opposing parties are from different states) or federal question (arising under Article II of the Constitution, which allows federal courts jurisdiction over all cases arising under the Constitution and laws and treaties of the United States). Like courts in general, federal courts require a jurisdictional amount in controversy. In other words, a certain amount of money must be in controversy in order for a federal court to have jurisdiction to hear a case. The present federal jurisdictional amount is a minimum of $75,000.

*Venue* refers to the place, or location, of the trial. Once the plaintiff determines that federal jurisdiction exists over the subject matter of the lawsuit, the plaintiff must decide in which federal district to file the suit. Generally, venue is permissible:

- Where any defendant resides, if all defendants reside in the same state;
- Where the events or omissions giving rise of the claim occurred or where property giving rise to the claim is located; and
- If there is no district in which the action may otherwise be brought, where any defendant may be found.

*Standing* is the legal right of a person or group to challenge the conduct of another person or group in a judicial forum.

*Legal capacity* is the requirement that, to bring suit, a person must be of sound mind, lawful age and under no restraint or legal disability.

PACE questions are federal-based and encompass many areas of the law. You are not expected to have advanced, specialized knowledge in any particular area. Of course, your experience will assist you in answering PACE questions. With that said, the drafters of PACE questions expect that you have some general, broad-based knowledge in many areas of law. The following is basic information for several areas of law which may appear on PACE. Some of these areas are expanded in greater detail at the end of this Manual.

<u>Basic Elements of Contract Law</u>

A *contract* is a promise or set of promises that is enforceable under law. Contract law is a combination of statutory and common law. A contract may be oral or written. In order for there to be a valid contract, there must be: (1) an offer; (2) acceptance; and (3) consideration. An offer is a promise to do something that is conditioned on the other party's promise to do something in return. The offeree must have the intent to be legally bound and have actual knowledge of the offer. Once an offer is made, the other party may accept, reject or counteroffer. An offer can be accepted by notification or by performance. Silence is not acceptance unless the terms specifically so provide.

*Consideration* is a bargained-for exchange and does not include a gift or moral consideration. Each party must give something of value as part of the bargain.

If a party fails to abide by the terms of the contract, a number of remedies are available, including rescission or cancellation of the contract, release or *novation* (substitution of a new contract to replace an old one). The offended party may go to court to seek monetary damages or equitable damages, such as specific performance.

Defenses include lack of legal capacity to form a contract due to age or mental capacity. Fraud is an affirmative defense used when one party made intentional or knowing misrepresentations or nondisclosures of material facts during the course of the negotiations. A contract is not valid if it was agreed to under duress. Contracts are not valid if they are illegal or unconscionable (oppressive and grossly unfair).

You should be familiar with the Uniform Commercial Code (UCC). The UCC is a code of laws governing various commercial transactions, including the sale of goods, banking transactions, secured transactions and other matters that were designed to bring uniformity to the laws of various states. With modification, the UCC has been adopted by all states and the District of Columbia.

The UCC is divided into sections that include sales, leases, commercial paper, bank deposits and collections, letters of credit, bulk transfers, warehouse receipts, bills of lading and other documents of title, investment securities and secured transactions. The UCC does not apply to real estate, insurance, bankruptcy or service contracts.

*Parol evidence* is a principle important to contract law. Under the parole evidence doctrine, a written contract may not be modified or changed by oral or verbal agreement.

*Basic Elements of Tort Law*

A *tort* is generally a private or civil wrong or injury resulting from a breach of a legal duty that exists by virtue of society's expectations, as opposed to a contract. Torts include battery, assault, infliction of mental distress, trespassing, appropriation, deceit, invasion of privacy, conversion, false arrest, false imprisonment, malicious prosecution and abuse of process.

There are various types of torts, the most common of which is *negligence*. *Negligence* is the failure to exercise that degree of care that a reasonable person would exercise under the same or similar circumstances. The elements of negligence are duty, breach of duty, causation and damages.

Damages are monetary compensation that the law awards to one who has been injured by the action of another. Damages may be *compensatory* (actually sustained), *punitive* (exemplary or compensation in excess of compensatory damages as a form of punishment) or *nomina*l (a trivial sum, usually $1, awarded in recognition of a legal injury where the amount is so small as not to constitute damages).

The law imposes a duty to act with "due care," or how a reasonable and prudent person would act in similar circumstances. The defendant's action must be the proximate cause of the plaintiff's injury. *Proximate cause* is the natural and continuous sequence of events unbroken by any of the intervening causes. Lastly, there must be damages resulting from the injury.

Pursuant to Fed. R. Civ. P. 8(c), an *affirmative defense* must be pled to be considered. Available affirmative defenses in tort law include *assumption of risk* and *contributory negligence*. Under the *doctrine of assumption of risk*, a plaintiff cannot recover damages related to an injury in which the plaintiff, knowing the danger and risk involved, chose to act as he/she did.

*Contributory negligence* is the act or omission amounting to a want of ordinary care on the part of the complaining party that, concurring with the defendant's negligence, is the proximate cause of the injury. Under the concept of contributory negligence, negligence is measured in percentages and damages are calculated accordingly.

While negligence consists of carelessness and unintentional acts, the law recognizes *intentional torts* in which the *tortfeasor* (the person who commits the tort) intentionally injures another. In such a case, the tortfeasor is subject to *punitive* or *exemplary damages* in addition to *actual damages*. *Punitive* or *exemplary damages* are damages on an increased scale award to the plaintiff over and above the amount that would compensate for actual damages.

Statutes sometimes provide for *treble damages*, punitive damages that triple the actual damages. Punitive damages are intended to punish the defendant and make an example of the defendant as a warning to others who may contemplate such acts.

Defenses to intentional torts include consent, self-defense, defense of third parties and certain privileges. These privileges include the law enforcement privilege that gives law enforcement authorities the right to use deadly force, the right to defend one's property and the right to invade another's property as a public necessity.

There are several defenses to the defamation torts, the most important and common of which is the truth of the statement or matter. Others include consent and privilege assertion, such as legislators' or governmental officials' privilege for comments made in carrying out their official duties. The law asserts an additional burden to the defamation plaintiff who is a public figure by requiring not only that the plaintiff prove the statements are untrue but, further, that they were made with "actual malice." Truth is not considered a valid defense to invasion of privacy.

Another legal concept related to tort liability is the doctrine of *strict liability*. The *doctrine of strict liability* declares an individual responsible for any injuries resulting from engaging in inherently dangerous activities (such as playing with explosives or keeping wild animals as pets), even though the activity may have been carried out in a safe and prudent manner.

<u>*Basic Elements of Estate Law*</u>

*Probate* is the process of proving that a will is valid and distributing the deceased person's estate property in accordance with that will and state law. An *estate* is the property (real and personal) that a person owns at the time of his/her death. This property is distributed in accordance with the person's will and state probate laws. A person who dies without a valid will is said to have died *intestate*. That person's property is then distributed in accordance with state probate laws. An *executor* is the person appointed by the testator (the person making the will) to carry out the directions and requests in the will. A *guardian* is the person who is given the duty and responsibility of managing the affairs of someone who is incapable of managing his/her own affairs, such as a minor.

Typically, a petition, the will and death certificate are filed in the appropriate probate court, along with the payment of a filing fee. *Letters Testamentary* are issued by the court giving the executor the power to pay the bills and distribute the assets of the estate.

Some aspects of probate may be avoided and taxes minimized by creating trusts. A *trust* is a legal relationship in which one party holds property for the benefit of another. Property is transferred to a trust fund, which is to be used for the benefit of a designated person or persons rather than being directly transferred to the person or persons as a part of the probate process.

*Basic Elements of Business Organizations*

You should have basic knowledge of the legal organization of business entities. The *sole proprietorship*, the simplest form of business organization, is a business owned by only one person. The number of employees is unlimited. Sole proprietorships are the extension of the individual owner, and all profits and losses are treated as personal profits and losses. Profits are taxed as personal income and the owner's personal assets are available to satisfy business related expenses.

A *partnership* is the form of organization in which two or more persons share ownership in a business. Partnerships operate under a partnership agreement. Like the sole proprietorship, the partnership pays no taxes; however, it must file a report to the IRS showing how the profits and losses were divided among the partners. Because each general partner is an agent of the partnership, the general partner assumes joint and several liability for the other general partners' actions in conducting the business of the partnership. Although the death or expulsion of a general partner dissolves a general partnership, most general partnerships are not liquidated, but are immediately restructured under a new partnership agreement among the remaining partners.

More formal than a general partnership, a *limited partnership* has at least one general partner and at least one limited partner. General partners manage the partnership and have unlimited liability, while limited partners are investors with no right to participate in the management and operation of the business and whose liability is limited to the amount invested. Like the general partnership, the limited partnership has a partnership agreement, but it must also file with the appropriate secretary of state a certificate of limited partnership.

A *limited liability company* (LLC) combines the flow-through taxation of the partnership with the ability of a member to participate in management of the company. The liability of a member, like that of the limited partner in a limited partnership, is limited to the amount invested. An LLC may be managed by its members or by managers chosen by the members. It is formed by filing *articles of organization* with the appropriate secretary of state.

The most common form of business organization is the corporation. A *corporation* is an association of shareholders created under law having a legal entity separate and distinct from the individuals who comprise it. Corporations may sue, be sued, hold and convey property, just as a natural person or individual may. The corporation's liability is generally limited to the corporation's assets and not those of its shareholders. Individual shareholders may have to accept liability through the process of piercing the corporate veil, in which courts ignore the corporate form and strip the shareholders of the limited liability they enjoy in a corporation. A corporation is formed when legal documents are filed with the office of the appropriate secretary of state.

A key legal document relating to a corporation is its *articles of incorporation.* The articles of incorporation must contain the name and address of each incorporator, the corporation's name, the purpose of the corporation, its share structure (number of shares authorized, classes and rights, and in some states, the par value of each share), as well as the name of the registered agent for service of process and address of the registered agent's office. Once a certificate of incorporation has been issued, the corporation is required to maintain certain records and file reports to appropriate governmental agencies.

A corporation's board of directors is responsible for managing the corporation. Officers of the corporation are elected by the board of directors. Directors have a fiduciary duty to act in the best interest of the corporation and its shareholders. Corporate capital typically comes from the sale of stock. Stock purchasers (called shareholders or stockholders) have voting rights in the election of the corporation's board of directors and receive distribution of part of the corporation's profits as directed by the board of directors.

*Basics of Intellectual Property*

The simplest explanation of intellectual property is that it is the product of a person's mind -- an idea. Intellectual property comes in three forms: patents, trademarks and copyrights. Article I, Section 8 of the United States Constitution gives us the Patent-Copyright clause, making those rights constitutionally mandated. In the late 1700's, Thomas Jefferson pushed for the adoption of trademark laws, but that legislation was not passed until 1870.

Patents

The mandate of the Constitution was implemented by Congress in 1790, when the first Patent Act was passed into law. Amendments since that time have been infrequent. The most dynamic was the codification of the Patent Law into Title 35 of the United States Code in 1952.

Webster defines the term "patent" as: "an official document conferring a right or privilege," *i.e.*, Letters Patent. Letters Patent are issued by the United States Patent and Trademark Office. The criteria for things that are patentable are set forth in 35 U.S.C. §101 as:

> Whoever invents or discovers any new and useful process, machine, manufacture, or composition of matter, or any new and useful improvements thereof, may obtain a patent therefor, subject to the conditions and requirements of this title.

One of the requirements of a patent application is for the applicant to disclose and discuss prior art patents. Because of that requirement, most patent practitioners perform a preliminary patentability search of the prior art at the Patent Office, in the various classes and subclasses, to determine what has been done previously in the particular field of endeavor. If it appears from the search results that patent protection might be available, then an application is written and filed with the Patent Office. There is a publication -- Manual of Patent Examining Procedure [MPEP] -- which sets out the form and content for applications. Once an application has been filed and the Patent Office has issued a "date of filing" and serial number, the application is then assigned to a Patent Examiner, who has expertise in the particular field and who will then proceed with the prosecution of the application. It is seldom that an application issues as a patent without office actions from the examiner, which contain various bases for rejection.

There are three categories of patents: [1] UTILITY which covers: useful process, machine, article of manufacture and composition of matter; [2] DESIGN which covers the ornamental characteristics; and [3] PLANT which covers a new variety of asexually reproduced plant. In today's world of advertising, there is much talk about "provisional patents." There are NO provisional patents -- there are "provisional applications." A provisional application can NEVER mature into an issued patent UNLESS the provisional application is converted to a full application within one year of the filing date of the provisional application.

If you are fortunate and your application issues as Letters Patent, this then gives you the right to exclude others from the manufacture, use and sale of the claimed invention. [35 U.S.C. 154] If you believe some other person or entity has infringed your patent, you may bring suit to protect your rights.

Preparing for patent litigation is similar to many other areas of civil litigation, but with other, far-reaching aspects added. That is a specialty part, which is discussed more fully in the Intellectual Property chapter of this Manual.

Trademarks

Thomas Jefferson pushed for trademark laws in the late 1700's. Unfortunately, that legislation was not passed until 1870. Even though the trademark law was not codified until Congress passed the Trademark Act of 1946, trademarks have been around for centuries. It was known then as "marking," and there is evidence of such marking going back as far as 3500 B.C.

The definition of a trademark is contained in §1127 of Title 15 [the Lanham Act] of the United States Code and states:

> [a] trademark includes any word, name, symbol, or device, or any combination thereof – (1) used by a person, … in commerce … to identify and distinguish his or her goods, including a unique product, from those manufactured or sold by others and to indicate the *source* of the goods, even if that source is unknown. [Emphasis supplied]

Ideally, a trademark consists of a word or symbol by which a business becomes recognized for its product's characteristics, such as quality, size or price or as the *source* of a particular product or service and, hopefully, both. A trademark in no way protects your product from being made by others. What it does is *identify the source of the product* as coming from a particular company or individual.

If a mark is only used in intrastate commerce, an applicant is entitled only to file for registration in the home state. If the mark is used in interstate commerce, then the applicant is entitled to file an application for federal registration. That application is filed with the United States Patent and Trademark Office. Only marks that are federally registered are allowed to use the designation ® with their mark.

It is the *use* of a mark that builds recognition and not its registration. It is not necessary to register a mark in order for it to be enforceable, but there are definite benefits. A more detailed discussion on trademarks is contained in Intellectual Property chapter of this Manual.

<u>Copyrights</u>

In the world of copyrights, everyone is familiar with the notices contained in books, at the end of the credits on movies, on computer programs, and, if you are a musician, on sheet music or books containing a large number of compositions. Some may not be aware of the fact that sculptures, lamp designs, patterns for clothing items, handbags, shoes, theatrical performances and performances of various musical compositions, both vocal and orchestral, are the subject of copyright protection.

Section 102 of Title 17 of the United States Code states that:

> (a) Copyright protection subsists, in accordance with this title, in original works of authorship fixed in any tangible medium of expression, now known or later developed, from which they can be perceived, reproduced, or otherwise communicated, either directly or with the aid of a machine or device…

Copyright protection is available on published, as well as unpublished works.

Works of authorship include literary works; musical works, including accompanying words; dramatic works, including any accompanying music; pantomimes and choreographic works; pictorial, graphic and sculptural works; motion pictures and other audiovisual works; sound recordings and architectural works.

Violation of the rights provided by the copyright laws is illegal, but the rights are not unlimited in scope. In some cases there are limitations and exemptions from liability. In order to claim the full measure of damages in a lawsuit, one must have a copyright registration prior to filing a complaint.

Applications for registration of copyrights are filed with the Copyright Office at the Library of Congress and can be done online or by U.S. mail. The Web site has forms, complete with line by line instructions for completion. The rules require that copies of the work be deposited with the Copyright Office, where they are stored. The instructions are clear as to how many copies of the item are required. Under the current state of the law, copyright protection extends for a period of 70 years beyond the death of the original author [the Bono Act].

<u>*Basic Elements of Bankruptcy*</u>

Bankruptcy is another federal-based specialty area. Bankruptcy is codified in Title 11 of the United States Constitution. The procedural aspects of bankruptcy are governed by the Federal Rules of Bankruptcy Procedure as well as local court rules. There is a bankruptcy court for each judicial district in the United States. Bankruptcy courts generally have their own court clerk office. The court official presiding over the federal bankruptcy courts is the United States bankruptcy judge, who is appointed officially by the President of the United States in a process similar to that of federal district court judges. Much of the bankruptcy process is an administrative process, carried out by a Trustee who is appointed to oversee the case. The fundamental goal of bankruptcy is to give debtors a "fresh start" from debt. There are five basic types of bankruptcy provided under the Bankruptcy Code. These types are commonly referred to by their chapter number in the Bankruptcy Code.

> Chapter 7 – Liquidation. In broad terms, the Trustee in a Chapter 7 liquidation reduces the debtor's assets to cash and distributes the money to creditors. The debtor has certain rights to exempt property and secured creditors receive distributions before unsecured creditors based on the Code. A creditor files a Proof of Claim with the bankruptcy court. At the end of most cases, the debtor receives a Discharge from the bankruptcy court for his/her dischargeable debts. The entire process many only take a couple of months.
>
> Chapter 9 – Adjustment of Debts of Municipality. Again, as the name implies, only municipalities such as towns, cities, counties and taxing districts may file under Chapter 9.
>
> Chapter 11 – Reorganization. Chapter 11 is used primarily by businesses who wish to continue operating the business while repaying creditors through a court-approved plan of reorganization. The Chapter 11 Debtor has the right to file his/her proposed plan within 120 days. The plan gives the debtor's business additional rights such as terminating burdensome business contracts and leases.
>
> Chapter 12 – Adjustment of Debts of a Family Farmer with Regular, Annual Income. As the name implies, this type of proceeding provides relief to family farmers. The process is similar to Chapter 13.
>
> Chapter 13 – Adjustment of Debts of an Individual with Regular Income. Chapter 13 is often preferable for individuals because debtors are able to keep valuable assets, such as a home. Chapter 13 allows the debtor to propose a plan to repay creditors over time (usually three to five years). At the confirmation hearing, the court either approves or disapproves the plan. Unlike, Chapter 7, the debtor in Chapter 13 does not immediately receive a discharge of his/her debts.

### *20.05 Prepare and/or coordinate the preparation of legal and factual documents, exhibits and evidence, and/or other information related to the client matter by compiling, creating, evaluating and organizing information to advance the client's goals and interests.*

Preparing legal and factual documents, exhibits and evidence requires knowledge of legal procedure as well as legal writing techniques and skills. Refer generally to the Federal Rules of Civil Procedure (Fed. R. Civ. P.) and the Federal Rules of Evidence (Fed. R. Evid.) for guidance. *See* Domain 40.00, Factual and Legal Writing.

*Case management*, or the organization and compilation of documents and evidence, is also essential in the development of a client matter. The system of organization you create in a client matter may vary from matter to matter, depending on case size and complexity. The system may be manual, on the computer database, or both. No matter the system, the goal is to locate and retrieve documents upon request, as quickly as possible.

As stated earlier in this Domain, the paralegal should know the law firm's practice and procedure for case organization, which is most commonly referred to as the *filing system.* Filing systems vary greatly from firm to firm. The best systems are those that are standardized so that each matter has the same basic format or organization. Subsidiary files would then be created as needed.

As discussed earlier in this Domain, if there is a standardized system of case management, follow it and create your case file. If there is no standard system, use organizational skills to determine the organizational system that best meets your case's needs.

The client's needs and resources should be a consideration in creating a case management system. The client that is a law firm or corporate legal department, for example, has obvious resources such as access to computerized legal research resources, law libraries, copy service resources and an established case management system. Determine the client's ongoing need for case documentation. Are you obtaining original copies of working or active files? Does the client have a business or personal need for case documentation on an ongoing basis? If so, your system of case management will have to allow for client access.

As in all aspects of legal practice, the creation of a case management system, as well as tracking legal and factual documents and exhibits, requires clear communication among the attorneys, support staff and the client. The task of case management typically falls upon you alone. You should, however, communicate to the attorneys the system in place and procedures for checking out documents. In some offices, a good rule is never permitting the attorney to touch an original document!

Some attorneys will want hard copies of many case documents for notations. This can be accomplished by creating an attorney working file or case notebook so that the attorney is able to write on or highlight those extra copies of the documents in his/her working file. The extra copies should be clearly labeled as "working copy."

In most law offices today, case management or the administration of a file is accomplished on the computer. A case management software package should have the capacity to:

- Search by date, document or action to determine if a docketed action occurred;
- Search by file name, matter name, party name, opposing attorney or co-counsel name;
- Determine the physical location of the file;
- Create reminders of deadlines with its tickler or calendaring function;
- Disallow the accidental deletion of material without proper security codes; and
- Report on status.

When should a case be computerized? It depends on the following factors:

- Volume of case documents and anticipated case documents;
- Complexity of the matter;
- Number of parties involved;
- Anticipated length of the matter; and
- Amount of damages sought.

Cost involved may also be a determining factor in deciding whether or not to computerize a matter. Costs include software, hardware, personnel, space and training.

You should be able to formulate and evaluate solutions to problems and arguments in support of specific positions, as well as apply legal authority to specific factual situations in the preparation of legal and factual documents to advance the client's goals and interest. Critical thinking skills are used in the analysis of any factual situation or the preparation of a document summary. General case organization or case management requires the utilization of critical thinking.

Preparing legal and factual documents, exhibits and evidence may require additional client or witness interviews. Document research to determine the production of responsive documents to another party will most certainly entail additional interviewing. These research interviews may be conducted in person or via telephone with the assistance of a fax machine or electronically-shared means. If the documents are voluminous and the witness is available, a person-to-person interview will be most productive.

Consider creating an investigation form for each document that requires research. This form should clearly indicate "Attorney-Client or Work Product Privilege" and contain document identification number, person(s) interviewed, telephone and fax number(s), date of the interview, notes and questions or issues raised. As with the initial client interview, preparation is essential to conduct research interviews. Documents should be fully reviewed and organized in a way that will make the interview proceed efficiently. Questions should be noted on the investigation form, which should be attached to the front of the document.

*Gathering and Collecting Documents*

Document requests should be in writing. Prepare a memorandum outlining what you want your client to provide, including information related to the source of that documentation. Document requests in writing provide a written trail of the document collection process that may be important in responding to discovery disputes or inquiries from parties, as in the case of third-party subpoenas. When responding to a grand jury or other government subpoena, it is essential that requests for documents be in writing so that there is no dispute as to what was or was not requested.

In the case of third-party subpoenas, attach the actual document request and definitions to your written request. Maintain a written record of those to whom you distributed the document request and be sure to calendar a reminder just after the due date.

Consider the following when drafting written document request letters for either informal or formal case discovery:

- Ask the client (particularly a corporate client) to assign a management-level employee to serve as your contact person. This person must be empowered to take the actions necessary to support the collection effort.

- Ask the client to identify the documents in its "possession, custody or control" that respond to the request. These are buzzwords because Fed. R. Civ. P. 34 allows for the production of all relevant documents in the party's possession, custody and control. *Control* refers to the legal right, authority or ability to obtain documents on demand.

- Ask for the source of the document. To control incoming documentation, it is essential that you know the source or who provided the documentation, including the source's organizational information. The easiest way to obtain source information is to ask in the collection letter that a collection memorandum be prepared by each person who provides documentation (each source).

- State a deadline (bolded and underlined in the memorandum) by which the documents are to be received. Include the specific address and telephone number of someone involved in the collection in case your client has any questions.

- Identify, as clearly and precisely as possible, the documents to be collected without limiting documentation that may be relevant. Consider including language concerning the following, common limitations:

> The search for documents should not be limited to those identified above. These categories are ____'s best effort as to the document types that may exist. You may know of additional document types that may be helpful. If so, please contact_____.
>
> The search for documentation should not be limited to formal or official company or client files. The search must extend to personal files, correspondence and reading files, informal working files, personal notes (including handwritten notes) and other forms of written or recorded materials (including documents stored on disk and in other forms of electronic mail) that might relate to the documents requested.
>
> The search for files should include all files maintained on site as well as those removed from your site, including storage or archiving. Your search should also include electronic-only stored files.

> The search should include not only written materials but recorded information in every other form, including writings, drawings, graphs, charts, photographs and other data compilations from which information can be translated.
>
> The collection effort should include exact or duplicate copies of documents found in other files, unless it is unreasonable to do so. (It is a good idea to inform the client that you do not consider a document with a handwritten notation or marking ever so slight, an exact duplicate.)

Instruct the client not to make additional notations, markings or alterations of any type on the documents being collected. Instruct the client not to erase anything from the documentation. If an explanation of the document is necessary, ask that the source provide an explanation on a separate piece of paper in the form of a memorandum addressed to the attorney with the following language: "Confidential, Attorney Client Privileged, Not Subject to Discovery."

Tell the client what you are going to do with the documents. For example, if the documents are being collected in response to a document request, mention that responsive documents that are not the subject of any privilege will be produced to ____ (insert party) after being reviewed. If you are requesting original documents, tell the client you will sequentially number each page and make copies of the documents provided. Use language such as: "The originals will be returned to you promptly and must be retained in the files at your location and not destroyed. The number placed on each original may not be removed." Provide the name(s) and number(s) of persons with knowledge of the collection effort so that questions can easily be directed to the appropriate person.

Your case management system should be in place before the requested documents arrive. Use forms, logs and file folders to track the documents collected. Indicate their source, date of receipt, etc. Consider separately numbering (commonly referred to as control-numbering) documents as they arrive. In a large, complex matter, the specific source of the document might receive its own control or *Bates*-number series. In most matters, the same series of control numbers may be used with the paralegal noting in chart or log form the source and number series provided by that source.

*Inspecting Documents*

You will be called upon to review client documents as well as those produced by the opposing party. When reviewing or inspecting documents, read everything on both sides of each page, including handwritten notes, drawings, invoices, etc. As you review client documents, consider whether a privilege may apply to the document and mark that document or note it accordingly.

Before you begin to review client documents, it is best to have a system of marking or noting documents in place. A common system is *color coding*, whereby you mark documents with colored flags such as red for privileged, green for responsive and orange for "needs further research," etc. You might want to select a color for hot documents or key documents. It is possible to segregate documents as you are reviewing them; however, this destroys the document order integrity of the files and documentation.

As you are initially reviewing client documents, remember that Fed. R. Civ. P. 34 requires that documents be produced as they are kept in the usual course of business or organized or labeled to correspond with the categories of the request. The most common method of production is in the *regular course of business*, which is another reason to maintain the document order integrity of the files being reviewed. Consider preparing or revising chronologies for the matter as you review the documents.

Maintain a detailed record of work performed during the document review. Take the time to prepare a detailed memorandum summarizing documents, or at least a summary of categories or file folders reviewed. This memorandum will be a permanent record in the file of your work.

*Disclosure Requirements*

Federal Rules of Civil Procedure require that, at the outset of the case, the parties disclose information "relevant to disputed facts," including witnesses (names, addresses, telephone numbers and subject of testimony/information), documents, damages and insurance policies.

Fed. R. Civ. P. 26(a)(1) does not require the parties to produce copies to other parties, but instead gives the parties the option of providing copies or a list or description by category and location of all documents in the possession, custody or control of the party that are relevant to disputed facts alleged in the pleadings. Local rules vary and some even opt out of the disclosure requirement. Be sure to check your local rules.

*Producing Documents*

At some point, you will be called upon to produce documents to the opposing party, either as a part of formal or informal discovery. In a less voluminous matter, and to speed the case along, a party may choose to produce documents as a part of the disclosure requirements addressed above. Parties may agree voluntarily to provide documentation to each other in an effort to resolve the dispute or for some other purpose. The most common reason for producing documents in a client matter in litigation is in response to a Request for Production of Documents pursuant to Fed. R. Civ. P. 34. Review Fed. R. Civ. P. 34 carefully when preparing to produce documents.

If a party is served with a request for production of documents under Fed. R. Civ. P. 34, they will have 30 days from service (plus three days if the request was sent by U.S. mail) to respond to the request in writing, stating that the documents will be produced or making appropriate objections to the request(s). The court can order shorter or longer response times. If you fail to serve a timely response, objections such as privilege may be waived. If confronted with a request for production, carefully review all requests and forward the request to the client. Determine any grounds for objections. Refer, generally, to Domain 20.07 for discussion of privileges. In addition, consider the following, commonly used objections:

- Overly burdensome, unduly expensive and sought for the purposes of harassment;
- Irrelevant to any issues in the lawsuit;
- Not calculated to lead to the discovery of admissible evidence;

- Overly broad, vague and ambiguous; and
- Confidential trade secret or confidential, competitive information.

Keep in mind that most court rules provide for *confidentiality* or *protective orders*. In cases where you are asked to divulge a trade secret or confidential information, object to the request, but agree to provide it if the parties agree to a protective order or confidentiality agreement.

It is not necessary to produce the documents requested at the same time a response is filed. If there is no objection to the request and there are documents responsive, state: "Documents responsive to this request shall be provided for copying and inspection at a time agreeable to both parties at the offices of ____ [your office]."

Fed. R. Civ. P. 34 requires inspection of the documents, not copying and delivery of the documents requested. In large document productions, the parties may agree to use an outside copy service for copying the documents produced at the requesting party's expense. Do not run up expenses to your client by offering to copy documents to be produced without an agreement as to the division of expenses. You will be responsible, however, for your client's copy of the documents produced, as well as other expenses such as *Bates*-numbering the documents produced.

At some point in your preparation to produce documents, you will segregate the client documents that are *responsive*, *non-responsive* and *privileged*. One system of organization previously mentioned involves control or Bates-numbering all documents received from the client in the order received. If this is done, the procedure would then be to copy all "responsive," "needs research," "privileged" and "to be redacted" documents. Documents to be produced will then receive a corresponding production number placed over the control number. You would retain both a control set of documents (in their original order as provided from the client) as well as a production set of documents (as produced to the opposing party).

The main advantage to this system is to maintain control of the documents and the integrity of the file. Researching whether you have produced a certain document becomes easy. This system may be too cumbersome in less voluminous matters. While control-numbering is less common in most matters, it is common and recommended practice to number the documents being produced.

Use logic to develop a numbering scheme. For example, if your party is Jones Electric, you may want your numbering scheme to begin with J0001 so that documents produced by Jones will be easily identified.

*Redacting Documents*

There may be times when you object to the production of only a portion of the document, such as a handwritten note or a confidential trade secret. In such cases, you may be called upon to *redact* or delete only a portion of a document and produce the remaining non-objectionable portions. Copies of documents to be redacted must be identified separately from other production documents. One practical tip is to use (or have the attorney use) a highlighter to indicate the words to be redacted. Physically redact out yellow highlighted portions of documents. As the documents are being physically redacted, place a "Document Redacted" stamp or sticker on the document. Copy and label the redacted documents for the production set, making sure the redacted data is completely removed.

*Preparing Legal Documents*

Several obvious types of documents prepared in the development of a client matter are outlined below, with the exception of litigation pleadings and discovery, which are discussed in Section 20.06. In preparing legal documents, locate and refer to the appropriate court or agency rules. For example, Fed. R. Civ. P. 56(e) outlines the form of affidavit to be attached to a Motion for Summary Judgment.

*Preparing Exhibits*

Exhibits may be used in conjunction with motions, depositions or at hearings or trial. Exhibits are evidence and therefore must be admissible in that the attorney must ultimately lay the proper foundation for admissibility of exhibits. Use court-approved exhibit stickers to mark your exhibits. (Check the local rules.) It is best to use a numbered copy of the document, such as one used in a deposition with a deposition exhibit sticker or a Bates-numbered copy, for chain of custody concerns in authentication. Do not cover any numbering, lettering or notation with the exhibit sticker. Double-check the copies to ensure that the exhibits are clear and accurately copied.

Before sequentially numbering the exhibits, discuss the organization of the exhibits with the attorney. Exhibits to motions are numbered in the order referenced in the motion. Trial exhibits should be organized in a manner that will allow you to locate the document easily. For example, documents may be organized by the person who is expected to authenticate the documents (*i.e.*, witness order), in simple chronological order or perhaps by subject matter.

Another technique is to number key documents early in the numbering scheme. Discovery responses are often marked as exhibits to motions -- such as a motion to compel discovery -- for ease of reference. Portions of deposition transcripts are often marked as exhibits to motions. Review local rules. When providing only portions of deposition transcripts, it is good practice to include the first page of the transcript showing witness name, date, etc., as well as the last page showing the court reporter's signature and fee statement.

*Preparing Affidavits or Declarations*

An *affidavit* is a written, *ex parte* statement made or taken under oath before an officer of the court or a notary public. A *declaration*, on the other hand, is not sworn to before an officer of the court or a notary public, but instead states that it is made under the penalty of perjury that the statements are true. Refer to local rules to determine the appropriate form of affidavit or declaration.

Affidavits and declarations must include language that the information presented is true and correct and based on personal knowledge. The remaining language of the affidavit or declaration obviously depends on the subject matter. Set out in paragraphs the information you wish to convey.

### *20.06 Prepare, file and serve documents related to the client matter by identifying relevant authority and procedure, assembling necessary documents and submitting documents in compliance with rules and regulations to advance the client's goals and interests.*

No matter the specialty area, paralegals are called upon to prepare, file and ensure service of documents in compliance with court or agency rules. Obviously, the first step is to determine which rules apply, whether it be Federal Rules of Civil Procedure or bankruptcy rules. Within most sets of broad rules, such as the Federal Rules of Civil Procedure, are local rules that may or may not alter the general rules, but also must be followed. You must be able to calculate deadlines in accordance with appropriate court rules. Fed. R. Civ. P. 6 provides general rules for time calculations that apply to the federal rules, local district courts, court orders and statutes.

Resources available in preparing court documents include form files available within the law practice (either personal form files or computer-aided files) and library reference form books such as *Modern Legal Forms, Am-Jur Legal Forms, American Jurisprudence Pleading and Practice Forms, O'Connor's Federal Forms* and *Moore's Federal Forms.* General legal Internet sites such as *FindLaw.com* contain links to online services providing state-specific forms, for example, US Legal Forms or LawDepot.com.

Drafts of similar documents created by another paralegal or attorney in your office furnish insight into the style of writing the attorney or firm may use, as well as providing a sample form. In instances in which cases are related by similar factual situations, language from the sister litigation may be copied "en masse," particularly definitions and instructions. Maintain your own form file library on your computer so that you do not have to recreate the wheel every time you draft a document. Forms located in the law library will provide specific information as to applicable court rules, case law and filing requirements. These resources should be tapped first before drafting a document.

Consider the client's needs and resources in the preparation, filing and serving of documents. Whenever possible, the client should receive, prior to filing but after the attorney has reviewed the document, a draft of the documents to be filed. Use your client's resources whenever possible. Law firm or corporate legal department clients may want to draft the documents, perform legal research or provide you with access to legal research at their reduced cost. More commonly, the client will be able to assist you in the compilation of matters to be used as exhibits or as factual reference points in the documents. Accounting summaries and damage calculations are common examples.

Computer principles and techniques used in the preparation of documents depend on the nature of the document. At a minimum, you must be able to utilize word processing tools available to prepare and revise the document. Depending on the situation, it may be more efficient to leave functions like graphs, charts and cleanup of headers and footers to support staff.

You may use the computer as a calendaring device. Use computer software to create and revise a calendaring, or tickler, system to keep the legal team aware of deadlines. You must apply legal principles and procedure to prepare, file and serve documents. Regardless of subject matter, basic principles in preparing documents include the correct construction of the case style or caption and the inclusion of all required segments and attachments to documents. For example, you must be aware that:

- The complaint must be accompanied by a summons and filing fee;
- Most court papers, other than those requiring service of process, must contain a certificate of service;
- All court papers (except draft orders) must be signed by the attorney representing the party; and
- All motions must be accompanied by a draft order for the court's consideration.

<u>*Calculating Deadlines*</u>

You must correctly calculate deadlines, imposed either by court order or court rule. Fed. R. Civ. P. 6 provides general rules for time calculations that apply to federal rules, local district courts, court orders and statutes. These basic rules are:

1. The date of the act, event or default from which the time begins shall not be included. In other words, start counting on the next day.
2. The last day of the period is included in the calculation, unless it is a Saturday, Sunday or legal holiday. If you are filing a document, this rule also provides for days in which weather or other conditions have made the court inaccessible.
3. When the time period is fewer than eleven days, intermediate Saturdays, Sundays and legal holidays are not counted.
4. Legal holidays are considered to be New Year's Day; Martin Luther King, Jr. Day; Presidents' Day; Memorial Day; Independence Day; Labor Day; Columbus Day; Veterans Day; Thanksgiving Day and Christmas Day; as well as state holidays and holidays enacted by the Congress or declared by the President.
5. When a party is served by U.S. mail, three days are added to any deadlines that follow. By the way, service by mail is considered complete when mailed.

The types of documents drafted depend on the client matter. The following is a basic explanation of legal principles and procedures related to the most basic legal documents.

The case *style*, or *heading*, includes the names of the parties, court case number and the name and location of the court. The heading should be inserted at the beginning of all documents served upon the parties or filed with the court. This information is also referred to as the case *caption*.

<u>*Pleadings and Complaints*</u>

A civil action is commenced by filing a *complaint*, the purpose of which is to give the defendant fair notice of the plaintiff's claims. The pleading must be clear enough to enable the defendant to answer or defend against those claims. *See* Fed. R. Civ. P. 3. The complaint must identify the defendant's full name and address, as well as a statement of jurisdiction, particularly federal jurisdiction if in federal court, the amount in controversy, a statement of venue and a statement of the claim, showing why the plaintiff is entitled to relief. *See* Fed. R. Civ. P. 8.

A complaint is a form of pleading. Pleadings set forth a claim for relief, whether an original complaint, *a counterclaim*, *a cross-claim* or *a third-party claim*.

Fed. R. Civ. P. 8 requires that all pleadings contain:

- A short and plain statement of the grounds upon which the court's jurisdiction depends;
- A short and plain statement showing that the pleader (person preparing the pleading) is entitled to relief; and
- A demand for judgment of the relief sought.

*Pleading Jurisdiction*

Federal courts have limited jurisdiction. In order for federal courts to hear a case, there must either be diversity of citizenship (opposing parties are from different states) or federal question (arising under Article III of the United States Constitution). Article III allows federal courts jurisdiction over all cases arising "under the Constitution, Laws and Treaties of the United States."

A certain amount of money must be in controversy to have a federal court hear a case. The present, federal, jurisdictional amount is $75,000.

The federal basis for jurisdiction, also known as *subject matter jurisdiction*, must be clearly stated in the complaint. The specific constitutional authority should be cited. Facts supporting subject matter jurisdiction should be cited in the complaint. For example, if diversity of citizenship is alleged, the complaint should include the states of citizenship of each party. Note that the requirement is citizenship, as opposed to residence.

*The Parties*

The caption of the complaint must contain the full names of all parties. Fed. R. Civ. P. 10(a).

*Venue*

The action may be filed in one of the following places:

1. Where specifically cited by statute;
2. If all defendants reside in the same state, where any defendant resides;
3. Where the events giving rise to the complaint occurred; or

4. If there is no district in which the action can otherwise be brought, where any defendant is subject to personal jurisdiction or may be found.

*See* 28 U.S.C. § 1391.

*Filing Documents*

The filing of a complaint commences a civil action. Before filing the lawsuit with the appropriate court, contact the court clerk to determine the amount of fees that will be required. Check the court rules or ask the clerk how many copies of the petition are required. Bring the petitions and copies, as well as a completed summons, along with a check for filing and service fees to the court clerk. At the time of filing, a *summons* will be issued. A summons or copies thereof shall be issued for each defendant to be served.

Fed. R. Civ. P. 5 outlines the procedure for filing documents in federal court. Review local or agency rules for additional procedures. This rule states that all papers required to be served upon a party shall be filed with the court within a reasonable amount of time after service. *Filing* means to file or deliver to the clerk of the court, although a judge may permit papers to be filed directly in their chambers. Local rules may permit filing via facsimile or other electronic means, so be sure to check the local rules. In most jurisdictions, documents filed with the court are required to contain a Certificate of Service.

*Service*

*Service* of the complaint and summons upon the defendant may be made by any person who is not a party to the suit and who is at least 18 years old. The plaintiff may request, however, that the court direct that service be made by a United States marshal, a deputy United States marshal or other person or officer specially appointed for that purpose. *See* Fed. R. Civ. P. 4(c)(2). Rule 4(d) allows the defendant to waive service under certain conditions. There is a time limit for service. Rule 4(m) allows the court, upon motion or its own initiative, to dismiss an action where service of the summons and complaint is not made within 120 days after filing the complaint.

The rules set forth regulations to follow in serving individuals within the United States and outside the United States, as well as infants and incompetents, corporations and the United States, its agencies, corporations and officers. *See* Fed. R. Civ. P. 4(e)(i).

Generally, service upon individuals within the United States may be made by: (1) delivering a copy of the summons and complaint to the individual personally; (2) leaving copies at the individual's home with a person of suitable age and discretion who resides there; or (3) delivering a copy to an agent authorized by appointment or law to receive service of process.

Fed. R. Civ. P. 4 sets out the requirements for service upon the United States government. Service upon a state, county or local government is effected on the chief executive officer of the entity or by state law.

Service upon corporations is effected by delivering a copy of the summons and complaint to an officer, managing or general agent or to any other agent authorized by appointment or by law to receive service of process. If the corporation has several offices in differing states, be sure to determine the appropriate office before trying to serve the pleading.

Court rules provide separate, more relaxed methods of service for pleadings and all other papers filed after the complaint. Fed. R. Civ. P. 5 provides that all pleadings subsequent to the complaint and every paper of discovery, written motion, written notice, appearance, demand, offer of judgment and similar paper be served upon each of the parties. Service is required to be made to the attorney representing the party, if the party is represented by an attorney and unless otherwise ordered by the court. Service shall be by hand-delivery or U.S. mail.

The rules allow that hand-delivery be made by directly handing the document to the attorney or party, by leaving it at the attorney's or party's office with a clerk or other person in charge or by leaving it at the attorney's or party's office in a conspicuous place. If the office is closed or the person has no office, the rules allow for service at the individual's house with a person of suitable age and discretion residing there. Service by U.S. mail is complete upon mailing. Remember to add three days in calculating deadlines when the proceeding papers are served by U.S. mail.

After the complaint, a certificate of service is required on most pleadings. A *certificate of service* is a paragraph typically located at the end of a court paper that certifies that a true and correct copy of the court paper was served upon all parties to the action as well as specifying the means of service (mail, hand delivery, facsimile). Certificates of service are required on all pleadings and court papers filed with the court, with the exception of the complaint or other documents requiring service of process.

*Ex parte communications*, or communications with the court that do not involve all parties to the matter, are prohibited. The Administrative Procedure Act defines an *ex parte communication* as "an oral or written communication not on the public record [for] which reasonable prior notice has not been given." 5 U.S.C. § 551(14). This concept applies to both oral and written communications with the court.

## <u>*Answers*</u>

### <u>Response to the Complaint</u>

The answer to the complaint is due within 20 days after service of the summons and complaint. Fed. R. Civ. P. 12(a)(1)(A). To determine the exact day, review Fed. R. Civ. P. 6, which details the rules for calculating deadlines. For example, if the 20th day falls on a Saturday or Sunday, the answer is due on Monday. If the 20th day falls on a legal holiday, the answer is due on the next business day following the legal holiday.

If there are appropriate grounds, a *motion to dismiss* pursuant to Fed. R. Civ. P. 12 may be preferred to filing an answer. Under Fed. R. Civ. P. 12, a successful motion to dismiss can terminate the lawsuit when any one of the following is successfully pleaded:

- Lack of subject matter jurisdiction;
- Lack of personal jurisdiction; or

- Failure to state a claim upon which relief can be granted.

A motion to dismiss may also raise procedural defects, which are usually curable and do not terminate the action. For example, a *motion for a more definite statement* asks the court to require the plaintiff to amend its complaint with a more definite statement. This motion must be filed prior to the answer deadline.

The Answer

On or before the 20th day after service of the summons and complaint, each defendant should file its answer. The purpose of the answer is to deny the allegations of the plaintiff as set forth in the complaint. If the defendant does not deny the allegations, they are treated as if admitted. *See* Fed. R. Civ. P. 8(b).

For this reason, the defendant should deny each allegation that can ethically be denied. While *general denials* are often used in state court actions, they are rarely used in federal court. The defendant should use specific denials, stating in plain terms its defenses to each of the plaintiff's allegations. If the defendant can deny only part of the allegation, he/she must specify the part admitted and deny only the remainder. *See Mann v. Smith*, 796 F.2d 79, 86 (5th Cir. 1986). If the defendant is without knowledge or information sufficient to form a belief as to the truth of the matter alleged, he/she must so state. Fed. R. Civ. P. 8(b).

An *affirmative defense* permits a defendant to avoid liability even if the plaintiff's allegations are true. By pleading an affirmative defense, the defendant alleges that other facts preclude liability. Rule 8(c) requires that the defendant raise any affirmative defenses in its answer, or the defense will be waived. Rule 8(c) lists 18 affirmative defenses. For example, alleging that the claim has been brought beyond the time allowed in the statute of limitations is an affirmative defense. *Laches* is another affirmative defense, referring to the doctrine that an unjustifiable delay in asserting a claim that causes prejudice to the defendant can cause the claim to be barred.

*Discovery*

The purpose of discovery is to ascertain the facts necessary to determine the merit of a party's claims and to preserve testimony and physical evidence to be used at trial. Simply put, the purpose of discovery is to find out the facts of the case beyond the court-ordered disclosures required pursuant to Fed. R. Civ. P. 26. The basic forms of discovery are:

- Interrogatories (Fed. R. Civ. P. 33);
- Requests for production (Fed. R. Civ. P. 34);
- Requests for admission (Fed. R. Civ. P. 36);
- Depositions by written questions (Fed. R. Civ. P. 31); and
- Depositions (Fed. R. Civ. P. 30).

Rule 26(b) sets forth the scope of discovery allowed in federal, civil matters, stating that a party may discover any information relevant to the subject matter of the suit that is not privileged.

Discovery Plan, Pretrial Conference and Scheduling Order

*See* Fed. R. Civ. P. 16 and 26. Once the suit is filed and the defendant(s) have appeared, Fed. R. Civ. 26(f) requires the parties to conduct a *case-management conference* where they discuss the claims, defenses and settlement, arrange for initial disclosures and develop a proposed *discovery plan*. The purpose of the discovery plan is to avoid deadlines for completing discovery and motions.

Once the court receives the proposed discovery plan, it holds a case-management or pretrial conference with the parties, either in person or by telephone. The court then enters a *scheduling order,* setting forth dates by which the parties will amend pleadings and join parties, file motions and complete discovery.

Initial Disclosure

Fed. R. Civ. P. 29(a) requires initial disclosures between the parties without waiting for a discovery request. The parties are to provide to the opposing party:

1. The name, address and telephone number of each individual likely to have discoverable information that the disclosing party may use to support its claims or defenses;

2. A copy description of all documents and other tangible things that are in the possession, custody or control of the party and that the disclosing party may use to support its claims or defenses; and

3. Damage compilations and insurance agreements.

Unless otherwise ordered by the court, these disclosures are to be made within 14 days after the case-management or pretrial conference. Rule 26 also requires disclosure of expert witnesses and reports; the name, address and telephone number of each trial witness; and trial exhibits.

Scope of Discovery

Rule 26(b) sets forth the standard or scope of discovery allowed in federal civil matters, stating that a party may discover any information relevant to the subject matter of the suit that is not privileged. The information sought does not have to be admissible as evidence, as long as the information is reasonably calculated to lead to admissible evidence. The rule also allows the court to set limits on the frequency and extent of the use of the various discovery methods, based on several factors to be considered, found in Rule 26(b)(2)(C).

Rule 26(b) was amended in 2006 to provide specific rules for the discovery of electronically- stored information. "A party need not provide discovery of electronically stored information from sources that the party identifies as not reasonably accessible because of undue burden or cost." The responding party has the burden of showing that the information is not reasonably accessible. The court can, nonetheless, order discovery of that information and set conditions on how that discovery is to be performed.

Interrogatories

*Interrogatories* are written questions used to acquire information from another party. Fed. R. Civ. P. 33. Unless otherwise ordered by the court or agreed to by the parties, parties are limited to propounding 25 interrogatories, including subparts. Interrogatories must be answered separately and fully, in writing, under the oath taken by the person answering. The rules allow for objections, which are signed by the attorney. Answers to interrogatories are due 30 days after service of the interrogatories.

Request for Production

Fed R. Civ. P. 34 allows a party to request production of documents, records and other tangible things in the possession, custody or control of the other party. The request must set forth, either by item or category, the items to be inspected and describe each with reasonable particularity. Notice that the language of the rule states "produce" and "inspect." This does not mean that the responding party must provide copies of documents requested.

The party upon whom the request is served is required to serve a written response within 30 days after service of the request. The response shall state, with respect to each item or category, that inspection will be permitted, as requested, unless objected. The party who produces the items may produce them in one of two ways: (1) as kept in the ordinary course of business; or (2) by request category.

Pursuant to Fed. R. Civ. P. 45, a nonparty may be required to provide documents through service of a subpoena. The nonparty may not be required to appear only to produce the requested documents – unless the subpoena specifically demands their presence.

Requests for Admission

Rule 36 allows a party to request another party admit the truth of any relevant, non-privileged matter, whether it is a fact or legal issue. Each matter shall be set forth separately. Unless the responding party objects or provides a written answer within 30 days after service of the request, the matter is deemed admitted. The answer shall specifically deny the matter or set forth in detail the reasons why the answering party cannot truthfully admit to or deny the matter.

Depositions by Written Questions

This method allows a party to present written questions to a witness, party or nonparty, who then answers the questions under oath. Depositions on written questions may be served on parties and nonparties. The most common use of this form of discovery is to obtain and authenticate the business records of a nonparty. Fed. R. Civ. P. 31 limits each party to ten depositions on written questions, but this limit may be increased by court order or written agreement of the parties.

Depositions

An oral deposition allows a party to ask questions to another party or nonparty, under oath, before the trial. Unless increased by court order or written agreement of the parties, Fed. R. Civ. P. 30 limits the number of depositions a party may make take to ten per side.

Unless amended by court order or written stipulation of the parties, a deposition is limited to seven hours in one day. Before a deposition may be taken, the rules require that the requesting party notify all parties, in writing, of the time and place of the deposition and the name and address of each person to be examined. If the person's name is not known, a general description is sufficient to identify the person or class/group to which the person belongs.

The rules further allow for the production of documents at the time of the deposition by the party being deposed. If documents are requested, the notice must detail the documents to be produced. If the deponent is a nonparty, a *subpoena duces tecum* must be served upon the person to be deposed. The list of materials to be produced, as set forth in the subpoena, must be attached or included in the notice of deposition.

Depositions are usually taken in person in the presence of a court reporter or videographer. Upon written stipulation of the parties, depositions may be taken by telephone or by other remote electronic means.

Subpoenas

A *subpoena* is a form of order compelling a person's attendance at trial or deposition. Fed. R. Civ. P. 45 governs the form and procedure of issuing subpoenas. As noted above, a *subpoena duces tecum* includes a request to produce certain documents or things. Disobedience of a subpoena may result in a finding of contempt of court and sanctions being imposed, including a monetary penalty, or in severe cases, by incarceration.

Motions

A *motion* is an application to the court requesting an order or rule in favor of the applicant. As noted above, a party can move to request that a claim be made more definite, or that a claim be stricken entirely. During discovery, a party can move the court to compel the other party to produce documents or things for which an objection has been raised or that the responding party has refused or simply failed to produce.

A motion for summary judgment is made when a party believes that after considering the undisputed facts and the application of the law, the moving party is entitled to judgment in its favor. Motions for summary judgment are typically accompanied by a concise statement of the pertinent facts, a memorandum of law and affidavits of witnesses, along with exhibits to provide evidence of the undisputed facts.

Following trial, a party may move the court for a judgment notwithstanding the verdict, otherwise referred to as "JNOV." In this motion, the party sets forth reasons why, in light of the facts presented to the jury and the applicable law, a reasonable jury could not have arrived at the verdict they did.

Motions may also be filed for routine scheduling matters, such as extending the deadline for completion of discovery. Check your local rules for whether routine motions are needed or whether a joint letter-request from counsel can achieve the same result.

The party moved against will have an opportunity to file a response, unless the motion is unopposed or the parties have discussed the matter and agreed to *stipulate* to the entry of a particular order. For certain motions, such as those for summary judgment, the moving party is allowed to reply to the opposing party's response. The moving party states in its motion whether or not they are requesting oral argument on the motion. The court has discretion in allowing oral argument; if allowed, a hearing will be scheduled for the parties to argue the motion before the court. The court's decision on the motion will typically be reflected in a written order.

## Meeting Time Deadlines

Follow established office policies and procedures in preparing, filing and serving documents. Most firms have established practices for obtaining firm checks for filing fees. Firms may prefer to use a certain process server. Some firms retain as support staff a person responsible for filing court documents. Due to filing complexity or time deadline, you may wish to file certain key court papers personally. In some venues, it is mandatory to file electronically with the court. Check your local rules.

Preparing, filing and serving documents are time-sensitive tasks, whose deadlines are often provided by court order or rule. You must be able to determine, calculate and meet these deadlines. You should calendar court-imposed deadlines either manually, through a tickler or calendar system, or through a computerized calendaring system so that the entire legal team is aware of each deadline. The basic deadlines are:

- Defendant's answer date: 20 days after being served with the summons. *See* Fed. R. Civ. P. 12(a)(1)(A).

- Responses to discovery (interrogatories, requests for production and requests for admissions): 30 days after service, unless otherwise ordered by the court.

Add three days to deadlines if mailed. Review the local rules for calculations relating to telecopied or electronically-filed documents.

## Other Areas of Law

In the areas of law besides litigation, there are often requirements on the form and substance of documents to be filed with recorders, registries, agencies or other entities. The particular entity will publish the rules applicable to filings with that entity. For example, deeds and other documents that affect interests in real estate must have certain information included in order to be accepted for recording in deed registries kept by the county recorder or county clerk. Each county may set forth specific requirements on the form of documents to be filed, such as reserving space for the recorder to add a recording index number or setting forth the name and address where property tax statements are to be sent. Although the requirements can be similar from location to location, the local rules should be researched to avoid having documents rejected.

***20.07 Prepare client, witnesses, experts, counsel and other individuals for legal proceedings and events through meetings, discussions, role-playing or other appropriate means to advance the client's goals and interests.***

*Preparing Counsel*

Your first and primary task as a paralegal is to prepare your attorney(s) for the legal proceedings at hand. This is accomplished by preparing notebooks containing all relevant documentation and research. The style and format of the notebook will depend on the proceeding. It is vital that the notebook contain important information in an easily accessible and labeled format.

*Preparing Witness Notebooks and Witness Files*

It is good practice to prepare witness notebooks or witness files containing the following information:

- Live pleadings;
- Protective or other discovery-related orders;
- Documents produced and perhaps documents collected that mention the witness;
- Deposition exhibits that mention the witness;
- Previous deposition testimony referring to or naming the witness;
- Discovery pleadings (interrogatories and disclosures) mentioning the witness; and
- Other research relevant to the case that relates to the witness, such as background searches, Secretary of State information and Google searches that mention the witness or his/her businesses or affiliates.

Gathering all documents related to a particular witness should be done well in advance of the deposition, meeting or witness preparation session. Typically, documents are organized chronologically. Key documents may be organized chronologically, by subject matter or both.

Determine the attorney's preference regarding the content of the witness file or notebook. Some attorneys prefer to see all documents mentioning the witness, while others may want you to cull down the documents to only key documents.

Once all of the information is researched and collected, paralegals might:

- Prepare summary highlights or memos of key information;
- Draft witness examination questions; and/or
- Prepare and mark copies of potential exhibits to be used in the proceeding.

In preparing questions for the witnesses, your attorney may:

- Ask the witness' name and background information relevant to the matter;
- Establish the witness' knowledge about relevant facts to which he/she will testify;
- Ask about facts or allegations you want to prove;
- Ask the witness to identify and introduce exhibits you want admitted through the witness; and
- Prepare to soften the blow of cross-examination questions by anticipating problems with the testimony. For example, if a prior deposition or statement appears to conflict with current testimony, ask the witness questions that elicit explanation for those inconsistencies.

In preparing questions for the opposing side's witnesses, the attorney may want to:

- Determine the probable purpose of the testimony;
- Anticipate direct examination questions and key facts and exhibits likely to be admitted through the witness (summarize that testimony);
- Review the witness file, paying special attention to previous testimony of the witness;
- Prepare leading questions to solicit information your side wants to prove; and
- Prepare leading questions to solicit inconsistencies in the witness' testimony. Note previous testimony references by page and volume and, if possible, by quoting the statement.

*Preparing Witnesses*

Testifying as a witness can be an unsettling experience, even for experienced expert witnesses. Paralegals are often asked to assist in preparing the client, witnesses and experts for legal proceedings. A witness who is prepared and knows what to expect will be more at ease testifying and will be a more effective witness.

Before the Witness Testifies

Contact the witness or client. Remind him/her of the proceeding's date, time and location, as well as last-minute contact information for any changes thereto.

Arrange a witness preparation time in the law office in advance of the proceeding. If such preparation is not necessary, provide the witness with directions to the courthouse and courtroom number and location.

Tell the witness where to meet you and/or the attorney. Determine if the attorney will want to spend time with the witness during a break or before the proceeding. If so, set up a meeting time and location.

Observe the layout of the courthouse. Where are the restrooms? The cafeteria? The best place for parking? The telephones?

If necessary, arrange for witness subpoenas. Also, determine if the witness has special needs that must be accommodated.

Witness Preparation Meeting

The purpose of the witness preparation meeting is not only to prepare the witness for his/her testimony at the proceeding, but also to put the witness more at ease concerning details such as procedure, attire, parking, courthouse location, etc. The time spent in preparation will obviously depend on the facts of the matter. A client's preparation time will be more exhaustive than that of a typical witness.

While communications with a client are protected from discovery under the attorney-client privilege, communications with witnesses are not protected. Keep this in mind throughout the witness preparation.

You will use your research, witness files and/or witness notebooks at the preparation meeting. Make sure all documents are easily and quickly accessible.

Most of the time, the attorney will prepare witnesses. There will, however, be times when the paralegal may be called upon to assist in witness preparation. Prior to the witness preparation, prepare an outline for the preparation session. The preparation session should provide the witness with information concerning:

- The status or review of allegations in the matter;
- Review of key documents;
- Review of documents to be admitted through the witness;
- Rough run-through of questions to be asked on the stand;

- Run-through of potential cross examination questions likely to be encountered; and

- Review of last minute details, such as time and meeting place and what to expect at the proceeding.

Role-playing is a technique utilized in preparing witnesses for proceedings. You may role-play both parties' attorneys by asking potential questions that will be asked on the stand. Role-playing the part of the opposing attorney cross-examining the witness is an important aspect of preparing a witness for a legal proceeding.

Preparing for Experts' Testimony

Preparing an expert for his/her testimony is very similar to preparing clients or witnesses except that the expert, as we have discussed earlier in this Domain, has specialized knowledge of a particular subject matter. Since experts are typically not fact witnesses, it is not likely that the documents produced and deposition testimony will refer to the expert. However, there are many Internet and other resource opportunities to investigate in preparing either your expert for a proceeding or preparing your attorney for an opposing expert.

In conducting research about the expert, start with the expert's resume. Use employer resources including databases, counsel association memberships and Internet resources to find out as much as you can about the expert, including obtaining any prior testimony. Consider purchasing any documents, articles or textbooks the expert has authored.

*Preparing for Hearings*

Once again, the topic or issues will determine the material you gather and most likely prepare in notebook format. If pleadings, motions or briefs were filed related to the hearing, you will want to include them, as well as all cases and statutes referred to in both parties' pleadings, motions and briefs. If you include cases, it is good practice to cite-check all cited cases and include the cite-checking data either as a separate tab or before each case tab. Live pleadings, relevant discovery motions (of a discovery related hearing), court rules and procedures may be included in the materials collected.

*Preparing for Administrative Proceedings*

Administrative agencies have far reaching power in many practice areas. In contrast to trial or court procedure, administrative agencies may conduct investigations, draft appropriate rules and hear testimony on their own in order to propose appropriate rules. Most of the day-to-day work of administrative agencies is less formal and have no need for hearings or formal proceedings. Typically, the process begins with the filing of paperwork, such as an application. Most decisions are made solely based upon the papers submitted. Formal hearings are most likely to occur when the agency's decisions are appealed, the agency seeks to impose a fine or take punitive action. Formal hearings may be required to resolve a dispute.

Preparing for administrative proceedings is similar to preparing for hearings and other legal proceedings. Procedures vary from agency to agency. With respect to federal agencies, always consult the appropriate written rules. The best source for agency rules in federal agencies is Code of Federal Regulations (CFR). Often, the agency rules contain dispute resolution procedures. Typically, when a dispute involves an administrative agency, the complaining party must first consult the agency before filing a lawsuit. This is known as *exhausting all administrative remedies.*

### *Preparing a Trial Notebook*

Remember that the purpose of a notebook is to have key information at your fingertips. Typically, a trial notebook may contain:

- Names, addresses and telephone numbers of the client, attorneys, court personnel and witnesses;
- Photocopies of pretrial orders, live pleadings, form for *voir dire*, key discovery, witness and exhibit lists for all parties, expert designations, orders on discovery or summary judgment, proposed jury instructions or any other pre-proceeding documentation required by the court;
- Photocopies of exhibits;
- Witness outlines with corresponding exhibits;
- Photocopies of key documents; and
- A notes section.

The volume of the exhibits and discovery materials may prohibit their inclusion in the trial notebook. If so, prepare separate notebooks for plaintiff's exhibits and defendant's exhibits, as well as discovery documents. Better yet, in this technological age, all exhibits are scanned, OCR'd and available in electronic format.

### *Preparing for Real Estate Closings*

Real estate law varies from state to state. Review state law before beginning preparation for a real estate closing. A closing is a meeting at which the seller, buyer and their attorneys or lending officials exchange the documents needed to finalize the sale of a piece of property. Necessary documents basically fall into one of four categories:

- Documents representing the agreement to purchase the property;
- Documents representing the sale of the property;

- Documents representing financing; or
- Miscellaneous documents.

It is a good idea to prepare a closing checklist detailing information such as: documents that must be delivered prior to closing; the party responsible for delivery; appropriate documents and the status of documents delivered. Summarize key information and dates in the closing checklist:

- The date of the contract;
- Notice of ownership due;
- Due diligence items due;
- Survey and title due;
- Survey and title objections due;
- Inspection period expiration; and
- Date of closing.

<u>*Additional Legal Terms*</u>

The *subpoena* is a procedural tool used in preparation for legal proceedings. A *subpoena* is a writ issued under the authority of a court to compel the appearance of a witness at a judicial proceeding. Check your local court rules and regulations to determine the procedure for obtaining and objecting to subpoenas. Fed. R. Civ. P. 45 specifies the procedures for the issuance, service and quashing of subpoenas in federal court proceedings.

You should subpoena a hostile witness or a witness who may not be cooperative in attending a proceeding. Your client or friendly witnesses may also require a formal subpoena (*e.g.*, to get off from work). Separately, subpoenas may also be used to secure documents from outside sources either before or at trial.

Be aware that Fed. R. Civ. P. 45 allows for subpoenas to be quashed if a nonparty deponent is made to travel more than 100 miles from his/her home or workplace.

A witness is presumed competent if he/she possesses the qualifications necessary to give testimony. A witness is incompetent for only two reasons: (1) lack of personal knowledge; or (2) lack of oath (*i.e.*, the witness has failed to promise to tell the truth).

***20.08 Assist the client, counsel and other individuals by attending legal proceedings and events and performing appropriate duties and actions to advance the client's goals and interests.***

The tasks you perform during legal proceedings will vary depending on the attorney and the case situation. You may perform the following tasks:

- Taking notes and observing;
- Assisting the attorney in developing strategies and analysis of evidence presented;
- Coordinating witness preparation and presentations; and/or
- Organizing and maintaining exhibits and materials, including tracking evidence.

Pursuant to rules and regulations, there will be deadlines imposed by the court. Determine those deadlines and calendar them so that necessary documents are timely filed. Calendaring or tickler systems vary from maintaining independent manual calendars to computerized calendaring systems that automatically notify members of the legal team by printed document or computer alert.

You and the attorney should determine the best way for the client to communicate to the attorney during legal proceedings. Many attorneys prefer not to have the client continually tugging on their sleeves throughout legal proceedings. As liaison, you may be called upon to intercept and decipher client notes and comments.

Legal proceedings tend to be pressure-filled. Effective, clear and concise communication is especially necessary during these situations. Before the proceeding, ask the attorney his/her preferences on communicating with the client and the legal team. All members of the team should understand each other's areas of responsibility and duties. Regular team meetings prior to and during the course of the proceedings, such as a regular meeting at the end of the day, will help facilitate effective communication amongst team members.

Team members' duties and responsibilities are better communicated if provided in written format. A simple memo or chart outlining team personnel, key telephone numbers and duties will serve as a help, reminder and communicator.

Use critical thinking skills to evaluate evidence presented during the proceeding. Take note of any deviation to the proceeding plan. For example, if a witness fails to establish a fact or evidence fails to be admitted through a particular witness, that fact or evidence must be established through another witness. Tracking and documenting evidence will assist you in this analysis.

Taking notes is an important role of the paralegal during legal proceedings, particularly those in which daily transcripts are not available. While the traditional method of taking notes has been the pad and pencil, computers are often now utilized. If computers are used in the courtroom, make sure that they are not disruptive. (For example, the alarm for a low battery should be muted.) Make sure that the notebook screen is not visible to the jury, judge, witness or opposing counsel so that confidentiality is maintained.

One of the obvious advantages of taking notes on a computer is that the document can quickly be cleaned up and word searches can be easily performed. The depth of notes will vary by attorney and proceeding situation. Special areas of concern are:

- Inconsistent testimony;
- Observations concerning jurors' reactions to witness testimony;
- Court rulings on motions, whether written or oral; and
- Court rulings on the admissibility of evidence.

Tracking evidence is another key role of the paralegal during court proceedings. In advance of the proceeding, prepare a chart on which to track and mark exhibits as they are presented, offered, admitted or denied. Objections should be noted and, if given, the reasons for denial.

In addition to the physical chart, you are apt to be responsible for the trial exhibits until they are admitted, at which time court personnel (court clerk or court reporter) retain possession of the evidence. Your notes and tracking chart will be a useful backup should a conflict of opinion occur as to what evidence has been admitted.

At the end of the proceeding day, it is a good idea to confer with court personnel concerning evidence admitted to date. Maintain your record of evidence admitted by party and then by numerical order. For example, plaintiff's exhibits should be stacked in numerical order separate from defendant's exhibits, which are also in numerical order.

Effective communication is especially important during pressure-filled court proceedings when tempers and sleep are often in short supply. Preparing a list of questions and concerns for discussion with the attorney each evening is a good idea and avoids miscommunication.

*Demonstrative evidence* includes maps, charts, summaries, videos, models and computer-aided accident reconstruction demonstrations. Paralegals often prepare or assist in the preparation of such demonstrative evidence. A picture can paint a thousand words!

In preparing demonstrative evidence, determine the most effective form of the evidence, whether you produce a blowup with highlights of key contract language, a model of a tractor or a computer-aided accident simulation. If your matter is before a tribunal, consider the admissibility requirements under the federal rules and plan the establishment of authenticity pursuant to Fed. R. Evid. 901 and 902, as well as relevancy pursuant to Fed. R. Evid. 104(b). Discuss these matters with your supervising attorney.

It is a good idea to have demonstrative or summary evidence prepared by the person who will eventually authenticate it at trial. Not only does this make the prove-up easier, it also adds to credibility.

*Evidence* is all the things that are submitted to establish or disprove any alleged matter of fact. Evidence includes witness testimony, the introduction of records, documents and exhibits for the purpose of inducing belief in the party's contention or allegation by the fact finder. Evidence is presented at hearing or trial, during arbitration or through pleadings and motions to the court.

An *allegation* is not evidence, but is something to be proved or disproved through the introduction of evidence.

Evidence is relevant if it has "any tendency to make the existence of [a material] fact... more probable or less probable than it would be without the evidence." *See* Fed. R. Evid. 401.

*Hearsay* is a statement or assertive conduct that was made or occurred out of court and is offered in court to prove the truth of the matter asserted. Hearsay may be oral or written. Hearsay is defined in the federal rules at Fed. R. Evid. 801. Evidence that falls within the hearsay definition is not admissible. Central to the concept of hearsay is the purpose for which the declaration is being offered.

There are *exceptions* to hearsay that are admissible. These are described in Fed. R. Evid. 801 (d) and include: (1) prior statements by witness; and (2) admission by party-opponent. Rule 803 outlines more than 23 additional exceptions.

The *business records exception* is the most common of the hearsay exceptions and one the paralegal should know. Business records meet the hearsay exception as long as:

- they record acts, events, conditions, opinions or diagnosis made at or near the time by a person with knowledge;
- they have been kept in the course of regularly conducted business activity; and
- if it was the regular practice of that business to make the records.

<u>*Trial Proceedings*</u>

Typical trial proceedings consist of the following activities:

*Jury selection* is the process by which a jury is seated in a jury trial or proceeding. Jury selection includes *voir dire*, which literally means "to speak the truth." *Voir dire* refers to the questioning of potential jurors by either the judge or attorneys to determine their qualification for jury service.

An *opening statement* is the statement made by the attorney for each party after the jury has been selected and before any evidence has been presented. Opening statements outline what the party believes that the evidence will be and presents the party's theory of the case.

The party who has the *burden of proof* (most often the plaintiff in a civil matter or the *prosecutor* in a criminal matter) then presents his/her *case in chief.* The attorney presents witnesses upon direct examination. Opposing parties have the right to *cross-examine* witnesses. Courts allow re-examinations known as *re-directs* and *re-crosses*.

At the close of the plaintiff's case, the defendant can make a *motion to dismiss* on the ground that the plaintiff has failed to establish its *prima facie case* or case in chief. This motion is often called a motion for directed verdict; which, if granted, the case is over.

If the defendant's motion to dismiss is denied, the defendant has the right to call witnesses and introduce evidence and exhibits. The defendant then rests his/her case.

Some courts allow the parties an additional turn to call or recall witnesses in their *rebuttal* case. Rebuttal is limited to evidence presented to refute prior testimony; not to introduce new evidence.

Once the parties have rested, the judge must charge or instruct the jury on what legal standards apply. The judge prepares the *jury charge* or *jury instructions*. The parties have the right to object to portions of the charge.

Before or after the charge is presented to the jury, each party makes a *closing statement* in which they summarize the evidence presented and state what they think their side has proved and the other side has failed to prove. Once the charge is presented and closing statements are concluded, jurors recess to a private room for deliberations. Occasionally, juries come back and ask the judge questions concerning instructions or perhaps request to rehear certain testimony. Once the jury has reached a *verdict*, it returns to the courtroom. The foreperson hands the judge the verdict and the verdict is read aloud in court.

In most instances, a party has a right to a trial by jury in this country. Sometimes a party will waive its right to a jury trial or statute specifically denies a jury trial. The judge will then sit in as judge of the law and finder of the facts. This is known as a *bench trial*. The portions of a bench trial are basically the same as a jury trial, with the exception of the court's charge and jury deliberations.

Fed. R. Civ. P. 39 allows trial by either jury or the court. Trial by jury must be demanded or requested. Issues not demanded for trial by jury shall be tried by a court.

You will use legal organization skills and techniques during a court proceeding. Typically, you will be responsible for all of the documents of the matter. This means you will be responsible for locating at a moment's notice all exhibits, deposition transcripts and other trial materials.

Trial notebooks are key organization tools. If not in the trial notebook, discovery, as well as a complete set of each party's exhibits, should be placed in other notebooks for easy reference. In addition, exhibits should be organized by exhibit number or sometimes by the witness through whose testimony you wish the exhibit to be admitted as evidence.

Exhibits and case documents, as well as deposition and hearing transcripts, can be loaded in full text onto a computer database system and utilized by the party alone or perhaps by all parties, the court and the jury. In such paperless trial situations, the judge and jurors can read admitted exhibits or deposition testimony from monitors in the courtroom, rather than the physical paper document.

*Impeachment* is to call into question the veracity of a witness by means of evidence offered for that purpose or by showing the witness is unworthy of belief.

*Leading questions* are those questions that suggest the answer to the witness. Leading questions are not proper on direct examination but may be used during cross-examination or the examination of a hostile witness.

*Judicial notice* is a rule of judicial convenience whereby the court takes note of certain facts that are capable of being known to a certainty, thereby relieving a party of the burden of producing evidence to prove these facts.

There may well be court-imposed deadlines that occur during and after the proceedings. You should continue to maintain a calendaring system to track these deadlines. For example, Fed. R. Civ. P. 59(b) requires that a motion for new trial be filed no later than ten days after the court has entered judgment in the matter. A response to a motion for new trial is due ten days after the motion is filed or 20 days upon agreement and showing of good cause.

*Arbitration* and *Mediation* refer to alternate forms of dispute resolution. In arbitration, parties agree to have their dispute put before an arbitrator, who typically is a person or panel of people who have knowledge of the area of law or business that the matter arises from. The proceedings follow a set of rules that may be similar to court rules; however, the emphasis is on reducing the expense and time it would otherwise take to resolve the dispute in court. Arbitration hearings are formal in some respects and less formal in other respects to court trials. Contracts may contain clauses requiring the parties to settle any disputes arising out of the contract through arbitration. An arbitration decision may be binding, that is, without opportunity for appeal. In other cases, the non-prevailing party may have the right to refer the matter to the court for a traditional trial. A paralegal's role in preparing for and attending an arbitration hearing will be much the same as that for a trial. Evidence is presented through witness testimony and exhibits, and these must be prepared, scheduled, organized and coordinated.

Mediation is a process whereby the parties to a dispute separately present their side of the case to a neutral third party. This third party -- the mediator -- moves back and forth between the parties to discuss each party's strengths and weaknesses and how a compromise might be formed. If the parties can agree to a compromise, they prepare agreements resolving the dispute. A paralegal may be involved in planning and preparing for the mediation by outlining strengths and weaknesses of the case, by charting potential damages or by preparing the client for the mediation session.

Settlement refers to resolving a dispute through an agreement and dispensing with the need for further court proceedings. The parties draft a document that refers to the court case, arbitration or simply the subject matter of the dispute and present the terms they have agreed to in resolution of the dispute. Settlement agreements are typically not public documents, thus allowing the parties to keep the details of the resolution off the record.

More information on Arbitration, Mediation and final disposition of matters can be found in Domain 20.09.

### *20.09 Facilitate disposition of a client's legal matter by negotiating within designated parameters to advance resolution of the client's legal matter or secure alternatives which are in the best interests of the client.*

Although this section is placed at the end of the development of a client matter, resolving the dispute as early as possible in the course of the dispute is in the best interest of the client.

More than 90% of all cases settle before going to trial. Judges prefer settlement and there has been a trend toward greater judicial involvement and influence in the settlement process. Judges use Pretrial Conferences to get the parties together and talking. Courts have standing orders requiring parties to mediate at some point during the course of the litigation.

Settling a case involves three basic steps:

1. Determining the case's settlement value;

2. Selling the settlement value to the other side; and

3. Getting the client to agree.

<u>Alternative Dispute Resolution, Mediation and Arbitration</u>

Most rules and regulations require attempts at dispute resolution. Fed. R. Civ. P. 16(c)(9) gives the court the authority to take appropriate action with respect to settlement. Rule 16 generally requires that a party or its representative be present or reasonably available by telephone to consider settlement of the dispute.

Resources are available in the selection of mediators and arbitrators.

- American Arbitration Association (AAA) is a national, nonprofit organization that, for a fee, helps the parties select arbitrators. AAA has drafted rules known as "AAA Rules," which often appear in contracts.

- Judicial Arbitration and Mediation Service (JAMS) is another national group that provides arbitrators and mediators.

- Most federal courts maintain a list of alternative dispute resolution (ADR) providers. Check with the district clerk's office.

- The courts may establish local agencies. For example, Texas maintains the Texas Registry of Alternative Dispute Resolution Professionals. Further, Texas statutes (Tex. Civ. Prac. & Rem. §152.002) provide for county dispute resolution agencies established by the courts.

- Mediation firms and brokers. Mediators have aligned themselves in firms to provide mediation and arbitration services.

Determine the client's resources with respect to ADR. Many clients have experienced arbitration or mediation in previous disputes. Some may even be trained mediators. While there is little doubt that it is in the best interest of the client to settle the dispute as early as possible in the life of the dispute, the atmosphere of allegations, threats and conflict sometimes breed a fight-until-death mentality. The legal team should encourage ADR early and at various points in the development of the client matter, educating the client as to all options available.

A variety of ADR methods are available, including:

- Settlement conferences, as emphasized by Fed. R. Civ. P. 16.

- Mediation, a structured settlement conference in which a neutral third party helps opposing parties reach their own settlement. Mediators are specially trained and establish ground rules at the beginning of the conference. The mediator typically meets with parties individually, going back and forth between them with issues and ideas for resolutions.

- Arbitration, a formal evidentiary hearing before a neutral third party arbitrator. Both sides present their cases to the arbitrator(s), who render an award. Unless the parties agree that the decision of the arbitrators shall be binding, arbitrations are typically non-binding. Parties are more likely to be required to participate in pre-arbitration discovery or at least the exchange of exhibits in an arbitration proceeding as opposed to any other form of ADR. Discovery is not mandated; however, arbitrators generally adopt rules of procedure that correspond to the complexity of the case.

- Mini-trials, a proceeding in which the parties present their abbreviated cases to a neutral third party who may issue an advisory opinion on the merits of the case. The opinion is typically non-binding, unless otherwise agreed by the parties or pursuant to a rule or regulation.

- Summary jury trials, in which the parties present their case in abbreviated form to a jury that renders a non-binding decision.

Determine applicable court rules with respect to ADR and the ADR proceeding in which you are participating. Contracts often contain language describing the ADR method parties should utilize in the event of a dispute. If the dispute is regarding a contractual matter, be sure to review the contract carefully for ADR provisions.

*The Paralegal's Role in Negotiating Settlements*

Paralegals are not authorized to practice law and, in the traditional role, do not have the authority to negotiate settlements on behalf of clients. Under certain parameters and in certain practice areas (*e.g.*, subrogations, collections), there may be times when paralegals play a role in negotiating the settlement of disputes.

The textbook approach is to negotiate and settle the dispute as early and as practical as possible. Some suggest that within three weeks of the escalation of the dispute, a face-to-face meeting amongst members of your side should take place to obtain the information necessary for preparing a negotiation strategy. The following are key points in the textbook approach to negotiating settlements:

- Identify the needs of the parties, issues, positions and alternative solutions, along with the strengths and weaknesses of your side's position.
- Contact the opposing side within several weeks of the escalation of the dispute to diffuse adversarial expectations and lay the groundwork for a face-to-face meeting.
- Listen to the other side's positions so that you thoroughly understand them. Listen, understand, and then talk.
- If you cannot reach a settlement, invite the opponent to consider alternative methods of dispute resolution, including mediation and arbitration.
- Establish a short deadline with your opponent at the beginning of the session.
- Be a good listener. Your body language will tell your opponent whether or not you are listening.
- Maintain eye contact with the speaker. Face the speaker and lean toward him/her.
- Avoid a closed posture with arms and legs crossed. Crossed arms and legs may signal negative, defensive thoughts.
- Try to keep your hands away from your face. Rubbing your eyes or covering your mouth are unconscious signals that you doubt what you are hearing.
- Unclench your fists and attempt to keep your hands open with palms exposed. This signals that you are open to your opponent's position.
- Maintain control of your emotions and you will maintain control of the negotiation. When you are getting steamed, manufacture a reason to take a time out, such as going to the restroom or making a phone call. Once outside, concentrate on taking slow, deliberate breaths until you feel your body calm down.
- Listen for:

    1. The issues (what your opponent thinks is the problem);
    2. Positions (who your opponent blames);
    3. The underlying interests (how your opponent feels about the dispute and what he/she needs); and
    4. The solutions (your opponent's proposed compromise).

- Summarize and restate the issues, positions, interests and solutions of your opponent so that he/she knows you are listening and understand his/her position. This should be a diplomatic summary.

- Never make a concession without getting one in return.

*The Paralegal's Traditional Role in Facilitating Settlements*

Traditionally, paralegals are not called upon to actually settle or negotiate the settlement of disputes. In a more traditional role, paralegals facilitate the settlement of disputes and closing of legal matters by preparing summaries and researching and presenting evidence and documentation by using presentation software and videos to prepare settlement brochures and video presentations.

Preparing for and assisting in settlement proceedings encompass the same skills and techniques involved in Domains 20.07 (Preparing for Legal Proceedings) and 20.08 (Assisting in Legal Proceedings). Be thorough.

*The Paralegal's Role in Closing the Matter*

The documents maintained and archived once a client's matter has been resolved will depend on court and/or ethics rules, office procedures, attorney's direction and the client's wishes. Most firms and corporate legal departments maintain pleadings, correspondence, testimony and work product (such as legal research memos) in archived storage for a designated period of time. Generally, law firms and corporations pay for the storage on monthly basis. Firms often seek the direction of the client as to what to do with client documents and documents produced. If the document is not work product, some firms send as much as possible back to the client so that it becomes the client's burden to archive and store. Certain materials may be maintained for the firm's use such as expert research and testimony.

Regardless of the documentation stored, it is important maintain archive logs with brief descriptions stating:

- where the documents are stored;
- when the documents are scheduled to be destroyed;
- the date and method for destroying the documents; and
- the date the documents are returned to the client.

Settlement contracts and documentation may require the destruction of documents related to the litigation. If the settlement contract requires the destruction of documents by a date certain, be sure to calendar this date on the firm deadline calendaring system. Throwing documents in your trash receptacle is not ethical. Documents should be shredded either by firm personnel or by using a professional document destruction service. Don't forget about destroying electronic evidence either in disk format or on firm software databases.

## SAMPLE QUESTIONS FOR DEVELOPMENT OF CLIENT LEGAL MATTERS

1. A paralegal conducts a client interview of a prospective client at a racetrack. The attorney ultimately does not accept the case. The prospective client tape records the conversation and later plays the tape for a roommate. Which fact is most likely to cause the conversation not to be privileged?

   a. The interview was conducted by the paralegal.
   b. The attorney did not take the case.
   c. The client tape-recorded the conversation.
   d. The client replayed the tape for a roommate to hear.

2. If asked the chances of recovery during a client interview, the paralegal should:

   a. refer the question to the attorney.
   b. answer the question honestly.
   c. avoid answering the question.
   d. tell the client that the answer requires legal research.

3. What is the most important component of a judicial decision when interpreting case law?

   a. date of decision.
   b. presiding judge.
   c. syllabus.
   d. court's opinion.

4. A paralegal serves as the primary liaison with the client. The paralegal returns the client's phone calls and works to answer the client's questions. The paralegal sometimes sends the client discovery material. After several years, the client matter is concluded in a manner that the client feels is unfavorable.

   a. The attorney should have been the primary client liaison.
   b. The attorney failed to convey to the client realistic expectations for case resolution.
   c. The paralegal failed to regularly keep the client informed of case developments.
   d. The paralegal's writing skills are poor.

5. For an enforceable contract to exist, there must be:

   a. an offer, acceptance and consideration.
   b. a reference to the appropriate statute.
   c. an accord and satisfaction clause.
   d. signatures of the parties.

6. Which statement is true of corporations?

   a. corporations may hold and convey property.
   b. corporate entities cannot be sued by individuals.
   c. all shareholders are equally responsible for the corporation's debts.
   d. officers elect the board of directors.

7. The major difference between libel and slander is:

   a. slander is statutory, and libel is common law.
   b. libel requires maliciousness and slander does not.
   c. slander is spoken and libel is written.
   d. libel has more elements than slander.

8. It is not appropriate to use a confidentiality agreement when:

   a. hiring an employee.
   b. contracting with a vendor.
   c. interviewing a client.
   d. allowing a third party to examine documents.

9. A paralegal is reviewing documents in preparation for an upcoming document production and comes across a responsive document with the client's handwritten note addressed to the attorney. The paralegal should:

   a. produce the document anyway, since the note is not damaging.
   b. not produce the document because it is protected by the attorney-client privilege
   c. not produce the document because it is protected by attorney work product.
   d. redact the handwritten note and produce remainder of the document.

10. A paralegal is very interested in obtaining documents reflecting financing arrangements that the opposing party considers a confidential trade secret. To obtain the document most cost effectively, the paralegal should:

    a. prepare a motion to compel production of documents.
    b. prepare and serve a request to produce documents.
    c. request the documents via a deposition notice *duces tecum.*
    d. ask for a hearing with the court.

11. A client wants to reduce legal fees by doing some of the leg work in a federal court matter. Instead of paying a process server to serve an amended complaint upon the opposing party, the client wants to do it. Under these circumstances:

    a. service is proper, assuming the client is at least 18-years-old.
    b. service is improper, since only court approved process servers perform service.
    c. service is improper, because the client is a party to the suit.
    d. service is improper, because the client is not a United States Marshall.

12. When preparing a client to testify at trial, a paralegal should:

   a. simulate the trial experience.
   b. expose the client to evidence to be produced at trial.
   c. review jury instructions with the client.
   d. advise the client to give comprehensive answers.

13. Your key witness is a 12-year-old child. When the child is called to testify, the opposing attorney objects on the grounds of competence. The court is likely to allow the child's testimony if the witness:

   a. takes the oath to tell the truth.
   b. is assisted in testimony by the client's legal guardian.
   c. is the child of another party to the suit.
   d. is so nervous that he/she cannot communicate effectively.

14. Under what condition is evidence admissible at trial?

   a. when proper foundation has been laid.
   b. after the judge has investigated its authenticity.
   c. after it has been authenticated by a neutral party.
   d. when copies are distributed to the judge prior to admission.

15. Impeachment refers to:

   a. calling into question the veracity of a witness.
   b. prohibiting a witness from testifying.
   c. disqualifying the trial court from hearing the case.
   d. asserting privileges during a witness' testimony.

*Answers:*

1–d. This question requires an understanding of confidentiality and the attorney-client privilege. The correct answer is option (d) because the client, by replaying the tape for a roommate to hear, waived his/her attorney-client privilege by disclosing information to an outside third party.

All jurisdictions have enacted statutes that address privileged communications arising out of certain relationships. These privileges grant the right to a designated person not to testify about or disclose a confidential communication. Statutes give certain persons the right to prevent others from testifying about or disclosing any confidential communication between them during the course of the attorney-client relationship.

Confidential communications between an attorney and a client/prospective client during the course of their relationship are privileged and protected from discovery. A communication is confidential if it is not disclosed or intended to be disclosed to third persons, other than those to whom disclosure is in furtherance of the rendition of professional services to the client, or those reasonably necessary for the transmission of the communication.

The privilege belongs to the client. Only the client may waive the privilege and consent to disclosure of confidential information.

The attorney-client privilege extends to representatives, agents and employees of the attorney, including paralegals or other members of a law firm or in-house corporate legal department.

Option (a) is not correct because it is perfectly appropriate for a paralegal to conduct a client interview, as long as the paralegal does not create the attorney-client relationship by accepting the case.

Option (b) is not correct because it is ultimately up to the attorney whether or not to accept representation.

Option (c) is not correct because it is within a prospective client's rights to tape record a conversation with counsel or an agent/representative of counsel.

2–a. This question requires an understanding of ethics. In particular, you should understand the unauthorized practice of law in the area of giving legal advice and of appropriate client relationships when conducting a client interview.

The correct answer is option (a) because giving a direct answer (for example, 50%) to the question requires the exercise of legal judgment that is appropriate only for a lawyer. Just as important is the fact that a lawyer would not be able to answer the question directly without much explaining and qualification. The answer would have to be based on an assessment of all aspects of the case: evidence, witnesses, nature of the case and relevant law on the issue -- some of which might not be evident at this stage of the case or even just before trial.

Option (b) is not correct because of the foregoing reasons. Any honest answer that is truly responsive to the client's concerns would require the careful legal judgment of a lawyer.

Option (c) is not correct because it is inappropriate to avoid answering a client's question. The client will not be satisfied with the representation if he/she asks questions to which the paralegal and/or attorney do not respond.

Option (d) is not correct because it does not address the client's concerns in a straightforward manner. While research may indeed be required, this answer merely delays the necessity of contacting the attorney to pass along the client's question.

3–d. We could say use your analytical abilities, but just use your common sense. What is the bottom line? -- The decision of the court. Where can you find the reasons for that decision? -- In the court's opinion. Remember the scenario refers to interpreting case law. Neither option (a) nor (b) nor (c) is going to mean a thing compared to the court's opinion.

4–b. Here, you must carefully analyze the fact scenario. According to the scenario, the paralegal's efforts to serve the client were proper and ethical, never crossing into the unauthorized practice of law. There is no indication that the paralegal should *not* have been the primary client liaison, so option (a) can be eliminated.

There is no evidence that the paralegal failed to keep the client informed either verbally or by sending written materials. You can reject option (c).

Nothing in the scenario indicates that the paralegal's writing skills were poor. You can reject option (d). (Even if they were poor, you can reason that this would not affect the way the paralegal returned the client's phone calls!)

Option (b) correctly lays responsibility on the attorney, which is where it belongs.

5–a. For a contract to exist, there must be agreement (*i.e.*, offer and an acceptance) and consideration (value exchanged between the parties to the contract). If these elements are missing, there is no enforceable contract. Option (a) is correct.

Although some statutes, such as the Uniform Commercial Code, impact on contracts, contracts are based on common law. There is no requirement to cite a statute for every contract.

"Accord and satisfaction" means that the parties have in some way amended or changed the contract in a manner mutually satisfactory to both. The contract is not the same as when the parties first entered into it, but the change is acceptable to all the parties.

"Accord and satisfaction" does not impact on enforcement, which is the issue the question addresses.

Verbal contracts may be valid and enforceable. There is no signature on a verbal contract.

6–a. Any layperson knows option (b) is wrong -- corporations are constantly sued by individuals! To choose the correct answer from options (a), (c) and (d), you must know basic corporate law.

Option (c) is not correct because shareholders are liable only for the amount of their investment. This limitation on shareholder liability is one reason the corporation is such a popular form of doing business.

Option (d) is not correct because officers do not have authority to elect directors -- officers are elected *by* directors, as a rule, and carry out the policy set by the directors.

This leaves option (a), which is indeed true. A corporation is a statutory person that may hold and convey property just as a natural person (*i.e.*, a human being) may.

7–c. To answer this question, you have to remember the difference in the two torts of libel and slander, which is exactly what option (c) states: slander is spoken and libel is written. Note that the question asks what the major difference is. Even if another option were correct, the *major* difference is that though both defame -- one defames by words spoken and the other by words written.

8–c. This question requires an understanding of the purpose and use of confidentiality agreements, which fall under the general category of confidentiality and attorney-client privilege.

The correct answer is option (c). This sample question is stated in the negative so the answers include three appropriate uses of confidentiality agreements and one inappropriate use. The inappropriate use is with the client himself/herself.

Agreements are used to remind persons working with confidential or privileged material of their obligation to maintain the confidentiality of that material. In the agreement, the employee, third party or vendor acknowledges this duty and agrees not to reveal any information seen or otherwise obtained during the course of the work.

Under the evidentiary rule of attorney-client privilege, the client has an unqualified privilege over communications between the lawyer and the lawyer's agents. Ethically, the client has extended protection over other material not necessarily covered by the attorney-client privilege. The client can voluntarily waive the privilege. While a client should be reminded not to discuss the legal matter with persons outside the firm, the client does not sign an agreement to that effect. The client cannot be forced to agree to maintain confidentiality of his/her own confidences and secrets.

9–d. This question requires an understanding of what may and may not be produced to opposing counsel.

Option (a) is not correct because the paralegal is not in a position to decide unilaterally whether the note is damaging or not damaging.

Option (b) is not correct because, while the handwritten note may fall under the attorney-client privilege, the document itself may not be protected simply because the note has been attached to it at some point.

Option (c) is not correct because the scenario in no way indicates that the document was generated by the attorney or the attorney's agents in anticipation of litigation.

Option (d) honors the client's privilege concerning the handwritten note, which only the client may relinquish, while being responsive to the request for document production.

10–b. The key to selecting the best answer to this question is the phrase "most cost effectively," making option (c) correct. You can simply ask for the documents by preparing and serving a routine form you have in your form files. This option involves the fewest persons and the least expense, giving it a cost-effective advantage over options (a), (c) and (d). Note that the question does not rule out using other options if the opposing party declines to produce the desired documents!

11–c. To answer this question, you must first decide whether service is proper at all. You can eliminate option (a) by knowing that the age of the client is irrelevant; Fed. R. Civ. P. 4 mentions the age of the person serving, not the age of the person served.

Service, then, is improper -- but for which of the three reasons offered? You can eliminate option (b) because you know that service may be made by anyone who is not a party to the suit and who is at least 18-years-old. You can eliminate option (d) for the same reason.

This leaves option (c), which is indeed correct because Fed. R. Civ. P. 4 bars anyone who is a party to the suit from serving complaint and summons. Your client is a party to a suit, which is the reason service is improper.

12–a. This is another question you can answer by critical thinking and eliminating incorrect answers. For instance, the word "advise" in option (d) eliminates (d) as a possible correct answer. Common sense will tell you that knowing the jury instructions, which can be quite technical, will not assist the client in preparing his/her testimony.

While both options (a) and (b) may seem reasonable, the paralegal is not in a position to carry out option (b). The paralegal can, however, simulate the trial experience through: (1) role playing; (2) a review of potential questions that may be put to the client; and (3) familiarizing the client with the physical appearance of the courtroom.

13–a. The Federal Rules of Evidence do not disqualify a witness simply because he/she is a minor. If the 12-year-old is mature enough to satisfy the judge that he/she understands the importance and gravity of an oath to tell the truth, the child's age will not disqualify the child. Options (b), (c) and (d) are irrelevant; particularly (d), which, when coupled with the scenario, is clearly incorrect.

14–a. To answer this question correctly, you must know what evidence is. One simple definition is "that which is used to prove or disprove a fact." To prove or disprove a fact, a proper foundation must be laid. The correct answer is option (a). No "authenticating" or distribution of copies will make evidence admissible if the attorney does not first lay a proper foundation for admission of the evidence.

15–a. This question requires you to know the meaning of impeachment, showing that the witness is not worthy of belief. This is often done by pointing up inconsistencies, contradictions or untruths in the witness' prior testimony and current testimony. Option (a) is correct. Options (b), (c) and (d) are simply fine-sounding distracters. You will disregard them if you know the meaning of the term "impeachment."

## 30.00 LEGAL RESEARCH AND WRITING

### *30.01 Communicate with the client, counsel and other individuals or entities by using appropriate means to relay or request information, or respond.*

Basic communication skills are invaluable to any paralegal. When you think about it, all legal professionals either request or provide information each time they speak or write. Legal arguments, ideas, instructions and questions, whether oral or written, must be understood to be effective. Follow a philosophy somewhat akin to Murphy's Law: what can be misunderstood will be misunderstood. Because much of what a paralegal does is to obtain or request information, it is critical to be easily understood, leaving no room for misinterpretation.

Almost 300 years ago, British author and politician Joseph Addison said:

> If the minds of men were laid open, we should see but little difference between that of the wise man and that of the fool. The difference is that the first knows how to pick and cull his thoughts for conversation... whereas the other lets them all fly out, indifferently, in words.

We are judged, however fairly or unfairly, by what we say and write, and how well we do it.

Research has shown that, in face-to-face communications, the voice carries 38% of that communication, the body carries 55% and the words carry 7%. To make your communication with others effective, your voice, body and words should convey confidence in what you are saying and how you say it. Although your words may sound as if you are calm and self-confident, your foot beating a rhythm on the floor indicates something altogether different. When speaking, consider your inflection, tone, facial expression, gestures and words; take into account the total impression you make.

Listening is a valuable communication skill. Regardless of whether you are listening to a client or to your supervising attorney as he/she gives you an assignment, it is critical that you be able to understand and translate what is said. To listen with understanding, you must envision the speaker's expressed idea from his/her viewpoint, sense how it feels to that person and use his/her frame of reference about the discussed topic.

Practice good listening techniques. If we do not clearly understand what is being said, we often do one of two things: 1) if we are interested in what the person has to say, we listen more closely to catch the meaning of what is said; or 2) if we become bored or distracted, our attention on the speaker wanders until we have no idea what the other person has actually said.

Here are suggestions for improving your listening techniques:

1. Pay attention to the answer given after you ask a question. Instead of listening to a response to our own question, we often concentrate on what we intend to say in response to the expected answer or think instead about our next question. Or, we may allow ourselves to drift into thinking about unrelated things, such as plans for after work or the weekend.

2. Maintain eye contact with the speaker to avoid allowing yourself to be distracted or allowing your thoughts to wander.

3. Avoid the tendency to anticipate or jump to conclusions about what is said before the speaker has finished. Instead, listen closely even if you think you know what the other person is going to say.

4. Sometimes people are so eager to show their enthusiasm or interest that they offer unsolicited solutions and suggestions without realizing that the speaker would prefer that they listen rather than give advice. That is not to say solutions or suggestions are never appropriate; of course they are. But first, be sure that you fully understand what you have been told before you offer any advice or suggestions.

5. It is nearly impossible to concentrate fully on someone's words while doing something else at the same time. You may take in the gist of what is said, but will probably miss the details. Stop what you are doing and give the speaker your full attention.

In all communications with clients and others, always use good manners and courtesy. Keep your temper under control too. Your behavior -- good or bad -- reflects not only upon you and your firm, but upon your client as well.

Sooner or later, everyone says the wrong thing. If you have blundered badly, simply say "I'm sorry" and move on to another topic. If you have only flirted with danger, however, veer away as fast as you can. Do not make a scene by making profuse apologies or by becoming flustered. Staying poised will help others do the same. If it is the other person who has blundered, help him/her out. Change the topic to a safer subject and then move on as if nothing had happened.

*Facilitating Client Communication*

One of the most important functions a paralegal can have is to facilitate communication between the attorney and client. Communication can quickly break down, however, when a client's telephone calls or e-mails are not returned within a reasonable amount of time. Clients, as well as others, become quickly irritated when someone repeatedly fails to respond.

A hectic and demanding schedule is no excuse for failing to return someone's telephone call or answering an e-mail. Have you ever tried to reach someone by telephone repeatedly, only to have them answer several days later and say, "I've been so busy, I just couldn't return your call?" Did you feel any irritation when you heard that response? If so, you can easily imagine how a client might react. If you cannot return a telephone call or e-mail or make any other contact on the same day it was received, apologize for the delay. The person on the other end will appreciate your consideration and professionalism.

*Communication Using Management Skills*

Most paralegals are not taught the basic management skills that are one of the most important forms of communication in any office. Many paralegals find it difficult either to give instructions, receive criticism or both. These are skills that can, and must, be acquired to achieve your greatest level of effectiveness and professionalism.

Sometimes you may feel that you have not received thorough instructions for an assignment or have not been adequately told what is expected by the supervising attorney. At times, instructions or guidelines are haphazardly given or overlooked because of a busy work environment. Attorneys sometimes neglect details that they assume a paralegal either knows or can figure out. Regardless of the reasons, this type of environment often leads to poor quality work and frustration for the lawyer and paralegal.

Remember that all communication between two or more persons is subject to each person's individual interpretation. It is impossible to control how others present information to us. We should work on our own listening and speaking skills to improve communication.

Listen carefully when instructions or assignments are given. Whenever possible, take notes, but only if you can do so without missing what is said. Do not interrupt with questions until after the speaker has finished. Then, paraphrase your understanding of the assignment by repeating the instructions in your own words while referring to your notes, if any. The supervising attorney can then quickly determine whether you have misunderstood the instructions and make whatever corrections or explanations are necessary.

Once the attorney has given complete instructions for the assignment, think before you speak or ask questions. Take a minute, and think about the assignment. Do you fully understand everything the assignment entails? Do you know where to find the files you will need? Are there unanswered questions left hanging as to whom to contact or how to obtain certain information? Do not try to second-guess the attorney's meaning or intentions. If you are not sure, it is better to ask for clarification than to guess.

Each of us wants to be regarded as a competent professional who can be trusted to complete any task efficiently and without mistakes. Perhaps we are afraid that, by admitting we don't know how to do something, our superiors or peers will think less of us. Those who have trouble saying, "I don't know," are often more afraid of putting their qualifications in doubt than of the embarrassment of failure.

There is no such thing as a stupid question. It is always better to admit you do not know how to do something than to flounder around trying to figure it out. At best, you will produce substandard work and, at worst, something unusable.

Even constructive criticism can be difficult to accept. Good management problem-solving requires that, when problems occur, they be fixed in two ways. First, deal with the current situation or problem, overcome it and go forward. Second, go back and find the cause of the problem and eliminate it. Constructive criticism should never be given or taken as a personal issue. Constructive criticism is not a personal insult; it is a problem-solving tool to keep a problem from resurfacing in the future.

*Workload Management*

Some attorneys, regardless of their legal knowledge and skill, are poor people managers. Often, their instructions will be vague or incomplete and they may blame your poor performance on your lack of skill rather than their lack of clear communication.

If a supervising attorney refuses to give you the instruction you need, request help from another paralegal or attorney who specializes in that area or is familiar with the case. In either event, you will have made your best effort to complete the assignment as accurately as possible and will have gained new experience in the process.

Many people find it extremely difficult to say "no" to any assignment even though their workload is already overwhelming. Yet, it may be impossible to accept an assignment from a senior partner and keep the commitments you have already made to other attorneys in the office.

Here is an example of what can happen when work assignment priorities become an issue: On Monday, you accepted an assignment from one of the firm's young associates to summarize fifteen depositions before the end of next week. On Wednesday, the senior partner asks you to monitor a trial that is related to a case in your office and take notes. The trial should last until the end of the following week. What can you do?

Take yourself out of the middle of this dilemma and ask the attorneys who gave you the assignment to decide whose work should come first. No support person should be placed in the position of deciding whose work takes precedence over another's.

Whenever you are working on one assignment and are approached to do another, ask: "What is the deadline?" It may be that there is no conflict in getting both assignments done on time. If it appears, however, that meeting the deadline for one assignment will interfere with the other, let the second attorney know about your prior assignment. Tell the second attorney that you would like to take on the assignment, but make it clear that you have already committed yourself to others and say what those deadlines are. Discuss the new assignment's deadline and how that will affect the other assignments you already have. If there is a conflict, the attorneys -- not you -- should decide whose assignment has priority and set the deadlines for both the new and old assignments. Or, if you are unable to take on the new assignment, tell the second attorney that, because of other commitments, you are unable to take on his/her assignment, but hope that the attorney will keep you in mind for any future assignments.

*Client Communications*

One of the most frequent complaints to bar associations is the failure of lawyers to communicate with their clients. Too frequently, lawyers fail to return their telephone calls, send copies of correspondence and pleadings or keep clients informed of developments in the case. These and other client communications can easily be delegated to a paralegal.

People hire attorneys because they have a problem. The worry and stress associated with this problem are commonly manifested by the need to stay in close contact. Most clients have no intention of making unreasonable demands on their attorneys' time. They may need only to ask a question, give some information or get reassurance that their case is receiving adequate attention. Few attorneys have the time or patience to respond to every inquiry from a nervous client. The simplest solution is for the lawyer to assign the paralegal the task of relaying communications directly to the client.

All contact with the client should be memorialized for the file, noting the date, time and the gist of the conversation. If you send something to the client by mail, use a cover letter – and copy, or blind copy, the attorney. If the contact with the client is verbal, such as a telephone call, a written record should be made for the client's file. This is a safeguard not only for the client, but for you as well should a dispute ever arise about what was said or done. This can be a quick note jotted on a piece of paper and put in the file or a more formal memo to the file. When verbal communication results in action to be taken, a confirmation letter is needed setting out your understanding of who will do what and when.

Whenever you, the paralegal, have any communication with a client, you must remember that you are never allowed to give legal advice. You may convey whatever your supervising attorney tells you to say or write -- even when it is legal advice -- if you do not elaborate on, or explain, the message. If pressed for an answer, simply say something like: "I cannot give you legal advice, but I will be sure to relay your question to the attorney."

<u>*Language Skills*</u>

Paralegals must possess above-average knowledge and competency with the English language. The human mind comprehends words as through a veil. When we use an unfamiliar word or phrase, or when our writing is unnecessarily complex or cumbersome, the reader either gets the meaning slowly or not at all. The law is an intensely complex subject and easy to misunderstand. Especially when writing about complicated things, we must keep our writing plain and simple.

Invest in a good grammar book, put it beside your dictionary and use it often. Some of the rules of grammar may seem picky to you, but to ignore them is simply unprofessional.

Like proper spelling, use of proper grammar, punctuation and capitalization is a sign of professionalism. Do not mistakenly think that readers miss small errors in any of these areas. If what you write is correct in every small detail, the reader knows he/she is reading something written by a careful craftsperson. As a result, your writing will be much more persuasive.

Avoid slang, profanity, fad words or other sloppy language. This type of language makes the speaker appear coarse and unprofessional. Consciously force yourself to find substitutes for these words and eliminate them from your speech.

<u>*Grammar Skills*</u>

This study manual cannot tell you all there is to know about grammar and punctuation, but it will address the major rules, as well as a few rules of capitalization. Using proper grammar is the mark of an educated and careful writer. Nothing will destroy the reader's confidence in you more quickly than an obvious grammatical error, for that will tell the reader you are either ignorant or careless, or both.

***30.02 Prepare and/or draft documents by using an appropriate format and means (including, but not limited to, computer entry and dictation) to advance the client's matter.***

As part of daily routine, paralegals draft a myriad of documents, such as correspondence, pleadings, contracts, legal memoranda and briefs filed with the court. All paralegals should possess above-average writing abilities. When paralegals write any type of document, it is for a definite purpose, often to give or request some kind of information to reach a specific result. Therefore, to communicate effectively as a paralegal, your writing must be clear, simple and concise.

It is critical that you leave a documented trail through every matter on which you work. Leave every file so complete that someone who knows nothing of the matter could pick up your file and work competently on it. This includes making sure that you do not keep the contents of conversations and telephone calls stowed away in your head. If you get sick or are unavailable for any reason, other people working on that file must have access to all the information relating to the case. They cannot read your mind.

Remember that it is very difficult to recall every detail of every matter on which you work. Six months after you have talked to the other side on some pending litigation, you may need to recall in detail what was said. You cannot be positive about who said what if you depend entirely on your memory. Moreover, if it comes to a dispute with another law firm about what was said, you will be far more convincing if you state what happened from notes made at the time of the conversation.

Make a written record of any conversation with an opponent, court reporter, judge's clerk, client or witness, etc., whether by phone or face-to-face, unless the conversation has absolutely no significance. If what you have just heard or otherwise learned is something you and your attorney need to process the case, you must get the information into the file. Regardless of whether you are sure a conversation is important, make a memo of it. Any substantive time you expend on a case -- and for which you will bill the client or someone else -- must be accounted for in the file.

*Using Samples and Forms*

Law libraries are full of form books containing volume after volume of sample writings for every occasion. Many law offices also keep samples of their own forms for future reference. These forms certainly have their place and can be useful in framing pleadings, contracts and other documents, including some types of letters. Much of their standard language, called boilerplate, is retained and used in every similar document.

However, be careful. Remember that no two legal matters are precisely the same. You may certainly use forms, but you must always be sure to tailor them to fit your precise purpose. Treat forms, especially letter forms, as models to be followed for general format and not necessarily for content. Your supervising attorney will tell you what standard language he/she wants retained in particular kinds of letters and what should be modified.

Some offices keep a file of sample documents to help new lawyers and paralegals with format; they can be very helpful. Better still, ask your supervising attorney about ground rules when you get the assignment; he/she is the one you must please. It helps to get a sample of a similar letter or document that the attorney has created. Use it as a model, but do not copy it. Remember, seldom are two documents exactly the same. Perhaps the best source of information on office forms and policy is an experienced legal secretary or paralegal.

*Memos to the File*

Whenever you are called by someone outside the firm on any matter, write a memo to the file or create a notation on the computer that is linked to the client's file. It takes only a few seconds to record this information. The rule here is: do it now. If you postpone recording the conversation, you increase the chance of forgetting exactly what was said.

What about writing a memo by hand? That will work, of course, but it is harder to read than a typed memo, and it takes at least as long to do. If your memos are handwritten, make sure you write them on a full-sized piece of paper, however short the memo. Little notes have a way of losing themselves in the file or falling out and disappearing forever. Also, make sure that the writing is legible and the meaning of the note can be understood. Many of us have our own shorthand or speedwriting that is easily read by us, but is undecipherable to anyone else. Keep in mind that any handwritten note to the file may also be referred to by others. Be sure to date the memo and include the case name at the top, in case the memo gets separated from the file.

Here is an example of a situation in which an internal memo to your attorney would be appropriate: the attorney has asked that you schedule a witness' deposition and has provided you with a list of dates and times when he/she will be available. Next, you call opposing counsel and, after explaining the reason for your call, agree on a specific date and time to hold the deposition. You then call to arrange for the court reporter.

Why could you not simply tell your boss when the deposition has been scheduled and go on to your next project instead of writing an internal memo? Something as important as a deposition -- or any event that requires the attorney's presence -- should be written down for the file and noted on the firm's tickler system. If you simply say to thc attorncy: "Thc dcposition has bccn sct for January 17th at 2 o'clock," one or both of you may forget when the deposition was scheduled.

Some offices keep a file of sample documents to help new lawyers and paralegals with format; they can be very helpful. Better still, ask your supervising attorney about ground rules when you get the assignment; he/she is the one you must please. It helps to get a sample of a similar letter or document that the attorney has created. Use it as a model, but do not copy it. Remember, seldom are two documents exactly the same. Again, the best source of information on office forms and policy may be an experienced legal secretary or paralegal.

*Letter-Writing Techniques*

As with any legal writing, you should always carefully proofread and edit any letter. Delete any unnecessary words or legalese. Write as you speak. Use plain English rather than legalese, and omit outdated phrases such as "the above-referenced case" or "enclosed herein." Your goal is to write letters that are easy to read and understand.

Although this has been stated in the previous section, it bears repeating here:

Like proper spelling, use of proper grammar, punctuation and capitalization is a sign of professionalism. Do not mistakenly think that readers miss small errors in any of these areas. If what you write is correct in every small detail, the reader knows he/she is reading something written by a careful craftsperson. As a result, your writing will be much more persuasive.

Avoid slang, profanity, fad words or other sloppy language. This type of language makes the speaker appear coarse and unprofessional. Consciously force yourself to find substitutes for these words and eliminate them from your speech.

As mentioned previously, all contact with the client should be memorialized for the file. If you send something to the client by mail, use a cover letter or enclosure memo.

Many lawyers write by opening a file and dictating the first thing that come into their heads. The result is often a confused mess in which topics and subtopics are all mixed together, leaving an irritated reader to waste time sorting everything out. It only takes a moment to make a note or two or an outline about what you want to say before you say it. Then you can write smoothly -- in short paragraphs -- dealing with one topic at a time.

Start by telling the recipient why you are writing. The "subject" line across the top of the letter will give the reader a general idea, but the first paragraph ought to specifically set out why you are writing.

Some legal professionals are fond of saying "in the above-entitled matter" or "in the above-referenced matter" at least once in any correspondence. Of course whatever he/she is writing about is "in the above-entitled matter." That is the reason for the subject line. Using "in the above-entitled matter" or "in the above-referenced matter is always unnecessary. Leave these out.

If you have not corresponded with the addressee before, introduce the firm before you state the purpose of the letter. For example:

> This firm represents the Estate of Mr. Charles Emory Martin, who, on May 14, 1992, was killed in a collision with a truck driven by your employee, Mr. Thomas A. Rodgers.

You will frequently need to ask the recipient to do something – sometimes several things. It is up to you to make certain that what you want done does not get lost in the rest of your letter. To be sure your addressee sees and identifies what is wanted, spell out what he/she must do and when it must be done. Put everything you want done in the same paragraph.

Numbering phrases or sentences does not lend itself to literary perfection, but it helps your reader pick up on those things he/she must take action on. A short paragraph like our example can then become a memo for action.

Always remember that what seems simple and routine to you may be complex and strange to a layperson. Take special care of correspondents who are elderly or unaccustomed to business or legal matters. Your efforts will help get things done smoothly and on time and your clients will appreciate your courtesy and attention to detail.

In the body of your letter, group similar things together. For example, suppose you are reporting on witness interviews, discussing what you found in medical reports, estimating the chances that your client will win or lose and asking the client to do something, all in the same letter.

In as many paragraphs as you need, deal with one topic only, such as the witness interviews. Finish that topic completely and then move on to the medical reports. Your letter will be easier for the reader to digest.

Bear in mind, by the way, that only the lawyer makes tactical judgments or predictions in a letter ("a 70% chance of winning"). You may never make such legal judgment calls yourself. If they are included in a letter, your supervising attorney must be the signer.

As a matter of style, some law offices will use headings for each topic, or will require that such headings be numbered. Others will require that each request be spelled out in a complete sentence or place other requirements on the format of letters. You must follow the office guidelines. In every case, however, you must try to organize each letter logically, making it as easy as possible for the addressee to understand and comply.

For simple letters covering one or two uncomplicated matters, you need not worry about careful organization and headings and such. If you are clear, your reader will understand without them. Even with short, simple letters, however, it is best to emphasize in the last paragraph anything the reader must do, supply or remember.

When you are answering a question posed to you in a letter from the correspondent, always restate that question, preferably in the exact words the reader used to you.

Limit the subject line to identifying the general subject matter of the letter and the file number. In this, as in all other matters of procedure and format, you will be guided by your attorney's preference.

When you write to the court about any case already filed with that court, always include the docket number of the case in your "subject" or "re" line. The docket number is the number assigned by the court administrator to identify each new piece of litigation.

Many offices require that the addressee's name appear at the top of the first page of a letter -- usually at the top left. If the letter is not sent by regular mail, show how the letter was transmitted.

If a letter has more than one page, make a header on the second and all subsequent pages by putting the name of the addressee at the top left. After the name, include the date of the letter and page number.

Always remember that there is no such thing as a "routine" letter. Every piece of correspondence has some importance. You should never treat correspondence casually, and you should not let a letter leave the office without reading it carefully in final form.

You will write thousands of letters every year. At first, especially, your supervising attorney may review some or all of them. Perhaps later, he/she may ask you to draft all of the correspondence in a given case or even to sign the attorney's name to some correspondence. Until your attorney pays you the compliment of giving you some latitude with correspondence, everything goes through him/her in draft.

*Common Errors in Letter Writing*

There are three common errors in letter writing. No matter what type of letter needs written, make every effort to avoid these three mistakes:

First, and worst, is writing so that your reader has trouble understanding you. Remember that your correspondent often knows little or nothing about the precise matter you are discussing. In any case, your knowledge is superior to that of your reader.

Second is talking down to your reader, insulting his/her intelligence or even giving that appearance. You must be sure your correspondent understands you, but it is unnecessary to explain the obvious or define a common term. Save your definitions and explanations of legal expressions and other unusual terminology.

Third is failing to be clear about the things you want your correspondent to do and when. Anticipate the reader's questions or possible misunderstandings. Deadlines or requests for action must be stated in such a way that the reader knows exactly what is expected and when. If there is a question in your mind as to whether the reader will know what you are talking about, do not leave anything to chance. Ambiguous letters are costly. You lose valuable time in writing second letters or making follow-up telephone calls and the additional time you spend solving the problem is passed on to the client in your fees.

Being Professional

Everything you write, whatever the subject matter and whoever the addressee, must be entirely professional in tone. Even when you are writing to a client you know well, do not say such things as:

> The insurance company just can't seem to get it together.

What is wrong with that sentence? To begin with, the expression is slang, and using slang is always a bad idea in formal correspondence. Worse, the line is vague; it does not tell the addressee what the problem is. Taken altogether, this language has an unprofessional tone, and every lawyer wants his/her paralegal to be always and entirely professional.

Sloppy English and careless writing also contributes to the impression of a lack of professionalism. Consider these lines, taken from an important letter demanding a large sum of money for an injured client:

> In addition, the facts of this case, as you very well know, are quite aggravated in view of the fact that your insured was driving his vehicle under the influence of alcohol and in concert thereof, fled the scene.

When we take this paragraph apart, you will find that it can be said more professionally in much fewer words:

- As you very well know is pure surplusage and a little insulting. Of course the other lawyer knows the facts and probably does not appreciate the condescending tone of the phrase.

- In view of the fact is a sure sign of careless writing. Because would have been better and saved four words.

- In concert applies to people acting together. What this writer meant was simply "and" or "and also." Thereof is advanced legalese and, in any case, it is wrongly used; therewith is the only word that fits with in concert and it too is pure legalese.

Altogether, the writer gave the other side the impression they were dealing with a confused mind -- a paralegal who could not be bothered with the details of an important letter. The attorney on the other side will not be impressed with his opponent's letter. Moreover, if this firm's client is intelligent and sees this letter, it could shake his/her confidence in his/her lawyer and the lawyer's support staff.

Sometimes you will write letters to people you know -- perhaps a paralegal or lawyer whom you see socially. Or, you will draft a letter for your attorney to someone the attorney knows well -- perhaps a law school classmate. Regardless, stay away from first names. Should your client also receive this letter, he/she simply may not understand how a lawyer can represent a client zealously and still call the other side's lawyer by a first name or nickname. Except in a purely social setting, address other legal professionals as "Mr." or "Ms.," no matter how well you and your attorney know them.

This principle applies to anyone to whom you write. Address everyone as Mr. or Ms., unless they have a title such as Judge, Reverend, Doctor, Major, etc., in which case you would use their title. Unless the person asks you to do so, never address anyone (even a personal friend) with whom you deal on behalf of your employer by that person's first name.

<u>Being Temperate</u>

Being temperate is really part of being professional. It means, simply put, to avoid sounding boastful and quarrelsome. Bombast and threats are not only highly unprofessional, but entirely unproductive. Here is a real-life example:

> I have been a trial lawyer in the city of X for … 18 years and hold the record for the highest jury verdict … awarded … in the sum of $2.1 million dollars.

The implication is, of course, that the opponent ought to give in and settle the suit immediately, but lawyers and other legal professionals are not intimidated that easily. Legal professionals' reactions to boasting such as this are usually quite different. They simply redouble their efforts to frustrate the writer's efforts to obtain whatever it is the writer wants. Any cooperation the writer might have otherwise received, he/she will receive no more, and the writer will acquire the reputation of a braggart in the bargain.

Being Understood

The secrets to being understood in writing are to:

- Delete every word that serves no function;
- Edit each verbose phrase that could be a short word;
- Delete every adverb meaning the same thing as the verb;
- Avoid the passive voice, which can leave the reader uncertain about who did what; and
- Use proper grammar and punctuation.

No matter whom the addressee, plain language is always best. The cardinal rule of legal writing applies here as it does everywhere else: if you don't say it, don't write it. Keeping it clear and concise helps ensure that everyone to whom you write will understand what you are talking about, no matter the level of the person's education.

Even if you do this, however, you must consider your audience. For a client with an eighth-grade education, you will have to take special pains to be clear. Short, simple writing may be the only thing that your addressee can easily follow. At the same time, you must be careful not to appear to talk down to people -- nothing is more insulting. Unless you are quite positive you are writing to somebody with sharply limited education or intelligence, ordinary language will do just fine for both layperson and learned lawyer.

Even when you are writing to an educated person, remember that he/she probably will not understand legal words of art and the jargon of other professional disciplines. Do not write glibly about *res ipsa loquitur* or "magnetic resonation" without telling your addressee what these terms mean.

Avoid legalese -- everywhere, of course -- but especially in letters. Fancy legal words add nothing but length and have a particularly discouraging effect on clients and other laypeople. They will not be impressed. "Whenever I read something and I don't understand it," said Will Rogers, "I know it was written by a lawyer." Most of the public share Rogers' opinion of lawyer's language, so be very sure you keep out all saids, hereinbefores and similar ancient terms.

Stay away from antique language, too. Oddly, many lawyers who normally speak good, modern English regress a couple of centuries when they write letters. "Yours of the 18th instant to hand" they write, instead of "I have received your May 18, 1994 letter." Paralegals, in a misguided attempt to sound more professional, may also adopt this writing style. The rule of thumb is: Keep it simple.

When composing correspondence, make every effort to be clear. Carefully say what you want, and proofread everything before you send it. Consider this example, written by a lawyer representing the plaintiff in a personal injury case. In this "demand letter," the lawyer for one side is telling the opposition about the client's damages and demanding a sum in settlement of the lawsuit.

> Moreover, she lost eight months of vacation if she would have stayed on the job as to an accrual in the sum of $981.60, including therein analogously sick leave for one day per month for a total of eight days in the sum of $785.28.

Imagine the dilemma of the addressee in trying to figure out what the writer wants!

"Eight months of vacation" -- does that mean she could have taken off eight months from work? Probably not as her vacation was worth only $981.60 -- or, was it? What is meant by "as to an accrual in the sum of $981.60?" Does that mean all her vacation was worth that sum -- or each month -- or what?

"Including therein analogously" -- a real mystery. Is sick leave included within vacation? It sounds like it, but if that is so, why is a separate value -- $785.28 -- placed on sick leave?

There may be circumstances in which you are called upon to respond to letters that are downright nasty. Do not be tempted to descend to the writer's level. Tell the attorney immediately, of course; he/she may wish to deal with the matter personally. In any case, you should remain entirely civil and professional. When an opponent becomes uncivil, sarcastic or abusive -- and sooner or later, someone will -- your first instinct is to strike back with the same weapons. Do not -- Ever. Your own cool professionalism will be appreciated by your attorney, the court and the client: it will stand out in sharp contrast to the actions of the other side.

Sometimes you must remind your addressee of a request made earlier which you have not yet received an answer. Be diplomatic. People are usually embarrassed when reminded that they forgot to do something important. Try words such as these:

> You will recall that on March 25, 2001, I asked for a copy of the inventory sheets for the first six months of operation in 1998. I need the sheets soon so that I may finalize our report. Please make arrangements for the inventory sheets to be sent to me before June 1, 2001. If you have any questions or need additional information, please do not hesitate to contact me.

If you have asked for something by telephone or in person and the matter is important, it is best to follow up your request by letter. You can often couch your follow-up gracefully in terms of a thank you note -- something like this:

> Thank you for agreeing to send me the maps of United Aggregate's gravel claims. Please let me know if there will be photocopying or other costs involved.

When you have arranged for someone -- say, your client or a witness -- to be in court or somewhere else at a particular time, always write a follow-up letter, no matter how alert and vigorous your addressee may be. Everyone forgets appointments and your reminder letter will be a handy memo for your correspondent. If a number of weeks or months will go by before the addressee has to do whatever-it-is, be both courteous and careful to send another reminder shortly before the event.

All the usual rules of good, readable legal writing apply to writing letters with double force. Short paragraphs are even more important in letters than they are in memorandums or briefs. Where the normal paragraph length in a memorandum should be fifteen lines or less, your paragraphs in a letter should not exceed eight or ten. The same goes for sentence length. Keep sentences short, preferably not more than ten or twelve words.

Remember the rule: if something you write *can* be misunderstood, it surely will be. Here is an issue of authority as an agent. When someone, other than your client, is represented by a lawyer, you must thereafter make any contact with that person through his/her lawyer. You may not call or write to that person directly. For example, when you are advised that Brown, the tenant your client is trying to evict, has retained Jones & Jones to represent Brown in the eviction dispute, you will thereafter deal with Jones & Jones in the matter. Your letters will be addressed to Jones & Jones, not Brown.

## Watching Your Language

By watching your language, we do not mean avoiding the use of vulgar language. We mean, rather, to always remember that what you write to someone today may come back to haunt you six months or a year from now.

Only your attorney can speak for the client on matters addressing the client's legal position, so you must avoid every appearance of doing so in any letter you personally sign. In this circumstance, as in all others, remember that you are a paralegal, not the attorney.

Be very careful of seeming to commit the firm to any course of action unless you have plain authority to do so. Even an estimate or "maybe" must be carefully considered before putting it in a letter. What can be misconstrued will be, especially by opposing counsel in a legal dispute. So, unless your attorney has authorized you to do so, make no promise or statement of fact to your client, a witness or opposing counsel without clearing it with your supervising attorney. If in doubt as to whether you have authority to make a statement, it is always better to ask.

Following the Golden Rule

The golden rule in letter writing is easy to remember:

> If you don't need to say it, don't say it at all.

Your letters are being read by busy professionals who do not have the time to wade through long, rambling missives. Make your point as succinctly as possible. Your brevity and clarity will be appreciated and will reflect well on you and your supervising attorney.

Do not put anything in a letter that does not have to be said to accomplish your purpose. Do not add gratuitous opinions. Do not give information you do not have to give. Do not make estimates unless the nature of your letter requires you to do so. If you do, you can be sure that someone may later try to bind you to any guess you made, any estimate you gave or any opinion you offered.

Being Human

Having said all these things about being careful, being professional and not using first names, there is still room for humanity. For example, if you know that your correspondent's spouse has been seriously ill, there is nothing wrong with adding -- even to the opposition -- "Best wishes from us all for your wife's speedy recovery." If a correspondent has been recently promoted, by all means congratulate him/her. There is nothing unprofessional about courtesy or concern for others.

### *30.03 Legal Writing – The Basics.*

*Keep It Simple*

The clearest writing we have ever seen is the stories we read in the first grade. Remember the two little children and the dog? Dick said to Jane, "Jane, there is Spot. He is a dog. He is running. See Spot run." You cannot beat that lean, plain writing for economy of words or for clarity. What is it about "see Spot run" writing that makes it so clear?

For one thing, there are no adjectives or adverbs. Most sentences contain little more than a subject, a verb and an object. The subject and the verb are together right up front, without unnecessary words inserted in between them. The more words we put between subject and verb, the less likely we are to make sense.

Compare these two, short paragraphs:

> The subject of this paragraph, Spot, our old, trusted family friend, an eleven-year-old male of variegated neutral colors, is a member of the canine species.
>
> This paragraph is about Spot, our faithful pet. He is a black-and-white, male dog.

In the second paragraph, in addition to cutting out the fancy words, we have moved the verbs next to the subjects. We find out up front what or who does the acting and immediately afterward we find out what he/she or it did. The second option is clearer because we got right to the point. By contrast, the first paragraph is harder to read and understand in one quick reading. We even have to wait to find out whether Spot is human; up until the 17th word, he could be the kid next door.

Simplicity has two other major enemies: pomposity and verbosity. When legal professionals write, most of us are sorely tempted to demonstrate the richness of our vocabulary for the entire world to see. When we talk together informally, we use ordinary words. After hearing a political debate, we say we thought one candidate "confused" the issue. That ordinary word, "confuse," is the common word for a concept everyone understands. Why, then, on the job, do so many legal professionals write "obfuscate" instead of old, commonplace "confuse?" Why do people write "facilitate" instead of "help" or "lead," as the case may be?

When we use an unfamiliar word or when our writing is unnecessarily complex or cumbersome, the reader either gets the meaning slowly — or not at all.

H. W. Fowler, perhaps the greatest writer on the English language, put his finger neatly on the great power of simple writing:

> There are very few of our notions that cannot be called by different names; but among these names there is usually one that may be regarded as the thing's proper name … the proper name … should not be rejected for another unless the rejector can give some better account … of his preference than that he thinks the other will look better in print.
>
> *Fowler's Modern English Usage* (Oxford University Press)

Be careful, too, of incorporating jargon from other businesses or professions into your writing. Sometimes you will need to use some unusual word that is common in a particular business. If you do, then translate it for your reader unless you know the reader is familiar with the particular business. Here is an example from a lawyer's letter to a client:

> Allegedly Mrs. Doe had a sensory deficit in the affected hip secondary to a prior surgery and could not detect that the hydrocollator was hot, and as a result sustained the aforedescribed burns.

Well, one can guess at "sensory deficit" -- that means she could not feel things. What about "secondary to a prior surgery?" Doesn't that mean "caused by" -- a nice, common English construction? And what is a hydrocollator? If the reader does not know what one of those is, all meaning is lost. (And before you leave this sentence, strike out the nonsense word "aforedescribed"; it is purest legalese). Write using the "proper names" of things, the language of everyday. Again, if you don't say it, don't write it.

Verbosity, or wordiness, is another major threat to simple writing. It is a terminal lawyer's disease, endemic in the profession. Much of the public is convinced that legal professionals talk and write far too much; sadly, that opinion is at least partially right. The fact that we have much to say and make clear does not excuse a single, unnecessary word.

Verbosity tends to produce windy letters like this example, a letter from one lawyer to another:

> Dear Mr. Jones:
>
> Due to my specialization in commercial law and related matters, I have been recently engaged by Mr. Brown to advise and additionally represent him regarding the above-referenced dispute. After reviewing the files on this matter, it appears to me that there are various ways in which the respective interests of our clients can be accommodated and settled as an alternative to the continuation of the pending litigation. Accordingly, I would appreciate your telephoning me at your earliest convenience so we can discuss the matter and pursue possible settlement of this case.
>
> I will be out of town on some unrelated litigation matters through Monday of next week, but will be available to discuss the matter with you after that time. I look forward to hearing from you.
>
> Sincerely,
>
> James Q. Dibell

Examine this letter for a moment and then decide what the lawyer is really trying to say. Now quickly write out the message the way you would put it. It ought to look something like this:

> Dear Mr. Jones:
>
> I represent Mr. Brown in this case. I think we can settle this matter. I shall be out of town through next Monday. Please call.
>
> Sincerely,
>
> James Q. Dibell
>
> Associate for the Firm

The rest of the original letter added nothing to the message, except to make it longer. Try to follow this guideline for all your correspondence: no more than ten to twelve words for each sentence and eight to ten lines for each paragraph.

Consider some of the ways this writer inflated a simple message. First, nobody cares why the writer represents the client; it is enough that he does. Second, of course Dibell represents Jones in the "above-referenced dispute"; what other dispute would it be but the one he writes about? Third, the reader does not care whether the writer has reviewed the files. Fourth, the reader is indifferent as to why the writer will be out of town; all the reader cares about is when he can be reached by telephone.

*Achieving Simplicity*

Simplicity is not always as easy to achieve as it was when improving the clumsy letter we just rewrote, but you cannot go far wrong if you follow a few simple rules. The rules set out below work in every situation, whether you are writing a letter, a memo or a brief. They work regardless of your audience.

### *Write the Way You Speak*

This cardinal rule has already been mentioned. Unless a word is a legal term of art with a specific legal meaning, do not use it in a brief or memorandum if you would not use the word in everyday conversation. Remember, no attorney or judge wants to waste time wading through sticky prose two or three times to ferret out its meaning. The judge will pick up the other side's brief to find out what the problem is; the lawyer will send your memo back, with terse directions to write something understandable.

### *Write in Short Sentences*

Keeping your writing simple is cousin to the second of the vital rules of good writing; and that rule is, keep it short. We have already talked about writing simply. Simple, common words are normally short words, one or two syllables long. Now we shall take those short, simple words and put them together.

As a general rule, the shorter the sentence, the easier it is to understand. A good writer will vary sentences in length and structure to avoid boring the reader. A sentence longer than about twenty words is almost surely harder to understand than it needs to be.

Of course, it is possible to write beautiful legal prose and be understood, but if you have to choose between grace and clarity, choose clarity every time. And for clarity, short is always better -- see Spot run. The best of legal writers have always known and practiced the "rule of short." Justice Cardozo was one of the most scholarly justices ever to grace the United States Supreme Court; he had an enormous vocabulary. But for clarity's sake, Justice Cardozo chose to write as simply as he possibly could:

> The defendant is a manufacturer of automobiles. It sold an automobile to a retail dealer.
>
> *MacPherson v. Buick Motor Co.,* 217 N.Y. 382, 384, 111 N.E. 1050 (1916).

Justice Cardozo's writing in *MacPherson* is almost telegraphic. To start, he uses short, plain sentences, each with the subject and the verb close together. There are no modifiers crammed in to lengthen and complicate these sentences. Toward the end of the passage, he varies his style. In one sentence, two short statements are coupled in a single sentence: since each could stand alone, they are joined by a semicolon. All of his thoughts come in bite-sized pieces. His prose may not be the stuff of which the Great American Novel is made, but is absolutely clear on one reading.

Justice Cardozo uses one sentence of 19 words, about as long as a sentence ought ever to be. But even that sentence is crystal-clear. Its words -- like the rest -- are the simplest possible. They are also the shortest possible; they are the common names of the ideas for which they stand.

Ordinary legal writers have an astonishing genius for using four words where one would do. "At this point in time" is a familiar example. What, in fact, does that phrase mean? What about "in fact?" Now -- say so. Get in the habit of looking at little clusters of words and asking whether there is a way to say the same thing with fewer words.

Cross out "on a regular basis," and substitute "regularly." Instead of "interpose an objection," write "object." Say "consider" instead of "take into consideration." Use "soon" rather than "in the near future." Erase "file an action against"; write "sue" instead.

Our common writing patterns are full of these obese phrases. Look for them and delete them mercilessly wherever you find them. Once you get in the habit, you will save yourself ten or fifteen percent of the verbiage you otherwise would use. It will be second nature to cut out "for the purpose of" and insert plain old "to."

Look for phrases containing redundancies, and cut them down to their bare essentials. For example, take "prior experience." Isn't all experience prior? Just say "experience." Or, take the expression "remand back," a redundancy often seen in lawyers' writing. "Remand" means "send back," so drop "back" and use "remand" alone. Cut "consensus of opinion" down to "consensus," for that is what "consensus" means.

Simply because they are so common, it takes practice to notice some of these everyday redundancies. Take "join together"; have you ever tried to join something apart? Do the same for "end result," "sum total," and "complete stop." Write "plan" instead of "preplan." (How can you plan after you do whatever-it-is?)

You can also streamline your writing by eliminating tautologies, several words that are commonly found together, but which mean the same thing. Here are some:

| | |
|---|---|
| bits and pieces | fair and just |
| whys and wherefores | free and clear |
| over and above | betwixt and between |
| pick and choose | various and sundry |
| ways and means | bound and determined |

The law has its share of tautologies, such as "null, void and of no effect." Rather than adopt this useless phrase, use "void" or "null" or "of no effect," but not all three together.

There are other ways to break your writing into small, digestible pieces. For example, you may separate short, complete thoughts by semicolons:

> American forces won the Gulf War with astonishing ease; speed, training and firepower again proved superior to numbers.

Or, you can achieve the same effect by using a dash.

> The motion for summary judgment should have been granted -- there were obviously no questions of fact remaining to be decided.

You may also state a proposition, close it with a colon, and then list subparts of the proposition, as:

> There are three elements required to prove first-degree murder: the killing of a human, by the accused, with premeditation.

Within a complete thought ended by a period, semi-colon or dash, careful use of commas will keep the parts of each thought set off from one another. As a general rule, insert a comma where you would pause if you read the sentence out loud.

As an example, take these classic lines from the Bible and read them aloud:

> Thou shalt not fear for any evil by night, nor for the arrow that flieth by day, for the pestilence that walketh in darkness, nor for the sickness that destroyeth in the noon day.

Note how this passage breaks naturally after each comma, precisely where you would hesitate when speaking the lines aloud.

Using a combination of these techniques, you may create clear sentences of varying lengths, easy to read and understand the first time through. Whatever you do, try to avoid big, fat dependent clauses and qualifying words hanging about in the middle of sentences. For example:

> The following clause dealing with the $5.00 payment which the parties correctly call "rental" instead of making it clear, as our opinion stated, that the $25,000 was paid not as a bonus but rental, makes the opposite clear. For, in addition to flatly stating that this $5.00 per acre stipulated for was "rental" while not calling the $12.50 rental because it was not, it shows that the $5.00 payment was not, as the $12.50 was, required absolutely and in all events but only as an alternative to drilling.

What? This horror was written by a United States appellate judge in a tax case. Granted, tax cases commonly have a general air of obscurity, but there was no reason to use only two sentences, cramming both full of qualifiers.

Just as bad is the next passage, in which a lawyer tried to state the "general rule" to be followed in cases such as the one he was arguing. In a laudable attempt to lay down a rule clearly, he produced the following mystery:

> Where there is a general plan or scheme adopted by an owner of a tract, for the development and improvement of the property by which it is divided into streets and lots, and which contemplated restriction as to the uses to which lots may be put, or the character and location of improvement thereon, to be secured by a covenant embodying the restrictions to be inserted in the deeds to purchasers, and it appears from the language of the deed itself, construed in the light of the surrounding circumstances, that such covenants are intended for the benefit of all the lands, and that each benefit thereof, and such covenants are inserted in all the deeds for lots sold in pursuance of the plan, a purchaser or his assigns may enforce the covenant against any other purchaser and his assigns if he has bought with actual or constructive

> knowledge of the scheme and the covenant was part of the subject matter of the purchase.

The whole statement is a single sentence that, if you read it repeatedly, turns out to have been carefully crafted. The trouble is that there are so many qualifications crammed into the sentence that it is impossible to understand. And this meandering sentence was taken from an appellate brief filed before the highest court in Texas!

What could the writer have done? Without reading farther in the text, take your pencil and try to edit this humongous sentence so that it is easier to read and understand.

It is always best to state the general rule or the result you are going to reach first, and then separately state qualifications or requisites. The sentence you have just read might be unraveled as something like this:

> Where a tract owner adopts a plan to develop and improve property and restrict its uses, a buyer of part of the property may enforce the restrictions against the buyer of another part of the property. The following preconditions must, however, be met:
>
> > First…
> >
> > Second…
> >
> > Third…

A related way to confuse the issue is to refer to modifying facts that are not stated anywhere in the writing; facts that the reader must stop and read someplace else. Consider this puzzle produced by Section 509(a) of the Internal Revenue Code:

> For purposes of paragraph (3) an organization described in paragraph (2) shall be deemed to include an organization described in section 510(c)(4), (5) or (6) which would be described in paragraph (2) if it were an organization described in section 501(c)(3).

No doubt the reader can go to the Code and read all these modifying sections, but while the reader is doing this, all understanding of Section 509(a) is totally lost. Such confusion is bad enough in a statute; it is unforgivable in ordinary writing.

The solution is to give the reader a rule or other statement and separately list any qualifications there may be, much as we did above for the tract-owner and the restrictions. Here are some other ways to accomplish this, setting each point off by numbering it. The process is called "signposting." Signposting is a structural tool in which elements of a particular rule or statement are categorized and numbered.

Use "first," "second" and "third" when the point you want to make is enumerated in complete sentences, as:

> The court focused on three things. First, it examined whether the defendant had breached his duty to the plaintiff-hotel clerk. Second, the court considered whether

> the defendant had breached the standard of care for store security. Finally, the court analyzed whether inadequate store security was the proximate cause of the plaintiff's injuries.

Look at the last example again and consider another way to write it. Signpost your points using numbers to set them off, but describe them in fragments by using "whether."

> The court focused on three things: 1) whether the defendant had breached his duty to the plaintiff-hotel clerk; 2) whether the defendant had breached the standard of care; and 3) the causal link between store security and the plaintiff's injuries.

If you can state your points briefly, you can simply spell them out in sentence form, signposting with numbers as before:

> The court focused on three things: 1) the defendant's duty to the plaintiff-hotel clerk; 2) the standard of care for store security; and 3) the causal link between store security and the plaintiff's injuries.

A common mistake is to signpost when the points are so brief that signposting is unnecessary. Look at this example of incorrect signposting:

> The court considered the child's: 1) age; 2) mental competence; and 3) maturity level.

In this example, it would have been more appropriate to separate these one- or two-word points by commas rather than semicolons, as:

> The court considered the child's age, mental competence and maturity level.

It is also possible to state points as a series of rhetorical questions, as in this example:

> The court asked three questions: 1) Did the defendant owe a duty to the plaintiff? 2) Did the defendant breach the standard of care? 3) Was the defendant's act the proximate cause of the plaintiff's injuries?

This technique tends to become awkward and cumbersome when making brief points.

A second, common mistake is stating too many points at once. Even though the next example is properly signposted and its points are stated in parallel construction, it becomes too long and cumbersome to be easily understood:

> The defendant made the following mistakes: 1) leaving blood on his hands; 2) taking a blood-stained shirt to the dry cleaner; 3) leaving blood-stained carpet remnants on his front lawn to be picked up with the garbage; 4) running a classified advertisement for the sale of his knife collection; 5) asking his next-door neighbor if he could borrow a shovel, a pick and a plastic bag; 6) donating his wife's blood-stained clothing to the Salvation Army; and 7) stopping by the police station to ask if he could be convicted of murder if the body could never be found.

When you list this many points, it is better to write them in indented paragraph form or to use bullet form.

Many people will tell you that an idea must be expressed in a single paragraph. Do not believe them. The real rule is this: do not express more than a single major idea in a single paragraph. If you need two or twenty short paragraphs to discuss an idea fully, by all means use them.

When you write dollar amounts, do not list zero cents when the number is rounded to an even dollar amount. For example, damages in the amount of $1,000,000.00 should be written as "$1,000,000." Unless the figure contains some odd number of cents, drop the ".00."

Many of the worst faults of legal writing can be traced to babble -- a sort of stream-of-consciousness writing that is long on sound and short on meaning. (Terminal babble is usually coupled with acute failure to proofread, a critical legal skill emphasized throughout this domain.)

Consider this example drawn from a real lawyer's letter:

> I have done as you have requested, and have reviewed the matter in my mind and have taken the time to review my file and the previous sets of interrogatories and defendant's answers, objections and responses thereto and I honestly am of the opinion, in good faith, that said interrogatories are not repetitive and that they are relevant and they were propounded before the effective date.

This rambling prose was obviously written in haste, probably while shuffling through papers in the case file. It was certainly never proofread and incorporates most of the worst features of bad writing. To start with, it is far too complicated. This passage is only part of a single sentence, 185 words long. It is studded with unnecessary words:

> "Reviewed the matter in my mind": of course it was in his mind. Where else?
>
> "Honestly of the opinion, in good faith": can anybody be honestly in bad faith?
>
> "Taken the time to review my file": doubtless it took time to review the file; why state the obvious?

And the whole letter -- well over a page, single-spaced -- is crammed with useless legalisms: "said," "thereto," "thereof," "therewith" and "aforesaid," none of which add anything -- especially clarity -- to the letter.

To be understood, we must choose our words carefully. Even if the reader can puzzle out what we really meant, a glaring malapropism makes the reader wonder whether we are really very bright and how much attention should be paid to the rest of our writing. This glitch, from a brief filed with a trial court, is an example:

> The Plaintiffs asserted due to the disillusion of the Defendant partnership … Where a partnership is in the process of disillusion...

The lawyer perhaps meant to write about the *dissolution* -- that is, the dissolving of the partnership. What the lawyer said was that the partners had lost their illusions. No doubt that was true, but it was not what the lawyer intended to say.

The reader probably was not misled. But what the reader learned was that the lawyer or paralegal who wrote this was careless. Either the writer did not know the difference between disillusion and dissolution, or did not care enough to proofread or both. And who wants to hire a careless lawyer or paralegal … or keep one?

A personal injury lawyer, writing to a corporate insurance client, produced this astonishing sentence:

> The mother testified that immediately after the March 1, 1978 vaccination, the child began a high-pitched scream that continued intermittently for years.

Think about the picture this lawyer has painted. Not only has the writer written something consummately silly, but the writer has left the reader confused. If the reader is trying to guess what reasonable damages in the case might be, surely he/she ought to know how often "intermittently" is.

If the child screamed once a month or so, damages might be reasonably low. If, however, "intermittent" means every few minutes, the insurance company is facing a major expenditure. The reader will certainly be on the telephone to the writer in short order; maybe he will start thinking of hiring another law firm as well.

Make certain that the words you choose are as accurate as possible. Your reader is most likely to be misled by words that are ordinary enough on their face and correctly assembled, but leave no clear picture of what they describe. For example, here is what one lawyer wrote to describe the demeanor of the key witness for the other side:

> During the plaintiff's deposition it became apparent that she creates a rather favorable impression … She apparently is a nice-looking woman, 28 years of age with three children and previously widowed … Having had conversation with [witness X] would conclude that he is an "everyday-type of person" whose testimony might not carry the same conviction.

Think, for a moment, about what a "rather favorable" impression might be. Is it less than favorable? Is it a little more favorable than the average, but not really engaging and persuasive, or what? The lawyer has left us with no notion of how this witness really comes across. The whole point of the letter was to advise a client of the relative strength of the client's case. Because the lawyer did not write a clear assessment of the witnesses, he/she failed entirely.

Equally mysterious is the statement "apparently a nice-looking woman." You are left with the feeling that the plaintiff is nice-looking (whatever that means), but that there is something that might detract from that impression. If there really is something about the plaintiff that detracts from her impact as a witness, it certainly is not specifically mentioned. Also, she has been "previously widowed," a rather intriguing expression. Can that mean she is no longer widowed?

Can somebody once widowed ever be un-widowed? Or does it mean, as it probably does, that she was a widow but has remarried?

The lawyer's correspondent must also have wondered what an "everyday-type of person" might be. Why should an everyday person somehow lack credibility? Perhaps there was something about Witness X that indeed made him/her less credible than some other witness; if there was, the lawyer surely did not describe the deficiency. All we know is that there is something wrong about Witness X; we have no inkling what that might be.

If you have the slightest doubt about the precise meaning of a word, pick up that most valuable office aid, your dictionary. It ought to be on your desk, not down in the library. Always make certain your meaning is right by the book. Even when common words are widely and popularly misused, people who are careful with their English will know the difference. Also, beware of all of the available online dictionaries: you should only refer to a trusted source, such as Merriam-Webster, *available at* m-w.com.

Be especially careful of commonly misused words such as "nauseous." Even more egregious is the common misuse of "lie" and "lay." "Lie" is what you do when you go to bed at night. "Lay" is its past tense, as in "Yesterday I lay down for a nap." Otherwise, "lay" is what a chicken does with an egg or what you do with something: for example, "lay the groceries on the counter." Writing "The doctor required her to lay down for an hour each day" marks you as darned near illiterate and spoils the effect and power of your writing.

Here are some similar traps for which you should be alert. Read them and see whether the differences in meaning between the first and second words are absolutely clear to you. Then, check your dictionary. You will find there are very broad differences in meaning between these words, even though many of the pairs sound, and even look, very similar.

| | |
|---|---|
| apprise | appraise |
| discreet | discrete |
| disinterested | uninterested |
| emigrate | immigrate |
| eminent | imminent |
| illusion | allusion |
| imply | infer |
| masterful | masterly |
| prescribe | proscribe |
| concise | precise |

Knowing both the difference and the precise meanings is not something nice to do. It is your responsibility as a professional, and nothing less.

There are dozens more of these treacherous words, many of which will sneak up on you because intelligent people all around you are also misusing them. Many people will not know this is happening, but some educated, careful readers will and they are your most important audience.

Then there are the jargon words we are tempted to borrow from other professions. Legal professionals are often tempted to use doctor's lingo when discussing medical matters, particularly the injuries involved in a lawsuit to recover for personal injuries or medical malpractice. The worst vice of this habit is using technical language, which means nothing to the average layperson. If you write about a "Colles fracture," you must tell the reader in ordinary terms what kind of break that is. Instead of "posterior to," write "behind." You will not sound like a doctor, but people will understand you better.

A few pages back we read a rather murky paragraph that dealt with burns from a hydrocollator. The lawyer who wrote it used the medical jargon "secondary to." It was unnecessary and could have been confusing. Doctors may say that "The patient Jones died secondary to a fifteen-story fall," but ordinary folk do not talk that way. We do not have to follow doctors' practice; it makes more sense simply to write that the fall killed Jones.

When you know your subject well, it is especially easy to get words out of order in a sentence. Sometimes the reader will instantly recognize your meaning, as when you write: "We only include doctors' bills already paid," instead of "We include only doctors' bills already paid." But, sometimes, inaccurate word order produces a silly result such as:

> In the presence of the judge, the district attorney announced that he knew of attempts to bribe the jury.

How can the reader possibly know what the writer meant? The little pronoun "he" is placed so that nobody can know what was intended. If the D.A. is telling the court that he has learned of attempted jury-tampering, good for him! He is doing his duty. If, however, he is telling the world that the judge knew somebody was fiddling with the jurors, then the D.A. had better be right; if he is not, he is in serious trouble with the judge.

How about this classic example of faulty word order:

> Being too stupid to understand directions, counsel argued that the defendant should not be held accountable.

In this case, the reader suspects that the writer meant the defendant was unusually dense, not the lawyer. Although not all meaning is lost, the reader's train of thought is interrupted when he/she hesitates to decide what the sentence means. Worse, the reader wonders how this law office let such a clunker out into the world; how else are they careless?

As legal professionals, our first duty is to be clear, simple and precise. That does not mean that our writing must be dull. It is possible to make our writing interesting, particularly when we are trying to persuade, as when we write a brief urging a judge to do a particular thing.

There are several useful ways to add interest and emphasis, and several others that should be used sparingly or avoided altogether. Here are a few to shun:

As a general rule, do not underline, italicize or otherwise emphasize a word. Likewise, do not put words or sentences in capital letters for the sake of emphasis. All caps can appear contrived, and gives your writing an unbalanced, amateur appearance. If your writing is well-crafted, the emphasis ought to be obvious. Artificial attention-getters tend to distract.

For the same reason, avoid emphasis by way of a great army of quotations. As we shall discuss more fully below, quotations should be used only rarely, and then only for how something is said, not for what is said. A plague of quotations gives your writing a cluttered, disconnected character.

*Positive Techniques*

Now let us examine the ways through which you can achieve emphasis and power, ways that add to the persuasive force of your writing. These techniques must not be overused; but, in moderation, they will improve the power of your writing.

When you repeat an important word or phrase, you add to its importance simply by driving it home in the memory of the reader. There are two ways in which repetition is used.

First, a single word may be used repeatedly in quick succession. The classic example is Sir Winston Churchill's great speech in the perilous summer of 1940:

> We shall fight in France; we shall fight on the seas and oceans; we shall fight with growing confidence and growing strength in the air; we shall defend our island, whatever the cost may be; we shall fight on the beaches; we shall fight on the land-grounds; we shall fight in the fields and in the streets; we shall fight in the hills; we shall never surrender.

All very well for a speech, you say; but, can a legal writer really use repetition this way? Consider this example:

> Never did Plaintiff make any effort to advise Defendant that the property was flooded; never did he write a warning letter; never did he visit the Defendant; never did he so much as place a telephone call.

You see the effect. The reader is left with the impression that the plaintiff was, at best, grossly negligent. He did absolutely nothing to help himself, and he failed to use any number of ways to tell the defendant that there was trouble so that the defendant could take some action. There is a great deal more power to the paragraph than there is in the flat, rather puny statement that "the plaintiff failed to notify the defendant."

The second way in which repetition may be used to strengthen writing is simply by writing a key word twice in quick succession. For example:

> By either definition, Defendant's actions were plainly reckless -- reckless of the lives and safety of everyone in the room.

Alliteration is the deliberate repetition of similar sounds close together. This emphasizes what you are saying in two ways: it makes your words smooth and appealing and its very sound can add a mood to what you write. Consider this example of how alliteration might be used in legal writing:

> However facile such a shallow analysis appears, it cannot survive the withering wind of close, careful, consistent scrutiny.

"Withering wind" is one use of alliteration: its "w" sounds add to the context of merciless examination. "Close, careful, consistent" is another: the repetition serves to emphasize the need for intense scrutiny.

Be careful not to overdo the use of alliteration. You are not writing classic poetry. But when this technique is applied sparingly, it adds both interest and emphasis to otherwise ordinary subjects.

Legal writing is not the place for purple prose. Ours is, or ought to be, a dignified profession dealing in facts and principles of law, not emotion and invective. That does not mean, however, that word choice and context are unimportant.

*Writing for the Court*

When you are writing for the court, you must do what you can in a dignified way to catch and hold the reader's attention. Even the most dedicated judge has trouble concentrating on banal, boring material. Consider this report from a real-world court in England:

> Proceedings were interrupted during a debt case at Bristol County Court yesterday when a solicitor discovered that his gown had been set alight by an electric fire. When he apologized for creating a disturbance, the [judge] said he was only too glad to have some interest introduced into the case.

Without departing from serious, professional speech to attract the court's attention, you certainly should consider the words you use to make your point and the context in which you use them.

Choice of Words

Consider the four common words below. They are very close to synonymous, but their impact on the reader is very different. All of them are ordinary words; all of them are simple. If you could use any one of them, which would you choose?

Dirty: the dust on the windowsill, the ring around the collar. Being "dirty" is probably no big thing. That is why we have washing machines.

Soiled: a little more serious, a little less appealing, perhaps a stain instead of some general dust. Nevertheless, "soiled" is not generally repulsive.

Grimy: this needs to be cleaned up immediately; nobody even wants to be around things that are grimy; the word implies ground-in, neglected dirt in quantity.

Filthy: *yech!* This is the apartment you will not even consider renting, the t-shirt you have to pick up with a stick, the cat-box that no self-respecting cat would use.

So, word choice does matter. Do not over-dramatize, but carefully consider the picture you are trying to paint for your reader. Choose the right word as you would choose the right color for a painting. Strictly within the bounds of honesty, your job is to persuade, and to persuade you must catch and hold the fancy of the reader. Vivid, precise language will help.

Consider the context in which you will use your words. What sort of impression are you trying to create? Suppose you are dealing with the question of whether a criminal defendant could have run six blocks fast enough to commit a crime at a particular time. If you wrote for the district attorney, you would probably characterize the distance as "only six ordinary blocks." On the other hand, a paralegal writing for the defense might call the same distance "six full-sized city blocks." Is there any real difference in the distance? Of course not. Is there not, however, a subtle difference in the impression left on the reader by these two contrasting statements?

Quotations

Quotations are the bane of the legal professional. Even the best of us are sorely tempted to lift from legal opinions whole squadrons of quotes and graft them onto our own writing. After all, if the court said this, it must be accurate and persuasive, right? Wrong.

There is never an excuse for quoting banal, commonplace language. There is nothing to be gained by quoting a court's statement that "the judgment is affirmed." You can say that just as well. In fact, you can almost always paraphrase what the court said and say the same thing more simply and in fewer words. Another reason to quote only occasionally is that using many quotations tends to produce dull prose. Moreover, a whole string of quotations gives a jerky, disconnected tone to any document.

Quotations also present a more subtle danger. It is rare that the case you are writing for matches exactly the case from which you are quoting. Therefore, it is essential that you are careful to explain the nexus between the two.

When should you quote, then? Quote when you cannot say whatever-it-is as well yourself, when the judicial language you quote expresses an important thought, perfect and memorably. How about this memorable opening to a Supreme Court argument:

> The question is whether a good Nazi can be a good American.

As an attention-getter, as a crisp, forceful statement of the problem, you cannot beat that line. Quote the sentence because it is well said. What it says is not nearly as important as the way it is expressed.

Proofreading

Failure to proofread is the most serious and unforgivable fault any legal writer can commit. It can produce simple nonsense, like this line from a lawyer's letter:

> He remembers leaks in the garden planters, but Mr. Jones had dirt pulled out of the planters and then repaired…

A proofreading lapse can also miss a truly memorable silliness such as this:

> In the index to this brief, the Court will find an extensive copulation of authorities on this subject.

This ugly mistake was made in a written argument filed with a federal appeals court. You can imagine the court's reaction to that line. No doubt the judges knew the writer meant "compilation" instead of what he/she wrote, but the mistake almost surely produced both a break in the reader's concentration and a serious question in the reader's mind about the competence and reliability of the writer.

Failure to proofread will also unleash on the world horrors such as this next example. This is particularly dangerous because it has two meanings, and there is no way for the reader to decide which meaning was intended.

> She had to replace her 1984 Buick Skylark, four door, with a 1985 Buick Skylark, four door, with the additional cost thereof which was not reimbursed by insurance… in the sum of $3,056.33.

"Thereof" (an unnecessary piece of legalese in any case) adds nothing to the sentence except confusion. Perhaps it refers to the '84 Skylark; maybe it means the '85 replacement. Is $3,056.33 the entire cost of the new car, or is it only the part not covered by insurance, or is it the difference between the value of the old car and the price she paid for the new one?

This sentence is a fine example of terminal babble, a piece of careless dictation never proofread. With just a little care, it might have come out something like this:

> She had to replace her 1984 Buick Skylark with a 1985 Skylark. The difference between the value of the old car and the cost of the new one is $3,056.33. This sum was not reimbursed by her insurance.

The writer could, and should, have caught and cleared away this confusion by careful proofreading. It was the writer's duty to make sure the writing was clear. The writer cannot delegate that task to a secretary or anyone else. When any of us writes something, the obligation to make certain the finished product accurately conveys the intention remains ours. Here are some time-tested suggestions for effective proofreading.

It is best to proofread not only what you have written yourself, but to have somebody else proofread as well. After spending time and effort on a memorandum or brief or pleading, the writer often will proofread for what ought to be on the page, not for what is already there. It is easy to miss typographical errors and ludicrous or misleading constructions.

To avoid this, have someone else read your writing. In the best case scenario, have that person read it aloud in your presence. Our language is only the spoken word reduced to symbols. You may be sure that if your writing sounds odd when read aloud, it needs some more work to read correctly. Never, ever be content with something that is "almost" right. We are judged by what we write, and our reputation rides on every line.

Most proofreading mistakes are made because we fail to read slowly enough to catch the errors. Force yourself to read slowly and look at each letter and punctuation mark. If necessary, use an old typesetting trick; using a pencil eraser, touch each character as you read to force yourself to read more slowly. You will eventually reach the point where you automatically proofread at a pace that allows you to spot each error. Proofreading is an acquired art that is mastered with patient practice.

Do not attempt to proofread anything immediately after you finish typing it -- wait at least an hour before you come back to it. This will also help you to avoid missing errors. Don't forget about the trick of reading from the bottom up and backwards; don't forget to proofread captions, headings, footnotes and footers.

When time permits, have an intelligent layperson read what you have written. That person may not understand the legal expressions in your writing, but the sense of what you want to say should come through. If it does, your writing has achieved its goal. If your reader turns to you and says, "I don't understand this," your writing needs more polish and editing.

### *30.04 Prepare and/or draft analytical documents by synthesizing information and using an appropriate format and means (including, but not limited to, computer entry and dictation) to advance the client's matter.*

This section deals with dissecting, understanding and applying legal authority. The process applies to statutes and regulations as well as to case law, and some very general rules apply no matter what you are trying to interpret.

First, both courts and legislatures ordinarily make no rule broader than is necessary to accomplish whatever it is they want to do. Courts follow the legal doctrine of *stare decisis,* meaning that, when a court has once laid down a principle of law applicable to certain facts, it will adhere to that principle in all future cases in which the facts are substantially the same even though the parties and property are different.

Second, language, either legislative or judicial, should be read in its ordinary sense unless, in a statute, that language is specifically defined as having some unusual meaning. In the sample brief of a case provided below, the court follows this rule and chooses the ordinary meaning of a term as the meaning intended by Congress in a statute rather than a strained and unusual meaning.

Third, as to statutes and regulations, courts prefer to read them in keeping with common sense rather than seeking some bizarre interpretation. Keep this in mind when deciphering language in statutes.

Fourth, if what a court says is susceptible to two meanings, you will normally choose the meaning that makes the opinion consistent with other decisions by the court. Appellate courts are normally reluctant to change existing law if they can decide a new case in similar harmony with cases they have decided in the past.

As long as you work in the law, remember that you can never accept someone else's idea of what particular legal authority means. Headnotes and other summaries are very helpful, and usually accurate. The same is true of discussions of an opinion in another case or in a law review article. Nevertheless, in the end, it is your analysis on which your attorney must rely. That means you must always read <u>any</u> authority on which you rely and make your own analysis of its effect.

*<u>Parts of a Brief</u>*

A *case brief* is a summary of the salient facts of the case, together with a succinct account of the court's decision and, especially, the rationale by which the court reached that decision. What are the steps you must take to write a brief?

Obviously, you must first read the case, initially without taking notes. Then, extract what information you need to take from the case to be briefed. Finally, read the case again, this time making notes. All the information you will need is contained within the opinion.

Note the title of the case, including the citation. You will need the citation for your brief or memo, or to return to the case to read it again or to check some detail. Note also the name of the court.

Note the parties in the case and identify them by name (*e.g.*, International Steel), by their relationship or by categorizing their identity (*e.g.*, employer and employee), or by their litigation status (*e.g.*, plaintiff and defendant or appellant and appellee). For cases involving two individuals, it is easiest to use first names (*e.g.*, Jim and Mary or Scott and Sam).

Just below the case name you will find: *"Certiorari* to the Circuit Court of Appeals for the Tenth Circuit." This line tells you where the case came from. *Certiorari* is the name of an ancient writ by which a higher court told a lower court to send the case up for review and is used today for the same purpose. Legal professionals informally refer to this as "*cert.*"

The date of decision is included in the citation. Note that, if the years of argument and decision are different, it is the year of decision that goes in the citation.

You should also include a brief mention of who is appealing (both sides do, sometimes), and what they are asking for. Usually, the plaintiff is seeking to obtain something from the defendant or is trying to stop the defendant from doing something. The defendant's objective simply may be to prevent the plaintiff from reaching that goal.

This information is usually found within the first few paragraphs of the opinion. If there is not a clear indication of what the parties' objectives are, you can infer them from the dispute or from any other clues you find in the opinion. If the opinion describes the plaintiff's objectives but not the defendant's, you may presume that the defendant's only goal is to prevent the plaintiff from obtaining his/her objective. Look for the ultimate objective -- the end result that the party hopes to achieve.

Most litigation occurs in stages. The first stage is from the time the lawsuit is filed until it goes to trial. The second stage is the trial itself, when facts are applied to the law. The litigation could end here, or the party who lost at trial might choose to appeal that decision. Then, should the appellate court remand the case to the trial court for further proceedings or a new trial; that would be the next stage, and so on. The stages of litigation that occur before the opinion is written are called prior proceedings or prior history. Likewise, any stages of litigation that occur after the opinion is written are called subsequent proceedings or subsequent history.

Not all opinions discuss prior proceedings. Those issued by trial court judges may not have any. It is also possible that the prior proceedings were not significant enough to merit mention in the court's written opinion. If there are prior proceedings mentioned in the opinion, note in your brief who brought the proceeding, summarize what that party wanted, identify the court that was involved and briefly state the outcome.

You do not need to show which attorneys represented which parties in the case. Omit that from your brief.

Next, you will note who wrote the opinion for the entire Court. There may be one or more opinions in any case. Briefly, these are the forms they may take:

- *Majority Opinion*: One justice writes for himself/herself and for the others who make up a majority of the judges hearing a case. This is the opinion handed down in the usual case.

- *Plurality Opinion*: An opinion written for the greatest number of judges who can agree on a single opinion. It is less than a majority.

- *Dissenting Opinion*: One or more justices opine that the case should be decided in a way other than the one chosen by the majority.

- *Concurring Opinion:* One or more justices agree that the result reached by the majority or plurality opinion is correct, but wish to add their own thoughts or reasoning.

- *Per Curiam Opinion*: "*Per curiam,*" which means "by the court," is a decision without a designated author. The term does not imply unanimity and normally appears in fairly routine matters.

When you are analyzing a less-than-unanimous opinion from a court in your own jurisdiction, it may be useful to note who wrote for the majority, who joined with that person, who concurred, who dissented, and so on. If the composition of the court has changed since the decision of the case you are analyzing, the change in personnel may indicate whether the court is likely to decide an identical case in the same way today.

Next, make a note of the reason for the litigation. What is the legal theory on which the plaintiff relies to recover against the defendant? This legal theory is not the injury for which the plaintiff seeks relief. Rather, it is a right recognized by the law that the plaintiff seeks to enforce: Is this a suit for breach of contract, or for personal injury caused by negligence, or for trespass to real property? The legal reason a plaintiff offers to support a claim is called a cause of action or, simply, a claim. Sometimes both sides will have claims against the other, as well as defenses to their opponent's claim.

Now, note the defense or defenses raised by the defendant. A *defense*, simply put, is a legal theory offered by the defendant to show why he/she has committed no legal wrong; therefore, the plaintiff should not prevail and the claim should be dismissed. A defense may assert a contrary theory of the principle of law relied on by the plaintiff. One type is known as an affirmative defense, which is basically the assertion that the defendant had the legal right to do whatever the plaintiff complains of in the Petition or Complaint. For example, in an action for the shooting death of the plaintiff's spouse, the defendant might assert the defense of justifiable homicide -- self-defense.

The most common defense is a denial of one or more facts necessary to support the claim. The denial is based upon a different view of the same rule of law raised by the opponent. The party asserting the denial is saying that the rule of law on which the claim is founded cannot be established because the other party has failed to prove an essential element of that rule.

Next, read the facts of your case. Your case brief begins with a summary of those facts. The facts must be stated in enough detail that you can easily remember what happened when you refer to your case brief again. Most lawyers agree that the facts of any legal matter are its most important component. Make sure you understand the facts of the case completely. Judicial decisions are fact-specific. Courts do not normally set out to lay down rules to solve cosmic questions of law. Rather, courts face a particular problem based on particular facts, and it is that question they address, on those facts. The rule is not intended to solve any question but the one presented in the case before the court.

The trick is determining which facts are the most important, because you will be including them in your brief. These are called key facts -- the facts upon which the court rested its opinion. In other words, which facts are so critical that, if they were changed, the holding of the opinion would have to be changed? Key facts are also sometimes referred to as "essential facts," "material facts" or "operative facts." You must be able to recognize these key facts and, during your research, determine whether the cases you found are relevant to the problem.

One way to find the key facts in an opinion is to note how the opinion discusses whatever prior proceedings occurred before the opinion was written. Sometimes an opinion discusses the prior proceedings, but only to the extent that it tells who won at trial and who is appealing the trial court's decision. If you are lucky, the opinion will discuss what happened. If so, then the court is telling you what facts it considered to be important (or unimportant) and whether it agreed with the decision made by the lower court and why.

Though judicial writers generally put the facts of the matter up front, you must watch for additional, important facts that are buried elsewhere in the opinion. Be especially alert for extra facts that appear only in a dissent or concurring opinion.

Not all facts in a case are important. In the beginning, however, follow this rule: If you are not sure whether a fact is important enough to include in your case brief, include. It is much better to have some extraneous facts in your brief than to omit something essential.

Nobody can give you an infallible rule that will tell you which facts to include and which to omit. Here are some rules of thumb that may help:

1. Your notes should show who the parties to the litigation are, what they want and what their relationship is. Maybe the plaintiff is a landlord, and he/she is suing his/her tenant for damage to the property. You might express these facts so:

   P-landlord v. D-tenant

   You will develop your own abbreviations. Many people use the Greek Delta (Δ) to mean "defendant" and Pi (π) to mean "plaintiff." By all means, use abbreviations; just be sure you can go back to your case brief later and understand what you wrote.

2. Your facts must also include what the litigation is about, that is, the cause of action on which the plaintiff is suing, *e.g.*:

   π landlord v. Δ tenant for damage to aptmt. & furn. caused by Δ's 12 cats.

3. If the defendant has raised some sort of defense to the suit and it bears on the question to be answered, include the facts that pertain to the defense:

   π landlord v. Δ tenant for damage to aptmt. & furn. caused by Δ's 12 cats. Δ relies on lease clause permitting keeping of pets & excusing damage from fair wear & tear.

Frequently, you will not need any more facts than this short paragraph; sometimes you will need more. Suppose, for example, the tenant wants to defend on the ground that the landlord assured him/her orally, contrary to the written lease, they could keep any number of pets and the landlord did not care what they did. The question would then be whether evidence of the oral assurance would be admissible. In that case, your facts might look like this:

> π landlord v. Δ tenant for damage to aptmt. & furn. caused by Δ's 12 cats. Lease says its entire agreement betw. parties bans pets, & holds Δ strictly liab. for all dam. Δ offers evid. of oral assurance by π that pets ok and π doesn't care what they do.

Sometimes the opinion itself will draw your attention to those facts the court itself considers most important. Such language as "the pivotal language of the lease," "it is critical that…" or "the case turns on the fact that…" points the way to facts that the court considered vital to its decision.

Make sure you understand, and write down, the precise question the court is deciding: legal professionals call that question the *issue*. An issue is a single, certain and material point, deduced by the allegations and pleadings of the parties, which is affirmed on the one side and denied on the other and may either be issues of fact or law.

Give the issue a separate, small paragraph of its own, putting it between the facts and the reasoning of the court. Some writers put it up higher in the brief, just after the title and history of the case.

There are usually several issues, or questions of law, in an opinion. Roughly, the issues will fall into two categories: substantive and procedural. A procedural question deals with the technicalities of bringing or defending the litigation, *e.g.*, the format of the complaint, the jurisdiction of the court and the admissibility of the evidence. Everything else is substantive, *e.g.*, the pollution of a river, the breach of a contract or the commission of a crime.

Some opinions contain only procedural issues. Some contain both procedural and substantive issues. Pay attention to the headings or subheadings in the opinion. These will most likely tell you what the issues are, *e.g.*, the appellant claims that Section 45 does not apply here, or the defendant asserts that this court lacks jurisdiction.

The issue is usually easier to understand if you put it after the facts. An issue statement might look like this:

> Issue: Does the legal domicile of a married, female Army officer follow the domicile of her husband, or is it determined by where she is stationed on military orders?

Your issue must be the precise question decided by the court. You cannot loosely state a proposition "like" the question the court decided; you must be exact.

After you formulate the issue, your next step is to decide <u>how</u> the court answered that question. The answer to the question is called the holding of the court. The holding is the legal principle to be drawn from the opinion or decision of the court.

Carefully formulate and write down the holding of the case. The holding is the court's answer to the issue, or the question the court set out to solve. The court's reasoning is why the court answered the issue as it did.

Some writers will put the holding right after their statement of the issue. Others put it at the end of the brief section dealing with the court's reasoning. Your statement of the court's holding should look something like this:

> Held: Where a female Army officer lives is decided by military orders. Therefore, her domicile is the place where she is stationed and is not affected by the domicile of her husband.

Next, you must deal with <u>why</u> the court answered the question in the way it did -- that part of the judicial opinion which applies law to fact to solve the question before the court. This is the rationale or reasoning of the court and must be reflected in your brief.

Condensing the court's reasoning into some manageable form is usually the toughest part of briefing a case. Oftentimes, the court's rationale will go on for pages. Always read the court's reasoning carefully -- at least once -- before you try to express it in your own words.

Headnotes in case reporters will often help you in understanding the court's reasoning. They can also assist you in formulating both issue and holding. For example, consider the headnote below, taken from a Nevada case, *McKinney v. Sheriff, Clark County,* 560 P.2d 151 (Nev. 1977).

In *McKinney*, a criminal defendant challenged an indictment by the grand jury. He claimed that he could not be indicted for murder in which he had conspired with other defendants to steal the victim's car, but did not know that the other conspirators murdered the victim and, in fact, ordered them not to use deadly force. The court disagreed, and one headnote summed up the court's decision this way:

> Where the purpose of the conspiracy is to commit a dangerous felony 'each member runs the risk of having the venture end in homicide, even if he has forbidden the others to make use of deadly force. Hence each is guilty of murder if one of them commits homicide in the perpetration… of an agreed-upon robbery…,' *supra.*

Suppose you are reading *McKinney* to solve the question whether a criminal conspirator may escape liability for a crime he did not contemplate and even forbade. *McKinney* obviously will help you since it deals with that very question. The headnote above plainly spells out both the problem the court addressed and the court's answer to that question: in short, it gives you both your issue and your holding.

A reminder: You may <u>not</u> rely entirely on a headnote to formulate your statement of the issue or the holding; a headnote is only an aid. Remember that your duty is to read the case and pull out the issues and holdings as they are formulated. Remember also, if you later reference a case in a memo or brief, you <u>never</u> cite to a headnote, but always to the opinion in the case itself. Likewise, never quote a headnote.

When you find a useful case such as *McKinney*, you will want to expand your research by running the case through *Shepard's Citator* to identify later cases that cited *McKinney*. In preparation for this, include in your case brief the number of the *McKinney* headnote dealing with the point of law in which you are interested. So, after you note the holding in *McKinney*, add this: (HN 4).

Not all questions raised in a judicial opinion are issues, and not all comments by the court are holdings. Remember that an issue is the ultimate question the court must answer to decide the case. Only the answer to that issue can be called a holding. Often the court will deliver itself of an opinion on some point of law, a non-binding comment that is not essential to the decision in the case. Such comments are called *dicta* (singular *dictum*), a shortened version of *obiter dictum.*

You need not include dicta in your brief, except if some dictum by a court supports or opposes whatever your firm is trying to accomplish. It may be persuasive to another court, even though it is not binding on that court.

Finally, after you have carefully stated the issue and written down the reasoning of the court and the court's holding, record what the court <u>did</u> with the case and the judgment it rendered, which is sometimes referred to as the court's disposition of the case. Often you can express that disposition in a single word: "affirmed" or "reversed." Sometimes the court will reverse the decision and "remand" it ("send it back") to lower court for some kind of further proceeding.

Sometimes you will want to include a dissenting or concurring opinion in your brief. A particularly well-written minority opinion may be persuasive to a court later considering the same or a similar problem.

In short, these are the elements of a case brief. As you get used to briefing cases, the process will become easier. You will almost automatically pick out the important facts and the reasoning of the court. The more you formulate issues and holdings, the better you will get this exacting task.

*Writing a Case Brief*

It is very important that you brief each case in your own words. If you copy what the court said word for word, your brief simply parrots the language of the opinion and you learn very little. Only if you grasp the meaning of the case and express it in your own way will you really understand what the opinion is all about. Extensive copying of the court's language only produces an overlong, uninformative attempt at a summary, although there is occasionally room for quotation in a case brief.

Use this format for case briefs, in this order:

1. Case Name and Citation;
2. Facts;
3. Procedural History;
4. Issue(s);
5. Holding(s);
6. Rationale(s); and
7. Judgment.

There is no need to type case briefs that are for your use alone. They can be handwritten, as long as your writing is legible. We suggest you write your case briefs on plain, three-hole paper. That way, you can keep a three-ring binder for your research and put in it all your case briefs, along with notes from your boss, photocopies of statutes and cases and so on. Your research material stays neatly together and none of it gets misplaced or lost. We also suggest you leave a three-inch margin in your case briefs for adding notes later as you discover new material or come to new conclusions about the law.

*Drafting Legal Memoranda*

The primary purpose of legal writing is to be understood clearly. Nowhere is this purpose more important than in writing a legal memorandum. Your supervisors will judge you by the clarity of your writing and by the research you have done before writing.

Distinguish between legal memorandums, internal to your law office, and briefs filed with the court in support of or in opposition to some motion or other matter. Legal memorandums -- also called memorandums of law -- are written within a law office to solve some problem that office faces. For example, it may be a question addressed to the firm by a client; it may be a problem raised by a case the office is trying; or it may be a query by an attorney who is devising a new provision for a will or contract. A legal memorandum attempts to answer a question by applying to it the pertinent judicial opinions ("cases") and statutes that your research has discovered.

The law constantly evolves. It does so as appellate courts address problems of legal interpretation and solve them in written opinions. With few exceptions, appellate courts do not take evidence; they deal with a case already tried and thus only consider questions of law. You will be most interested in appellate opinions from your own jurisdiction -- your state. Or, if your case is a federal one, you will look to the federal appellate area -- the "circuit" -- in which your case will be tried.

Rely on cases decided as recently as possible. Reason from cases which are -- factually -- as close as possible to your own. You will seldom find a case exactly like yours, or "on all fours." "On all fours" is most commonly used when a particular case is in all aspects similar to another because the facts are similar and the same questions of law are involved.

As you write your memorandum, always tell the reader where you got the ideas and propositions of law you are discussing. When you first mention a case or statute, give your reader the full citation of that case or statute. The citation is the combination of words and numbers that tells your reader exactly how to locate the case or statute.

As you discuss a case, refer to the specific page on which you found the reasoning you are discussing. This is called "spot" or "short" citation, and is even noted in online references. It helps the reader who wants to read the case go directly to the critical part of a case on which you rely.

The whole idea of a memorandum is to predict, from the law as it is, what a court -- or administrative panel -- would do with the situation about which you are writing. Would a particular piece of evidence be admitted? Would a contract be interpreted by a court as your client thinks it should be? Would a special will provision achieve your client's goal if it were challenged in court?

Whatever the question is, you will write about it in the same general format. We have given you a useful format, below, which includes all the essential elements. Your law office may have its own approach. If it does, it will not be very different from ours, because any good memo must contain certain critical parts. Here is a sample:

MEMORANDUM

TO: Senior Partner

FROM: Pat Paralegal

DATE: [The Date of Completion of the Memorandum]

RE: [Brief Reference to Issue or Question]

FILE: [Identity of Client and File Number]

INTRODUCTION

[Optional]

Keep this brief, no more than one or two paragraphs. Briefly explain what has already happened in the case, bringing the reader up to date, or explain why you were ask to write the memo, or how the issue arose. Do not include any legal citations.

STATEMENT OF FACTS

This section should set out all of the facts needed to understand and solve the problem -- whether by someone familiar with the situation or by somebody who knows nothing about it except what is contained in the memorandum. Your attorney may come back to your memo weeks or months after you have written it, or other attorneys in the office may pull it out of the brief bank and rely on it at a later date.

Use only those relevant facts that are necessary to the reader's understanding of the issues. The facts must be written objectively and accurately. Don't adopt an adversarial tone (arguing for one side or the other). Point out pros and cons in a dispassionate manner. Do not attempt to interpret the facts in their best light for your client. You may state the facts most favorable to your client in more vivid language than those that favor the other side, but never omit a fact because it supports the opposition. Do not include any legal citations.

QUESTION(S) PRESENTED

Keep this section brief, usually only one sentence in question form. This is a legal question, not a factual statement. Omit legal citations unless necessary to state the problem to be solved. You may need to do some preliminary reading before you even draft the questions, particularly when the problem is in an area you do not know well. Careful drafting of the question(s) will help you as you proceed with your research. State the question in the present tense (and also for your answer).

The *question presented* should look something like this:

Question: Is the residence of a female military officer determined by the residence of her husband?

Having asked the question as briefly and clearly as possible, answer it in the same way, without citations, as:

Brief Answer: No. Because she moves on military orders directed to her, her residence is the place where she is stationed, or another place where she intentionally establishes and keeps residence.

When there are many issues or questions presented in your memo, you may wish to state each question at the beginning of the analysis of that issue.

Many legal memos will involve interpretation of statutes or regulations. Paraphrase those statutes in this manner: "The statute requires that…" You may quote from the statute; but, if you quote a sizable section, you may lose your reader. If you must include longer passages from a statute, place it as an appendix at the end of the memo for the reader's reference.

When you quote from a statute or case law that remains in the main body of the document, it should be block-indented, *i.e.*, single-spaced and indented on both margins so that it stands out. The *Bluebook* requires block-indenting when the quotation is 49 words or more. We think the better rule is this: if something is worth quoting, it is worth block-indenting if it is more than a few words.

BRIEF ANSWER

This is a summary of the answer to the question presented. It gives the reader a quick "yes" or "no" to the question raised, with a brief statement of the reason for the answer. Again, omit legal citations.

DISCUSSION

This is the heart of the memorandum -- your discussion of the law as it applies to your question. Use the past tense throughout, except when you state what the law is; that goes in the present tense.

This is where you will begin your research. Once you have gathered the case law and any pertinent statutes, you will sit down to write the *Discussion* of your memorandum. Do not save your best cases for last. Lead your discussion with your most compelling authority, analyze it, and apply it to your own facts. Discuss cases in the order of their importance.

When discussing each case:

1. State the facts and holding in the case;
2. Give the court's rationale -- its reasoning -- for its holding; and
3. Compare the facts of that case to your own case situation.

Never forget that your legal memorandum should educate the reader. Lead the reader through a logical progression of thought. Remember that you should presume that the reader knows nothing. Do not make any jumps in logic from point A to point C expecting your reader to follow your train of thought.

Do not merely say that "*Kirkland* held..." Tell the reader the facts of the case, the court's holding and the court's reasoning. Show the reader why the case is relevant to the question presented. Then, explain the similarities or the differences between the cited case and your client's situation. Be convincing, clear and methodical. At the end of your analysis, the reader should be subconsciously nodding his/her head in agreement.

Remember that statutes are mandatory authority. If a statute applies to your problem, discuss it first and then any case law that it interprets.

Start the discussion section by: 1) repeating the first question presented; and 2) discussing the legal analysis of the issue the question raises. Begin with any statutory authorities, following with case law.

<u>Never</u> submit a memorandum that merely makes statements about the law and then follows those statements with citations alone. That is the equivalent of asking your reader to take the statements you make on faith alone. For each case you cite, you must tell your reader what the facts were, the court's reasoning and the court's holding.

The discussion achieves three main goals:

1. It collects and preserves your legal research;

2. It educates the reader as to what he/she must know to understand the law that applies to each of the questions presented; and

3. It should methodically show the reader the writer's rationale or reasoning used to reach the answer.

Above all, your discussion should be impartial. You should give an unbiased, judicious analysis of the problem assigned to you. Do not take sides; do not identify with the client. Try to approach the problem as if it had nothing to do with real people. Sometimes the best service you can render a client is to create a clear, well-reasoned memorandum concluding that the client has no case and should save his/her money.

<u>CONCLUSION</u>

The Conclusion is a summary of the analysis of the discussion and the answer to the questions presented. It may also recommend action to be taken based on the result reached. The conclusion should answer the questions presented and touch on the major legal issues that must be resolved to reach that conclusion. It may be that your research indicated that there was no general consensus among the various courts as to how an issue should be decided. If so, set forth the status of the law relating to the question presented by pointing out that some courts have held one way while others have come to a different -- perhaps opposite -- conclusion.

Briefly restate the general points made in the discussion and give the overall result.

To return to your discussion and analyses of the cases:

The length of the body of your memorandum -- which is the Discussion section -- depends on the complexity of the problem and on the amount of useful authority available. Sometimes you will have an abundance of authority. Generally speaking, four or five good cases ought to be enough to reach a conclusion on any question. Whatever the problem that is the focus of your memo, the process of analyzing and applying case law should work about the same in every memorandum.

What is a good case? Remember, as we discussed above, it is a case that is as close as possible to your question factually, as recent as possible and, when possible, in your own jurisdiction. Sometimes you will want to show your reader there are other important cases in addition to those you fully discussed and applied. To do this, you may use string citations.

Your research may have unearthed several opinions from other courts (jurisdictions) that followed the same rationale and have come to the same conclusion. When you cite each of those cases to emphasize your point, that successive chain of cases is called a *string cite*. They are separated by semicolons and preceded by a signal such as "*see*" (which means the citations that follow are to cases generally reaching the same result as the cases just discussed).

Your string cite might look something like this:

> *See Henderson v. State*, 546 P.2d 11 (Okla. Crim. Ct. App. 1968) (defense of isolated barn with spring gun unlawful); *State v. Johnston*, 288 N.E.2d 429 (Ohio 1962) (spring gun killing in vacant house is homicide, but dictum that gun might be justified in occupied dwelling where inhabitant could have fired if personally present).

You will see that each citation in this string cite is followed by an abbreviated summary of the case in parentheses. These are called *parentheticals*, and help the reader understand why the cases are similar in import to the ones you analyzed at length. Never string cite without using parentheticals, even though the signal will tell the reader something about the cases that follow. Normally, parentheticals should not exceed two lines in length and may omit articles and other words not crucial to meaning.

Do not string cite more than four cases together. If you do, the result is likely to be a confusing, unwieldy mass of words and numbers in which the significance of the cases is lost. Instead, in that rare instance when you want to tell your reader there is a whole regiment of similar cases available, put them in an appendix and simply refer your reader to the back of the document.

Nobody can predict how long a memo will be. Many are only a page or two; others may reach 15 or 20 pages. Obviously, as with everything else you write, brevity is a virtue in writing, but you cannot sacrifice clarity and completeness just to use fewer words. Keep the analysis simple and it will remain clear, no matter how many pages you have to use to cover the subject adequately.

You are writing an analysis of, and an answer to, a specific question or questions. Your reader wants the answer and the reasons for it. He/She wants an analysis of the authorities that are important to <u>this question</u>, not a general treatise on the law. Stick with what is germane to your problem; forget tangential matters, however interesting.

Omit cases that are ancient history and no longer apply to the law as it stood at the time of the cause of action. History may be interesting, but not on the client's money and the firm's time. What the law is not, but used to be, is occasionally useful in understanding the law as it is now. Otherwise, history has no place in your memorandum.

*Using Designations*

Designating a specific name for each of the parties or other actors -- or for some other important event, document or thing -- helps to make the text of any document more readable and understandable. Lawsuits, and the documents generated from them, deal not only with the parties but also with contracts, legal descriptions, events and dates. Commonly, they are described in lengthy and cumbersome legalese. Use designations whenever a particular person, such as a party or thing, appears repeatedly throughout a document.

There are three basic ways to refer to parties in a case:

1. By the party's name or abbreviation of the name;

2. By a "functional" or descriptive name; and

3. By their relationship in the lawsuit -- Plaintiff or Defendant.

Here is how it works. Suppose that the case involved one plaintiff and one defendant and both are individual persons. You could refer to the plaintiff as "Plaintiff," "Plaintiff Rebecca Caufield" or "Plaintiff Caufield" and to the opposing party as "Defendant," "Defendant James Baxter" or "Defendant Baxter." The style of the case clearly shows the relationship of the parties. Use one designation or the other.

Here is how you show the reader the designation assigned to each of the parties:

> Plaintiff Rebecca Caufield ("Plaintiff") sued Defendant James Baxter ("Defendant").

It is obvious to the reader that the designation within the quotation marks and parentheses means "hereinafter referred to as." That onerous bit of legalese is unnecessary, and should always be omitted. After you have formally designated how you will refer to each of the parties, be sure that you consistently refer to the party in that way throughout the document.

When there are multiple plaintiffs or defendants, we suggest avoiding designations by plaintiff or defendant without adding something to help the reader distinguish between which plaintiff and which defendant. Instead, use a descriptive name, such as "plaintiff-driver" and "plaintiff-passenger." If the party is a corporation or some other type of business entity, use an abbreviation of the company's name, such as "GM" for General Motors.

Functional names are descriptive names that indicate the relationship between the parties, such as "landlord" and "tenant," "manufacturer" and "distributor," or "buyer" and "seller." Functional names work especially well when you want to refer to a group of plaintiffs or defendants with a common characteristic ("limited partners"), or when the party's technical name is too lengthy or difficult to abbreviate ("union" or "school district").

Do not refer to you client <u>in their case</u> by abstract names such as "defendant," "accused" or "appellant." Call him/her "Mr./Ms. Brown" or "Rev. Davis," or refer to the "Bosco Corporation" or "the school." This is especially useful in impressing on the reader that your client is a "real" person with whom the reader will be able to empathize.

However, refer to other players in your client's case according to their status: "petitioner," "claimant" or "defendant." Using these impersonal terms also helps keep them separate from the characters in your own case when your case is being compared with an authoritative case.

Up to this point, we have talked only about designations of the parties or other actors in the litigation. Litigation also involves events, contracts, etc. If your case involves a police union for an alleged breach of the Collective Bargaining Agreement in a contract entered into by two parties, designations might be the "City" and the "Union."

How would you designate the Collective Bargaining Agreement, one of the key factors of the lawsuit? You could call it simply the "Contract" or refer to it by its initials, "CBA." Or, if the date of the contract was pivotal to understanding the event that brought about the lawsuit, or if there is more than one floating about, you might want to refer to it as the "6/10/94 Contract" or "6/10/94 CBA."

The same thing works for finding designations for the two amendments. Each was signed at a different time, so you could use that to differentiate between them: "First Amendment" and "Second Amendment." It is better, however, to use the date the document was signed or became effective, like this: "7/10/94 Amendment" and "10/10/94 Amendment." If one dealt with health benefits and the other with wages, you might refer to them as "Benefits Amendment" and "Wage Amendment," especially if benefits and wages are part of the issue being litigated.

Designations will help your reader only when you keep them short and make them sufficiently descriptive so that the reader understands immediately to what you refer. Designations are useless if you fail to use them consistently throughout the document. Once you designate an identity for something or someone, stick with it until you reach the "*prayer for relief*," or final closing paragraph of the document. Then, because you adopt a slightly more formal tone to ask the court to give you whatever it is you want, drop the designation and substitute the full names or titles of the litigants, like this:

> WHEREFORE, Plaintiff Rebecca Caufield requests that this court deny Defendant James Baxter's Motion for Summary Judgment.

*<u>Legal Authority</u>*

The authors of Domain 30.00 have discussed the different sources of legal authority. Remember that the usual source on which you will rely is called *primary authority*. There are two basic kinds.

First, there are statutes passed by the Congress, a state legislature or local government or administrative agencies of the executive branch which issue regulatory rules and regulations. Second, you will use case law. These cases are almost always the opinions written by appellate courts, with one important exception: the federal district courts. Although federal district courts are basically trial courts, their published opinions are also valuable as authority.

While primary authority is any law (*e.g.*, statutes, constitutions and case law) on which a court could rely in reaching its decision, *mandatory authority* is any primary authority that a court must follow in reaching its decision. *Secondary authority*, on the other hand, is any non-law on which a court could rely in reaching its decision.

Although primary authority usually decides legal questions, do not ignore secondary authority. This authority includes treatises on the law and articles in legal journals. While these authorities will not compel a result in any case, they may be very persuasive to a court, as well as a fine starting place for your research.

*Briefs, Generally*

Briefs are formal, written, adversarial arguments. They are presented to the court to persuade it to rule in a way favorable to the writer's client. Commonly, the opposing party then submits a brief in response that attempts to defeat the other side's argument and persuade the court to rule for its client.

Briefs are an essential advocacy tool. Because a brief gives an attorney the chance to state the client's argument without objection by opposing counsel or questions from the bench, it must be well-written and carefully researched. Everything in a brief has but two purposes: to educate and persuade the court.

> Lawyers make the mistake of assuming that the judge knows all the law, which … is a violent assumption. It should be remembered that a judge sitting in a trial term must necessarily often decide questions of law on the spur of the moment and without the thoughtful and careful consideration which an appellate tribunal has an opportunity to give to its decisions.
>
> Moscowitz, *Glimpses of Federal Trials and Procedure*, 4 F.R.D. 216, 223 (1946).

Legal memoranda (sometimes called "case briefs"), discussed above, are an objective and unbiased summary of a case. The briefs discussed here are adversarial, that is, argumentative in your client's favor and are filed with the court. Every part of the brief is written to present your client's position in the most favorable light. As you will see, it is permissible to write the brief so that it emphasizes the facts favorable to your client and minimizes those that are not.

Sometimes briefs are supplemented by oral argument before the court, sometimes not. Especially in the appellate arena, the enormous press of business has forced the courts to restrict the time for oral argument or abolish it altogether. Hence, the importance of power and precision in writing briefs is greater than ever. The brief may be the only chance the attorney has of educating and persuading the court.

You may be asked by your attorney to write a first draft of a brief. Your writing must be clear and persuasive beyond question. It is not uncommon for many state trial court judges to have only one law clerk, or none at all, to help them wade through the mass of paper they must negotiate each day. Judges and their clerks simply do not have time to ferret out the point in a complex, murky brief. The court wants to know what the problem is, the issue presented for decision, the legal considerations and authority controlling that decision.

If you do not tell the court clearly and concisely what your issues are, along with the facts and supporting authorities, the court will turn to the other side's brief for enlightenment. That, of course, is precisely what you do not want. You want the court to learn about the case from your persuasive argument and reasoning, not your opponent's.

Although in writing briefs, as in all things, you will follow the orders of your supervising attorney, the procedures of your office and the court rules, we can offer one word of general advice. If you have the chance to submit a brief on some point, but are not required to, *do it*, even if your attorney will argue the matter in person. The reasons for this are quite practical.

A great many legal questions are not decided on the spot. A judge will often wish to mull over a decision and will "take the matter under advisement." That means he/she will think it over before deciding how to rule, in chambers, the judge's office or at home. At such a moment, you want your firm's written argument close at hand so that the judge may consult it again before ruling.

*Court Rules*

The court rules determine the format you will use to prepare your brief, *e.g.*, cover sheet, table of contents and table of authorities. Generally, the local court rules supply the most information about a court's requirements for briefs. Local rules will tell you things such as which motions require supporting briefs or whether the court has a limit on the number of pages. Follow the rules exactly. Do not put your attorney in the position of asking leave to file a brief that is on the wrong size paper, too long or out of time. You handicap your attorney and your client by trying to file a brief that may be disregarded by the court because it is too late or too long.

Each jurisdiction has its own set of local rules, and the requirements for briefs may change from one court to another. It is not unusual for a brief to be governed by two sets of rules -- state court rules and local court rules -- at the same time. Unless you are familiar with all of the requirements for each brief, it is easy to overlook something.

*Brief Banks*

It may be helpful in developing your expertise to study briefs your attorney or others in the law firm have written. If your firm does not already have a brief bank, you may wish to create one to use as a reference tool. A brief bank is like a form file in which briefs may be filed by types, *e.g.*, a brief accompanying a motion for summary judgment, or filed by the area of law to which it applies. A well-organized brief bank can also be an effective research tool. It is also a good idea to read the bar journals and add to your brief bank copies of cases that either clarify or redefine the areas of law in which you work.

*Trial Briefs*

As the name implies, a brief is generally filed in support of, or opposition to, some question that arises in connection with litigation, present or pending. In some jurisdictions, trial briefs are called "memoranda of points and authorities" or simply "memoranda of law." A trial brief may be filed before, during or just after trial and addresses one or several of a broad range of questions connected with the trial.

Distinguish trial briefs from briefs filed on appeal, after a case has been decided in the trial court. These are, logically, called appellate briefs and are quite formal in tone. They tend to be longer and more complex than trial briefs and even more closely controlled by court rules.

Related to the trial brief, but not quite the same, are briefs filed in support of motions made at other stages of the litigation, such as a brief in support of a motion to compel the opponent to answer discovery. Briefs such as these, filed contemporaneously with a motion as "support" for that motion, are referred to simply as "supporting briefs."

When the court allows, submit a trial brief to help you and your attorney prepare for trial, if for no other reason. The trial brief will help to formulate a clear concept of the facts and inform your attorney of anticipated points of law to be argued at trial, as shown by the example told below by a federal district court judge:

> A case comes to mind in which plaintiff's attorney argued a point of law without preparing himself on the subject matter. I asked him if he had any authorities to sustain his contention, to which he replied, "Well, your honor, this is elementary." I stated, "It may be elementary, counselor, but not to me. I would appreciate it very much if you would go to the library tonight and check on this law which you regard as so elementary." The following morning he came into my chambers a little bit crestfallen with his adversary and admitted that the decisions revealed him in error … [H]e was wiser for having had the experience of learning what the preparation of a trial brief would have accomplished.
>
> Moscowitz, *Glimpses of Federal Trials and Procedure*, 4 F.R.D. 216, 223 (1946).

The trial brief's length depends on the complexity of the issues to be decided at trial and the number of pages allowed by the court rules. Some are quite short, especially if they address a single issue.

Brevity is a special virtue in a trial brief since you are writing for a busy judge who does not have time for long, complex submissions. Whatever its length, the trial brief will <u>always</u> contain citations of authority and applications of that authority to the question or questions to be decided by the court at or before trial.

Often, in addition to the discussion of authority contained in the brief itself, wise legal professionals will, where the court permits, append photocopies of one or two decisive cases. If the judge wants to read the whole case in addition to your discussion of it, he/she will appreciate not having to look elsewhere to dig it out. Many judges would rather not break their concentration to go and find a case, or have their clerk (if any) do so. Hence, include anything critical, especially if it is not easily accessible by the judge.

In some courts, counsel may thoughtfully highlight or underline the decisive parts of the opinion. In other courts, this practice may be considered too informal. Be guided by local custom, your boss' preference and court rules.

Suppose your attorney is representing a defendant in a criminal matter. Your client, Jones, has killed a man named Slivovitz in a barroom fight. Slivovitz was a big man, but unarmed. Your client, somewhat smaller, was being beaten when he grabbed a beer bottle and hit his antagonist over the head with it. Jones hit Slivovitz too hard and has been charged with second-degree murder.

You have learned that Slivovitz was a real hoodlum whose hobby seems to have been beating up people whenever he got a few drinks inside him. He has quite a history of this behavior. If you can get this evidence before the jury, you have every chance of an acquittal.

Assume that the law in your jurisdiction permits such evidence on the issue of who was the aggressor. The law requires, however, that to get the evidence in, you must show a substantial pattern of violent behavior by the dead man, a pattern extending over time to a point reasonably close to the time of his death. The prosecution will object to the introduction of Slivovitz's violent history. The court has called for briefs from both sides. Your task is to persuade the judge -- through a motion *in limine* and supporting brief -- that the evidence should come in.

### The Cover Page, Table of Contents and Table of Authorities

Depending on the court rules, your brief may have a cover page that will follow the format dictated by the court. The cover usually sets out the case number, the style of the case, the title of the brief, the name, address and telephone number of the attorney filing the brief, whom he/she represents and the date the brief was filed. Appellate brief covers may also include the name of the trial judge and the jurisdiction from which the case came or order on appeal.

The cover is made from slightly heavier paper stock, a little like the cover of a softbound book. Oftentimes, the court will have requirements about the color of the cover stock. If there are no rules governing the color, use either off-white, tan, navy, light blue or red. Avoid pastels or neon colors, which look unprofessional. Even when a cover is not required, it is a good idea; it adds formality to your brief. *See* next page for an example.

Case No. CRF-92-877W

IN THE DISTRICT COURT OF CLEVELAND COUNTY

STATE OF OKLAHOMA

THE STATE OF OKLAHOMA,

Plaintiff,

vs.

ROBERT THOMAS JONES,

Defendant.

TRIAL BRIEF OF DEFENDANT

ROBERT THOMAS JONES

Name of Attorney
Attorney I.D. No.
Firm Name
Street Address
City, State, Zip Code
Telephone Number
[Fax Number - Optional]
[E-mail Address – Optional]

Attorneys for Defendant Robert Thomas Jones

[Date of Filing]

The caption or style of the case is the first information the court will read -- it must be accurate. Be sure that the parties' names are correctly spelled and listed. Always proofread the case number for accuracy. A transposed number could easily cause your brief to be misfiled by the court clerk.

Depending on court rules and local custom, the next section of the trial brief will often be an index of the headings and subheadings within the body of the brief called a Table of Contents.

TABLE OF CONTENTS


| | | |
|---|---|---|
| TABLE OF AUTHORITIES | | ii |
| INTRODUCTION | | 1 |
| STATEMENT OF THE CASE | | 2 |
| ARGUMENT AND AUTHORITIES. | | 4 |
| I. | EVIDENCE OF THE DEAD MAN'S HISTORY OF CRIMINAL ACTS SHOWS A PATTERN OF VIOLENCE | 4 |
| II. | EVIDENCE ON THE ISSUE OF WHO WAS THE AGGRESSOR SHOULD BE ADMISSIBLE AT TRIAL | 7 |
| CONCLUSION | | 9 |


-i-

The next section will normally be a Table of Authorities, sometimes called a Table of Cases. The applicable court rules will tell you whether a Table of Authorities is required. If it is, the rules will also prescribe its format.

The order for citing legal authorities in a Table of Authorities is:

1. case law (in alphabetical order, regardless of jurisdiction or reporter);
2. constitutional law (in sequential order, beginning with the smallest number to the largest);
3. statutes (federal statutes first if your case is in federal court; state statutes first if your case is in state court);
4. court rules; and
5. other authorities.

Cases are always listed in alphabetical order, regardless of their jurisdiction or reporter. When listing each case, include the number of the volume of the reporter and the page on which the case begins, but not pages within the case used as spot cites throughout the brief.

Wrong:

*Anderson v. United Finance Co.*,
666 F.2d 1274, 1278 (9th Cir. 1982) 14, 15, 16

Correct:

*Anderson v. United Finance Co.*,
666 F.2d 1274 (9th Cir. 1982) 14, 15, 16

A citation found within a quote is never listed in the Table of Authorities because it is not the citation upon which your argument is based.

Constitutional law, statutes and court rules should be listed in their separate categories in sequential order, from the smallest number to the largest. An example is shown in the Table of Authorities found below.

TABLE OF AUTHORITIES

| Cases: | Page |
|---|---|
| *Aspen v. State,* 73 Okla. Crim. 244, 221 P.2d 665 (1941)[1] | 3 |
| *Cameron v. State*, 561 P.2d 211 (Okla. Crim. App. 1978) | 4 |
| *Marshall v. State,* 680 P.2d 827 (Okla. Crim. App. 1981) | 5 |
| *Sciani v. State,* 762 P.2d 4 (Okla. Crim. App. 1990) | 2, 5 |
| Statutes: | |
| 21 Okla. Stat. 384 (Supp. 2002) | 3, 4, 6 |
| 21 Okla. Stat. 386 (Supp. 2003) | 5 |

-ii-

The Introduction

The Introduction to your brief is short, but nevertheless important. It is never a required component of any brief, but it can be a useful mechanism to "introduce" the lawsuit to the judge who may not recall anything at all about it. By clearly stating these points at the beginning of your brief, you have set the stage for a logical explanation and argument by which the judge will consider your brief and request. Designate names to help the

[1] The *Aspen* citation differs from the others because *Aspen* was decided before Oklahoma stopped publishing its official reporter. Remember that when you cite a state case in a court of that state, you must include both official and unofficial citations if the case was reported in both.

court identify each of the important players, events or things and use those designations consistently throughout the brief.

The Statement of the Case

Usually, a Statement of the Case includes both facts and a procedural history of the case, when that history is important. A procedural history is required in appellate briefs. It may be unimportant in a trial brief, and local rules may not require that it be mentioned at all.

The Statement of Facts

The Statement of Facts relates to the court those facts necessary to decide what must be determined. The judge relies on the parties' briefs to present the facts of the case as succinctly and clearly as possible. Use the statement of facts as one more way to further educate the court about why your client should prevail.

As in all legal writing, the facts are the crux of the case. Remember that the court may not attach the same importance to a piece of testimony that you did. The judge may even have forgotten it, even though most judges have prodigious memories for the evidence presented in a case. In either event, you must remind the court of the facts that will be used. You need not rehash all the facts in the case, just those that affect the question you are arguing.

Because you want the brief to be as persuasive as possible, narrow the facts -- without distorting or misrepresenting the entire picture -- to those that will lead into your legal analysis. Do not include dates, legal descriptions or other factual details unless they are pertinent to the issues. You can, and should, state the case in such a manner as to emphasize the facts in your client's favor and minimize those that are not. There is nothing to gain by concealing or ignoring damaging facts. Instead, confront them and then explain them. Although you may slant the facts to fit your argument and stated purpose, be ethical. Misstated court decisions and exaggerated factual statements only hurt your cause.

Your statement of the facts should be clear, concise, and interesting. Tell the facts in such a way that the reader is intrigued and acquires an interest and sympathetic curiosity about what will be said next. The statement of the facts should persuade the reader without appearing to do so. If you want to emphasize a word or phrase, put it at the end of the sentence and make sure that the sentence is in the active voice. If you wish to de-emphasize something, put it at the middle of the sentence and use the passive voice.

An imaginary case, *State v. Jones*, will clarify this discussion. Our fact statement in the example below is stated in the nature of an offer of proof. That is, we are going to set out those things we expect to prove, showing the court the pattern the law requires to admit the whole history of Slivovitz's violent past.

Statement of Facts

Through testimony and records of conviction, the defense will show the extensive criminal history of Bernard Slivovitz. In particular, the defense will show that Slivovitz committed violent assaults at these times and places:

1. At Muskogee, Oklahoma, on June 15, 1988, he assaulted John Kerrigan without provocation, breaking Kerrigan's nose and two ribs. He was not tried for this offense because he reached a private settlement with Kerrigan.

2. At Weatherford, Oklahoma, on December 11, 1989, he struck Arthur Running Deer with a chair, fracturing Running Deer's skull. Slivovitz was convicted of aggravated assault for this offense, and served six months in the county jail as a result.

3. At Oklahoma City, Oklahoma, on...

Notice something important about the Statement of Facts above. The language used, like the language in any good trial brief, is terse, plain and simple. Remember, you must both illuminate and convince in one reading, without confusion. In the example, both sentences and paragraphs are short. We used strong verbs and ordinary nouns, and avoided adjectives and adverbs. Short and simple is always best.

Even so, pay attention to the language you use and how you designate your client and the opposing party. In our example, the dead man is designated as simply "Slivovitz." You could call him the "victim," as the prosecution will. That term may arouse sympathy, and certainly mischaracterizes the dead man: after all, your point is that Slivovitz is the villain of the piece, not your client. We also used the term "violent assault." Strictly speaking, there is some sort of real or threatened violence in any assault, so perhaps "violent" is redundant. Even so, we used the word to reinforce the impression of Slivovitz's lawlessness and brutality.

The Argument and Authorities

The Argument and Authorities is the body of your trial brief. It will normally follow your Statement of Facts. If your trial brief is lengthy, you may wish to precede the argument with a special, short section -- a Summary of the Argument. Even where this section is not required, it is a powerful addition to your brief.

The Summary of the Argument is a short, hard-hitting capsule of your argument -- a blunt summation of what your client wants and why the law says he/she should prevail. Although this section is sometimes excluded, many appellate court rules require this section. Regardless, we think the Summary of the Argument is the most powerful section of a brief and we recommend its use. The Summary of the Argument is short and simple -- a page or less -- and is usually written after the Argument and Authorities section has been completed. It omits all citations and simply states your major arguments briefly, succinctly and powerfully: "we win *because*." But, if you have a statute or case that unquestionably requires the result you seek, by all means say so here. The Summary of the Argument is discussed in greater detail under the section on Appellate Briefs, below.

Remember that the reader will give the most emphasis to statements that appear either at the beginning or end of a sentence. The same is also true for paragraphs and a strong, clear quote will often make more of an impression on the reader than the same information in narrative form.

Drafting Propositions

The Argument and Authorities section is broken down by headings known as propositions. These sections contain a discussion of each of your arguments and sub-arguments in outline form. The proposition is simply a trenchant statement of the argument to follow, terse and hard-hitting. It is stated positively and argumentatively, flatly asserting the law as you think it is or ought to be. The tone of the proposition should be partisan, although each argument must be reasonable to have any chance of acceptance by the court.

Your argument will begin with your proposition -- your first proposition, if there is more than one. Then, you will argue the point made in your proposition by answering the question raised and explaining why it must be so. Do not save the best for last -- lead with your best arguments and your best authorities. First impressions here will be important.

Think of a proposition as a heading -- normally a single sentence -- which states the question for the court. Generally, the judge who reads the brief will know the problem already; often he/she will have called for briefs from both sides. Nevertheless, you should begin with the proposition; it reminds the judge of the precise issue in question. Do so affirmatively and plainly, putting your best argument forward.

Sometimes the matter you have briefed will be decided by a judge who knows nothing about the matter except what you tell him/her. This happens in jurisdictions where the matter will be decided by a "law and motion" judge -- one who hears all manner of preliminary questions from dozens of different cases.

Again, the first proposition should be the best and strongest of all of the propositions in your brief. It may be followed by subheadings, or sub-propositions, some of which will also have subheadings. Each of the subheadings should flow from the major premise of the proposition and each should logically follow the last. If written correctly, the reader should be able to follow your argument easily by reading the propositions and sub-propositions in order as they appear in the Table of Contents.

Insert a new proposition or sub-proposition where you begin a distinctly new and important point. Avoid inserting a heading or subheading when the discussion of that point lasts only a paragraph or two. Still, it is better to use too many than to use too few and thereby misplace the force and logic of your argument in an unbroken river of words. The best briefs have an inexorable quality about them, flowing steadily and logically toward the writer's goal, carrying the reader along. Headings will help this flow.

Note that the proposition is stated affirmatively -- as if it were absolutely so -- not as a question. You are telling the court what you think the law is and requires. There is no rule against stating the question the court will decide as a question; however, your brief is much stronger and more persuasive if you put the proposition positively, as a fact. For example:

I. EVIDENCE OF THE DEAD MAN'S HISTORY OF ASSAULTS IS ADMISSIBLE BECAUSE IT SHOWS A PATTERN OF AGGRESSION LEADING UP TO THE OFFENSE CHARGED.

As any useful proposition should, this one not only states positively what the court ought to do with the question, but why: "because it shows a pattern of aggression..." The proposition can take two forms: "X should happen because of Y," the pattern we used above or, "because of Y, X should happen." Use whichever form seems smoothest and most persuasive, but always make the proposition say why the court should rule as you want.

Using the example of our homicide case, let us suppose that your client, "the defendant," has taken the position that Slivovitz was killed in self-defense. In your trial brief, you want to take the position that your client's self-defense theory is fairly raised by the evidence and you want the court to instruct the jury on that issue. How do you state your proposition?

I. WHETHER DEFENDANT IS ENTITLED TO A JURY INSTRUCTION ON SELF-DEFENSE.

Blah. The issue is stated, but it is so broad and drab that it neither informs nor arouses. Try again.

I. WHETHER A DEFENDANT MAY STRIKE AN UNARMED MAN IN SELF-DEFENSE.

No better, and a little worse. The issue is more specific, but it is still dreary and sounds as if the other side wrote it.

I. WHETHER DEFENDANT, THREATENED BY AN ANGRY, LARGER MAN, HAD THE RIGHT TO DEFEND HIMSELF.

Much improved, but we can still do better.

I. WHETHER A SMALL MAN, THREATENED WITH SERIOUS INJURY BY AN AGGRESSIVE, LARGER MAN, MAY SHOOT TO DEFEND HIMSELF.

Now this is a fair summary of the question, but it states the case from your client's perspective. If you can, you want to state the proposition not only fairly, but in such a way that persons reading it will answer instantly as you wish them to.

Here is another example: Your supervising attorney represents a municipality in a civil appeal by a criminal defendant who was convicted on his own confession. The defendant filed the case below alleging that his constitutional rights were violated because he was not warned of his right to say nothing to the police. When the defendant was first interviewed by the police, a police detective asked his name and address, at which point he gave both and gratuitously added: "I did it." You could state the proposition something like this:

I. WHETHER THE POLICE MUST GIVE A MIRANDA WARNING TO THE ACCUSED BEFORE ASKING ANY QUESTIONS OF HIM.

Stated like this, the proposition is vague, divorced from the facts of the case, and does not begin to state your theory. Start over.

I. WHETHER A DEFENDANT MUST BE WARNED BEFORE ANYTHING HE SAYS MAY BE USED AS EVIDENCE AGAINST HIM.

Nothing -- same old flat proposition, restated. Try one more time.

I. WHETHER A CRIMINAL DEFENDANT'S VOLUNTEERED CONFESSION MUST BE EXCLUDED BECAUSE THE POLICE DID NOT WARN HIM, BUT ONLY ASKED HIS NAME AND ADDRESS.

Now you have something more useful. It fairly states the question, but it states it in your words. A word of caution: keep the length of your proposition to four or six single-spaced lines. More than that, your proposition becomes intimidating rather than persuasive. Delete all unnecessary words that do nothing to convey the meaning of what you are trying to say. If you feel that you simply cannot state the proposition adequately within this limit, it may be a signal that subheadings are necessary.

If the rules of the court permit, you may wish to depart from the "whether" format to make your propositions a little stronger. You might state your proposition in our last example like this:

I. THERE IS NO REASON TO INCLUDE A VOLUNTEERED, UNWARNED CONFESSION WHEN ALL THE POLICE ASKED WAS THE DEFENDANT'S NAME AND ADDRESS.

Always be scrupulously fair when stating any proposition. The court will lose confidence in your brief if it appears that you are slanting the issues or embroidering on the basic question before the court.

Use of Authorities

Start with your controlling authority. If it is a statute, discuss it first. Then, follow with any case law that interprets the statute, beginning with your best case. It is not necessary to cite every case that interprets your controlling authority.

> A few good cases on point with sufficient discussion of their facts to show that they are relevant are much to be preferred over a profusion of citations.
>
> *Practitioner's Guide*, United States Court of Appeals for the Tenth Circuit.

Lead your discussion with your most compelling authority, analyze it and apply it to your own facts. Discuss cases in the order of their importance. Once again, remember to whom you are writing. The judge or clerk who picks up your brief will be in a hurry and may not read the entire argument to get to the "heart of the matter." This is not the time to wax eloquent -- be clear, concise and persuasive.

Look at the example below to see how the argument might begin in our hypothetical homicide.

I. EVIDENCE OF THE DEAD MAN'S HISTORY OF ASSAULTS IS ADMISSIBLE BECAUSE IT SHOWS A PATTERN OF AGGRESSION LEADING UP TO THE OFFENSE CHARGED.

In *Sciani v. State,* 762 P.2d 4 (Okla. Crim. App. 1990), the defendant killed a man who attacked him without provocation. The attacker beat the defendant with his fists. The defendant then picked up a piece of scrap lumber and struck the attacker, killing him.

The dead man in *Sciani* had a history of unprovoked assaults, just as Slivovitz did in the case at bar. The court held that evidence of the dead man's penchant for violence was admissible on the issue of who the aggressor was. *Sciani* at 4. The court reasoned that a demonstrated propensity for violence is relevant to establish who started the fight that led to the killing. The court stated that such a propensity "[s]urely makes it more probable than not that the dead man began the affray." *Id.* at 5.

Specific incidents of violence are admissible so long as (1) they form a pattern of physical aggression; and (2) the last incident in the pattern occurred "reasonably near" the time of the killing being tried. *Id.* at 6-7.

In *Sciani*, the defense offered to prove five separate incidents of aggressive violence by the dead man. The last of these took place about six months prior to his death at the hands of the defendant. The pattern in the case at bar is even more pronounced than the pattern in *Sciani* -- six incidents of unprovoked assault in as many years.

The last of these occurred only four months before Mr. Jones defended himself by killing Slivovitz. An attack occurring six months before the killing satisfied the "reasonably near" requirement in *Sciani*. *Id.* at 5. It follows that Slivovitz's attack only <u>four</u> months before assaulting Mr. Jones surely meets the "reasonably near" requirement with ease.

*Sciani* is only the most recent in a substantial line of well-reasoned cases supporting admission of a pattern of aggressive conduct by the dead man in a homicide case. The seminal case in this long-established line of cases is *State v. Aspen*, 73 Okla. Crim. 244, 221 P.2d 665 (1941). In *Aspen*, the court held that…

You get the idea. Note that the whole tone of the brief is partisan and argumentative. This is not the impartial analysis you make when you write memoranda of law for your attorney. It is a strong statement of what result the court ought to reach, and an explanation -- based on case law and other legal authority -- of why the law compels that result.

In writing a brief, just as in writing a memorandum of law, the reader must have enough facts to know why the case is similar to the case at bar and therefore persuasive. You must also give your reader the holding in the authority case and the rationale, or reasoning, of the court. Then, you must apply the case; that is, reason from its rationale to the facts of your case.

When discussing each case:

1. State the facts and holding in the case;

2. Give the court's rational -- its reasoning -- for its holding; and

3. Compare the facts of that case to your client's situation.

Frequently, a statute will affect the outcome of your problem. When a statute is substantially involved in your case, it is good practice to include it verbatim someplace in your brief, just as you do in writing a memo. If you have a pertinent statute no more than a couple of lines long, you can include it at the bottom of your index, or add a section just before or just after the facts called "Pertinent Statutes."

Do not, however, quote a statute of any length up front. Remember, the first part of your argument is liable to have the greatest effect on the court. You do not want to interrupt that persuasive effect by giving the court a long, statutory quotation to read.

Avoid footnotes -- or worse, endnotes -- in a brief. For that matter, avoid using them any place in legal writing unless you are writing an article for a scholarly journal. Nothing breaks a train of thought and interferes with comprehension like a plague of footnotes. If you have material, such as a verbatim statute, that needs to be included, but is not essential to understanding the argument, put it at the back of the brief.

Often, the pertinent authority will not be entirely on your side. There may be some very strong cases that reach a conclusion opposite to the one you seek. Like bad meat, hostile authority gets no better with age. You cannot ignore opposing authority; you cannot afford to let the first mention of it be by the other side.

One of your jobs, therefore, is to attack the authority on which the other side relies and show why it should not be followed. Normally, you deal with hostile cases by distinguishing them, showing that they are not persuasive. Usually, this is done by showing that the opposing cases are so different in their facts from your own case that they need not be applied.

Be careful. You cannot simply dismiss an antagonistic case from your own state by saying it was "badly decided" or "inequitable." That may be so, and the trial judge may agree with you. Even so, he/she must follow the law laid down in that case if it was decided by a court in the same jurisdiction and superior in rank.

For this reason, you must concentrate on showing the judge that, factually, the other side's case is different enough from your case -- the case at bar -- that it need not be followed. An exception to this rule is the case that just does not fit the holdings in other cases by the same court or other courts of equal or greater rank. A case like that can sometimes be written off as an aberration or a maverick case, or a case that has been implicitly overruled if you have no other means of getting around it. Even here, however, it is best to distinguish on the grounds of factual dissimilarity if you can.

The Conclusion

The conclusion of a trial brief is short, no more than a medium-sized paragraph for each proposition. This summary should briefly review each major point of your argument. It is simply a restatement, with few or no citations, of what your client wants and why he/she ought to prevail. Finally, close with a prayer -- a formal request for relief.

> CONCLUSION
>
> Our evidence will show that Slivovitz assaulted other people regularly over the last eight years. The last assault occurred only four months before the attack on Mr. Jones. These assaults form a clear pattern of calculated brutality, culminating in the attack on Mr. Jones. Under *Sciani* and the other cases cited, this evidence is admissible on the issue of who the aggressor was.
>
> For the reasons and arguments given above, Defendant Robert Thomas Jones requests that this court admit evidence at trial of Mr. Slivovitz's violent history to show a pattern of aggression leading up to the offense charged.

Usually, the conclusion is followed by a boilerplate line such as "Respectfully submitted," and the signature block of the lawyer or firm representing the client, something like what is shown:

Respectfully submitted,
NAME OF LAW FIRM

By: ____________________________

Attorney's Name, Bar Number
Law Firm's Address
City, State, and Zip Code
Telephone Number
Fax Number

ATTORNEYS FOR DEFENDANT
ROBERT THOMAS JONES

*Drafting Appellate Briefs*

Many of the same considerations that influence trial briefs apply to appellate briefs. There are, however, significant differences.

Most obviously, the appellate brief is written only after a matter has been disposed of by a trial court. This means that the appellate court is deciding matters of law, not fact. Appellate judges will not second-guess a decision made on the facts by the trial judge or jury unless there was no competent evidence on which the trier of fact could have decided as it did. In the normal case, that is a very hard thing to show. It is seldom any good complaining on appeal that the jury or judge decided wrongly on the facts.

The questions on appeal will therefore be questions of law. For instance, whether the court gave legally appropriate instructions to the jury, whether evidentiary rulings were legally correct or whether some procedural rule was strictly followed.

Having said all of that, let us add that, on appeal, the facts are still critically important. The appellate court knows absolutely nothing about the facts of the case except what it is told by counsel or whatever its clerks can dig out of the record. Therefore, you must pay particular attention to telling the court the facts clearly, fully and succinctly.

Here's what a veteran Supreme Court Justice had to say about the importance of the facts:

> The main purpose of a hearing is that the court may learn what it does not know, and it knows least about the facts. It may seem paradoxical but most legal contentions are won or lost on the facts.
>
> Jackson, *Advocacy Before the Supreme Court*, 37 A.B.A.J. 801 (1951). (Reprinted by permission). (Emphasis supplied).

Appeals are controlled rather strictly by statute and/or court rules. Not everything that happens in the trial court is appealable. Sometimes certain fundamental errors can be appealed without having been raised in the trial court. Generally, however, little can be appealed that was not saved at trial as part of the record, usually by appropriate objection.

Other rules proscribe the time within which an appeal may be taken and the prerequisites to filing one. Suffice it to say that the time to prepare for an appeal is immediately after trial. Formal notice of intention to appeal is not always required, but other procedures must be followed immediately post-trial such as designating portions of the record of the trial proceedings to be transcribed.

Appellate Brief Cover Pages, Table of Contents and Table of Authorities

Know the appellate court rules. Appellate rules and statutes prescribe not only time periods and other requirements or limitations, but often such things as page format and citation form. For example, Rule 32(a)(2) of the Federal Rules of Appellate Procedure requires that the cover page of an appellate brief contain:

> Except for filings by unrepresented parties, the cover of the appellant's brief must be blue; the appellee's, red; an intervenor's or amicus curiae's, green; any reply brief, gray; and any supplemental brief, tan. The front cover of a brief must contain:
>
> (A) the number of the case centered at the top;
>
> (B) the name of the court;
>
> (C) the title of the case (see Rule 12 (a));
>
> (D) the nature of the proceeding (*e.g.*, Appeal, Petition for Review) and the name of the court, agency, or board below;
>
> (E) the title of the brief, identifying the party or parties for whom the brief is filed; and
>
> (F) the name, office address, and telephone number of counsel representing the party for whom the brief is filed.

Remember that the rules differ from jurisdiction to jurisdiction and you must know the ones that apply to you. The rules for covers and cover pages also vary a little from one jurisdiction to another.

Just as with any other document filed with the court, the appellate brief is the first information that the court will read. It must be correct. Incorrect captions seem to be a particular problem of appellate briefs rather than trial briefs.

The style of the case remains the same when the lawsuit is appealed. It is the designation of the parties that changes. The party bringing the appeal is the appellant, regardless of whether that party was the plaintiff or defendant in the district, or trial, court. The party against whom the appeal was filed is the appellee, again regardless of his/her previous status. If the appellant was the defendant in the lawsuit (see example, below), make the distinction by showing the designation in the caption as "Appellant/Defendant." The court will appreciate your attention to detail.

The appellate brief requires a Table of Contents, while the trial brief may or may not. The Table of Contents may or may not include your propositions, but it will always show the beginning page for all the sections of the brief.

TABLE OF CONTENTS

Table of Authorities ii

Questions Presented 1

Interest of the *Amici* 1

The American Association of University Professors 2

The Faculty Senate of the University of Oklahoma 3

The Faculty Council of Oklahoma State University 4

Statement of the Case 4

Argument and Authorities 5

I. Oklahoma's Law Recognizes Tenure Rights As Customarily Defined by Colleges and Universities Throughout the United States 5

A. Colleges and universities make express offers and guarantees of tenure to attract faculty of quality with promises of economic security and academic freedom 5

B. Oklahoma law authorizes tenure, which creates a property interest by the Due Process Clause of the Fourteenth Amendment 9

II. Oklahoma May Honor the Tenure Rights of Faculty Serving in the State's Public Colleges and Universities Without Violating the Constitution's Balanced Budget Mandate 11

III. When a Public College or University Dismisses a Faculty Member in Violation of Tenure Rights, Oklahoma Law Requires a Remedy That Protects the Faculty Member's Expectation Interest 15

Conclusion 19

The Table of Authorities is an index, showing all the cases, statutes and other authority you mention in your brief. All authority is listed by full, formal citation, according to the rules of the court to which you are appealing. Generally, all citations should be in *Bluebook* form, but some local rules require special citation for particular authorities. Some rules may require that your propositions -- your arguments -- be shown in the Table of Authority, followed by the authority in support of each proposition.

Some jurisdictions may require that you list U.S. Supreme Court cases first, followed by other federal cases and then state cases. Within each subdivision of case law, it is customary to alphabetize the cases by appellant's/plaintiff's -- or the first litigant's -- name. Cases are followed by statutes, then by secondary authority such as legal periodicals and treatises.

Show the pages on which each authority appears, just as you did in the index to the trial brief:

TABLE OF AUTHORITIES


| Cases: | Page |
|---|---|
| *Bietzell v. Jeffrey*, 643 F.2d 870 (1st Cir. 1981) | 8, 9 |
| *Hamburger v. Cornell University*, 148 N.E. 539 (N.Y. 1925) | 5, 8 |
| *King v. University of Minnesota*, 774 F.2d 224 (8th Cir. 1985) | 6, 10, 11 |
| *Levin v. Harleston*, 770 F. Supp. 895 (S.D.N.Y. 1991), *aff'd in part, vacated in part on other grounds*, _ F.2d __, 1992 WL 122106 (2d Cir. 1992) | 6, 10, 11 |
| *Oliver v. Xavier University*, 553 So.2d 1004 (La. Ct. App. 1990) | 8, 12 |
| *Price v. Oklahoma College of Osteopathic Medicine & Surgery*, 733 P.2d 1357 (Okla. Ct. App. 1986) | 7, 8 |
| *Thorne v. Monroe City School Board*, 542 So.2d 490 (La. 1989) | 8, 9, 11 |
| Other Authorities: | |
| William Van Alstyne, *Tenure: A Summary, Explanation and "Defense,"* AAUP Bull. 328 (1971) | 6, 7 |
| AAUP, *General Report of the Committee on Academic Freedom and Tenure* (1915) | 7 |
| *FACULTY TENURE: A REPORT & RECOMMENDATION BY THE COMMISSION ON ACADEMIC TENURE IN HIGHER EDUCATION,* 256 (1973) | 7 |


-ii-

Let us discuss a few points about *Levin v. Harleston* in the example above. First, notice how the "subsequent history" of the case is shown. "*Aff'd in part, vacated in part on other grounds*" tells us that the appellate court affirmed a portion of the decision made by the court below in *Levin* and vacated another part of that same decision.

If we are citing *Levin* as an example of how we think our court should decide our case, then seeing affirmed is good news. Note, however, that the *Levin* decision was vacated in part on appeal. Vacated means the decision, or a part of it, was annulled or set aside. Never cite a case with negative history such as vacated, reversed, limited, superseded, overruled or modified, without first thoroughly reading the case and determining that the negative treatment does not affect the point of law for which you are using the case.

In the example above, we could have said "*aff'd in part, vacated in part*," and left it at that. If, however, we add "*vacated on other grounds*," we tell the reader that, yes, a portion of the court's decision was vacated, but not on the issues for which *Levin* is used in our brief.

Questions Presented

The *Questions Presented* is a short section, not always formally required but quite important. Required or not, we recommend that a questions presented section always be included.

Just as with the trial brief, you will argue one or more propositions -- argumentative, partisan statements of the law -- as you believe it to be and as you want the court to decide it is. These will lead off each major topic raised in the body of your brief and may also, if required by the court's rule, appear in your Table of Authorities.

The questions presented section, however, is something different. It is simply a statement of the questions the court must answer on appeal, stated as the court might state them for itself, impartially and without bias. The questions should help the court to ascertain precisely what problems it is called upon to solve.

Appellate judges will tell you that what many lawyers fail to do is isolate and define the legal issues to be decided on appeal. These issues are, along with the facts, the most important things the court wishes to know. A United States appellate judge put it this way:

> The most aggravating brief is the one which is unfocused. Counsel should strive to state and define the issues with as much precision as possible.

One appellate judge told the story of handing a lawyer-friend three sets of briefs and asking him to define the issues in the cases. The lawyer could not, because the brief writers had not clearly written exactly what everybody wanted the court to decide. The lawyers who wrote those briefs failed to fully serve either the court or their clients.

Issues are generally stated in a single sentence beginning with "whether." Remember, they must be as specific as possible and tied to the facts of your case. Let us consider a few.

"Whether the court's instructions were erroneous." This is the sort of amorphous issue statement about which the judge complained in the quotation just above. This may be the question, surely, but it is stated in such a general and non-specific fashion that it does not help the court.

Below are statements of three issues as they appeared in a real-world brief. If you carefully define the issues as in this example, not only will you help the court, but you will also enhance your chances of success. Your brief will strike the court as highly professional and everything else you say will be read with all the more attention and respect.

QUESTIONS PRESENTED

I

Whether faculty who have earned tenure at Oklahoma's public colleges and universities enjoy tenure protection as customarily defined by colleges and universities throughout the United States.

II

Whether the contract rights of tenured faculty serving in Oklahoma's public colleges and universities are abrogated, nullified or impaired because of the balanced budget provisions of the Constitution of the State of Oklahoma. Okla. Const., art. 10, § 23.

III

Whether a faculty member, who is dismissed in violation of tenure rights by a public college or university in Oklahoma, is entitled to a remedy that protects his/her expectation interest in performance of the contract.

## The Statement of the Case and the Statement of the Facts

The Statement of the Case tells the court what happened in the case so far. Normally, it will recite when the case was tried, the result and the steps taken -- including dates -- to perfect the appeal. Recite the procedural history in chronological order.

Sometimes you may elect to combine this section with the next one -- the Statement of Facts -- and call both the Statement of the Case. You will ordinarily choose to do this when your statement of facts is reasonably short. Even when you combine the two sections, you may wish to separate by short subheadings the history of prior proceedings from the facts.

In the Statement of the Facts, set out as concisely as you can the facts that the court will need to render its decision. You must presume that the court will know nothing of the facts of the matter on appeal except what you relay. The court has a right to expect, and will expect, a fair statement of the facts for both sides, not a one-sided rendering of those facts that favor only your side.

Many judges call the Statement of Facts the most important part of the brief. Remember the quotation from Justice Jackson and *The Practitioner's Manual* for the United States Court of Appeals for the Tenth Circuit we gave you above? As you state the facts, you must tell the court where the facts can be found in the record of trial, like this: (R.119). This is a citation to page 119 of the transcript produced by the court reporter at trial.

In the Statement of Facts, as everywhere else in the brief, keep your sentences and paragraphs short and crisp, your subjects and verbs close together, your language plain. The example below shows part of the Statement of Facts from a brief in a state supreme court. The example also shows how the Statement of the Case may be combined with the Statement of Facts into a single, clear, succinct section.

STATEMENT OF THE CASE

> William P. Brown ("Professor Brown") served as Chair of the Horse Management and Training Program at Murray State College (the "College") from January 1982, until his termination in 1989. As conceded by the College, "[p]laintiff [Brown] had tenure." Defendant Murray State College's Trial Brief ("College's Trial Brief"), page 1.
>
> Professor Brown was forced to resign without a hearing in 1989. In January 1989, the College's Director of Occupational Education notified Professor Brown that a female colleague had filed a written complaint against Professor Brown. The Director asked for Professor Brown's resignation. The Director added that, if Brown did not resign by defined deadlines, Brown's employment would be on a probationary basis. Also, if Professor Brown did not resign, the Director said the President of the College would initiate an investigation of the allegations, which could lead to Professor Brown's dismissal. In subsequent correspondence, the President of the College reaffirmed the College's position.
>
> Initially, Professor Brown denied the allegations, demanded a hearing and refused to resign. However, six days later, Professor Brown sent a memorandum submitting his resignation effective as of June 30, 1989. The President accepted the resignation on behalf of the Board of Regents.
>
> Two months after the President accepted Professor Brown's resignation, Professor Brown made a formal request to rescind his resignation. The request was denied, and the Board of Regents terminated Professor Brown's employment on June 30, 1989.
>
> Professor Brown sued the College and several individual defendants, alleging that his resignation was the result of duress and coercion. Professor Brown's claims against the College for breach of contract and tortious breach of contract were tried to a jury, which rendered a verdict for Plaintiff, Professor Brown, and awarded damages in the total amount of $100,000. The trial court entered judgment for the full amount plus attorneys' fees and post-judgment

interest. Both the College and Professor Brown filed cross-appeals in this Court.

There were no references to the record in the example above. This was because the form of the verdict at trial in this case framed the issue on appeal without requiring reference to the trial transcript.

## The Summary of Argument

Normally, a Summary of Argument section is not required by any rules of court. Next to the Statement of Facts, however, it is the most important part of any brief and you should include it if your attorney concurs.

The Summary of Argument is simply a concise, hard-hitting statement of why your client ought to win. It is especially useful in a case in which the argument itself -- the body of the brief -- is relatively long and complex. Usually, the summary should be no more than two pages long, preferably a single page. It should not discuss any authority unless you are convinced that a single case or statute compels the result you want; in that case, your summary will urge that case or statute as the decisive factor in the appeal.

The great value of the Summary of Argument is that a judge or his/her clerk, before reading the body of your brief, gets a strong, simple statement of what your client wants and why the client ought to prevail. It can be read again just before deciding the case, or just before your attorney goes before the court for oral argument, or both.

Write your Summary of Argument only after you have finished writing the rest of your argument. Since the summary is your argument condensed to a fine essence, you must have a tight grasp on your theory of the case before your summary can approach the perfection of clarity and force it needs to carry the day. Avoid the tendency of many legal professionals to regurgitate the headings and subheadings contained within the body of the brief. This is not only boring, but wastes an additional opportunity to restate your theory of the case in a fresh and interesting manner.

This restatement may include a complete re-sequencing of the points contained within the body of your argument. All judges understand that an argument made within one or two pages of a brief may, by necessity, be structured differently from an argument made within the following 20 to 30 pages.

## The Argument and Authorities

The Argument and Authorities section is the body of the trial brief. Here, you apply the law to the facts and show the court why your client ought to prevail. As shown in the next example, it begins with your proposition, the argumentative statement we discussed above. Next comes a subheading (sub-proposition), if appropriate, and the argument itself.

## ARGUMENT AND AUTHORITIES

I. OKLAHOMA LAW RECOGNIZES TENURE RIGHTS AS CUSTOMARILY DEFINED BY COLLEGES AND UNIVERSITIES THROUGHOUT THE UNITED STATES.

A. *Colleges and universities make express offers and guarantees of tenure to attract faculty of quality with promises of economic security and academic freedom.*

> Academic tenure is a "status granted, usually after a probationary period, which protects a teacher from dismissal except for serious misconduct, incompetence, financial exigency, or change in institutional programs." *Price v. Oklahoma College of Osteopathic Medicine & Surgery*, 733 P.2d 1357, 1358 n.1 (Okla. Ct. App. 1986).
>
> Though tenure is often perceived as a commitment to employ a professor until death or retirement, the commitment is not absolute in any sense. "Tenure … lays no claim whatever to a guarantee of lifetime employment." William Van Alstyne, *Tenure: A Summary, Explanation and Defense,* AAUP Bull. 328 (1971) (emphasis in original). Instead, academic tenure is appropriately and precisely defined as "an arrangement under which faculty appointments in an institution of higher education are continued until retirement … subject to dismissal for adequate cause." *FACULTY TENURE: A REPORT & RECOMMENDATION BY THE COMMISSION ON ACADEMIC TENURE IN HIGHER EDUCATION,* 256 (1973).

More often than not, you will see citations to case law appear as the reference to *Price* does: a statement of what the case held followed by a *Bluebook* citation. When the case you are discussing is a powerful one for your side, however, we recommend you discuss it in some depth before applying it to your facts.

First, tell the court what the case held, much as the writer did for *Price.* Then give enough of the case's facts that the reader can see the important similarities -- or differences -- between that case and the case at bar. Next, tell your reader what the court's rationale was.

> In *United States v. Pretzinger*, 542 F.2d 517 (9th Cir. 1976), the court held that the warrantless installation of a "beeper" on an airplane was not a search because the owner of the airplane had consented to the installation the day before the airplane was sold to the defendant. Consequently, the *Pretzinger* court concluded that no warrant is needed to justify installing a beeper unless Fourth Amendment rights would … have to be violated in the initial installation. *Id.* at 522.

Note that all facts were eliminated save those essential to understanding and applying the case. We know that a beeper was installed on an aircraft and that the owner of the plane had consented to that installation before selling the craft to the defendant. For these reasons, said the court, there was no search in the Constitutional sense. Obviously, there were more facts involved in the case, including much procedural maneuvering. Nevertheless, we gave the court what it needed to decide this question, whether the beeper installation in this case was, under these particular circumstances, a search.

Next, apply the authority to the facts of your own case. You might use *United States v. Pretzinger* like this:

> The rationale of the *Pretzinger* court in rejecting monitoring as a Fourth Amendment search was that one flying an airplane has no reasonable expectation of privacy in his movements. *Id.* at 522. Since aircraft are already tracked on radar, the aircraft has no Constitutional protection against affixing a "beeper" to it.
>
> However, the reasoning of *Pretzinger* compels a different result in the case at bar. Here the vehicle was an ordinary automobile, a vehicle not ordinarily tracked by the government or anybody else. Therefore, it should have, unlike an aircraft, Constitutional protection from warrantless searches.

Which cases do you use, and how many? Sometimes there will be dozens of useful cases, sometimes dozens on both sides. Which ones do you choose, and how many? There is no court-imposed requirement to use some specific number of authorities. Sometimes many are available, sometimes very few.

First, as to which ones to use, the guidelines are much like those we followed in talking about the trial brief. Choose cases from the highest court of your own jurisdiction whenever possible. Choose cases dealing with the question of law raised in your case and choose cases with facts as close as possible to those of the case at bar.

Second, as to how many: you do not need a lot of cases if you choose the best ones. The courts believe that quality outweighs quantity in choosing cases, but judges also want a brief to give enough facts to show why those cases should persuade the court.

Three or four good cases should be enough to prove any legal point. Choose them according to the guidelines above. Try to find suitable cases decided as recently as possible. Include, whenever there is one, the seminal case -- the well-known case that subsequent decisions regularly cite for the proposition you are discussing in your brief.

After you have fully discussed and applied your major cases, you are free to string cite a few other good cases, if you choose. Give the proposition for which they stand, their full citation and a parenthetical -- an abbreviated sentence telling your reader something about each case's facts and rationale.

Treat hostile authority exactly as we discussed under the subject of trial briefs. Do not lead off with an attack on the other side's authority; if you do that, you over-emphasize its importance. Rather, start with your own affirmative argument, stated as powerfully as possible. Only when you have made your own points fully will you distinguish dangerous authority on the other side. Here is a sample of how it is done:

> In *United States v. Hufford*, 539 F.2d 32 (9th Cir. 1976), the court *held ....* *However,* the facts of *Hufford* are inapposite here. A warrant had already been issued for the installation of a "beeper" on the defendant's truck. Moreover, the ... installation had been consented to by the owner ...

The best way to nullify an opposing case is to show that it is so different on the facts from the case at bar that it does not apply, or at best is unpersuasive. The example above does exactly that, stating that *Hufford* is hostile authority, but arguing that it does not apply because it was decided on very different facts.

Keep in mind that no appellate court likes to "overrule" a prior case, even when it does not want to follow the case. The court would much rather decide that the case simply does not apply because it is factually different from the case at bar.

The appellate rules are not mere guidelines that are nice to follow: they are requirements. Most appellate rules put page limitations on the length of briefs. Courts do not take kindly to litigants trying to circumvent these limitations by hiding argument in annexes and appendices. Put your argument in the body of the brief, where it belongs, and obey the court's strictures on page length.

## The Conclusion

The conclusion section of an appellate brief is short. It may include a very short summary of the heart of your argument, no more than a medium-sized paragraph for each proposition. Just as it does for any brief, the conclusion closes -- and closes the body of the brief -- with the prayer, or formal request for relief. A typical prayer might look something like this:

> For the reasons set forth above, Plaintiff respectfully requests that the judgment of the trial court be reversed, and that the motions to suppress the evidence and to issue an order dismissing the second count of the indictment be granted.

In the alternative, the conclusion may be in the form of a simple invitation to the court to grant the relief asked for, without a formal prayer:

> This Court should vacate the judgment and remand the case with instructions to the trial court to fashion a remedy which will vindicate Plaintiff's expectation interest in the performance of the tenure contract.

*Brief Checklist*

Here is a checklist of steps to take, after the brief is written, to finalize and prepare it for filing with the court clerk:

1. Shepardize and cite-check every citation. Look up every statute to be sure that: (1) it is the correct reference for that point of law; and (2) the numbers have not been transposed.

2. Proofread all quotations. Double-check citations to quotations. Every quotation should have a cite showing the page number where it appears in the opinion.

3. Proofread the brief for sense, typographical mistakes or grammatical errors; check for internal consistency such as:

    (A) Appendix ("App. ___.");

    (B) Record ("R. ___.");

    (C) Exhibit ("Ex. ___.");

    (D) Short form/abbreviated references to parties or name of motion -- the name designated at the beginning of the brief;

    (E) Propositions/sub-propositions;

    (F) Any dates given, *e.g.*, dates of contracts or dates a pleading or other paper was filed with the court; and

    (G) All references to exhibits, transcripts, depositions, appendices.

4. Review the appropriate court rules. Some examples of points to check are listed below:

    (A) Does the brief comply with any page limitation?

    (B) Does the brief need a Table of Contents or Table of Authorities?

    (C) Should the brief be bound and, if so, is a specific color required for the outside cover stock?

    (D) Is the brief in the proper format as required by all of the rules applicable to that court?

5. Prepare the cover page, Table of Contents, and Table of Authorities in the format set out in the applicable court rules. Check to be sure that each document is arranged in accordance with the rules.

6. Return a revised draft to the supervising attorney for final approval.

7. Determine the number of copies to be filed with the court and to be mailed to counsel of record listed on the Certificate of Service. (Be sure that the date and time for any hearing on the motion is shown on the copies mailed to counsel of record.)

8. Proofread the finalized draft to be sure that all changes have been made accurately.

9. Have the appropriate color of cover stock printed or copied for the cover page and have the necessary number of copies of the brief bound according to the applicable court rules.

10. Make a notation on the file copy that copies of the brief were mailed to counsel as shown on the Certificate of Mailing (pc: all counsel of record, the date and your initials). If the brief was e-filed with the court, attach the confirmation e-mail showing the date and time the brief was filed to the file copy.

11. Docket/calendar the response or reply dates, or the date and time set for the hearing.

**SAMPLE QUESTIONS FOR LEGAL RESEARCH AND WRITING**

1. In preparing a response brief, the paralegal should:

    a. Evaluate the cost-effectiveness of responding to the brief.
    b. Critique the writing style of the opposition's brief.
    c. Furnish appropriate objections to the opposition's brief.
    d. Distinguish cases upon which the opposition relies from the case at bar.

2. An interrogatory requests the names and addresses of all those who have provided medical care to the plaintiff in a case involving an automobile accident. The paralegal's best response would be to:

    a. Observe that the question is overly broad and provide a list of relevant caregivers.
    b. Observe that the question is overly broad and covered by the physician-patient privilege.
    c. Provide a complete list of all caregivers.
    d. Observe that the question is irrelevant.

3. A complaint based on diversity may be filed in federal court if:

    a. Two different state supreme courts issued conflicting opinions and the amount in controversy exceeds $50,000.
    b. The plaintiff's principal place of business is in a diverse jurisdiction and the amount in controversy exceeds $50,000.
    c. The controversy is between residents of different states and the amount in controversy exceeds $10,000.
    d. The controversy is between citizens of different states and the amount in controversy exceeds $75,000.

4. A letter sent to the defendant's insurer that summarizes the plaintiff's injuries, lost wages, medical treatment and medical bills, and requests monetary compensation is commonly known as:

    a. a statement of damages.
    b. a demand letter.
    c. a memorandum of law.
    d. an opinion letter.

5. Which of the following would appear on a court docket?

    a. document production.
    b. affidavit.
    c. continuance.
    d. a personal injury plaintiff's medical examination by the defendant's expert.

6. To obtain medical records from a treatment facility in time for a deposition, the records manager may be served with a:

   a. subpoena *duces tecum.*
   b. summons.
   c. motion to compel discovery.
   d. subpoena *ad testificandum.*

7. A memorandum of law must include:

   a. all facts, issues and analysis.
   b. all pleadings previously filed.
   c. persuasive authority.
   d. all previous cases litigated.

8. Which of the following is a researched discussion of a hypothetical fact situation?

   a. law examination.
   b. legal memorandum.
   c. dissenting opinion.
   d. treatise.

9. When it is determined that there is no material dispute between the parties regarding the facts, the best way to remove a case from jury consideration is by means of a motion for a:

   a. directed verdict.
   b. summary judgment.
   c. voluntary dismissal.
   d. judgment on the merits.

*Answers:*

1–d. Although it is always a good idea to try to keep the client's costs as low as possible, it should not have any impact on whether a response brief is written and filed in a case. Even if you and your attorney believe that the opposing party's brief lacks the necessary elements to prevail, a response should always be filed. If you did not, it would leave your client's side of the story untold -- or worse, told by the opposite side.

Critiquing the writing style of your opponent would be waste of the court's time; the court looks to the arguments and authorities within a brief to decide the case, not the brief's writing style. Although there may be valid legal objections to the opposition's brief, objections alone are not persuasive. You must back them up with legal authorities.

The correct answer to this question is: (d) distinguish cases upon which the opposition relies from the case at bar. In your response brief, you want to knock down the other side's argument. In other words, you want to persuade the court that the authorities relied upon by the opposition either do not really support the other side's position or there are other, more relevant cases upon which the court should rely in making its decision.

2–a. The correct answer to this question is option (a).

The question is overly broad. Suppose your client, the plaintiff, had sustained back and neck injury in a car accident. Suppose also that your client had several foot surgeries that were unrelated to the car accident. If you followed (c) and provided a list of all medical care providers, you would provide the name and addresses of the client's foot doctor and the hospital where the foot surgeries were performed -- information that has no relevance in this lawsuit. The question is neither irrelevant (a non-word, at any rate) or covered by the physician-patient privilege.

Under Fed. R. Civ. P. 35, whenever a plaintiff claims that the acts of the defendant caused him/her physical or mental injury, the defendant has the right to determine the genuineness of the condition, its extent and causes and to develop a prognosis. This is not only true as to a plaintiff, but applies equally to a defendant who asserts his mental or physical condition as a defense to a claim. Further, by placing a mental or physical injury in controversy as part of the lawsuit, the plaintiff automatically waives his/her physician-client privilege. To maintain the privacy of a plaintiff's medical records, the parties could enter into an agreed protective order that prohibits the defendant and defendant's counsel from disseminating the information contained in the medical records to anyone other than the court.

3–d. The correct answer is option (d).

This question requires an understanding of 28 U.S.C. § 1332(a), a common jurisdictional statute for federal cases, which relates to the diversity of citizenship or to the dollar amount of the controversy:

(a) The district court shall have original jurisdiction of all civil actions where the matter in controversy exceeds the sum or value of $75,000, exclusive of interest and costs, and is between:

(1) citizens of different States;
(2) citizens of a State and citizens or subjects of a foreign state;
(3) citizens of different States and in which citizens or subjects of a foreign state are additional parties; and
(4) a foreign state, defined in section 1603(a) of this title, as plaintiff and citizens of a State or different States.

4–b. The correct answer is option (b).

A memorandum of law is an internal memorandum written to solve a legal problem by applying pertinent cases and statutes. An opinion letter is a letter written by an attorney to the client giving a legal opinion about specific issues. A statement of damages, without a demand for settlement or payment, would be ineffective.

5–c. The correct answer is option (c), the continuance.

A court docket contains a listing of documents filed with or issued by the court, as well as hearings, court minutes and orders and the payment of court fees. A document production and the plaintiff's medical examination are events that occur during the course of a lawsuit; they are not documents filed with the court. An affidavit alone is rarely, if ever, filed as a separate document; it normally is attached to a motion or brief to support statements made in that document.

6–a. The correct answer is option (a), subpoena *duces tecum.*

Fed. R. Civ. P. 45 provides for two different types of subpoenas: a subpoena *ad testificandum*, commonly just called a subpoena, and subpoena *duces tecum*. A subpoena is used to require a person who is not a party to the lawsuit to appear and give testimony at his/her deposition or at trial. A subpoena *duces tecum* is used to require a person who is not a party to the lawsuit to bring to his/her deposition certain documents or things in that person's custody or control that are material and relevant to the facts at issue in the lawsuit. Fed. R. Civ. P. 34 allows service of a request for production only on a party, not on a <u>non-party</u> witness. A subpoena *duces tecum* is the <u>only way</u> to obtain documents or other tangible things from a non-party.

7–a. The correct answer is option (a): all facts, issues and analysis.

A memorandum of law, or legal memorandum if you prefer, is an internal[2] memorandum written to solve a legal problem by applying pertinent cases and statutes. For example, it may be a question addressed to the firm by a client; it may be a problem raised by a case the office is about to try, or is actually trying; it may be a query by an attorney who is

[2] In some jurisdictions, a Memorandum of Law must be filed simultaneously with certain briefs.

devising a new provision for a will or contract. A legal memorandum should contain: (1) all the relevant facts necessary to the reader's understanding of the issues; (2) a clear statement of the legal, not factual, question(s) the memo is intended to solve; and (3) a section commonly called the "Discussion" that gives an impartial analysis of the law as it applies to the question answered by the legal memorandum.

8–b. The correct answer is option (b), the legal memorandum.

The paragraph above explains the purpose of a legal memorandum. A dissenting opinion is a separate opinion written by a judge that disagrees with the majority opinion. A treatise is a type of secondary authority that focuses on a particular area of the law, such as *Restatement (Second) of Torts*.

9–b. The correct answer is option (b) summary judgment.

Under Fed. R. Civ. P. 56(c), the moving party is entitled to summary judgment only "if there is no genuine issue as to any material fact" and "the moving party is entitled to a judgment as a matter of law." Do not confuse a motion for summary judgment with a motion for judgment on the pleadings, which is a device for disposing of cases when the material facts are not in dispute and only questions of law remain. A "judgment on the merits" is like a dismissal with prejudice -- the party whose case has received a judgment on the merits cannot bring the same suit again. A directed verdict occurs within a trial when the judge rules that the party with the burden of proof has failed to make a *prima facie* case. A voluntary dismissal may be accomplished by a plaintiff without leave of court if it is filed before the defendant's Answer is filed, or by stipulation signed by all parties after the defendant's Answer is filed.

## 40.00 OFFICE ADMINISTRATION

### *40.01 Manage personnel through recruiting, hiring, training, counseling, supervising, evaluating and/or coordinating activities to create an efficient and effective work environment.*

The law practice has the potential to be either highly successful or to fail based on the type of personnel hired to be on the legal team. It is important to hire individuals who will work efficiently and effectively with the attorneys as well as with the staff members. When interviewing a candidate, the hiring party should determine whether the recruit is a team player and whether the candidate will fit into the firm's culture. The main purpose of recruitment is to find the best possible candidate for the job. Paralegals searching for employment should keep in mind that the way to get a good reputation is by being a good paralegal and by being active in the profession. Paralegals who participate in paralegal association activities become well-known throughout the legal community. This is not only good for you, the paralegal; but, it is also beneficial to your employer.

Law practices, primarily, fall into three categories:

- In-house corporate legal department;
- Legal department of governmental agencies; or
- Law firm.

*In-House/Corporation Legal Department*

Corporate legal departments are often headed by the general counsel. Working with the general counsel may be an associate general counsel, associate counsel and paralegals. The corporate legal department generally handles the legal affairs of the corporation or hires outside law firms to handle the corporation's legal matters.

*Legal Department of Governmental Agencies*

Governmental agencies' legal departments are headed by an attorney (*i.e.*, county attorney, city attorney, state attorney). Working with that attorney may be assistant attorneys, paralegals and legal secretaries. The governmental legal department generally handles the legal affairs of the governmental agency it represents or it hires outside law firms to handle certain legal matters.

*Law Firm*

Law firms can be any size and can be formed in a variety of ways:

- *Sole Practitioners* – These attorneys can be legal generalists or their practice may specialize in a particular area of law;
- *Partnership* – The partners/shareholders share the profits, losses and the decision-making;

- *Professional Corporation (P.C.)* – The practice operates as a corporation, and the shareholders are protected from personal liability. Incorporating safeguards personal assets and saves on taxes. The professional corporation has a board of directors or executive committee.

The law firm usually has a managing partner and each department or practice area has a department chair. The attorneys can be partners, associates or staff attorneys. Additionally, there are paralegals, sometimes paralegal managers/coordinators and the legal staff. The legal staff includes the firm administrator, legal secretaries, receptionists, accounting personnel, marketing personnel and other staff members. It is important that every member of the legal team works together for the success of the organization.

*Accounting Procedures within the Law Firm*

Although many paralegals are not exposed to the financial part of the business, it is important that they be familiar with the firm's accounting procedures and budgets. It is vital that the paralegal understand the purpose of trust accounts. The law firm's monies are kept in an *operating account* and the clients' funds are kept in a *trust account*. It is illegal to co-mingle the clients' funds with the law firm's funds. Often, several trust accounts are maintained simultaneously.

The accounting department may be comprised of just a few or many employees; this generally depends on the size of the law firm. The accounting area may include:

- The data processor, who inputs time;
- The billing assistant, who reviews the bills;
- The accounts receivable/payable clerk who is responsible for processing invoices owed to and owed by the firm;
- The payroll clerk, who calculates and processes payroll and tracks vacation and sick time used by the employees;
- The comptroller, who oversees the activities of all of the accounting personnel mentioned above; and
- The financial manager, who is responsible not only for overseeing the entire accounting department, but also for strategic financial planning and financial forecasting. (Oftentimes, the firm's managing partner also acts as the firm's financial manager.)

Although the billing assistant reviews the bills before they are forwarded to the attorneys for review, it is imperative that the paralegal and attorney keep accurate time records. With consumer revolution causing clients to review bills more closely, many are not willing to pay for a paralegal's on-the-job training. In light of this, the learning curve must be short, or valuable business may be lost.

Additional legal service providers not previously mentioned include:

- Law clerks;
- Office manager;
- Human resources director;
- Benefits coordinator;
- Director of management information systems (MIS);
- Litigation support manager;
- Computer programmer; and
- Library personnel.

### *Communication Skills*

Whether communicating verbally or in written form, you must always identify yourself as a paralegal. A paralegal cannot give legal advice even when the client requests it, cannot sign a legal pleading and cannot set fees. A paralegal cannot make court appearances, except in specific instances when authorized by statute, by court order or by the authorizing agency (*e.g.*, Social Security Administration).

A good communicator not only knows the importance of speaking clearly and in terms that others understand, but knows that listening is a very important part of communication. Good written communication skills are of equal importance.

### *Computer Skills*

Computer knowledge is essential. The paralegal should be proficient in various software programs because better computer skills will help to work effectively and efficiently. This will reflect positively on the professional performance of the employer and will best serve the client. The law is information-intensive and data must be organized for easy access. There is no substantive area of law that cannot benefit from computer utilization, including timekeeping and billing organization, indexing and coding materials and legal research. Computer support provides a higher quality of service to clients. Paralegals need to be on the cutting edge of computer systems, applications and techniques. At times, you may actually perform data entry; but, many times, you will supervise the input so that you are free to analyze and summarize the data.

While some paralegals may be afforded the luxury of having support staff or an entire department devoted to database systems and preparation, most paralegals must have a basic knowledge of the language of computers, the application of computer concepts in the law and an understanding of the legal work to be done. And hybrid paralegal positions require paralegals to be competent in administrative procedures and processes, as well as paralegal processes. Once those concepts have been mastered, the client can benefit from enhanced service at a lower cost.

You must analyze and understand the task at hand prior to setting up a database that will benefit the client and be useful in your case. It is common to use outsource scanning, imaging and coding of documents. In order to obtain the best result, the paralegal should unitize the documents prior to scanning the documents. Unitizing simply means to organize the documents so that all pages of a document are scanned in together. Of course, many programs offer the ability to add or delete pages of documents to existing documents or scans, such as in Adobe PDFs. An experienced paralegal, knowledgeable in computer systems that are most beneficial to his or her particular practice area, can be quite valuable to the client and the employer.

Additionally, database management systems are computer software programs designed to facilitate the creation and management of a database containing large volumes of data. This includes adding and deleting data, editing, sorting, searching and preparing hard copies. Many paralegal specialty areas, by nature, require that paralegals have extensive computer knowledge and work with databases

There are a number ediscovery databases and ediscovery certifications available to assist in complex litigation matters that require the paralegal to have extension knowledge and understanding of the attributes and differences so as to recommend the most appropriate database for the matter at hand to their attorney. This also requires detailed knowledge of metadata (the hidden data within electronic documents) and how to respond to and draft specific requests for same. Databases will be discussed in more detail in the Technology Section of this Review Manual.

*The Paralegal as an Employee*

One of the greatest considerations in any law office is that of employee benefits and administration. Vacation, sick time, paid time off, health insurance and bonuses are some of the key benefits that are a vital part of employment. Other benefits may include:

- Paid parking;
- Flexible hours;
- Pension plan;
- 401(k) plan;
- Flexible spending account;
- Health savings account;
- Structured bonuses;
- Profit sharing;

- Firm credit card for business expenses;
- Meal allowance;
- Health club membership;
- Professional dues;
- Pro Bono Participation;
- Continuing legal education seminars;
- Mileage reimbursement;
- Employee assistance program; and
- Education reimbursement.

According to the U.S. Department of Labor (DOL), "The Fair Labor Standards Act (FLSA) is a federal law that requires that most employees in the United States be paid at least the federal minimum wage for all hours worked and overtime pay at time and one-half the regular rate of pay for all hours worked over 40 hours in a work week."

There are exceptions to this requirement that are set forth in Section 13(a)(1) of the FLSA. This Section exempts minimum wage and overtime pay for certain "executive," "administrative," "professional" and "outside sales" personnel. There is a similar exemption allowance in Section 13(a)(17) pertaining to certain "computer" employees. It is important to note that the job title does not determine whether the job is exempt. In order for an exemption to apply, an employee's specific job duties and salary must meet certain the requirements of the DOL's regulations.

Prior to revision of the Fair Labor Standards Act in 2004, many paralegals were salaried employees and received no overtime pay. Although many paralegals are pleased with the 2004 FLSA change from exempt to nonexempt status, others have experienced a downside following this change. Some employers used the opportunity to lower or cut other benefits because they are now required to pay overtime. Although the overtime pay is appreciated, many paralegals prefer to retain their exempt status because they have lost the flexibility of managing their own time. In addition, many say there has been a noticeable lack of respect since being moved to the nonexempt status

*Aspects of Employment Law*

To ensure a complete understanding of employee benefits, you must understand the different aspects of employment law. Those laws include, but are not limited to, the Civil Rights Acts of 1964 and 1991, the Americans with Disabilities Act, and the Family Medical Leave Act of 1993.

Civil Rights Acts of 1964 and 1991

Title VII of the Civil Rights Act of 1964 makes it unlawful for an employer to discriminate against any applicant or employee as to hiring, firing, compensation, promotion and/or all terms, conditions or privileges of employment on the basis of race, color, religion, sex or national origin. 42 U.S.C. § 2000e(b). Title VII further prohibits covered employers from limiting, segregating or classifying employees in any way that would tend to deprive individuals of employment opportunities or adversely affect their employment status. 42 U.S.C. § 2000e-2(a)(2). Title VII also prohibits sexual harassment and pregnancy discrimination.

Sexual harassment, gender abuse or other discriminatory, unfair treatment is not allowed in the workforce. Such actions are illegal under federal, state and city laws. Sexual harassment has been defined by the Equal Employment Opportunity Commission (EEOC) Guidelines as unwelcome sexual advances, requests for sexual favors and other verbal or physical conduct of a sexual nature when, for example:

- Submission to such conduct is made either explicitly or implicitly a term or condition of an individual's employment;
- Submission to or rejection of such conduct by an individual is used as the basis for employment decisions affecting such individual; or
- Such conduct has the purpose or effect of unreasonably interfering with an individual's work performance or creating an intimidating, hostile or offensive working environment.

Sexual harassment does not refer to socially acceptable behaviors. Improper sexual advances and behaviors should be immediately reported to the personnel or human resources director. If you become aware of a possible sexual harassment or discriminatory situation against a co-worker, it should be reported to a supervisor or personnel director. Reports of this nature should be kept confidential throughout the ensuing investigation.

Retaliation against a party who reports a possible sexual harassment or discriminatory offense is a serious violation of the policy and must not be permitted. Such acts of retaliation should be reported and investigated promptly. Such inappropriate behaviors demand that responsive action be taken. Responsive action may include:

- Training;
- Referral to counseling;

- Disciplinary action (verbal or written);
- Reassignment;
- Temporary suspension without pay; or
- Termination.

The Civil Rights Act of 1991 (CRA § 91) amends the following federal statutes:

- Title VII of the Civil Rights Act of 1964 (Title VII);
- Section 1981 of the Civil Rights Act of 1966 (Section 1981);
- Title I of the Americans with Disabilities Act (ADA);
- The Age Discrimination in Employment Act (ADEA); and
- The Rehabilitation Act of 1973 (Rehabilitation Act).

The amendments effectively reverse several U.S. Supreme Court decisions that had narrowed the scope of these statutes. The key provisions are that the CRA § 91 adds new awards of compensatory and punitive damages under Title VII and the ADA for victims who were intentionally discriminated against. The Act sets the following caps on the recovery of these damages:

- For employers with 15-100 employees: $ 50,000;
- For employers with 101-200 employees: $100,000;
- For employers with 201-500 employees: $200,000;
- For employers with more than 500 employees: $300,000.

Immigration Reform and Control Act

Asking an interviewee the wrong question can result in a discrimination suit. Therefore, it is important that the interviewer be educated concerning proper and improper questions to ask at interviews. Improper interview questions may include asking any questions related to the recruit's age, marital status, religion, medical condition, family information or whether the applicant has ever received workers' compensation. Based on the 1986 Immigration Act, it is unacceptable to ask an applicant the name of his/her native country; however, it *may* be permissible to ask if the applicant is a United States citizen. This is allowed because the Immigration Reform and Control Act, 8 U.S.C. §§1101 *et seq.*, prohibits the knowing employment of aliens not lawfully authorized to work in the

United States, or of legal non-immigrants whose classification does not permit them to be employed in the United States.

The Americans with Disabilities Act

The Americans with Disabilities Act (ADA), 42 U.S.C. § 12101, impacts all employees. The ADA covers employment, public accommodations, transportation and telecommunications. As of July 1994, it affects the employment, training, promotion, compensation and termination policies of every employer having 25 or more employees. It also affects the provision of goods and services by both private and public entities. Additionally, the ADA applies to public accommodations and services operated by private entities, which encompass businesses that are open to, or cater to, the public. 42 U.S.C. § 12111(5)(A).

An employee who demonstrates that the employer acted "with malice or reckless indifference to the federally protected rights" of the employee is eligible for punitive damages under Title VII and the ADA. In cases where the employee feels that his/her rights under the ADA have been violated, and the violation involves the provision of a "reasonable accommodation," the employer can avoid liability for compensatory or punitive damages if it demonstrates "good-faith efforts" to accommodate the individual's disability. Good faith must include consultation with the disabled individual seeking the accommodation.

The Family and Medical Leave Act

The Family and Medical Leave Act of 1993 (FMLA) states that employees who have worked for the same employer for at least one year and at least 1,250 hours in the previous twelve months are entitled to take up to twelve weeks of unpaid leave during any twelve-month period for any of the following reasons:

- for the birth and care of the newborn child of the employee;
- for placement with the employee of a son or daughter for adoption or foster care;
- to care for an immediate family member (spouse, child, or parent) with a serious health condition; or
- to take medical leave when the employee is unable to work because of a serious health condition.

The Age Discrimination in Employment Act

The Age Discrimination in Employment Act of 1967 (ADEA) prohibits covered employers from discriminating against any individual 40 years of age and above on the basis of age. 29 U.S.C. § 631. The ADEA also prohibits discrimination because of age against one person in the protected age group in favor of another person also within that same age group.

Similar to Title VII, the ADEA applies to all terms and conditions of employment. The ADEA covers such practices as employment advertising, pre-employment inquiries, hiring, terms and conditions of employment and termination of employment.

Older Workers Benefit Protection Act

The Older Workers Benefit Protection Act, 29 U.S.C. §§ 623 and 626, amends the ADEA by extending the coverage of ADEA to all employee benefits, whether or not provided pursuant to an employee benefit plan. In addition, this Act codifies the "equal benefit or equal cost principle," which holds that the only justification for age discrimination in employee benefits is the increased cost to the employer in providing the benefits. Finally, the Act prohibits all waivers of ADEA rights unless the waiver is knowing and voluntary.

The general rule is that ADEA prohibits mandatory retirement at any age. One very limited exception, however, allows for the mandatory retirement of individuals who are *bona fide* executives or in high policy-making positions, who: 1) are at least 65 years of age; 2) have held their position for two years immediately preceding retirement; and 3) are entitled to retirement income of at least $44,000. 29 U.S.C. § 631(c)(1).

The Equal Pay Act

The Equal Pay Act (EPA), an amendment to the Fair Labor Standards Act, 42 U.S.C. § 201 *et seq.,* requires that men and women receive equal pay for equal work. The EPA declares it illegal for an employer to discriminate by paying employees of one sex lower wages than those paid to employees of the opposite sex employed in the same establishment for work requiring substantially equal skill, effort and responsibility and performed under similar working conditions. The statute protects men as well as women. It is not a violation of the EPA if unequal payments are due to:

- A seniority system;
- A merit system;
- A system that measures earnings by quantity or quality of production; or
- Any factor other than sex.

Additional Federal Statutes

The *Employee Retirement Income Security Act of 1974 (ERISA),* 29 U.S.C. §§ 1001 *et seq.,* governs pension and health and welfare benefit plans.

The *Occupational Safety and Health Act* (OSHA), 29 U.S.C. § 651 *et seq.,* was enacted to ensure "safe and healthful working conditions" for "every working man and woman in the nation."

The *Fair Credit Reporting Act,* 15 U.S.C. § 1681 *et seq.,* governs the activities of consumer reporting agencies and users of information procured from such agencies to ensure its use in a manner that is fair and equitable to the consumer.

The *Consumer Credit Protection Act,* 15 U.S.C. §§ 1601 *et seq*., prohibits, among other things, an employer from discharging any employee be reason of the fact that his or her earnings have been subjected to garnishment for any one indebtedness.

The *Jury System Improvement Act*, 28 U.S.C. § 1875, protects employees from discrimination for their attendance or scheduled attendance in connection with jury service. Employees cannot be penalized for jury service.

The *United States Bankruptcy Code,* 11 U.S.C. §§ 25 *et seq.,* prohibits private employers from terminating the employment of, or discriminating against, any individual who is or has been a debtor or bankrupt. 11 U.S.C. § 25(b).

The *Health Insurance Portability and Accountability Act (HIPAA)*, 45 CFR Part 160 and Part 164, Subparts A and C required the Secretary of the U.S. Department of Health and Human Services (HHS) to develop rules and regulations protecting the privacy and security of certain health information.

*Job Enhancement*

There are steps you can take to be a great paralegal. These include:

- Familiarize yourself with the basic principles of a myriad of practice areas;
- Stay up-to-date on legal technology in order to assist attorneys in delivering quality legal services the most cost- effectively;
- Know and understand general legal terminology;
- Stay abreast of changes in the law;
- Know the policies and procedures of your office;
- Know the ABA *Model Guidelines for the Utilization of Paralegal Services*:
- Know the Professional Guidelines of your jurisdiction;
- Know the *NFPA Model Code of Ethics and Professional Responsibility*;
- Communicate effectively and clearly, whether orally or in writing;
- Calendar all deadlines and reminders;
- Regularly attend Continuing Legal Education (CLEs), including ethics;
- Delegate routine tasks to subordinates, if appropriate;

- Be organized and avoid clutter;
- Bill your time efficiently and accurately:
- Communicate with the paralegal manager when the paralegal workload is too light or too heavy;
- Mentor a junior paralegal;
- Assist with in-house training;
- Network with other legal professionals; and
- Participate in routine evaluations of yourself and take corrective measures, as needed.

*Financial Aspects*

While paralegals may not be involved in the financial planning of the employer, one fact remains clear: the more productive and profitable the paralegal is, the happier and more marketable he/she is. Likewise, the more productive and profitable the paralegal is, the more valuable he/she becomes to the firm.

In all matters, a fee agreement should be signed before work is commenced on a client matter. The fee agreement should state:

- Fees, including whether or not a fee increase will be included;
- An estimate of possible costs; and
- Whether the client pays disbursements directly or at a markup.

If you are managing a large matter, you may have responsibility for supervising other paralegals, temporary paralegals and support staff. In that event, it is essential for you to understand that supervising is a responsibility and that all work product, regardless by whom it is performed, ultimately, is your responsibility.

***40.02 Acquire technology and materials by identifying needs, available resources and cost factors; negotiating acquisition; overseeing installation and training; and managing resource use to provide quality and cost-effective legal services.***

Negotiating with outside vendors for services and products is a skill you will need to improve as you attempt to negotiate. When you obtain goods and services for a client, give the same degree of attention you would pay when obtaining goods or services for an employer. A request for services may be sent to numerous vendors to determine which will give the best, most economical service. The quote should always be in writing so that the interests of the client are protected at all times.

The interviewing process should be conducted in a fair manner. Each potential service provider should be asked the same questions and be given the same written proposal format to present.

While negotiating contracts, the goal is to obtain the best product available for the lowest cost; that may mean utilizing various vendors' services. It may also mean having to make a decision against a vendor that you have frequently used, but who has not put in the best bid. Along those same lines, paralegals must be careful not to allow vendors to offer them perks in return for contracts for goods or services. Confidentiality agreements with vendors and temporary employers are an absolute must.

Many times hardware and software are purchased for the use of a specific client. This purchase should be discussed with the client before it is made. The client should be a part of the entire process, particularly when the client is paying for the service. All transactions should be in writing, and the client should be informed each step of the way. If the client is presented with a memo outlining the needed materials and services in order to prevail in the dispute, it is more likely that the client will agree to pay for the needed materials and services.

A cost analysis should be prepared and reviewed with the client; the negotiation strategy of the purchase can also be discussed with the client. In many instances, clients have contacts that they are able to utilize to enhance the purchase of materials and/or services needed. Keeping the client updated is a key to client satisfaction. However, a word of caution: be mindful and careful about what is committed to in writing, both on disk and hard copy, as that information may be discoverable.

The important things to remember in negotiating are: give all the necessary information and know how far your authority goes. An employer will often have specific policies and procedures regarding the acquisition of computers and other materials, how those items are to be paid for, who will be responsible for the training on the utilization of those new items and how to ensure that the goods and services are cost-effective and maintained in good quality. Failure to understand and abide by office policies and procedures could put your job at risk. Never make a decision on your own without consulting others so that you can see how your decision will affect your employer.

As long as you are honest while negotiating, you should not find yourself in any ethical quandary. It is unethical, however, for you to contract for services or goods in return for favors from a vendor. This can include accepting tickets to events, a gift or money. The rule of thumb is: take the best offer that gives you the most for your money, but take nothing else.

Once the negotiation is complete, it should be memorialized in writing with copies to all involved parties. Keep the writing short and to the point. As with everything you prepare, give special attention to grammatical and structural correctness. Failure to clearly state the agreed-to terms may result in confusion, disappointment or even default.

***40.03 Coordinate and utilize vendor services by identifying needs, available resources and cost factors; negotiating and managing services; and evaluating vendor performance to provide quality and cost-effective legal services.***

Depending upon the mission statement of the employer, there may be times when the utilization of outside vendor services, whether it be in the form of temporary employees or goods, is needed. Once a thorough evaluation has been completed and a decision is made to contract with outside vendors, a request for services bid form should be prepared. While all needs for outside vendors may not require an out-and-out bidding process, any time you are bringing temporary employees in for an extended period of time or, have a large copying, imaging or other voluminous project, it is helpful to issue a bid request to ensure that you are getting the lowest possible cost for the client. Once you have obtained those costs, you can bill the client directly. Or, if you are putting a proposal together for a client, the information you receive will assist in budgeting your costs better.

Before any vendor contracts are signed, you should check to determine if there is an employer policy regarding who can sign the contracts, how long they should last and who notifies the client. It is also important to check whether the client will be directly billed for disbursements or whether they will be billed through the firm.

Equally important is evaluating the performance of the vendor's services. If you are using a copy service or document retrieval service, were they prompt in the pick-up and delivery of the data? Did they check the data to determine the accuracy of the data? Is there a clear chain of custody? Was the mirror imaging for the devices captured correctly? If you are using a temporary paralegal agency, what quality of services was provided? Were the people provided to you qualified and trained? Did they exhibit quality work ethics?

Before utilizing any outside services, it is always preferable to check what the employer and client can provide and their preferences. For example, if you have a corporate closing and have thousands of documents to be scanned, perhaps the corporate legal department can have the documents scanned in-house at a much lower cost to the client. Likewise, if you are looking for additional employees for a special project, perhaps other staff can assist, making it unnecessary to go outside to bring in people unfamiliar with the matter.

Sometimes the needs of the client do not become apparent until the last minute and result in the need to utilize temporary outside help or goods. All this communication should take place with the client before any commitments are made. How will the billing be done? Many firms now have billing guidelines in place for expenses that exceed a certain dollar amount, so checking the employer's billing policies is also a good idea. Most important, the client should be asked whether they can handle a project in-house. Generally speaking, it is easier and less expensive to accomplish tasks inside than to resort to external resources.

The key to success in a legal environment is communication. When contracting with outside vendors, communication should be followed up in writing so that there is no confusion as to who is responsible for what, how much the services will cost and when payment will be due. Additionally, assignments are generally performed better when they are made in writing so that there is no confusion as to expectations.

Many times following an assignment, outside vendors will ask you to evaluate their services. Always take advantage of this opportunity. If you were unhappy, you must communicate exactly what was wrong to the vendor or it may continue to happen. Simply failing to use the vendor again is not the answer. The vendor wants to improve its services to you and cannot do so if you will not communicate what went wrong.

Since every legal specialty has special databases that can be set up and different systems and techniques that can be used, it is essential for the paralegal to communicate what his or her expectations are for computer usage. Many paralegals in the real estate and corporate areas use a calendar and docketing system to keep track of document arrival and departure so they can determine whether or not they can actually follow through with a closing. In the estates and trusts area, wills can be tracked on a specialized database. Many times the client will want you to have the same computer capabilities it has so you can communicate by disk or by electronic mail.

Each specialty area is developing its own types of computer usage, and databases are continually specialized for each area of law. In immigration, for example, a database can be used to track expiration dates for visas or interviews with the Department of Labor. A paralegal wanting to excel in a specialty area would be wise to learn the database systems in that area. Knowledge of databases is very important because, in addition to saving the client's money by performing work yourself or in-house, often you are able to see what exhibits or documents will look like by exploring bars, charts and graphs. More information about Databases can be found in the Technology Section of this Review Manual.

When dealing with outside vendors, you have an ethical responsibility to obtain the lowest possible prices for services, while meeting the needs of the client, with total disregard for your own personal benefit. If time permits, it is always preferable to interview outside vendor services or obtain written bids for their services. In the case of temporary paralegals or support staff, it is essential that these people be interviewed just as you would interview for a regular paralegal position. The goal of the interview is to get the best possible people for the position. Once again, you should not discount the opportunities that may be available by using your client's resources or, if you are in a big legal environment, by utilizing other departments. Networking through paralegal associations can also be helpful in finding temporary solutions.

When using outside vendor services, in addition to making sure they understand legal jargon, you must understand their language. If, for example, you are attempting to get a bound volume prepared after a closing, you need to understand that you will have to select the material for the cover and what binding to use. You will need to know various terms of art in the book binding business.

If you happen to be dealing with a bank, it is essential that you understand banking terms because those terms may not be consistent with the same terminology you use. In all instances, you need to have a complete understanding with the vendor so that there is no room for confusion. It is helpful to memorialize any agreement in writing.

Many legal entities have policies for utilizing outside vendor services and, particularly, support staff. Understand policies regarding issues such as:

- Who is authorized to supervise outside support staff?
- Is outside support staff permitted to work on the premises without direct supervision?
- What are the policies for safe transportation and overtime meals?
- Who will approve the work product of outside support staff?

- What tasks are they allowed to do?
- Where are they allowed to be in the employment setting?
- What hours are they to work?
- Is there a sign-in, sign-out policy?
- Who is monitoring outside support staff on confidentiality issues?
- What is the policy toward their use of the telephone?
- Is there any general information policies about which outside support staff should be told?

If there are specific policies and requirements of outside vendors, either with services or temporary employees, these policies and requirements should be communicated in advance -- preferably in writing, but most definitely with clarity. Evaluations can be done mid-project to make sure that both parties are happy with the work product. Finally, if the services are not acceptable, you can withhold payment of invoices until the situation has been rectified. In many instances, this may involve being given credit on future projects or being given the use of someone to fix the incorrect project.

Because many different departments within a legal environment may be utilizing outside services, before contracting for any outside services, check with your employer to see if you can obtain a lower cost by using multiple requests. It is helpful for all people utilizing outside services to communicate with each other to evaluate the services that have been provided and to be certain there are no conflicts of interest. Sometimes vendors are hesitant to sign a conflict of interest form because they fear a loss of business. Do not leave without a confidentiality agreement and ensure that any agreements with third-party vendors are in full compliance with the HIPAA Privacy Laws[3].

### *40.04 Legal and factual research to promote quality and efficient legal services.*

The type of legal environment within which you practice will determine what kind legal and factual research is required from the paralegal. It is of utmost importance to protect client confidentiality when creating template forms and using research from one matter to the next. Particular attention should be paid to redacting any identifiable information to protect the integrity of each client. Take special care when using forms to make sure that the form is changed from client to client. Additionally, if an ethical wall is in effect, the forms file should be protected from unauthorized use by individuals blocked by the ethical wall.

Keeping up-to-date with the latest technological advances in legal research, as well as database maintenance, will keep your employer at the forefront of the legal community. By communicating with other paraprofessionals, paralegals can make sure that they have state-of-

[3] The HIPAA Privacy Rule is composed of national regulations for the use and disclosure of Protected Health Information (PHI) in healthcare treatment, payment and operations by covered entities. https://www.hhs.gov/hipaa/for-professionals/privacy/index.html
(Last accessed August 10, 2025)

the-art research materials and knowledge. Of course, client names and information should not be discussed with those outside of the law office.

It is the responsibility of each paralegal to learn as much about computerized legal research as possible. Lexis® and Westlaw® both offer many training sessions and give instruction on their various databases. Many forms templates are usually maintained on various database systems so that all members of a legal environment can share information. Again, it is extremely important to protect the confidentiality of each client by making sure that after each template form is used, the client's is scrubbed from the form before the template is used again. In addition to Lexis and Westlaw, nonlegal database search services are beneficial systems with which to be familiar.

It is the responsibility of the employer to make certain that the integrity of all research libraries and template forms are maintained. Specific areas in the work environment may be set up for the template forms in the various areas of law. Attention should be given to where and how files are stored to ensure proper security protocols are in place to that they are not vulnerable to overwriting by the common user . If there is an ethical wall setting in the employment situation, special care must be taken to abide by the guidelines for ethical walls.

There should be procedures in place for the individuals responsible for updating any template forms so that outdated content or formatting within the templates can be replaced or deleted. Embarrassment can be avoided by keeping the templates updated so that a lawyer does not utilize an outdated template.

Before appearing in any court, confirming the local rules of the court on the Court's website or contacting the court clerk for a specific Judge's requirements, is common sense and avoids undue embarrassment.

Because legal research and published case law is readily available on the internet, most firms have done away with in-house libraries and library staff. To assist lawyers with legal research, an understanding of the court system and cite checking procedures is necessary. You should know how to autocite and Shepardize cases, as well as how to use *Bluebook* format when citing cases. Reporters, the *Federal Register*, reports from federal agencies, digest systems, citators, loose-leaf services, legal periodicals, treatises, restatements of law, legal encyclopedias, forms books, legal dictionaries, directories, legal newspapers and trade and professional publications are but of the publications needed in legal research. More information about legal research and writing will be found in the Legal Research and Legal Writing Section of this Review Manual.

The paralegal must understand the employer's file preservation policy and have an organized plan for updating files, naming conventions of files and maintaining current databases. Some offices continue to retain hard file records and/or efile records. Always be sure to understand the expectation about how client files are maintained and who is in charge of file maintenance.

The paralegal must know how to utilize various databases for both legal and nonlegal research. Every paralegal must be adept at "surfing the 'Net.'" Additional Lexis and Westlaw courses can aid you in learning short-cuts that will save both the client's money and the lawyer's time.

### *40.05 Develop and maintain a billing system by tracking time, services and expenses to ensure sound business practices and maintain accountability.*

Maintaining accurate financial records is extremely important since many individuals may have access to the funds. Most employers will limit the number of people who are authorized to sign checks so as to minimize potential embezzlement or other unauthorized use of funds. Any time you submit a request for reimbursement, attached your receipt regardless of the amount.

Different billing systems can be used to charge for legal services. Paralegals should be familiar with what system is used in their employment structure or for individual matters.

A *contingency fee* is a percentage of what the client is awarded as a result of the lawyer's work. In this system, the fee is directly contingent upon the client's settlement award. There is some risk involved for the lawyer in taking a matter on a contingency basis. If the client does not prevail, the attorney receives no payment. On the other hand, a contingency matter can be financially rewarding, as it is common practice to take 33% if a matter is settled before trial, and 40% if it goes to trial.

A *percentage fee* is another form of billing in which the attorney takes a percentage of what the client eventually receives. This fee is common in the collection practice.

A *fixed fee* is paid for a particular service, such as a real estate closing, drafting a simple will or incorporating a new business.

An *hourly rate* is generally charged by litigators and corporate attorneys. The hourly charge depends upon who is performing the work. Generally, a partner or an associate's hourly rate is higher than that of a paralegal. The recent trend is toward a blended rate, where the billing rates of all who work on a matter are averaged and the average rate is charged, regardless of whom is performing the work.

Paralegals working in law offices will usually bill time, while their corporate counterparts may not. Accurate timekeeping is important. It is essential that timekeeping be done daily by those billing time to a matter. For example, if you are sitting in on a document production on behalf of one client while proofreading a mortgage for another client at the same time, you cannot bill both clients. If you are performing simultaneous, multiple functions, the time should be split between the clients.

Since the ABA guidelines clearly state that travel time spent outside normal work hours is not billable for lawyers; it is likewise not billable for paralegals. Paralegals should follow the same rules of ethics that lawyers follow. Depending upon employer policies, you may be able to bill travel time to the office administrative account. How paralegal travel time is compensated is a question that could be asked when you are interviewing.

The Supreme Court has given some basic guidelines for paralegals who bill their time[4]:

[4] *In Missouri v. Jenkins,* the United States Supreme Court held that in setting a reasonable attorney's fee, a legal fee may include a charge for paralegal services at "market rates" rather than "actual cost" to the attorneys. Source: https://supreme.justia.com/cases/federal/us/491/274/ (last accessed August 10, 2025)

- The services performed must be legal in nature rather than clerical[5];
- The fee statement must specify in detail the qualifications of the person performing the service (to demonstrate that the paralegal is qualified by education, training or work to perform the assigned work); and
- The evidence that the work performed by the paralegal would have had to be performed by the attorney at a higher rate[6].

Generally, paralegals are billed at an hourly rate that is calculated based on education, experience and location. Be familiar with hourly rates in your area and keep your employer up-to-date on these statistics. Law firms usually define how many hours their paralegals are expected to bill and the consequences of not being able to meet that number. Depending on the law firm, a paralegal may be expected to generate between 800 and 2,000 billable hours per year[7]. For paralegals close to the 1,800/2,000 billable hours per year mark, some employers may or may not provide an allowance for vacations, sick time or holiday hours to be excluded from this amount (requiring the paralegal to "flex" or "make up time" should they take time off).

It can be very difficult to track and capture billable time in an efficient manner that affords enough description that the client understands the tasks completed on their case. How do you know what should be billed? When do you start and stop your billable time for a given task? Will your employer rely on an automated, electronic billing system or will you be expected to keep track of your time/tasks manually such as in an excel spreadsheet? Are your billable hours prorated for sick time or vacation? Is there a billing code or accounting mechanism to keep track of administrative time that cannot be billed to the client, community service or pro bono volunteer hours, or for attending CLEs? These are all questions you should address with the attorney/employer at the onset of the matter. More details about Billable guidelines can be found in the Ethics Section of this Review Manual.

Another popular method is the "flat fee" by which lawyers vie for clients by promising to do work for a certain cost. This method clearly runs a risk for the lawyers if they cannot deliver the services for the amount they have quoted. This flat fee process is not unlike what other businesses, such as contractors, encounter but is gaining popularity

Because of the demand for quality legal services at lower prices, alternative billing rates are frequently proposed to clients. While billing time by the minute, tenth of an hour or quarter hour may no longer be the norm, it is still a consideration.

Retainers and advances may be given to attorneys to handle all matters that come up during a certain period of time. This arrangement can be beneficial because it is guaranteed income.

Many professional associations keep lawyers on retainer to handle their month-to-month problems. An advance may be given on anticipated costs such as filing fees, corporate service

---

5 *See* eg *In re Dimas, LLC,* 357 B.R. 563, 577 (Bankr. N.D. Calif. 2006).

6 Comment to Guideline 8 - ABA Model Guidelines for the utilization of paralegal services.

7 https://supreme.justia.com/cases/federal/us/491/274/ (last accessed August 10, 2025)

fees, bank fees or other costs that might have to be advanced by the attorney. These fees should be deposited into the firm's trust account until they need to be paid.

Prepaid legal services have been used by some professional groups where the groups contract with attorneys to provide specific legal services for their members. A prepaid service is not unlike an HMO. It may also offer supplementary services (beyond the specified prepaid services) at a lower than market rate.

Statutory fees vary from state to state. They are set by the legislature and are most common in real estate or probate transactions. They are percentage fees based on the total value of the assets being handled.

Generally, the lawyers and the client will determine how frequently the client will be billed. The client will not pay for time after the fact when it had arranged to receive a monthly bill.

To keep the billing process manageable, many firm administrators receive reports on a weekly or monthly basis. The administrator then determines the financial outlook for the employer.

Since cash flow is always important to an employer, the pressure is on the attorneys to collect their outstanding billings. It is incumbent upon paralegals and attorneys to bill their time and disbursements in a timely fashion. Because paralegals are infrequently involved in the accounting process, they do not realize how important it is to bill their time and expenses promptly. For example, failure to accurately record photocopy charges, postage, filing fees or service fees can result in a delay in billing the client. Thus, the paralegal may cause the employer to lose money.

The more you know about the billing system of the employer, the more prepared you will be to obtain a client billing history, understand it and explain it to the client. Do not bill the client for your time, or even put it on the client's bill as a "no charge." Routine time spent with a client with regard to questions about a bill should never appear on a client invoice.

While it is important for you to understand how the billing system and different databases in the financial area work, it is most important to remember that you must record time accurately, as it is being performed, or in "real time." Always be sure to include enough detail to help you recall the activity in the event your billable time is questioned, by either an attorney or the client.

### *40.06 Unauthorized Practice of Law.*

Both paralegals and lawyers are covered by criminal statutes prohibiting theft, fraud and obstruction of justice. Paralegals are told not to participate in the unauthorized practice of law (UPL), but without a definition of the practice of law, steering away from UPL is sometimes difficult. With the addition of non-traditional paralegal roles, such as Virtual, Freelance, contract and temp paralegals, it has become even more important that paralegals be aware of potential UPL and when they may be crossing a line. More details regarding UPL and non-traditional paralegal roles are addressed in the Ethics Section of this Review Manual.

A lawyer may not delegate to a paralegal:

1. Responsibility for establishing an attorney-client relationship.

2. Responsibility for establishing the amount of a fee to be charged for a legal service.

3. Responsibility for a legal opinion rendered to a client.

Guideline 3, ABA Model Guidelines for the Utilization of Paralegal Services.

A paralegal shall not engage in the unauthorized practice of law. *EC-1.8, NFPA Model Code of Ethics and Professional Responsibility and Guidelines for Enforcement.*

You are only authorized to perform functions permitted under law that are not in violation of the unauthorized practice of law statutes within the applicable jurisdiction. You are expressly prohibited from providing legal advice. *(Discussed in further detail below.)*

Ethical responsibilities of paralegals include:

- Not Giving Legal Advice
- Not Accepting Cases or Setting Fees
- Rules Against Solicitation of Clients
- Requirement for an Appropriate Level of Attorney Supervision
- The Paralegal as a Supervisor/Colleague of Others
- Obligation to Work Competently and Promptly
- Contact with Parties and Witnesses
- Communications with the Court and Jurors
- Candor and Honesty in Dealing with Binding and/or Relevant Authority
- Improving the Delivery of Legal Services
- Staying Current in Your Area
- Promptly Alerting Your Attorney of Potential Conflicts of Interests

During an interview, you can quickly determine whether or not a conflict of interest may exist by maintaining a list of all matters on which you have worked. If one exists, an ethical wall can be created. *See* the Administration of Client Matters Section for more detailed information on creating an ethical wall.

Although the ABA Model Rules permit attorney advertisement in newspapers, television and radio, a lawyer local jurisdiction may have more or less restrictions on direct attorney advertising.

### *40.07 Manage work flow by prioritizing activities and events and monitoring task completion to ensure that legal services are provided in a timely manner.*

Paralegals not only work for a variety of clients, but generally work for a number of different lawyers. The lawyers do not necessarily keep track of all the work you are performing for other people. When they ask you to do work on a project, the lawyer has no idea how much is on your agenda unless you communicate your current workload capacity. Failure to communicate your workload may result in the attorney being unhappy with your performance.

A suggestion for dealing with a very active work flow is to specifically identify the attorneys, their projects and their deadlines. Have those attorneys determine what project needs to be completed first. In many instances, you will find that a project which has been alleged to be a top priority matter -- in reality -- does not need to be done immediately. The only way this information reaches the attorney is by you informing the attorney of what you are doing.

Admittedly, there are many times when, because you have developed such a good reputation, every attorney wants to use you. There are just not enough hours in the day for you to get everything done in the effective and efficient manner that has established your reputation. You must communicate to the lawyers that you cannot get all the work done. Rather than just saying, "I can't do all this work," devise an action plan. Tell the attorney that you can get part of the project done by the deadline and that the rest will be coming within a certain period of time. The most essential fact to remember is not to panic.

The burden is on you to make certain that you have communicated effectively about your workload and all the projects that you must complete. Attorneys can re-prioritize the workload they have given to you. If you communicate clearly, whether in writing or verbally, about the workload you have and put the attorneys in the position of having to make a decision as to whose work gets done first, they may realize that some of the set deadlines are artificial.

You have an ethical responsibility to the client and your employer to make sure that, when you realize you have too much work, or you do not understand how to do the work, that someone knows and furnishes assistance to you as soon as possible. It is not a crime to ask for help!

Sometimes, no matter how organized you are, an emergency will arise and with an already excessive workload, the work just cannot be completed on a timely basis. In that case, the assigning attorney must be advised immediately and, with the assistance of a paralegal coordinator, if available, assistance can be obtained to complete the projects so that emergencies are handled efficiently and effectively.

To manage work flow, you may need to obtain assistance from other employees. You need to know what process to go through to obtain this assistance. There are undoubtedly specific procedures that must be complied with before assistance is obtained from outside the department and/or firm.

In a legal environment, employees may be so departmentalized that they fail to cross lines even if there is an emergency. You must understand the organization of the employment situation and what must be done to obtain assistance to complete work. A complete understanding of doing whatever it takes to get the job done may include asking people to cease work on their current projects and assist you with a more imminent deadline. You must understand how the employer operates so you can do whatever it takes to accomplish work for the client in the most expeditious way. If overtime is involved, you must know the employer's overtime policy.

Understanding that flexibility is the key to strategic planning will assist you in prioritizing your workload. Utilizing calendaring systems will help you to help others get you what you need and avoid a crisis. By using a calendaring system and advising people days in advance of pending deadlines, there is a possibility that work sent to you will be done in a timely fashion.

When all is said and done, if you manage time correctly, you will be able to handle even a last minute crisis. Many paralegals have daily to-do lists and complain that they never get to the bottom of the list. But, if they are continually marking items off the list, then progress is being made.

When you are given a project, your job should be to analyze all of the component pieces of that project and to start the wheels in motion to make a logical progression through the project's completion. A logical progression will help you to supervise staff that may be assisting in various phases of the project.

One reason for confusion over deadlines results from the failure to give clear instructions. While we are often pushed into giving directions verbally, it never hurts to follow up by putting project directions and deadlines in writing. Writing leaves no confusion as to the deadlines or how a particular project will be handled.

## SAMPLE QUESTIONS FOR OFFICE ADMINISTRATION

1. In 2004, the Fair Labor Standards Act was revised, changing the status of many paralegals from __________ to __________:

    a. Professional to Qualified.
    b. Exempt to Nonexempt.
    c. Administrative to Professional.
    d. Nonexempt to Exempt.

2. Paralegals can most effectively assist attorneys in client development by:

    a. sending holiday cards to prospective and current clients.
    b. talking about the firm's successes.
    c. generating a newsletter with articles analyzing current trends and regulations.
    d. advertising the firm's services in the paralegal association newsletter.

3. Billable, routine tasks for which the amount can be estimated easily in advance are best represented on a paralegal's bill as a(n):

    a. flat fee.
    b. contingency fee.
    c. fixed fee.
    d. hourly fee.

4. All of the below are actions attorneys should not delegate to a paralegal, except:

    a. responsibility for establishing an attorney-client relationship.
    b. responsibility for establishing the amount of a fee to be charged for a legal service.
    c. responsibility for document management on a case.
    d. responsibility for a legal opinion rendered to a client.

5. While negotiating contracts, the goal is to obtain the best product available for the lowest cost; what other requirement is an absolute *must*?

    a. Confidentiality agreements with vendors and temporary employers.
    b. Obtaining all services through the same vendor.
    c. Question potential service providers differently.
    d. Vary proposal formats depending on the vendor, not the service.

6. A paralegal whose firm is representing a celebrity and who informs a neighbor of that fact has violated:

    a. the work product rule.
    b. conflict of interest rules.
    c. the rule of confidentiality.
    d. attorney-client privilege.

7. The supervising paralegal in a large securities firm has been approached by a paralegal who reports an instance of "inappropriate behavior" by one attorney. The best course of action for the supervising paralegal is to:

    a. ask the paralegal to write down what happened and review the written document to determine whether the firm's policies have been violated.
    b. discuss the complaint with firm management without identifying either of the parties involved.
    c. forward a copy of the relevant firm policies and a summary of the complaint to the firm management.
    d. discuss the complaint with the alleged perpetrator and then present a balanced report of the comments of both parties to the firm management.

8. Which of the following is it permissible to ask an applicant during a job interview?

    a. religious or other group affiliation.
    b. previous arrests.
    c. age and marital status.
    d. previous work attendance record.

9. A paralegal preparing a profit and loss statement for a merger would use a:

    a. database program.
    b. billing program.
    c. word processing program.
    d. spreadsheet program.

10. It is appropriate to use a confidentiality agreement when:

    a. interviewing a prospective employee.
    b. contracting with a vendor.
    c. interviewing a client.
    d. accessing information provided by a client.

*Answers:*

1–b. Exempt to Nonexempt.

Prior to revision of the Fair Labor Standards Act in 2004, many paralegals were salaried employees and received no overtime pay. With the revision; paralegals changed from exempt to nonexempt. Neither (a), (c), or (d) are correct because they are descriptive factors of a paralegal. For example, a paralegal is a person qualified through education and training to perform substantive legal work that requires knowledge of the law and procedures. A paralegal is also a professional that may be required to handle some administrative duties.

2–c. Keeping clients up-to-date with current trends in the law and legal technology assists their understanding of the legal services being delivered to them.

By creating a client newsletter and writing articles, the paralegal can assist in developing the client's understanding of legal issues. Option (a) might be interpreted as client solicitation. While word-of-mouth and advertising are standard marketing techniques, neither will assist the client.

3–c. A fixed fee arrangement is best suited to routine and repetitive tasks because you are paying for a particular service for which the cost can be estimated based upon prior practice. None of the other three options offer this advantage.

4–c. Of the items noted, the only activity that the attorney may delegate to the paralegal is the responsibility for document management on a case. The other three items are strictly prohibited from delegation from the attorney to the paralegal.

5–a. Confidentiality agreements with vendors and temporary employees are an absolute must. A vendor confidentiality agreement is a contract between a vendor and an organization, where one or both parties agree to keep certain information confidential. The confidential information is the property of the firm and may not be kept by or removed by the party without express permission of the organization. If the vendor violates the agreement, he or she is subject to adverse action, which may include civil or criminal penalties.

6–c. Quite simply, it is an ethical obligation and expectation of every client -- whether a celebrity or not -- that his or her legal affairs will be kept in the strictest of confidence. Legal issues, the cost of the service and parties involved cannot be expressed without the consent of the client. This confidentiality continues even after the end of a lawsuit, and/or if you leave that firm.

Option (a) is not an appropriate answer because work product was not involved in the verbal remark. Option (b) is not an appropriate answer; no conflict of interest issues were raised. While attorney-client privilege comes under the umbrella of confidentiality, option (c) is the most appropriate answer.

7–c. When "inappropriate behavior" is suspected, the paralegal supervisor must be certain that the firm is put on notice and follows appropriate procedure. The pertinent firm policy, with a summary of the complaint, must be given to the appropriate firm management body, which may be a standards committee. In many firms, there are very specific procedures, generally outlined in a policy/procedures manual, that directs the actions when a violation is alleged to have occurred.

8–d. It is perfectly permissible to ask a job applicant about his or her previous work attendance record during a job interview. This candidate will be part of a team and the team must be able to function as a smooth unit. Work attendance records indicate the level of dedication a candidate brings to a job. Continually leaving early or arriving late indicates a potential team player who may let the team down. Asking about any of options (a), (b) or (c) is not permissible under law.

9–d. Spreadsheet programs clearly indicate, in many different landscapes, pertinent information. It is quite easy to determine whether a company has shown a profit or loss by laying out a spreadsheet program. Spreadsheet information translates more easily to lay people, particularly a jury. Neither the database program nor the word processing program offer the advantages of option (d), the spreadsheet program. Option (b) is irrelevant to the question; one's billing does not affect the client's proposed merger.

10-b. In order to avoid any conflicts with vendors, it should be a matter of course to have them sign confidentiality agreements. In some areas of law, the choice of vendors is limited and both parties may end up using the same one. You may have an employee sign a confidentiality agreement as a condition of employment, but that will take place after you have offered the prospective employee a position and it is accepted. Remember that a client holds the privilege and does not sign an agreement to that effect. The client cannot be forced to agree to maintain confidentiality of his or her own confidences and secrets.

# 50.00 BANKRUPTCY

## *50.01 What is a Bankruptcy?*

A bankruptcy is the legal procedure, authorized by the United States Constitution, for dealing with debt problems of individuals and businesses under one of the chapters of title 11 of the United States Bankruptcy Code. (11 U.S.C. § 101-1330). The intent of bankruptcy is to give debtors a fresh start financially.

Bankruptcy proceedings are filed in the U.S. Bankruptcy Court in the federal district where the debtor resides. The Bankruptcy Abuse Prevention and Consumer Protection Act of 2005 (BAPCPA) has imposed the requirement for all those filing a personal bankruptcy to participate in budget and credit counseling. Exigent circumstances are grounds for a deferral request from this requirement.

The bankruptcy estate consists of all the legal or equitable interests of the debtor in property at the time of the filing of the bankruptcy. The estate consists of all property in which a debtor has an interest, even if it is jointly owned or held by another party.

Every debtor must provide detailed financial information, which includes household income, living expenses and a complete listing of all assets and creditors. Documentation such as tax returns, financial statements, pay check records and real estate documentation will also need to be provided by the debtor.

One of the primary purposes of bankruptcy is to discharge certain debts to give an honest individual debtor a "fresh start." As a result, the debtor has no further liability for discharged debts.

There are two types of bankruptcy available to individual debtors. A Chapter 7 bankruptcy is called a "liquidation," while a Chapter 13 bankruptcy is frequently referred to as a "reorganization." Debtors whose income exceeds the median for the state in which they are domiciled may be required to convert their case to Chapter 13, which means they could repay a portion of their debts by making payments to the trustee though a plan from their excess income. Let's look at the types of bankruptcy in more detail.

## *50.02 Bankruptcy Relief.*

A bankruptcy petition is the document filed by the debtor (voluntary) or by the debtor's creditors (involuntary), which opens the case. Once the petition has been filed, an interim trustee is assigned and a first Meeting of Creditors (a Section 341 Meeting) is scheduled. The debtor must appear before a trustee with their counsel and submit to the trustee's questions under oath. Notice of the Section 341 Meeting is given to all creditors and they may appear and ask questions of the debtor.

In a Chapter 7 bankruptcy, depending on the information provided and the non-exempt assets of the debtor, the trustee will file his/her report of no distribution or a notice of possible assets. When a Chapter 7 is determined to be an asset case, the non-exempt assets of the debtor are sold and notice is issued to all creditors to file a claim on the proceeds by a date certain. The proceeds are distributed pro rata among the creditors who file priority and unsecured claims in the Bankruptcy proceedings. Secured claims are not paid in a Chapter 7 bankruptcy by the trustee; however, the secured creditors still have rights with respect to their collateral.

A claim is a creditor's written assertion of a right to payment from the debtor or the debtor's property. Claims are filed in the bankruptcy in a Chapter 7 case upon a determination of an asset case, or in a Chapter 11, 12 or 13 case upon confirmation of a plan by the court.

Such debts as mortgages and car liens may be "reaffirmed" by signing an agreement to retain and continue paying payments on the secured property. Reaffirmation agreements are filed with the Bankruptcy Court.

Many forms are needed to file for bankruptcy. In order to complete the official forms that make up the petition, statement of financial affairs and schedules, the debtor must provide a list of all creditors; the amount and nature of their claims; the source, amount, and frequency of the debtor's income; a complete list of all of the debtor's assets; and a detailed list of the debtor's monthly living expenses, *i.e.*, food, clothing, shelter, taxes, utilities, transportation, medicine, etc.

Married individuals must gather this information for their spouse regardless of whether they are filing a joint petition, separate individual petitions, or even if only one spouse is filing. In a situation where only one spouse files, the income and expenses of the non-filing spouse is required so that the court, the trustee and creditors can evaluate the household's financial position.

The Bankruptcy Code allows an individual debtor to protect some property from the claims of creditors because it is exempt under federal bankruptcy law or under the laws of the debtor's home state. Many states have taken advantage of a provision in the Bankruptcy Code that permits each state to adopt and utilize its own exemption laws rather than the federal exemptions. In some jurisdictions, the individual debtor has the option of utilizing either the federal package of exemptions or the exemptions available under state law. Thus, whether certain property is exempt is often a question of state law. There is no presumption of exemption … that is, in order to claim an exemption, the debtor must state the claim on the appropriate schedule to the bankruptcy petition. Under Chapter 7, claims of exemption are allowed for certain property. Non-exempt property may be taken by the trustee and sold with the proceeds paid pro rata to creditors.

A married couple may file a joint petition or individual petitions. Even if filing jointly, a husband and wife are subject to all of the document filing requirements of individual debtors.

Under BAPCPA, certain documents are required to be filed with the Bankruptcy Clerk. These include the Credit Counseling certification, "Payment Advices" for the past 60 days (with all but the last four digits of social security numbers redacted from pay stubs) and the last statement from any educational IRA, state section 529 account or equivalent.

Prior to the first Meeting of Creditors, tax and income information must be gathered. The following should be provided for any account of any nature in which the debtor had an interest: a complete copy of the most recent tax return for the preceding year, including all forms W-2,

1099 and Schedules; proof of current income; and copies of bank statements for the last three months.

A domestic support obligation (DSO) generally relates to child support, spousal support or alimony payments. The trustee is required to send notice to the recipient of any DSO. At the first Meeting of Creditors, the trustee will request -- and the debtor should provide -- the complete name, address and telephone number of the DSO claim holder. Under BAPCPA, domestic support obligations are now considered first-level priority claims following only the allowed administrative expenses of the trustee.

Many debtors are engaged in workers' compensation, personal injury, class action or medical malpractice claims. They do not think to tell their bankruptcy counsel about the claim. This is problematic as the case progresses. Debtors must report any judgments rendered in their favor as well as any complaints for any legal proceedings filed by the debtor. This also applies to any divorce decrees in addition to any estates in which the debtor may have an interest. The name and contact information of the attorney representing the debtor and/or the estate will be required to determine if the debtor may have an interest as a result of a litigation which could constitute property of the bankruptcy estate.

A person who knowingly and fraudulently conceals assets, or makes a false oath or statement under penalty of perjury (either orally or in writing), in connection with a bankruptcy case is subject to a fine, imprisonment or both. All information supplied by a debtor in connection with a bankruptcy case is subject to examination by the United States Attorney General acting through the Office of the United States Trustee, the Office of the United States Attorney and other employees of the Department of Justice.

*Chapter 7*

The Chapter 7 liquidation is designed for those in financial difficulty who do not have the ability to pay their existing debts. Debtors who have primarily consumer debt are subject to the "Means Test" to determine if they should be permitted to proceed under a Chapter 7. The Means Test is documentation that supports the household's living expenses. Those expenses primarily relate to private school tuition, private educational expenses and extra home heating expenses for the debtor or the debtor's dependents. Husbands and wives may file jointly or separately, but income of both filing and non-filing spouse in the household is considered in the Means Test. If the individual debtor is married but filing individually, copies of documents used to complete the spouse's portion of the Schedule of Income will also be considered in the Means Test.

Section 707(b)(2) of the Bankruptcy Code applies the Means Test to determine whether an individual debtor's Chapter 7 filing is presumed to be an abuse of the Bankruptcy Code requiring dismissal or conversion of the case (generally to Chapter 13). Abuse is presumed if the debtor's total current monthly income over five years and net of certain statutorily allowed expenses is more than $10,000, or 25% of the debtor's non-priority, unsecured debt, as long as that amount is at least $6,000. The Means Test is not a pass/fail test … the result of "failing" is a presumption of abuse. The debtor may rebut a presumption of abuse only by a showing of special circumstances that justify additional expenses or adjustments of current monthly income.

If the debtor's income is greater than the median income for the state of residence and family size, it is possible for the United States Trustee to file a motion requesting that the Bankruptcy Court dismiss the case under §707(b) of the Bankruptcy Code. Improper conduct can cause denial or revocation of a discharge. Debts may not be subject to discharge if they arise from fraud, breach of fiduciary duty, theft, death or personal injury caused by operating a motor vehicle while intoxicated from alcohol or drugs and certain debts which are not properly listed in a bankruptcy petition. Student loans, most taxes, child support obligations and property settlement obligations generally are not subject to discharge.

To qualify for relief under Chapter 7, the debtor may be an individual, a partnership or a corporation. Relief is available for a corporation or other business entity under Chapter 7 regardless of the amount of debt or whether the debtor is solvent or insolvent.

If, during the preceding 180 days, an individual had a prior bankruptcy petition dismissed due to the debtor's willful failure to appear before the court or comply with orders of the court, the debtor cannot file for relief under Chapter 7 or any chapter of bankruptcy. The same rule also applies if the debtor voluntarily dismissed the previous case after creditors sought relief from the Bankruptcy Court to recover property upon which they hold liens.

No one may be a debtor under Chapter 7 or any chapter of the Bankruptcy Code unless s/he has received credit counseling from an approved credit counseling agency either in an individual or group briefing within 180 days before filing. There are exceptions in emergency situations or where the U.S. Trustee has determined that there are an insufficient number of approved agencies to provide the required counseling. If a debt management plan is developed during required credit counseling, it must be filed with the court.

The "automatic stay" is an injunction that automatically stops lawsuits, foreclosures, garnishments and all collection activities against the debtor from the moment a bankruptcy petition is filed. The automatic stay is invoked upon filing a petition, which stops all adverse action against the debtor. Due to BAPCPA, there are exceptions to the automatic stay. If the debtor has had a pending case dismissed within one year of filing, the stay is only in effect for the first thirty days unless an order continuing the stay is requested and approved by the court. If the debtor has had two or more proceedings dismissed within a year of filing, the stay does not go into effect at all.

During the stay, creditors cannot repossess property, evict or foreclose, garnish wages or shut off utilities. Any bank accounts that are frozen, or garnished funds, must be turned over to the bankruptcy trustee during the automatic stay.

A Chapter 7 case begins with the debtor filing a petition with the Bankruptcy Court in the District where the debtor lives, or where the business debtor is organized, has its principal place of business or principal assets. In addition to the petition, the debtor must also file with the court a schedule of assets and liabilities; a schedule of current income and expenditures; a statement of financial affairs listing the prior year's income, business transactions, payments to creditors, law suits and other pertinent information; as well as a schedule of executory contracts and unexpired leases and a listing of co-debtors.

Individual debtors with primarily consumer debts have additional document filing requirements. They must file a certificate of credit counseling and a copy of the debt repayment plan developed through credit counseling, if any; evidence of payment from employers received 60 days before filing; a statement of monthly net income and any anticipated increase in income or expenses after filing; and a record of any interest the debtor has in federal or state-qualified education or tuition accounts.

Debtors must also provide the assigned case trustee with a copy of the most recent year's tax return or transcripts, as well as tax returns filed during the case. This includes any tax returns for prior years that had not been filed when the case began.

It is important for the debtor to cooperate with the trustee and to provide any financial records or documents that the trustee requests. The Bankruptcy Code requires the trustee to ask the debtor questions at the Meeting of Creditors to ensure that the debtor is aware of the potential consequences of seeking a discharge in bankruptcy such as the effect on credit history, the ability to file a petition under a different chapter, the effect of receiving a discharge and the effect of reaffirming a debt.

### Chapter 7 Discharge

A *discharge* is the mechanism that releases individual debtors from personal liability for most debts and prevents the creditors owed those debts from taking any collection actions against the debtor. Excluding cases that are dismissed or converted, individual debtors receive a discharge in most Chapter 7 cases. Unless an interested party files a complaint objecting to the discharge or a motion to extend the time to object, the Bankruptcy Court will generally issue a discharge order relatively early in the case, typically within 60 to 90 days after the date first set for the Meeting of Creditors.

The grounds for denying an individual debtor a discharge in a Chapter 7 case are narrow and are construed against the moving party. The court may deny the debtor a discharge if it finds that the debtor failed to keep or produce adequate books or financial records; failed to explain satisfactorily any loss of assets; committed a bankruptcy crime such as perjury; failed to obey a lawful order of the bankruptcy court; fraudulently transferred, concealed, or destroyed property that would have become property of the estate; or failed to complete an approved instructional course concerning financial management.

Secured creditors may retain some rights to seize property securing an underlying debt even after a discharge is granted. Depending on individual circumstances, if a debtor wishes to keep certain secured property (typically a home or automobile), the debtor may decide to "reaffirm" the debt. A reaffirmation is an agreement between the debtor and the creditor that the debtor will remain liable and will pay all or a portion of the money owed, even though the debt would otherwise be discharged in the bankruptcy. In return, the creditor promises that it will not repossess or take back the property so long as the debtor continues to pay the debt.

An individual receives a discharge for most of his/her debts in a Chapter 7 bankruptcy case, but not all debts are discharged in Chapter 7. Debts not discharged include debts for alimony and child support, certain taxes, debts for certain educational benefit overpayments or loans made or guaranteed by a governmental unit, debts for willful and malicious injury by the debtor to another entity or to its property, debts for death or personal injury caused by the debtor's operation of a motor vehicle while the debtor was intoxicated from alcohol or other substances and debts for certain criminal restitution orders. The debtor will continue to be liable for these types of debts to the extent that they are not paid in the Chapter 7 case.

Debts for money or property obtained by false pretenses, debts for fraud or defalcation while acting in a fiduciary capacity and debts for willful and malicious injury by the debtor to another entity or to the property of another entity will be discharged unless a creditor timely files and prevails in an action to have such debts declared non-dischargeable. This is accomplished by the creditor filing an adversary proceeding which is a separate lawsuit in the bankruptcy case.

The court may revoke a Chapter 7 discharge on the request of the trustee, a creditor or the U.S. Trustee if the discharge was obtained through fraud by the debtor, if the debtor acquired property that is property of the estate and knowingly and fraudulently failed to report the acquisition of such property or to surrender it to the trustee. Discharge may also be revoked if the debtor (without a satisfactory explanation) makes a material misstatement or fails to provide documents or other information in connection with an audit of the debtor's case. Not every Chapter 7 case is audited; only those which the U.S. Trustee has reason to believe there may be just cause or by random selection are audited.

In a Chapter 7 case, a discharge is only available to individual debtors, not to partnerships or corporations. Although an individual Chapter 7 case typically results in a discharge of debts, the right to a discharge is not absolute. Moreover, a bankruptcy discharge does not extinguish a lien on property.

Conversion

The Bankruptcy Code allows the debtor to convert a Chapter 7 case to one under Chapter 11, 12 or 13, which affords the debtor complete relief as long as the debtor is eligible to be a debtor under the new chapter. A condition of the debtor's voluntary conversion is that the case has not previously been converted to Chapter 7 from another chapter. The debtor will not be permitted to repeatedly convert a case from one chapter to another.

A corporation or partnership may not be a Chapter 13 debtor. However, any individual, even if self-employed or operating an unincorporated business, is eligible for relief under Chapter 13 so long as the individual's unsecured debts are less than $307,675 and secured debts are less than $922,975.

An individual cannot file under Chapter 13 or any other chapter if, during the preceding 180 days, a prior bankruptcy petition was dismissed due to the debtor's willful failure to appear before the court, comply with orders of the court or was voluntarily dismissed after creditors sought relief from the bankruptcy court to recover property upon which they hold liens. In addition, no individual may be a debtor under Chapter 13 or any chapter of the Bankruptcy Code unless the debtor has received credit counseling from an approved credit counseling agency either in an individual or group briefing within 180 days before filing.

*Chapter 13*

Chapter 13 of the Bankruptcy Code is the proceeding that provides for adjustment of debts of an individual with regular income. It is a repayment of all or part of the debts of an individual with the ability to pay their debts in installments over a period of three to five years. Chapter 13 is an action typically filed to preserve assets such as a home or vehicle and also to reduce debt.

The debtor must propose a repayment plan within 30 days of filing the case. The plan must then be approved by the Bankruptcy Court and must propose to make regular payments to the trustee. This process is referred to as "confirmation" of the plan. Confirmation is the judge's approval of a plan of reorganization in a Chapter 13 or 12 payment plan and/or liquidation in a Chapter 11 proceeding. The plan must be completed within three to five years to cure payment arrearages, reduce the balance on secured property, discharge debt which may not be dischargeable under Chapter 7, repay tax liabilities or to reorder priorities into classes which are paid according to the plan and are binding on both the debtors and creditors.

Protection for co-debtors and/or co-signers not available in Chapter 7 is provided in a Chapter 13 proceeding. After completing a plan, a discharge is generally awarded; however, it may not be applicable to all debts, including certain debts for acts that caused death or personal injury and certain long-term secured obligations.

Like a Chapter 7, the Chapter 13 case begins by filing a petition with the Bankruptcy Court serving the area where the debtor resides. Unless the court orders otherwise, the debtor must also file with the court the schedules of assets and liabilities, a schedule of current income and expenditure, a schedule of executory contracts and unexpired leases and a statement of financial affairs. The debtor must also file a certificate of credit counseling and a copy of any debt repayment plan developed through credit counseling; evidence of payment from employers, if any, received 60 days before filing; a statement of monthly net income and any anticipated increase in income or expenses after filing; and a record of any interest the debtor has in federal or state-qualified education or tuition accounts.

The debtor must provide the Chapter 13 case trustee with a copy of the tax return or transcripts for the most recent tax year as well as tax returns filed during the case. The debtor must also include tax returns for prior years that had not been filed when the case began.

A husband and wife may file a joint petition or individual petitions. In order to complete the official bankruptcy forms that make up the petition, statement of financial affairs and schedules, the debtor must compile a list of all creditors and the amounts and nature of their claims; the source, amount and frequency of the debtor's income; a list of all of the debtor's property; and a detailed list of the debtor's monthly living expenses, *i.e.*, food, clothing, shelter, utilities, taxes, transportation, medicine, etc. Married individuals must gather this information for their spouse regardless of whether they are filing a joint petition, separate individual petitions or even if only one spouse is filing. In a situation where only one spouse files, the income and expenses of the non-filing spouse is required so that the court, the trustee and creditors can evaluate the household's financial position. This does not vary from the Chapter 7 petition.

When an individual files a Chapter 13 petition, an impartial trustee is appointed to administer the case. The trustee evaluates the case and serves as a disbursing agent, collecting payments from the debtor and making pro rata distributions to creditors.

Filing the petition under Chapter 13 also automatically stops most collection actions against the debtor or the debtor's property. Filing the petition does not, however, stay certain types of actions listed under 11 U.S.C. § 362(b). If a stay is granted, it may be effective only for a short time in some situations. The stay arises by operation of law and requires no judicial action. As long as the stay is in effect, creditors generally may not initiate or continue lawsuits, obtain wage garnishments or even make telephone calls demanding payments. The bankruptcy clerk gives notice of the bankruptcy case to all creditors whose names and addresses are provided by the debtor.

Chapter 13 also contains a special automatic stay provision that protects co-debtors. Unless the bankruptcy court authorizes otherwise, a creditor may not seek to collect a "consumer debt" from any individual who is liable along with the debtor.

Individuals may use a Chapter 13 proceeding to save their home from foreclosure. The automatic stay stops the foreclosure proceeding as soon as the individual files the petition. The individual may then bring the past-due payments current over a reasonable period of time. The debtor may still lose the home if the mortgage company completes the foreclosure sale under state law before the debtor files the petition. The debtor may also lose the home if s/he fails to make the regular mortgage payments that come due after the Chapter 13 filing.

The Chapter 13 debtor will be required to attend a Meeting of Creditors where the trustee places the debtor under oath and both the trustee and creditors ask questions. The debtor must attend the meeting and answer questions regarding his/her financial affairs and the proposed terms of the plan. If a husband and wife file a joint petition, they both must attend the Meeting of Creditors and answer the questions.

To participate in distributions from the bankruptcy estate, unsecured creditors must file their claims with the court within 90 days after the first date set for the Meeting of Creditors; however, a governmental unit has 180 days from the date the case is filed to file a proof of claim.

A Chapter 13 debtor is entitled to a discharge upon completion of all payments under the plan so long as the debtor certifies that all domestic support obligations that came due prior to making such certification have been paid (if applicable); has not received a discharge in a prior case filed within a certain time frame (two years for prior Chapter 13 cases and four years for prior Chapter 7, 11 and 12 cases); and has completed an approved course in financial management. The court will not enter the discharge until it determines, after notice and a hearing, if necessary, that there is no reason to believe there is any pending proceeding that might give rise to a limitation on the debtor's homestead exemption. The discharge releases the debtor from all debts provided for by the plan or disallowed with limited exceptions. Creditors provided for in full or in part under the Chapter 13 plan may no longer initiate or continue any legal or other action against the debtor to collect the discharged obligations.

Typically, the discharge releases the debtor from all debts provided for by the plan or disallowed, with the exception of certain debts. Debts not discharged in Chapter 13 include certain long-term obligations (such as a home mortgage), debts for alimony or child support, certain taxes, debts for most government-funded or guaranteed educational loans or benefit overpayments, debts arising from death or personal injury caused by driving while intoxicated or under the influence of drugs and debts for restitution or a criminal fine included in a sentence on the debtor's conviction of a crime. To the extent that they are not fully paid under the Chapter 13 plan, the debtor will still be responsible for these debts after the bankruptcy case has concluded. Debts for money or property obtained by false pretenses, debts for fraud or defalcation while acting in a fiduciary capacity and debts for restitution or damages awarded in a civil case for willful or malicious actions by the debtor that cause personal injury or death to a person will be discharged unless a creditor timely files and prevails in an action to have such debts declared non-dischargeable.

The discharge in a Chapter 13 case is typically broader than in a Chapter 7 case. Debts dischargeable in a Chapter 13, but not in Chapter 7, include debts for willful and malicious injury to property (however not to a person), debts incurred to pay non-dischargeable tax obligations, and debts arising from property settlements in divorce or separation proceedings.

Hardship Discharge

After confirmation of a Chapter 13 plan, circumstances may arise that prevent the debtor from completing the plan. In such situations, the debtor may ask the court to grant a "hardship discharge." Such a discharge is available only if the debtor's failure to complete plan payments is due to circumstances beyond the debtor's control and through no fault of the debtor; creditors have received at least as much as they would have received in a Chapter 7 liquidation case; and modification of the plan is not possible. Injury or illness that precludes employment sufficient to fund even a modified plan may serve as the basis for a hardship discharge. The hardship discharge is more limited than the discharge described above and does not apply to any debts that are non-dischargeable in a Chapter 7 case.

### *50.03 Common Bankruptcy Terms.*

A 341 meeting, commonly referred to as the "first Meeting of Creditors," is required by section 341 of the Bankruptcy Code. At such meeting, the debtor is questioned under oath by creditors, a trustee and/or the U.S. Trustee about his/her financial affairs.

An adversary proceeding is a lawsuit that arises in (or is related to a bankruptcy case) or that is commenced by filing a complaint with the Bankruptcy Court.

The bankruptcy schedules are official forms containing detailed lists filed by the debtor along with (or shortly after filing) the petition showing the debtor's assets, liabilities and other financial information.

A Chapter 7 bankruptcy typically involves consumers who cannot pay their existing debts, which mainly relate to education and expenses related to the home.

A Chapter 9 action provides for reorganization of municipalities (which includes cities and towns, as well as villages, counties, taxing districts, municipal utilities and school districts).

A Chapter 11 action is a reorganization for a business and is also available to consumer debtors.

A Chapter 12 bankruptcy action is reserved for a family farmer or fisherman. This Chapter is also a repayment. Its eligibility requirements are quite restrictive in that the majority of the family income must come from family farming or commercial fishing.

A Chapter 13 bankruptcy is filed by an individual with regular income to preserve assets -- such as a home or vehicle -- and adjust debt payments over a period of three to five years.

Chapter 15 deals with cases of cross-border insolvency.

Consumer debts are debts incurred for personal, family or household expenses, as opposed to business needs.

Current monthly income is the average monthly income received by the debtor over the six calendar months before commencement of the bankruptcy case, including regular contributions to household expenses from non-debtors and income from the debtor's spouse if the petition is a joint petition, but not including social security income and certain other payments made because the debtor is the victim of certain crimes.

A discharge is release of a debtor from personal liability for certain dischargeable debts set forth in the Bankruptcy Code. A discharge releases a debtor from personal liability for certain debts (known as dischargeable debts) and prevents the creditors owed those debts from taking any action against the debtor to collect the money owed. The discharge also prohibits creditors from communicating with the debtor regarding the debt, including telephone calls, letters and personal contact.

Exempt property is certain property owned by an individual debtor that the Bankruptcy Code or applicable state law permits the debtor to keep from unsecured creditors. For example, in some states, the debtor may be able to exempt all or a portion of the equity in the debtor's primary residence (homestead exemption), or some or all "tools of the trade" used by the debtor to make a living (*i.e.*, auto tools for an auto mechanic or dental tools for a dentist). The availability and amount of property the debtor may exempt depends on the state the debtor lives in.

A fraudulent transfer is a transfer of a debtor's property made with intent to defraud, or for which the debtor receives less than the transferred property's value.

The means test is a mechanism devised to determine whether an individual debtor's Chapter 7 filing is presumed to be an abuse of the Bankruptcy Code under Section 707(b) requiring dismissal or conversion of the case (typically to a Chapter 13). Abuse is presumed if the debtor's combined current monthly income over five years, net of certain statutory allowed expenses, is more than $10,000 or 25% of the debtor's non-priority unsecured debt, as long as that amount is at least $6,000. A debtor may rebut a presumption of abuse only by a showing of special circumstances which justify additional expenses or adjustments of current monthly income.

A motion to lift the automatic stay is a request by a creditor to allow the creditor to take action against the debtor or the debtor's property that would otherwise be prohibited by the automatic stay. Typically, a lift is filed with regard to repossession of real estate and/or vehicles.

A no-asset case is a Chapter 7 case where there are no assets available to satisfy any portion of the creditors' unsecured claims.

A non-dischargeable debt is a debt that cannot be eliminated in bankruptcy. Examples include debts for alimony or child support, certain taxes, debts for most government-funded or guaranteed educational loans or benefit overpayments, debts arising from death or personal injury caused by driving while intoxicated or under the influence of drugs and debts for restitution or a criminal fine included in a sentence on the debtor's conviction of a crime. Some debts, such as debts for money or property obtained by false pretenses and debts for fraud or defalcation while acting in a fiduciary capacity, may be declared non-dischargeable only if a creditor timely files and prevails in a non-dischargeability action.

An objection to dischargeability is a trustee's or creditor's objection to the debtor being released from personal liability for certain dischargeable debts. Common reasons include allegations that the debt to be discharged was incurred by false pretenses or that debt arose because of the debtor's fraud while acting as a fiduciary.

A trustee's or creditor's objection to the debtor's attempt to claim certain property as exempt from liquidation by the trustee to creditors is a pleading filed with the Bankruptcy Court entitled "Objection to Exemptions."

A preference or preferential debt payment is made to a creditor in the 90-day period before a debtor files bankruptcy (or within one year if the creditor was an insider) that gives the creditor more than the creditor would receive in the debtor's Chapter 7 case.

A priority claim is the Bankruptcy Code's statutory ranking of unsecured claims that determines the order in which unsecured claims will be paid if there is not enough money to pay all unsecured claims in full. Under the Bankruptcy Code's priority scheme, money owed to the case trustee or for pre-petition alimony and/or child support must be paid in full before any general unsecured debt (*i.e.*, trade debt or credit card debt) is paid.

A proof of claim is a written statement on an official form verifying documentation that is filed by a creditor describing the reason the debtor owes the creditor money.

A reaffirmation agreement is an agreement by a Chapter 7 debtor to continue paying a dischargeable debt (such as an auto loan) after the bankruptcy, usually for the purpose of retaining the collateral. The collateral which secures the debt would otherwise be subject to repossession.

A secured creditor is a creditor holding a claim against the debtor who has the right to repossess and hold or sell certain property of the debtor in satisfaction of some or all of the claim.

A secured debt is backed by a mortgage, pledge of collateral or other lien for which the creditor has the right to pursue specific pledged property upon default (*i.e.*, home mortgages, auto loans and tax liens).

The Servicemembers Civil Relief Act applies in bankruptcy cases. The Act provides protection to members of the military against the entry of default judgments and gives the court the ability to stay proceedings against military debtors.

The trustee is the representative of the bankruptcy estate who exercises statutory powers, principally for the benefit of the unsecured creditors, under the general supervision of the court and the direct supervision of the U.S. Trustee or bankruptcy administrator. The trustee is a private individual appointed in all Chapter 7, 12, 13 and 11 cases. The trustee's responsibilities include reviewing the debtor's petition and schedules and bringing actions against creditors or the debtor to recover property of the bankruptcy estate. In a Chapter 7 case, the trustee liquidates property of the estate and makes distributions to creditors. Trustees in Chapter 12 and 13 have similar duties to the Chapter 7 trustee and the additional responsibilities of overseeing the debtor's plan, receiving payments from debtors and disbursing plan payments to creditors.

U.S. Trustees are officers of the United States Justice Department responsible for supervising the administration of bankruptcy cases, estates and trustees. It is their duty to monitor plans and disclosure statements, creditors' committees, fee applications and perform other statutory duties.

An unsecured claim is a claim or debt for which a creditor holds no special assurance of payment -- a debt in which credit was extended based solely upon the creditor's assessment of the debtor's future ability to pay.

Installment payments or a request for waiver of fees are available for those who cannot afford to pay the full filing fee at the time of filing. If approved by the court, this allows the debtor to pay the filing fee over a period of four to six months. For those who cannot afford to pay the filing fee at the time of filing or in installments, a request can be made for a waiver of the filing fee. The judge may waive the fee only if the debtor's income is less than 150% of the official poverty line applicable to the debtor's family size.

**SAMPLE QUESTIONS FOR BANKRUPTCY**

1. The bankruptcy estate consists of:

   a. All property in which the debtor has an interest, including jointly owned property or property held by another party.
   b. All legal or equitable property of the debtor.
   c. Only those assets listed on the debtor's petition and schedules.
   d. All property titled in the debtor's name or possession on the date of filing of the petition and schedules.

2. The Bankruptcy Code allows an individual debtor to protect some property from the claims of creditors:

   a. Because it is exempt under the laws of the debtor's state of residence.
   b. Because it is exempt under federal bankruptcy law.
   c. Because the debtor has claimed the appropriate exemption on the schedule filed with the bankruptcy court and federal and/or state law allows for such exemption.
   d. Because the debtor needs the property to maintain his/her lifestyle.

3. The automatic stay stops lawsuits, foreclosures and all collection activities against the debtor the moment the petition is filed and remains in place until:

   a. The bankruptcy is finalized.
   b. The first thirty days.
   c. Until the debtor has had the opportunity to receive a fresh start financially.
   d. During the pendency of the bankruptcy action unless exceptions are invoked due to BAPCPA rules.

*Answers:*

1–a. Property transferred by the debtor to another party in anticipation of filing bankruptcy is still looked upon by the court as being property of the bankruptcy estate, regardless of who has possession of the property.

2–c. There is no presumption of exemption. It must be claimed under the correct exemption statute.

3–d. Debtors' actions and any prior filing will bring into play the provisions of the Bankruptcy Abuse Prevention and Consumer Protection Act of 2005. This could vastly affect the automatic stay by either shortening the stay period or causing it not to go into effect at all.

# 60.00 BUSINESS LAW

## *60.01 Introduction to Business Law.*

Business law is a broad and complex topic. It encompasses not only the types of business entities and their functions, but also includes contracts, employment and labor, products and services, dispute resolution, property -- including real and intellectual -- and much more.

Any number of federal, state and local statutes and regulations may regulate a typical business. For example, a financial institution, such as a bank, will have to comply with federal agencies and regulations such as the Securities and Exchange Commission, Federal Deposit and Insurance Commission, Federal Trade Commission, Department of Labor (with respect to employment issues), Internal Revenue Service, Department of Housing, Environmental Protection Act, Occupational Health & Safety Act and Family Medical Leave Act, as well as contractual issues which may be multi-jurisdictional.

For the purposes of this study manual, business law covers the various types of business entities and how they relate to work a typical paralegal might perform in the law firm or corporate environment. The paralegal studying for PACE should review additional resources to become more familiar with business entities, how they function and the common legal issues confronting them.

There are primarily four types of business forms in the United States today: sole proprietorships, partnerships, corporations and the newest forms, the limited liability company (LLC) and the limited liability partnership (LLP). This section will cover the benefits of each type of entity, the manner in which the business is created and operated and the dissolution of the business. Public Corporations, while regulated by state laws, may also be regulated by the Securities and Exchange Commission (SEC) and other government agencies. Corporations subject to SEC governance and the rules and regulations of publicly held corporations will be the primary focus of this section as they fall under "federal" agency law and relate to paralegal work. Joint ventures, franchises and cooperatives will also be included on a limited basis.

There are advantages and disadvantages of the various forms of business. Those who wish to start a business must consider the following: 1) tax ramifications; 2) ownership control; 3) potential liability to the owners; 4) cost and formalities; and 5) ability to transfer interest. A person or persons wishing to start a business should consult an attorney as well as a Certified Public Accountant or tax attorney in order to be aware of all the legal and financial advantages and disadvantages of each of these business types.

## *60.02 Business types.*

### <u>Sole Proprietor</u>

The simplest type of business form is the *sole proprietorship.* There are few formalities in creating this type of business. Typically, a person who chooses to start a business will file the appropriate documents in the location where they wish to operate the business. In many jurisdictions, the sole proprietor will obtain a business license, publish a fictitious name and complete any documents regarding local taxes to which s/he may be subject. There is minimal government regulation or legal requirement.

The sole proprietor has total control of the business, is responsible for all debts and retains all profits. Any profits are taxed as personal income. The business is not "transferable;" however, the business or its interest could be sold to another individual or business entity.

*Partnership*

According to the Revised Uniform Partnership Act (RUPA), a *partnership* is "an association "carry on a business for profit." A *partnership* that is created may be a general partnership or a limited partnership.

General Partnership

Under a general partnership, all partners are equally responsible for the management of the business, share all profits, and are equally responsible for any debts incurred by the partnership. The partners should execute a partnership agreement setting forth the initial contributions, their management roles and/or contribution of services. In the event the general partners contribute unequally, each partners' share should be documented in the partnership agreement, including how profits are to be distributed. The Revised Uniform Partnership Act will control any distributions in the absence of a partnership agreement.

A well-written partnership agreement includes the following:

- Name and address of the business (partnership);
- Names and addresses of the partners;
- Purpose and duration of the partnership;
- The amount and type of investment of each partner;
- Management and voting rights of each partner;
- Responsibilities and duties of each partner;
- Type of accounting system, financial institution, authority to deposit and withdraw funds, etc.;
- Authority to borrow money for the company, as well as whether partners may borrow from the company;
- Employee and employment responsibilities and information; and
- How profits and losses will be shared.

The partnership will file a partnership return with the Internal Revenue Service (IRS) showing any profit or loss of the business. The partnership does not pay taxes itself.

Profit is shown in its derivative share and each partner pays personal income taxes on his/her share of the profits. If the partnership loses money, each partner is allowed to deduct the derivative share from his/her personal income tax. Should the business fail, all partners have unlimited personal liability and will be held responsible for all debts of the partnership out of their personal resources.

A partnership may be terminated or "dissolved and wound up." This process is simpler than it is for a corporation. A partnership can be terminated when one partner wishes to leave the partnership, when the business is sold, the partnership agreement expires or when the business goes bankrupt. Dissolution of the partnership prevents any new business from taking place. Winding up the business allows the business to finalize all transactions, pay any debts, divide any profits and distribute remaining assets. While the general partnership is not transferable to another, the business or its interests may be sold.

Limited Partnership (LP)

A *limited partnership* must have at least one general partner and can have one or more limited partners. RULPA (2001) governs the manner in which the partnership is formed and must function. The general partner manages the business and is responsible for paying all debts and distributing all profits. He or she is liable under the same standards of the General Partnership as discussed above. The limited partners are investors and are liable only to the amount of their investment. Additionally, the limited partners may be natural persons, however, they could also be trusts, estates, associations, corporations, or other business entities.

There are two primary types of limited partnerships: Limited Liability Limited Partnership (LLLP) and Limited Liability Partnership (LLP). Under an LLLP, the general partner and the limited partners all have the same liability, which is to the amount of the investment made by each partner. Professionals who wish to form a common business typically form an LLP. Doctors, and particularly medical or legal specialists, often form an LLP. The advantage of an LLP is that if one partner is sued, the business will continue to function; the partners are not jointly and severally liable.

Another *type* of limited partnership is a Family Limited Partnership. The primary purpose of this type of partnership is for estate planning and tax deference benefits. Typically, parents (this includes siblings, spouses, and other family members) will be the general partners and the children of the general partners are the limited partners.

Limited Partnerships are usually registered with the Secretary of State in the state where they will be primarily conducting business. The partners should have an attorney prepare, and they should execute, a partnership agreement that states the purpose of the limited partnership and the contributions made by each partner. The form must also state who will be the general partner, along with his/her fiduciary and management responsibilities to the partnership. A registered agent for service of process must also be provided.

Limited Liability Company (LLC)

A *Limited Liability Company* (LLC) may be created by one or more individuals, who are referred to as members. There is no limitation to the number of members in an LLC. The members choose a name and file the articles of organization with the Secretary of State in the state where the business will be primarily conducted. As with the LLP, the information about the registered agent for service of process is provided.

An operating agreement outlining responsibilities, voting rights and the management of the LLC should be prepared and signed by all members. The members may contribute money, real or personal property, contracts for services, promissory notes and intellectual property in order to fund the LLC. The members have total control over the management of the business. Liability is limited to the amount of the capital contribution. The members are protected from personal liability, whether arising out of contract or tort, by the company or any individual member.

The LLC does not pay taxes; all money is passed through the business to the individual members. The individual members must report any profit or loss on their income tax. The accounting method should be set up properly for this type of business entity.

*Corporations*

A *corporation* is defined as an entity formed and authorized by state law to act as a single person and to raise capital by issuing stock to investors who are the owners of the corporation. Regardless of the number of persons who own or share in the corporation, the corporation is treated as a single entity. In most cases, the corporation protects the individual shareholders from personal liability. A corporation is considered a "person" and this it pays taxes.

The most common types of corporations in the "business" world are *Closely Held Corporations* and *Publicly Held Corporations*. Many of the same laws apply to both closely held and publicly held corporations. Professional and limited liability corporations have gained popularity and will be discussed as well.

There are many more formalities required of corporations. Not only do by-laws need to be created and amended, but the corporation must elect a board of directors, appoint officers or manager who manage the business on behalf of the shareholders, vote on actions, maintain records and minutes, and manage the daily business and activities of the corporation.

Closely Held Corporation

The largest numbers of corporations in the United States are *Closely Held Corporations*. They are considered private corporations. The shares are not traded on any of the national securities exchanges. They are often owned by family members, close friends or small groups of people who have incorporated to "protect" the individuals from liability. The owners or shareholders will, usually, also be the officers, directors and managers of the corporation. Articles of Incorporation are filed with the Secretary of State, bylaws are prepared, officers elected, meetings held and minutes prepared; any other type of business is performed as set forth under the Articles and the bylaws. The bylaws must state that the shareholders have limited ownership to the initial stockholders in order to be considered a *Closely Held Corporation.* Thus, the original owners retain total control of the corporation.

Subchapter S Corporation

The *Subchapter S Corporation* is considered a "hybrid" of the corporation and a partnership. It is created and operated much as a regular corporation; however, it is treated as a partnership for tax purposes; the shareholders are taxed rather than the corporation. The IRS states that a *Subchapter S Corporation* must: 1) have no more than 100 shareholders, all of whom are individuals, estates or certain types of trusts, and none of whom is a nonresident alien; 2) issue only one class of stock; 3) not be a member of an affiliated group of corporations; 4) it is not a bank, insurance company, or domestic international sales corporation; and 5) all shareholders must consent. Shareholders must sign a consent agreeing to the *Subchapter S* election, which is filed with the IRS. The "S" election must be made within a specified period of time (currently the "fifteenth day of the third month of the corporation's tax year."

A Subchapter S Corporation may also qualify under IRC §1244, known as "qualified business stock," if it has no more than $1 million in stock, which are entirely employee owned. This Section eliminates the "double taxation" that is often a detriment to creating a corporation.

Nonprofit Corporation

*Non-profit Corporations* are formed by individuals who have like interests and who want to protect a board of directors and individual members from liability. These corporations are formed by charitable organizations or benevolent groups (sports, travel, recreation and environmental groups, to name a few) who have like interests or causes. Paralegals may be involved in the preparation of documents for such corporations. The nonprofit group must qualify as such under the appropriate IRS codes.

Professional Corporation

It has only been of late that professions have allowed their members to "incorporate" and, thus, this is a relatively new concept and area of law. The *Professional Corporation* is a type of corporation is created for doctors, dentists, accountants, lawyers and other professionals in order to take advantage of tax deductions, particularly for health and pension plans, which are allowed. While states differ in their definition of "profession" must follow the Model Professional Corporation Act, which limits the formation of a corporation to those professions that must be licensed within that state. Since it is considered contrary to public policy to grant professionals limited liability for negligence, the "owners" of the professional corporation are not afforded that same protection allowed in other types of corporations. Professionals are personally responsible for wrongful acts and/or those performed under their supervision and control.

Domestic, Foreign, and Alien Corporations

These "corporations" are terms of art for the location of incorporation as well as where the corporation does business:

- *Domestic Corporation* -- a corporation described in terms of where it was formed and where the Articles of Incorporation are filed.
- *Foreign Corporation* -- a corporation that is incorporated in one state, but which does business in another state.
- *Alien Corporation* -- a corporation formed in another country, but which does business in the United States or its territories.

Publicly Health Corporations

A *Publicly Held Corporation* is a corporation whose stock is sold or traded on one of the national securities exchanges. The shareholders in this type of corporation are strictly investors. The management and control of the corporation is maintained by the Officers and Directors, who may also be shareholders.

Due to an increasing "global" economy, many *Multinational* or *Transnational Corporations* have been created. The stocks may be traded on the securities exchanges of numerous countries. The managers may be citizens of different countries.

All 50 states, the District of Columbia, Guam and Puerto Rico have their own incorporation statutes. A corporation may incorporate in any state it chooses. Over half of the Fortune 100 companies are incorporated in the State of Delaware. Delaware's Supreme Court is considered the most liberal and influential with regard to corporate governance. Thus, anyone who manages, merges or sues a Delaware corporation is subject to Delaware laws, both statutory and case law.

The initial document filed to incorporate is the *Articles of Incorporation.* The appropriate fees are paid upon filing. In most states, the Articles are filed with the Secretary of State. The Articles must include, at a minimum, the name of the corporation, the name(s) and address(es) of the incorporator(s), the resident agent and his/her address, the purpose of the corporation and the kind, number and face value of stock issued by the corporation. Many corporations use the Revised Model Business Corporations Act (RMBCA) as a guideline for financing, managing, operating and dissolving a corporation.

Bylaws are the governing documents of the corporation. They are the rules for governing the management and operation of the business of the corporation; they must be consistent with the articles of incorporation and also cannot be in violation of any state or federal statutes or regulations. The bylaws should be presented at the first organization meeting of the corporation. The bylaws should also contain provisions relating to the directors and officers of the corporation; who they are – such as President, Vice President, Secretary, Treasurer, etc. - as well as the duties and authority of each officer and/or director. The bylaws should also state the frequency of meetings, how the notice of meetings should be given, requirements for calling special meetings, the definition of a quorum, filing empty positions, if officers and/or directors are to be compensated, action(s) that may be taken without a formal meeting, the removal and replacement of officers and directors, and information about the shareholders – the types as well as voting rights. This is not an exhaustive list by any means, but the basic requirements for creating corporate bylaws.

The corporation must have capital in order to operate. Those funds can be acquired by two methods of financing: debt financing, which refers to loans; and equity financing, which is the selling of shares or an interest in the business, otherwise known as stocks. Stock is defined as the capital that a corporation raises through the sale of shares that entitle the holder(s) to certain rights of ownership. Many publicly held corporations create capital using a combination of these two methods. The IRS looks carefully at corporations that rely strictly on debt financing. While interest payments on loans are deductible by the corporation, the IRS may take the position that the loans are capital contributions by shareholders if the corporation is too thinly capitalized.

The shareholders are the owners of the corporation. They have the right to control the corporation by voting how the corporation is run. They also vote on how ongoing income or dividends will be received. The shareholders will typically receive a pro rata share, based on the percentage of their investment, upon the corporation's dissolution. The shareholders also elect members who will represent their interests on the Board of Directors. The shareholders who are unable to attend board meetings may also give their proxy to a board member who will vote on their behalf.

As indicated above, the Articles must state the type, number and the value of the shares to be issued by the corporation. The corporation is not required to issue all of the authorized shares immediately. There are two classes of stock: common stock and preferred stock. A corporation must have at least one class of stock issued that allows the shareholders voting rights, which include the power to elect directors and make other business decisions that affect the corporation. The corporation must also provide a class of stocks that will provide that the shareholders receive profits and/or residual assets if the corporation is dissolved.

- Common stock is defined as a class of stock that entitles the owner to vote for the corporation's Board of Directors, to receive dividends and to participate in the net assets upon liquidation of the corporation.
- Preferred stock is defined as a class of stock that entitles the owner to receive special preference with regard to either dividends or the distribution of assets.

Common stock has traditionally carried the most rights, as well as the highest risk of loss. A shareholder who owns common stock has the right to vote, the right to receive dividends and the right to receive net assets upon dissolution. An individual owning preferred stock does not typically have the right to vote (or those rights may be limited) and will receive "preference" when dividends are paid. The payment will be in the form of either dividends or assets, and will be paid to the preferred shareholder before the common shareholders are paid. Preferred shareholders may convert or exchange their preferred stocks to common stock upon request. Some corporations will designate only one type of stock. In that event, only common stock will be issued.

A stock is issued at *par value*, which is defined as the nominal or face value of a stock or bond. The total par value of the stock initially issued or offered by the corporation is considered the stated capital. During the initial offering, the consideration paid may be in the form of money, property, past services, promissory notes and/or future services. The company may also issue a stock warrant. A *stock warrant* is a document that authorizes its holder to purchase a stated number of shares at a stated price, usually for a specific period of time. Stock warrants may be freely traded.

A *stock option* is when an employee is granted the right to purchase shares (or warrants) at a stated price. Those options cannot be traded, but they can be sold back to the corporation. The buyback of shares is governed by the Financial Accounting Board of the SEC, which amended the rules effective July 2005 as a result of *Enron* and numerous other securities fraud cases.

There are three groups that have a voice in the operation of a corporation: the shareholders, the Board of Directors and the corporate officers. The shareholders elect the Board of Directors, who is responsible for the policy and management of the corporation. The Board of Directors also elects the officers who carry out the day-to-day operation and policies of the corporation. The state's statutes, and thus the bylaws of the corporation, outline the officers to be elected (*e.g.*, president, vice president, secretary and treasurer). Some corporations elect a chief executive officer (CEO) and/or a chief financial officer (CFO) instead of or in addition to the previously listed officers. Additionally, there may be several vice presidents who oversee various functions.

The Officers and Board of Directors have a fiduciary responsibility to the shareholders. The *corporate opportunity doctrine*, which was established by case law, states that corporate officers, directors and agents cannot take personal advantage of an opportunity that in all fairness should have belonged to the corporation. The RMBCA at §§8.30 and 8.42 provide for the standard of conduct in performance of those duties:

> (1) In good faith; (2) with the care an ordinarily prudent person in a like position would exercise under similar circumstances; and (3) in a manner he reasonably believes to be in the best interests of the corporation.

A *conflict of interest* may also occur when an officer or director, who has a personal interest in a matter, enters into a transaction with the corporation. The RMBCA provides governance on defining a conflict of interest for the individual and/or corporation. Additionally, the *business judgment rule* states that corporate officers and directors are not liable for honest mistakes of business judgment.

## Amendments

Amendments to the Articles must be made by a majority of stockholders, although some state statutes allow a two-thirds vote, particularly with regard to changing or eliminating the rights of minority shareholders or the rights of non-voting classes. Voting will usually occur by class or voting groups.

The power to make amendments is governed by individual state statute. However, the RMBCA provides "recommended" powers to amend as follows:

- To increase or decrease the number of authorized shares;
- To exchange, classify, reclassify or cancel shares, whether or not previously issued;
- To limit or cancel the right of shareholders of a class of shares to receive dividends;
- To create new classes or shares whether superior or inferior to shares that are outstanding or change designation of shares on the preferences, limitation or rights of classes of shares, whether or not previously issued; and/or
- To change voting rights of outstanding shares, eliminate the power to vote cumulatively or assign multiple or fractional votes per share, and deny power to vote entirely to a class of shares, whether or not previously issued.

The Board will usually recommend the adoption of any amendments, mergers, consolidations, sale of assets and/or dissolution that require shareholder approval.

To learn more, review the Sarbanes-Oxley Act of 2002 and/or take a continuing education course regarding this topic. The Act was created because of the numerous corporate fraud cases that were heard by the federal courts in early 2000. Since the law was enacted, CEOs and CFOs have become accountable, having to sign under penalty of imprisonment, that all financial statements and reports are accurate. Corporate accounting firms and their relationships as advisors and auditors to large corporations have come under scrutiny as well. A Public Company Accounting Oversight Board was created to regulate accounting firms. The SEC has enacted new regulations giving additional powers to file administrative and civil actions against corporate officers who attempt to defraud the corporation and the shareholders.

## Mergers and Consolidations

A *consolidation* occurs when two corporations disappear and a new corporation is created. A *merger* occurs when one corporation supersedes another. If Corporation A and Corporation B merge, Corporation A disappears and Corporation B survives. Corporation B will assume all assets and liabilities of Corporation A. Shareholders will receive the consideration specified in the merger plan. The IRS calls this a Class "A" reorganization. The IRS, in fact, has two additional classifications of restructuring of corporations.

A Class “B” reorganization occurs when one corporation exchanges its voting shares for all or most of the outstanding shares of the other corporation. Most state corporation codes refer to this as a stock purchase or acquisition. The disadvantage of this type of merger or reorganization is that there can be a large number of shareholders (sellers) and the acquired business remains liable for unknown or undisclosed liabilities, including taxes.

A Class “C” reorganization is also called an asset purchase or acquisition. This occurs when a corporation exchanges its voting shares for the assets of another corporation. The assets purchased can be all of the assets, a majority of them or the assets of a particular line of the business. The acquired corporation will remain in existence after the transaction, during which time the assets from the proceeds of the sale, as well as liabilities, are not still assumed by the purchasing corporation. At some point, the acquired corporation will liquidate, pay any remaining liabilities and pay the net remains to the shareholders. The acquired corporation may, however, stay in existence and operate as a holding or investment corporation.

While the IRS has its classes of reorganization, the courts have, through case law, established three types of mergers: horizontal, vertical and conglomerate. These mergers are described as follows:

A *horizontal merger* is between two or more companies producing the same or a similar product and competing for sales in the same geographic market. For example, two banks or supermarkets that merge in the same state are considered a horizontal merger.

A *vertical merger* is one that integrates two firms that have a supplier-customer relationship. For example, a manufacturer of electronics may merge with a retail store that sells electronics. A vertical merger in which the manufacturer or supplier acquires the retailer is called a forward merger. A backward merger occurs when the retailer acquires the manufacturer or supplier.

A *conglomerate merger* is one in which the businesses are totally unrelated. The courts look carefully at these types of mergers to determine whether they are a violation of the Clayton Act. The criteria is whether the acquiring corporation had intended to move into that area of business prior to the proposed merger, rather than only as a means of affecting competition among those who are already competitors.

Another type of merger that has become more prevalent is a triangle merger. This type of merger has the acquiring corporation forming a “wholly owned subsidiary” in which cash is “dropped” (the corporation may also contribute stock) and then merges an acquired corporation with the subsidiary. This type of merger eliminates the corporation from being responsible for liabilities of the acquired company.

Mergers between parent corporations and their subsidiaries are either called "upstream" or "downstream" mergers. A surviving corporation is the "upstream," while the subsidiary corporation -- if it survives -- is the "downstream."

A corporation may use this method if it wishes to change its state of incorporation. The corporation would create a wholly owned subsidiary in the state where it would like to be incorporated. It would then merge "downstream" with the subsidiary. All shares and financial interests would be mirrored in the subsidiary. The shareholders do not need to vote if less than the amount set forth by the corporation or statute is merged with the subsidiary. This type of merger does not offer any protection to the minority shareholders as they are unable to block the merger. The terms of the merger may be unfair to the minority shareholders, while being advantageous to the majority shareholders.

The Justice Department created "Merger Guidelines" in 1968 and carefully scrutinizes mergers of publicly held corporations. The Guidelines were amended in 1984 to include foreign competition. The Hertindahl-Hirschman Index (HHI) is used to decide whether to challenge a merger. The Justice Department considers the level of the market index (HHI) prior to the merger and the effect after the merger.

A corporation may be the target of a hostile bid or takeover. A hostile bid is an offer that is opposed by the management of the target company. A tender offer is a public offer made by an individual or corporation directly to the shareholders of the targeted corporation in order to acquire the targeted corporation at a specific price. The bid is usually to gain at least 51% of the shares of the corporation in order to gain control. There are specific rules governing these types of takeovers. The Securities and Exchange Act §§13-14 provide the framework for tender offers and hostile bids.

Winding up/Dissolution of the Corporation

Most state statutes provide for a streamlined process of dissolving corporations if the vote to dissolve is unanimous among the shareholders. Typically, a resolution to dissolve or wind up is adopted and approved by the majority, or other percentage specified in the bylaws or by statute, of the shareholders.

Some states require the filing of a notice of intent to dissolve, after which the affairs of the business are "wound up." Notice must be given to creditors, any franchise and/or contractual obligations must be resolved and taxes paid. Directors have a fiduciary responsibility to pay, discharge or make provisions for all corporate liabilities prior to liquidation and distribution of assets to the shareholders. The articles of dissolution are then filed with the Secretary of State.

Most states provide statutes for a period in which a corporation may be sued on pre-dissolution claims. Post-dissolution claim litigation is often a problem when a product injures an individual after the company has dissolved. In that event, the normal statute of limitations often has expired. However, if another company purchased assets, including the right to manufacture a product, the claimant may bring a cause of action against the new company under the theory of de facto merger or continuity of enterprise.

It is recommended that a paralegal studying for PACE should also review the Revised Model Business Corporation Act, the Revised Limited Liability Partnership Act, and the Uniform Limited Liability Corporation Act.

## SAMPLE QUESTIONS FOR BUSINESS LAW

1. Tom is injured using a widget manufactured by ABC Corporation. Tom's attorney learns that ABC Corporation dissolved last year. Tom has filed his claim within the appropriate statute of limitations. What remedy, if any, may be available to Tom?

   a. Tom is out of luck; ABC Corporation is gone and there is no one to sue.
   b. He could determine if another company or corporation acquired the right to manufacture the widgets and then sue them.
   c. Sue the directors of ABC Corporation as they had a fiduciary responsibility to Tom.
   d. File a claim with the Securities and Exchange Commission requesting that the shareholders pay his claim.

2. A paralegal is directed by the attorney to prepare the following documents for a corporation that will distribute medical supplies: Articles of Incorporation; bylaws; minutes of first meeting naming a wife, who is a medical doctor, as president, secretary and a director, and naming husband as vice president, treasurer and a director; an initial offering of $50,000; and stock certificates giving the husband and wife 200 shares each, at a par value of $1.00 each. What type of corporation is being created?

   a. common.
   b. professional.
   c. closely held.
   d. publicly held.

3. A chief executive officer (CEO) of an accounting firm contacts a law firm about creating a new corporation to sell widgets. The paralegal learns while gathering additional information that the officers and directors of the corporation are the spouses of the CEO and the chief financial officer (CFO) of the corporation to whom the new corporation will sell the widgets. The paralegal should:

   a. notify the Securities & Exchange Commission.
   b. draft the documents as it is perfectly legal.
   c. notify the attorney as it is illegal.
   d. notify the Department of Justice.

*Answers:*

1–b. The correct answer is b), according to the Corporation: Nutshell Series. In a corporate merger or acquisition, the company acquiring will typically acquire all assets and debts of the company. This means that even though the acquired corporation was dissolved, the acquiring corporation will likely bear responsibility for Tom's injuries, particularly if they are still manufacturing the widget.

2–c. See Glossary for types of corporations.

3–c. The accounting firm is committing an illegal act under Sarbanes-Oxley. The paralegal should inform the attorney, and the attorney should report the breach to the Securities & Exchange Commission and the Department of Justice if this is a publicly owned corporation. In the event the attorney does not take the appropriate action, then the paralegal may follow through with other action. (Reference: See *Kubasek, et al.*)

## 70.00 AGREEMENTS AND CONTRACTS

### *70.01 The Basics of an Agreement.*

A contract is another name for an agreement. An agreement, in essence, is an arrangement between one person or entity to provide a product or service to another person or entity. There are elements which must be included in every transaction, but usually the contract you enter into can be as simple as buying your morning coffee, or as complex as selling the franchised business that sells your morning coffee -- or that Marital Settlement Agreement you worked on yesterday -- or the Real Estate Sales Contract you'll be working on this afternoon. No matter what area of law you work in, you may be involved with some type of agreement, contract, transaction and contract law, so it helps to understand the basics elements of a contract.

What will determine whether you have made an agreement, whether simple or complex, will depend on whether all of the following items are present:

- Offer;
- Acceptance;
- Consideration;
- Legality of subject matter;
- Contractual capacity; and
- Contractual intent.

Most agreements usually are not as simple or straight forward as buying a cup of coffee, which is why a paralegal will frequently be drafting or reviewing agreements or contracts for the clients' different activities.

*Offer*

The *Offer* is the tangible or intangible goods or services which are being sold or traded. It should be as specific, descriptive, detailed and as rational as possible, covering at least these four elements:

- the price;
- the subject matter;
- the parties; and
- the time of performance.

Note that the time of performance must be a certain, reasonable time, and not something abstract.

The person making the offer to purchase or obtain -- the *offeror* -- must clearly state that he/she wants to obtain the goods or services. The offer may be made in writing or orally, or both; if the offer is made in more than one manner, make sure each is the same offer. If you retain superseding offers, ensure that the most recent offer is made in writing and dated, and that the agreement includes language noting that it supersedes all previous offers.

*Acceptance*

*Acceptance* is when the party agrees to accept, through purchase or otherwise, the tangible or intangible goods or services. The party accepting the offer -- the *offeree* -- must let the offeror know that they accept the offer. This acceptance may be made orally, in writing or by action, so the offeree should be careful. Or, the offer or agreement may provide a provision that if the offeree does not respond, or cashes the check or accepts the goods, the offeree has accepted the offer. Once this action has occurred, the offeree has little recourse to say it did not accept the offer.

The offeree may decide that it likes most of the offer, but is not happy with the price. The offeree may make a counteroffer agreeing to accept the offer if the offeror lowers the price. If the offeror agrees to the counteroffer, then the parties will proceed with the transaction. Should the offeree make a counteroffer, they should do nothing to appear that they have accepted the original offer or that could defeat their options in making the counteroffer.

*Consideration*

*Consideration* is the amount that will be exchanged between the parties. That amount can be money or something else given in exchange for the goods or services. It is important to note that each party is providing consideration: the party that gives the goods or services and the party which gives the money for the goods or services. There are, however, restrictions on what constitutes consideration. An example of a restriction is: Money given in the past, not specified for any purpose, cannot be used as payment for a present purchase.

*Legality of Subject Matter*

If the parties are not entering into a legitimate transaction to begin with, then it will probably not be considered binding. One well-known type of transaction which does not meet the legality of subject matter criteria is a drug deal; which, although it can meet the elements of a legitimate contractual transaction, would not be considered legal since it violates the law in most jurisdictions.

Generally, two types of contracts fall in this category:

- contracts which may violate public policy or are morally reprehensible (*malum in se*); and

- contracts which violate a local, state or federal law, ordinance or regulation (*malum prohibitum*).

*Contractual Capacity*

The party who makes the offer should be legally able to make that offer and the party accepting the offer should be legally able to accept the offer. Federal and state laws define parties which have contractual capacity for individual or corporate purposes when creating contracts; but, generally age, mental capacity, signing under duress and whether the person is under the influence of alcohol or drugs may affect whether a person has the legal capacity to enter into the contract. Also, it is important that if a person is signing on behalf of a corporation, the corporation has granted the person authority to sign the agreement on its behalf. Occasionally, extra verifications, such as witnesses or notary publics, will be required to confirm that a signatory has the contractual capacity to enter into the contract.

*Contractual Intent*

Did the parties intend to enter into the agreement or contract as discussed above? Can you show that each of the elements required to be met for an enforceable agreement have been met? Or, did one or both of the parties make a provable mistake in entering into the agreement; or, did a party misrepresent an issue relevant to the contract or commit fraud, which could void the contract? Whether there actually was an agreement or contract, or if it can be voided under one of the other elements discussed above, may lead to arguments and litigation, sometimes making people wish that a handshake was good enough to seal the deal.

### *70.02 Elements of the Written Contract.*

It is important to know what the client wants in the agreement, or has discussed or maybe agreed to, instead of just putting every possible provision in the agreement. If the agreement contains a lot of provisions the client will not abide by, then there is no reason to create a complex agreement for the client. There will be specific provisions in the agreement relating to the arrangement and there may be some general provisions that should be in the agreement to avoid confusion later. A well-written contract should set forth the intentions of the parties in its provisions well enough for either party to understand each provision; and, if it comes to that point, a judge or jury can understand each provision. The written contract should name each party, explain the intent of the parties, what each party is required to do, when the parties are required to perform their responsibilities and what the parties will receive for what they are doing. Depending on the type of agreement you are preparing or reviewing, there may be other provisions. Discussed below are some of the common provisions you may see or want to include in an agreement.

*Addresses and other contact information*

The contract may either have a formal Notice provision, which states how and when the parties will notify each other if certain events occur; or, at the very least, it should include the address and telephone number for each party to the contract so that if one party needs to contact the other for any reason, they have a place to begin.

*Effective Date*

Even though the offer requires that a time of performance be stated in order to be valid, parties occasionally overlook stating a specific date when the time of performance begins. Consider including a statement like: "the effective date of this agreement shall be the date the last party to sign this document signs," without providing a method for either party to date their signature. Whenever possible, include a stated Effective Date in the first or last paragraph of the agreement to save a few headaches. If the Effective Date is contingent on an event to be performed in the future, be sure that you have a letter or some other method of memorializing that date, kept with the contract.

*Termination or Expiration Date*

Just as you need an Effective Date, you may need or want a Termination Date. If the agreement has a specific term noted, then specifying the Termination or Expiration Date is useful, so -- as noted above -- there is no argument when the term of the agreement expires. It is also helpful to have a Termination or Expiration Date so that you have a method of ending the agreement if you wish to end the relationship, or a way to renew the relationship on updated terms at another time period.

*Automatic Renewal of Contract*

Some parties add a provision stating that, unless one party notifies the other, the agreement will not terminate on the Termination Date, but will continue for another amount of time. This can be a useful provision if you want to monitor it; but, if you forget about it, then you could be stuck in an agreement or it could be difficult to renegotiate a new agreement with the party. To help their options, if there is automatic renewal of the contract, parties might also include provisions which allow changes to pricing, volume requirements, type of equipment, or other things that can bring the terms of the agreement more current with their other agreements or customers.

*Termination With or Without Cause*

Additional provisions can allow either party to terminate with cause. Or, depending on the bargaining power of one of the parties or type of contract, a party may not want the other party to have any rights to terminate the agreement without cause. Occasionally, a contract will allow a method for cure of certain breaches of the contract.

*How a Contract May be Voided*

Certain types of contracts must include -- per state or federal law -- how the consumer or purchaser may terminate or rescind the contract. When drafting or reviewing agreements, you should know the industry you are dealing with; and, as with any other aspect of your job, you should review pertinent statutes or regulations to determine if there are statements which should be in the agreement regarding how or when the parties may terminate or rescind the agreement.

*Survival of Provisions*

There may be provisions in the agreement regarding non-competition, payment of amounts due, governing law or other items. One or both parties may want to assure that these provisions continue whether or not the contract was terminated with or without cause. Adding a statement of the provisions which survive termination of the agreement assist in meeting this goal.

*Assignment*

The Assignment provision is a provision which is overlooked in many agreements. Including a provision about whether the agreement may be assigned is occasionally required; but, if it is not, it may help to include one for a few reasons.

- One, depending on the industry you work in, you may not want a party that you are contracting with assigning the contract to a competitor, so a provision in the contract stating that the other party needs your permission to assign the contract may be prudent.
- Two, your client may be an individual and want the latitude to assign the contract to a corporation it creates for its benefit without the approval of the other party, so that clause can be helpful.
- Three, a party may not want the other party assigning any of its right, title and interest in any property it obtains from the agreement to another party, so including a provision that debars this is helpful.

*Indemnification*

One party may indemnify the other party, or indemnification may be mutual. The parties indemnify each other for claims from other parties or monies which may be lost because a product fails to perform, events occurring before the contract is executed, or other eventualities.

*Insurance or Security Bond*

Instead of indemnification, a party may request insurance coverage or a security bond. For example, a company that is retaining temporary employees may want a provision in the agreement with the other party to cover it for any loss of property should a temporary employee steal money from it and agree that proof that the other party has insurance coverage covering employee crime is acceptable. In other industries, such as the construction industry, a security bond, which is different from insurance coverage, may be required to assure that the contractor will complete its provision of services, such as constructing the building by a certain date at the amount quoted to the builder. If the contractor does not complete the building construction according to the terms of the contract, then the builder has the option of using the security bond to finish construction of the building.

*Special, Consequential, or Liquidated Damages*

You do not want to pay more money than you have to, so a damages provision which limits or states only when damages may be paid could help. If the agreement includes a provision which allows for early termination of the agreement and one party is expecting to make a certain amount of money from the agreement for several years, a provision which allows it to obtain money if the other party terminates the agreement early -- liquidated damages -- may be included.

*Delivery of Goods*

This section can read like alphabet soup, FOB, FAS, COD; and trying to decipher the alphabet can be frustrating. It can also be frustrating if you have a contract covering delivery of goods and do not specify who will pay for delivery fees and have those added on top of payment, or taken from the payment you were expecting. Knowing what the alphabet means and how to use it can buy you instant credibility in several industries.

*Mediation, Arbitration, and/or Litigation*

Including a method or methods for resolving disputes can be helpful. There is one thing to watch out for that some parties may try to slide in: waiver of jury trial. If your client wishes to waive the right or it is mutual, that may be acceptable, but this is another important thing to watch for. Since the dispute resolution and litigation provisions usually come near the end of the contract, concentration may flag in the review process.

*Governing Law, Jurisdiction, and Venue*

Probably overlooked as often as putting in an Effective Date is adding which law will govern the agreement. With a document this important to your client, why leave how it will be interpreted to chance or argument? Whichever federal, state or county law applies, specify it in the agreement whenever possible. Also, identifying jurisdiction and venue can help, especially if you want to keep litigation or other actions in a locale which is close to where your client is located or with which you are familiar.

*Execution*

Usually, both parties sign an agreement or contract, but there are certain types of agreements, such as Promissory Notes, which may be signed by only one party. Statutes, regulations and even case law may specify who must sign a document, if it must be witnessed or notarized, whether an individual's or a company's seal must be used on the document, whether a separate document must be provided confirming that the signatory is authorized to sign the document and other execution needs. Since an executed document is an important asset for the client, assuring that both parties execute the document, and execute it correctly, is a very important part of the contracting process. If you have ever had to follow up on getting any type of document signed, you also know that obtaining a fully-executed copy can turn out to be a difficult and time-consuming task.

### *70.03 Uniform Commercial Code.*

The Uniform Commercial Code (UCC) has been adopted in part or in whole in almost every state, although it is a model law which is fairly uniform throughout the states. One purpose of the Uniform Commercial Code is to promote commerce, governing contracts and agreements between merchants, yet it also governs contracts which involve non-merchants. The UCC consists of several Articles, each numbered by a Roman numeral, with Articles I, II and IX being the ones which are most pertinent to contracts.

In transactions, state law will apply unless the UCC supersedes; however, unlike some structured transactions, ~~if~~ the parties to the contract may agree they have more leeway to vary the UCC law provisions which may be found or required in their contract. Also unique to UCC transactions is a little more liberal interpretation of UCC Articles applied to agreements than interpretation of normal case laws applied to other state and federal statutes or regulations.

#### Article I

Article I imposes three obligations on the parties contracting; which, although they seem like common practice, the parties are still required to perform:

- in good faith;
- in a reasonable time; and
- according to past business dealings and practices.

#### Article II

The sale of goods over $500, not services, is covered by Article II. Article II also has several provisions which protect the buyer or consumer. Occasionally, the seller will have language in its UCC agreements attempting to mitigate its responsibility should any of the following events occur:

- *Strict Liability* – if the product is defective, the maker or seller may automatically be liable to an injured party.
- *Warranties – Express or Implied*
    - *Express warranties* are created either by a statement in the contract, a description in the contract or collateral material, such as marketing material, or a sale model which is used to consummate the sale.

There are two types of Implied Warranties: *Warranty of Merchantability* and *Warranty of Fitness for a Particular Use*. Under a *Warranty of Merchantability*, the seller is guaranteeing that the goods it is selling to the purchaser are fit for the purpose they are being sold and purchased for, naturally within reason. The second, *Warranty of Fitness for a Particular Use*, is a guarantee that the purchaser can use the goods for the purpose specified to the seller for which the goods were bought.

*Article IX*

Many different types of agreements can create secured transactions -- a transaction which creates a security interest in tangible or intangible property. Article IX covers any agreement which is signed with the expectation that the parties, both knowingly, will enter into the relationship where one party is providing the tangible or intangible property, or collateral, to secure a loan from the other party. This Article provides the party loaning the money certain rights should the party which borrowed the money fail to repay the loan on time.

## SAMPLE QUESTIONS FOR AGREEMENTS AND CONTRACTS

1. Morton and Jimmy enter into an agreement. Morton assumed that the terms of the contract were $500 for the purchase of 500 canisters of salt, while Jimmy thought the terms of the contract were $500 for 500 canisters of pepper. After Morton pays Jimmy $500 and receives his pepper, he contacts Jimmy and requests that Jimmy return his money. Morton returns the pepper, and they cancel the agreement. Jimmy and Morton agree to do this because of the concept of:

    a. provable mistake.
    b. warranty of merchantability.
    c. rescission for liability.
    d. unilateral voidance.

2. Two parties sign a contract dated June 1, 2007 for the purchase of computer software. The agreement states that the agreement will be effective on the date that the software is delivered to the purchaser. The purchaser began using the software on June 12, 2007. There is a letter attached to the contract signed by the purchaser stating that the seller shipped the software on June 3, 2007 and the purchaser received the software on June 5, 2007. The Effective Date of the contract would be:

    a. June 1, 2007.
    b. June 12, 2007.
    c. June 3, 2007.
    d. June 5, 2007.

3. In drafting an agreement for a trademark licensing from Party A to Party B, a paralegal might include which of the following provisions to assure that Party B will not have to pay expenses of litigation if a third party claims that it does not have rights to use the trademark Party B is being licensed rights to by party A.

    a. Collateral.
    b. Insulation.
    c. Indemnification.
    d. Security bond.

*Answers:*

1–a. Provable mistake is the correct answer. Both parties agree that they made a simple mistake in understanding the terms of the agreement, which makes this the correct answer. This transaction arguably could be a transaction which falls under Article II of the Uniform Commercial Code, so Morton receiving pepper instead of salt could allow Morton to terminate the agreement under the warranty of merchantability. However, since both parties agree that it was an innocent mistake, the warranty of merchantability is too stringent for this scenario. Rescission might be applicable if this were an instance where Morton had any right to rescind the contract, but he did not have any under the agreement. Also, as noted above, both parties agree they both made a mistake, so a rescission by one party is not acceptable in this instance and rescission of liability would not be applicable since, as discussed above, neither party has any liability to the other. Unilateral voidance would only allow one party to void the agreement; both parties wish to cancel the agreement.

2–d. June 5, 2007 is the correct answer. The agreement states the effective date is the date the software was delivered to the purchaser, or it received the software, which is June 5, 2007. The date on the agreement, software shipping date, and date the purchaser began using the software are not pertinent here.

3–c. Indemnification is the correct answer. Indemnification allows for one party to pay expenses which the other party incurs if claims are filed against them or if they are sued for events occurring due to their activities under the contract which they have signed with the party. Since this is not an agreement where one party is loaning money to the other, granting the other a security interest and providing collateral does not apply. A security bond would not apply because this is not a situation where one party is making a promise to finish its responsibilities under the agreement in a situation in which the security bond would normally be issued. Insulation is not a legal concept.

# 80.00 ETHICS

## *80.01 Conflicts of Interest.*

<u>*General Background Concerning Conflicts of Interest*</u>

> A lawyer should take reasonable measures to prevent conflicts of interest resulting from a paralegal's other employment or interests.
>
> *Guideline 7, ABA Model Guidelines for the Utilization of Paralegal Services.*
>
> A paralegal shall avoid conflicts of interest and shall disclose any possible conflict to the employer or client, as well as to the prospective employers or clients.
>
> *EC-1.6, NFPA Model Code of Ethics and Professional Responsibility and Guidelines for Enforcement.*
>
> A paralegal shall avoid conflicts of interest that may arise from family relationships and from personal and business interests.
>
> *EC-1.6 (c), NFPA Model Code of Ethics and Professional Responsibility and Guidelines for Enforcement.*

A conflict of interest arises when the duties of loyalty and/or confidentiality to a client are threatened. As a paralegal, you possess information about a client's transactions, the attorney's strategies, thought processes, work product and/or other client proprietary or privileged information. Conflicts of interest involving paralegals usually result from personal and business relationships outside the work environment or from your work on legal matters at a prior place of employment.

Your supervising attorney is obligated to determine whether there is a conflict of interest between you and the client or legal matter.

You should abide by the decisions made by the supervising attorney or the firm's conflicts committee or ethics counsel. If, however, you feel uncomfortable continuing to work on a matter on which your employer determined a conflict does not exist, you should discuss the matter further with the appropriate authority in your firm or organization.

Examples of potential conflicts of interest are:

- Changing jobs -- when you work at one law firm that is handling, or has handled, a legal matter on behalf of a client, then go to work for another law firm that is handling either (a) the opposite side of the same legal matter or (b) a matter in which a former client is involved as an adversary.

- Family and personal relationships -- when you are related to or are close friends with a party, a client, an attorney, a paralegal or someone on the opposite side of a legal matter.

Business interests and professional relationships outside employment -- if you are involved either within a legal professional organization or in another business entity where you have a dual role that may cause your work as a paralegal to be influenced or compromised, such as owning stock in a client's company.

*Conflicts Involving Simultaneous and Successive Representation*

> A paralegal shall act within the bounds of the law, solely for the benefit of the client, and shall be free of compromising influences and loyalties. Neither the paralegal's personal or business interests, nor those of other clients or third persons, should compromise the paralegal's professional judgment and loyalty to the client.
>
> *EC-1.6 (a), NFPA Model Code of Ethics and Professional Responsibility and Guidelines for Enforcement.*[8]

> A paralegal shall avoid conflicts of interest that may arise from family relationships and from personal and business interests.
>
> *EC-1.6 (c), NFPA Model Code of Ethics and Professional Responsibility and Guidelines for Enforcement.*

An attorney is prohibited from concurrent (sometimes called simultaneous or dual) representation of clients whose interests are adverse to each other. Interests may be adverse even when litigation is not involved. Simultaneous representation is prohibited when a lawyer's responsibility to one client may inhibit or materially limit the attorney's ability to represent a second client.

While the responsibility for accepting or declining representation lies with the attorney, that attorney may rely heavily on information obtained by the paralegal. No matter how minute the information may seem, be sure to share everything with your attorney.

A conflict in successive representation arises when an attorney is asked to represent a party whose interests may be adverse to those of a former client of the attorney. While not as serious a conflict as simultaneous representation, such a conflict is still a source of ethical problems. The general rule is that an attorney is disqualified from successive representation only if the interests of the former and current client are truly adverse *and* if the past and current matters are substantially related.

An *issue conflict* may occur when an attorney represents two clients on unrelated cases and urges a legal position for one client that, if the position prevails, will have negative consequences for the second client. Such conflicts do not usually require an attorney to withdraw from representation; however, many attorneys do not handle matters that may result in such conflicts, because clients are not comfortable with this situation or because the attorney believes that the conflict impairs his/her effectiveness.

[8] Non-traditional and special designation paralegals, such as virtual, freelance, contract and temp paralegals, must be held to the same ethical requirements, in fact, they should be more stringent because of the inherent independence and distance from attorney supervision of their positions.

You should be familiar with these possibilities to alert the attorney to possible ethical violations. Likewise, you should be familiar with NFPA's *Model Code of Ethics and Professional Responsibility and Guidelines for Enforcement*, available at: https://www.paralegals.org/files/Model_Code_of_Ethics_09_06_rev12-9-14.pdf (last visited Aug. 30, 2018).

*Conflicts from Personal or Business Interests*

> A paralegal shall avoid conflicts of interest that may arise from family relationships and from personal and business interests.
>
> *EC-1.6 (c), NFPA Model Code of Ethics and Professional Responsibility and Guidelines for Enforcement.*

You may encounter conflicts involving:

- Business transactions with clients, such as lending money to a client or investing in a client's business;
- Gifts from clients;
- Payment of fees by a third party who may seek to control the representation;
- Persons related to you or the attorney, *e.g.*, a close relative working on the opposing side of a case; or
- Trading in stocks of companies represented by your firm.

If your employer is serving as counsel to the issuer or the underwriter in connection with an initial public offering, you must never invest in the underwriters' original allotment. This constitutes "insider trading" which is not only unethical but is illegal under the Securities Exchange Act of 1934.

You must never buy or sell securities of any publicly held entity without complying with your employer's trading procedures. You must never buy or sell securities of any publicly held entity about which you have material non-public information.

You must never provide another person with material non-public information regarding any publicly held entity. "Tipping" such information is also an ethical and criminal violation.

You must never engage in speculative trading such as:

- Trading a client's securities on a short-term basis;
- Purchasing a client's securities on margin;
- Selling a client's securities short; or
- Buying or selling puts or calls involving the client's securities.

Prior to effecting any transaction in the securities of a publicly held entity, contact your employer's conflicts department. A conflicts department should maintain a list of publicly held clients and other publicly held entities about which your employer may possess material non-public information.

The conservative securities trading policy applies to transactions in securities of mutual funds, but not to transactions by the mutual funds themselves in securities of other entities. In other words, you should ascertain whether a mutual fund in which you wish to invest is on the conflicts list of your employer. You need not worry about whether securities bought or sold by the mutual fund are on the list.

Once you have determined -- through appropriate inquiry to the conflicts department -- that a mutual fund in which you have invested through a broker-directed discretionary account is not on the list, further investment in that fund by your broker without the broker's prior consultation with you does not have to be cleared against the list. However, giving your broker discretionary authority to effect other types of trading through your account does not obviate the need to comply with your employer's securities trading policy.

*Imputed Disqualification*

> A paralegal shall keep those individuals responsible for the legal representation of a client fully informed of any confidential information the paralegal may have pertaining to that client.
>
> > *EC-1.5 (e), NFPA Model Code of Ethics and Professional Responsibility and Guidelines for Enforcement.*
>
> A paralegal shall avoid conflicts of interest that may arise from previous assignments, whether for a present or past employer or client.
>
> > *EC-1.6 (b), NFPA Model Code of Ethics and Professional Responsibility and Guidelines for Enforcement.*

Imputed (or vicarious) disqualification is based on the idea that all persons in a firm know everything about all the clients and cases being handled by that firm. When strictly applied, disqualification of any one lawyer or paralegal would mean disqualification of the entire firm -- a difficult result for clients who select counsel on a matter-by-matter basis and for legal professionals who wish to maintain job mobility and career progression.

In some cases, the use of screening and ethical walls, discussed below, will avoid imputed disqualification[9].

[9] Imputed disqualification does not apply to nonlawyers, including paralegals, according to the new Comment 4 to Rule 1.10 of the recently revised ABA Model Rules https://www.americanbar.org/groups/professional_responsibility/publications/model_rules_of_professional_conduct/rule_1_10_imputation_of_conflicts_of_interest_general_rule/comment_on_rule_1_10/ (last accessed August 10, 2025)

ABA Informal Opinion 88-1526 distinguishes between screening an attorney and screening a paralegal. This opinion reads in part (formatting added for clarity):

> A law firm that employs a nonlawyer who formerly was employed by another firm may continue representing clients whose interests conflict with the interest of clients of the former employer on whose matters the nonlawyer has worked, as long as the employing firm screens the nonlawyer from information about or participating in matters involving those clients and strictly adheres to the screening process described in this opinion and as long as the nonlawyer to any person reveals no information relating to the representation of the clients of the former employer in the employing firm.

It is important that nonlawyer employees have as much mobility in employment opportunity as possible, consistent with the protection of clients' interests. To so limit employment opportunities that some nonlawyers trained to work with law firms might be required to leave the careers for which they are trained would disserve clients, as well as the legal profession. Accordingly, any restrictions on the nonlawyers' employment should be held to the minimum necessary to protect confidentiality of client information

<u>*Screens and Ethical Walls/Consent*</u>

An ethical wall, sometimes called a screen or cone of silence, is an imaginary boundary placed around an individual who has a conflict of interest. This imaginary boundary is designed to bar all communications and influences, written or verbal, between the members of the legal team handling a matter and the person. The primary purpose of erecting an ethical wall is to protect the client's confidences and secrets from being revealed or used inappropriately.

An ethical wall is erected not because the person with whom the conflict exists would reveal the client's privileged information, but simply to guard against this opportunity and to avoid the appearance of impropriety. The ethical wall is erected to ensure that there is no opportunity for the client's confidences and secrets to be revealed to anyone other than those working directly on the client's legal matter.

As previously mentioned, a legal professional's job mobility is not limited because of a conflict by erecting an ethical wall. Similarly, a legal professional's continued employment is not in jeopardy as long as the boundaries of the ethical wall are never crossed.

Once it is established that a conflict of interest exists, the affected clients' consents for continued representation in the matter must be obtained. If you are working in a traditional setting, the attorney will obtain that consent.

Then, a screen should be put in place. A memorandum should be immediately sent concerning the conflict of interest to alert all employees who may work on the matter or have access to the files or other information. The memorandum should advise employees that they are not permitted to communicate any information about the file with, or in front of, the person with whom the conflict of interest exists.

To remind people about the ethical wall, you should maintain copies of the memorandum establishing the wall in both the hard and electronic file. A memorandum placed in each file folder will also be a defense in case a challenge to the wall is made by an adversary or some other individual. Place an obvious tag or some other visible notation on the file folder that reminds everyone working on the matter that a wall has been erected. Appropriate comparable restrictions on computer access to files should also be put in place.

In some instances, it may be appropriate to move the files to another physical location away from the affected individual. The affected individual should not work on other matters with the team handling the walled matter because of the risk of inadvertent disclosures of confidential information.

***80.02 Conflicts Checks.***

> In order to be able to determine whether an actual or potential conflict of interest exists, a paralegal shall create and maintain an effective recordkeeping system that identifies clients, matters and parties with which the paralegal has worked.
>
> > *EC-1.6 (d), NFPA Model Code of Ethics and Professional Responsibility and Guidelines for Enforcement.*
>
> A paralegal shall reveal sufficient non-confidential information about a client or former client to reasonably ascertain if an actual or potential conflict of interest exists.
>
> > *EC-1.6 (e), NFPA Model Code of Ethics and Professional Responsibility and Guidelines for Enforcement.*

As new clients, staff and legal matters come into the office, and new parties are added to a litigation case already underway, a conflict check must be conducted to determine if real or potential conflicts exist. Know and follow your firm's policy for conflict checks. Virtual, Freelance, contract and temp paralegals must pay close attention to potential conflicts and have conflict check processes and policies in place to prevent conflicts arising when accepting new work from attorneys.

Upon receiving a job offer, cooperate with your potential employer in obtaining and reviewing a list of legal cases or matters that the employer is handling. You can reasonably expect the potential employer to initiate this process to protect itself from possible disqualification or sanctions.

If the attorney/firm does not do so, however, you must take the initiative and request such a list for review. You should review that list to identify the names of clients, parties in litigation, acquaintances, friends or family members. Compare the list of all legal cases and matters on which you have worked against the potential employer's list. If you work in litigation, review the names of attorneys representing various parties. You must then advise the potential employer of any matters in which you suspect you may have a conflict of interest, providing only enough information about the matter for the employer to determine whether or not a conflict exists. Usually, the client name or matter name is sufficient to assess potential conflicts.

Despite best efforts, a matter or client in which you have a possible conflict of interest may slip through. If this happens, bring the possible conflict to the attorney's attention as soon as you become aware of it.

### *80.03 Crisis of Conscience: Personal, Religious, or Political Conflicts.*

Can paralegals do their best work when they disagree morally, politically or religiously with what the client represents? Some commentators espouse that every individual is entitled to representation and those in the legal profession cannot always choose a "side," but must make a strong commitment to basic constitutional principles.

Increasingly, paralegals are confronting situations that force them to review their value system and to make decisions about whether strongly held beliefs -- be they moral, political or religious -- would prevent them from doing their best work. This presents the same ethical dilemma as jury service, where oaths are taken to base verdicts solely on the evidence presented, regardless of personal beliefs.

As society adopts a more activist mentality, these crisis-of-conscience situations have become more prevalent. Paralegals working on controversial cases may not always be able to put aside their personal feelings and beliefs and rise to the occasion.

To some extent, lawyers can pick and choose the kinds of cases on which they work, but paralegals cannot. Some legal scholars believe that paralegals should follow the same principles attorneys do in deciding to represent a client -- specifically, that everyone has a right to fair legal representation, regardless of counsel's personal feelings about the case. Other scholars believe paralegals should not be asked or expected to represent clients zealously, as do attorneys, because paralegals have not taken an oath to do so.

Virtually everyone agrees that paralegals have an obligation to speak up when they are presented with a crisis of conscience. Sometimes, simply talking with the attorney may resolve the conflict. Even if the conflict is not resolved, the attorney should appreciate your honesty, since anything that interferes with your ability to do good work could damage the case.

Additionally, the ABA Model Rules of Professional Conduct instruct lawyers to ensure that people working under their supervision honor the ethical obligations of the law. Anything paralegals do that might violate those obligations is imputed to the lawyers for whom they work.

If you are hesitant to approach your supervising attorney about these types of conflicts, you may find help through your paralegal association. Many associations have ethics committees that can help members talk through personal conflicts and possibly resolve them without alerting others in the paralegal's place of employment. Such avenues, however, must be used carefully to avoid any breach of confidentiality.

Having strong personal feelings and being morally opposed are two different things. You must not let outside influences get in the way, including friends and family members who may have strong opinions about a case in which you are involved.

Every paralegal enters the profession with a set of moral principles that has been developed over his/her lifetime, and everyone's set is different. You must know in your heart what is important and what cannot be compromised.

### *80.04 Confidentiality.*

*General Background Concerning Confidentiality*

> A lawyer is responsible for taking reasonable measures to ensure that all client confidences are preserved by a paralegal.
>
> *Guideline 6, ABA Model Guidelines for the Utilization of Paralegal Services.*
>
> A paralegal shall preserve all confidential information provided by the client or acquired from other sources before, during and after the course of the professional relationship.
>
> *EC-1.5, NFPA Model Code of Ethics and Professional Responsibility and Guidelines for Enforcement.*
>
> A paralegal must protect the confidences of a client and must not violate any rule or statute now in effect or hereafter enacted controlling the doctrine of privileged communications between a client and an attorney.
>
> *Canon 7, NALA Code of Ethics and Professional Responsibility.*
>
> A paralegal shall not use confidential information to the disadvantage of the client.
>
> *EC-1.5 (b), NFPA Model Code of Ethics and Professional Responsibility and Guidelines for Enforcement.*

Confidentiality is one of the oldest precepts of legal ethics. It is a principle grounded in the concept that any attorney must know all of the facts of a matter if the attorney is to represent the client effectively. Without the assurance that incriminating or embarrassing information will not be revealed outside the attorney-client relationship, a client may be reluctant to fully disclose information needed by the client's attorney.

Confidentiality is also grounded in agency law. The attorney, as agent, has a fiduciary relationship with the client, as principal. An agent owes to the principal loyalty, confidence, good faith and accountability.

The duty of confidentiality is broader than the attorney-client privilege. The work product rule encompasses both. *(Discussed in further detail below.)*

The confidential nature of matters with which a paralegal comes into contact cannot be stressed strongly enough. Anything you hear or learn as a result of your professional duties, whether or not it is client-related, is strictly confidential.

A client's business -- and, indeed, the fact that the firm is representing a particular client -- ought not to be communicated in public places. A firm's or company's internal correspondence, communications, and publications are also confidential.

*Attorney-Client Privilege*

A client who seeks an attorney's advice or assistance may invoke an unqualified privilege not to testify and to prevent the attorney from testifying as to communications made by the client in confidence to the attorney. The client's privilege lasts indefinitely. The privilege belongs to the client. Only the client may waive the privilege and consent to disclosure of privileged information. Although the client holds the privilege, the attorney is obligated to advise the client of such privilege.

The attorney-client privilege extends to all nonlawyers working on client matters, including paralegals, and covers employees, vendors and independent contractors. See Section 50.02.

Before attending client meetings, check with the supervising attorney to determine whether note-taking is desirable or whether a follow-up memorandum is warranted. Your notes or memoranda may be discoverable, *i.e.,* requested by and produced to the other side in response to a *subpoena duces tecum.*

You should not disseminate communications from a client to anyone other than someone in your firm who has a clear need to know, such as an attorney who has been assigned to the matter. You must never discuss client matters in public areas where a conversation may be overheard, on cell phones that can be overheard easily by individuals passing by, or in general conversation with individuals not employed by the firm.

A stamp marked "Privileged" should be used to protect the privilege. Courts are more willing to uphold the privilege of a document if they *see* the document so designated.

While carbon copies themselves are no longer in use, be careful of sending copies or blind copies and of using notations on letters to indicate their distribution. When counsel is in a position to discover documents from an opponent, he/she will probably request the original file copy of all letters to determine who may have been copied or blind-copied on the correspondence.

An expert witness will normally be advised not to place anything in writing prior to a verbal report of his/her findings. It is advisable for an expert to proceed with picture/note-taking, but to keep such pictures and notes to a minimum. Suggest that the expert enter the report on a computer, but to withhold printing of the report until the attorney has so directed. Electronic reports may be revised and printed once all revisions have been made. Thus, one hard copy of the report exists, with no preexisting written drafts.

*The Work Product Rule*

The work product doctrine was acknowledged in a 1947 case, *Hickman v. Taylor*, 329 U.S. 495. The doctrine was codified in Federal Rule of Civil Procedure Rule 26(b)(3), which is the model for the work product rule in many states.

In *Hickman*, the Supreme Court created a qualified immunity from discovery for a lawyer's trial preparation. In this opinion, *mental impressions* -- the attorney's ideas on how to conduct the case in strategy and theory, including legal research -- were covered by an unqualified privilege. *Informational material* -- factual research material -- was covered by a qualified privilege.

If the opposition finds such informational material essential to its case and does not have an effective substitute, it may obtain the material by court order. However, the work of paralegals in preparing litigated matters is protected by the work product rule.

The life of the work product rule varies from jurisdiction to jurisdiction. The client may also waive such protection by actual or implied consent.

*Confidentiality with Technology*

> A paralegal shall preserve all confidential information provided by the client or acquired from other sources before, during and after the course of the professional relationship.
>
> *EC-1.5, NFPA Model Code of Ethics and Professional Responsibility and Guidelines for Enforcement.*

> A lawyer may transmit information relating to the representation of a client by unencrypted e-mail sent over the Internet without violating the Model Rules of Professional Conduct (1998) because the mode of transmission affords a reasonable expectation of privacy from a technological and legal standpoint. The same privacy accorded U.S. and commercial mail, landline telephonic transmissions, and facsimiles applies to Internet e-mail. A lawyer should consult with the client and follow [his or] her instructions, however, as to the mode of transmitting highly sensitive information relating to the client's representation.
>
> *ABA Standing Committee on Ethics and Professional Responsibility Formal Opinion No. 99-413, March 10, 1999.*[10]

[10] See: https://www.americanbar.org/news/abanews/publications/youraba/2017/june-2017/aba-formal-opinion-477r--securing-communication-of-protected-cli/?login (last accessed August 10, 2025)

Cellular Phones and Faxes

Computer-generated information must be protected in the same manner and to the same degree as hard copy files and verbal exchanges. There are special risks concerning computers and faxes with respect to confidentiality.

When you speak to a client using a cellular or cordless phone, the client should be advised that the communication may be overheard and is more easily intercepted, so sensitive information should not be discussed. For those same reasons, do not use cellular or cordless phones to pick up your voice mail.

When faxing confidential documents, special care should be taken to be certain an appropriate person is at the receiving end. Privileged communications should be clearly and obviously marked as such with a warning to others not to read. You and those you supervise must guard against misdirected faxes.

Computers and Cyberspace

Care should be taken in using computers to protect confidential information stored on them. Appropriate passwords are needed. Deletion and back-up software must be used. Screens should be covered so that passers-by cannot see what is on them. Laptops should have special protection in case they are stolen.

Communication with a client via computer may result in waiver of the attorney-client privilege. If you transmit confidential information to a client via e-mail and the client has given (intentionally or inadvertently) a large number of people access to that e-mail, it is likely that the confidential information will be deemed to have lost its privileged status immediately upon arrival at the client's insecure installation.

If the client is an individual (contrasted with a client that is a business entity, such as a corporation or partnership) and only he/she can access his/her e-mail, the privileged character of the transmission is protected. However, no one, unfortunately, can guarantee protection against a skilled and determined hacker.

Before sending confidential or privileged information by e-mail, it is advisable to ask the client what security provisions have been made on the client's end. Also, be sure to obtain the client's express consent to use e-mail as a means of communication.

In a recent ABA opinion, Formal Opinion 477 , (updating Formal Opinion 99-413, issued in 1999), reflects changes in the electronic communication as well as the 2012 changes to the ABA's Model Rules of Professional Conduct, focusing on the duty of technology competence in Model Rule 1.1 and changes to Rule 1.6 regarding client confidences:

> However, cyber-threats and the proliferation of electronic communications devices have changed the landscape and it is not always reasonable to rely on the use of unencrypted email. For example, electronic communication through certain mobile applications or on message boards or via unsecured networks may lack the basic expectation of privacy afforded to email communications.

> Therefore, lawyers must, on a case-by-case basis, constantly analyze how they communicate electronically about client matters, applying the [above] factors to determine what effort is reasonable.[11]

For the purposes of e-mail and listserv communications, confidential information includes a client's or party's name or other information relating to a client or the client's legal matter that could, in any way, identify the client or the matter.

Another important consideration with respect to paralegal cyber communication is preserving client confidences and secrets. Federal communications laws have been applied concerning interstate commerce via electronic transmission through cyberspace.

Conversely, as noted in the Wiretap Act and amended by the Electronic Communications Privacy Act, 18 U.S.C.A. §§ 2510 *et seq.* (1988), reading, intercepting and/or disclosing electronic mail messages, exchanged over public e-mail systems by anyone other than the sender and receiver, is a felony. The attorney-client privilege is preserved under this federal law, which provides that no otherwise privileged wire, oral or electronic communication intercepted in accordance with, or in violation of, the provisions of this chapter shall lose its privileged character.

Proper security measures should be evaluated by any legal professional to ensure that e-mail messages are not intercepted, altered or otherwise misused. One well-accepted form of security is encryption; however, there is no evidence that it will secure all Internet communications.[12]

In an effort to preserve the confidential nature of electronic communications by adding a disclaimer on client e-mail communications is it is highly recommended that a disclaimer be added to client email when appropriate, such as:

> E-mail communication on the Internet may NOT be secure. There is a risk that this confidential communication may be intercepted illegally. There may also be a risk of waiving the attorney-client and/or work-product privileges that may attach to this communication. DO NOT forward this message to any third party. If you have any questions regarding this notice, please contact the sender.

But be wary of blanket disclaimers that dilute the efficacy of a disclaimer.

> DO NOT read, copy or disseminate this communication unless you are the intended addressee. This e-mail communication contains confidential and privileged information intended only for the addressee. If you have received this communication in error, please call us (collect) immediately at [inset phone number] and speak to the sender of the communication. Also, please notify

---

[11] See Ethics: Email Communications with Clients 4/17/13 https://www.americanbar.org/publications/law_practice_magazine/2013/january-february/ethics/ABA Formal Opinion 477R Securing Communication of Protected Client Information Revised 5/22/17 https://www.americanbar.org/news/abanews/publications/youraba/2017/june-2017/aba-formal-opinion-477r--securing-communication-of-protected-cli/?login (last accessed August 10, 2025)

[12] ABA Formal Opinion 477R Securing Communication of Protected Client Information Revised 5/22/17 https://www.americanbar.org/news/abanews/publications/youraba/2017/june-2017/aba-formal-opinion-477r--securing-communication-of-protected-cli/?login (last accessed August 10, 2025)

immediately via e-mail the sender that you have received the communication in error.

Additionally, most states consider attorney websites as advertising and require a disclaimer stating such. See § 6157(c) of the California Business and Professions Code and "communication" as defined by Rule 1-400(A) of the California Rules of Professional Conduct.[13]

As a result of these potential risks, legal professionals should take appropriate steps to ensure internal security within a law office or legal department with respect to access to computer terminals and passwords, etc. Legal professionals should also establish procedures and/or policies to ensure that confidentiality is protected in public or quasi-public posts.

*Confidentiality Agreements*

Confidentiality agreements are intended to protect against disclosure of protected information. The well-drafted confidentiality agreement requires the signer not to disclose such information and to make all efforts to prevent others from disclosing such information. Many firms now require all employees, contractors, and vendors to sign written agreements in which they agree not to reveal any confidential information about a client or to misuse such information.

It is not unusual for vendors to be asked to sign such agreements. You may be charged with evaluating and selecting vendors to provide the most cost-effective services for a client. The same ethical considerations that apply to you must apply to a vendor and its employees, with particular stress on the confidential nature of documents in a large document case. A large number of documents does not mean any one of them is less confidential or privileged.

The ethical vendor or independent contractor should not object to signing a confidentiality agreement. Paralegals working as independent contractors, including those identified as virtual or freelance paralegals should include confidentiality and work product clauses in the engagement letter he/she presents to a client.

### *80.05 Protecting Client Confidentiality When Creating Standard Forms or Using Prior Research.*

When using a document prepared for a particular client as a template, check multiple times to ascertain that all references to the original client and matter have been expunged from the draft document. When redacting a document, use the same thoroughness to make sure all confidential or identifying references have been marked out. Many legal professionals avail themselves with redaction tools within office software to redact confidential text. Once redacted, the documents are then "flattened" and the references are scrubbed when the metadata is wiped from the document, protecting not only the seen data but the hidden data of the document.

### *80.06 Document Retention Policies.*

Confidential papers, materials, and documents that are being destroyed should be shredded or otherwise properly disposed of. This is also applicable to electronic files. You should ascertain your employer's policy with respect to closing out client files. The integrity of the files must be

[13] See also: Advertising in a Digital Age: The Do's and Don'ts of Attorney Websites 3/26/18 https://www.njlawconnect.com/wp-content/uploads/2018/03/NJ-Attorney-Website-Advertising-Rules.pdf (last accessed August 10, 2025)

maintained. An index, or some other record, must be made prior to sending the file to storage or purging materials. Original documents must not be destroyed. Clients should be contacted to see if they want to take possession or make other arrangements for retention of the documents. In any event, confidential information must remain confidential through the storage and dismantling of any records.

### *80.07 Specific Ethics for Paralegals.*

<u>Disclosing Your Status as a Paralegal</u>

> A lawyer may identify paralegals by name and title on the lawyer's letterhead and on business cards identifying the lawyer's firm.
>
> *Guideline 5, ABA Model Guidelines for the Utilization of Paralegal Services.*
>
> A paralegal's title shall clearly indicate the individual's status and shall be disclosed in all business and professional communications to avoid misunderstandings and misconceptions about the paralegal's role and responsibilities.
>
> *EC-1.7 (a), NFPA Model Code of Ethics and Professional Responsibility and Guidelines for Enforcement.*
>
> A paralegal's title shall be included if the paralegal's name appears on business cards, letterhead, brochures, directories and advertisements.
>
> *EC-1.7(b), NFPA Model Code of Ethics and Professional Responsibility and Guidelines for Enforcement.*
>
> A paralegal shall comply with the applicable legal authority governing the unauthorized practice of law in the jurisdiction in which the paralegal practices.
>
> *EC-1.8 (a), NFPA Model Code of Ethics and Professional Responsibility and Guidelines for Enforcement.*
>
> A lawyer is responsible for taking reasonable measures to ensure that clients, courts, and other lawyers are aware that a paralegal, whose services are utilized by the lawyer in performing services, is not licensed to practice law.
>
> *Guideline 4, ABA Model Guidelines for the Utilization of Paralegal Services.*
>
> Disclosure of a paralegal's status as a nonlawyer extends to verbal communications (telephone conversations and in-person contacts) as well as written communications (original documents, letters, memoranda, e-mail and faxes). Appropriate titles should be used to reflect the paralegal's status.
>
> Avoid use of the term "my client," as such phrase suggests you are personally representing the client. "Our firm's client" makes it clear that the representation rests with attorneys.

Disclosure applies to all parties you encounter in the course of the firm's representation. This includes the staff of public agencies and records custodians.

*Avoiding Unauthorized Practice of Law (UPL)*

General Background Concerning UPL

A paralegal shall comply with the applicable legal authority governing the unauthorized practice of law in the jurisdiction in which the paralegal practices.

*EC-1.8 (a), NFPA Model Code of Ethics and Professional Responsibility and Guidelines for Enforcement.*

A lawyer may not delegate to a paralegal:

(1) Responsibility for establishing an attorney-client relationship.

(2) Responsibility for establishing the amount of a fee to be charged for a legal service.

(3) Responsibility for a legal opinion rendered to a client.

Guideline 3, ABA Model Guidelines for the Utilization of Paralegal Services.

A paralegal shall not engage in the unauthorized practice of law.

EC-1.8, NFPA Model Code of Ethics and Professional Responsibility and Guidelines for Enforcement.

You are only authorized to perform functions permitted under law that are not in violation of the unauthorized practice of law statutes within the applicable jurisdiction. You are expressly prohibited from providing legal advice. *(Discussed in further detail below.)*

Not Giving Legal Advice

You must distinguish between relaying legal advice from an attorney and giving (or originating) legal advice. The former is accepted as a client service. The latter is the unauthorized practice of law. Even when you know the information you would give is correct, the actual advice must come from the attorney as a direct, or substantively accurate, quote to be transmitted to the client by the nonlawyer without embellishments or additions.

No Accepting Cases or Setting Fees

> A lawyer may not delegate to a paralegal:
>
> (a) Responsibility for establishing an attorney-client relationship.
>
> (b) Responsibility for establishing the amount of a fee to be charged for a legal service…
>
> Guideline 3, ABA Model Guidelines for the Utilization of Paralegal Services.

Adding to the dilemma are the social ethics of paralegals communicating through social media.[14]

Rules Against Solicitation of Clients

> A lawyer can neither split legal fees with a paralegal nor pay a paralegal for the referral of legal business. A lawyer may compensate a paralegal based on the quantity and quality of the paralegal's work and the value of that work to a law practice, but the paralegal's compensation may not be contingent, by advance agreement, upon the outcome of a particular case or class of cases.
>
> *Guideline 9, ABA Model Rules for the Utilization of Paralegal Services.*

Direct in-person or telephonic solicitation of clients is prohibited by ethics rules in all jurisdictions. Lawyers cannot use agents, such as paralegals, to make solicitations.

Requirement for an Appropriate Level of Attorney Supervision

> A lawyer is responsible for all of the professional actions of a paralegal performing services at the lawyer's direction and should take reasonable measures to ensure that the paralegal's conduct is consistent with the lawyer's obligations under the rule of professional conduct of the jurisdiction in which the lawyer practices.
>
> *Guideline 1, ABA Model Guidelines for the Utilization of Paralegal Services.*

Be certain that the attorney is reviewing your work. If you have any reason to believe your work product is not being reviewed, it is your duty to report this breach to a supervisor according to the office policy (*e.g.*, paralegal/office manager or managing

[14] See NFPA Informal Ethics and Disciplinary Opinion No. 16-1 What are the general ethical duties of a paralegal when communicating via social media? https://www.paralegals.org/page/positions-issues-ethics (last accessed August 10, 2025)

partner). Again, non traditional or freelance paralegals must be even more vigilant against an attorney not reviewing their work.

The Paralegal as a Supervisor/Colleague of Others

The paralegal that is in a supervisory position bears a double responsibility. Besides keeping watch on his/her own ethical conduct, he/she may be consulted by individuals being supervised. Even when there is no occasion to consult, the conduct and appearance of the supervisor clearly influences the conduct and appearance of those being supervised.

Be alert to potential problems in your colleagues and those whom you supervise. Substance abuse, for example, and personal and financial problems are potentially dangerous in the legal workplace. Warning signs may include:

- Not managing one's workload;
- Emotional outbursts;
- Unexplained disappearances without telling others;
- Irregular attendance or tardiness; or
- Evidence of financial difficulties, such as repeatedly asking for advances in salary.

Excessive devotion to political or religious causes may interfere with a paralegal's wholehearted contribution to the case.

Obligations to Work Competently and Promptly

> A paralegal shall perform all assignments promptly and efficiently.
>
> *EC-1.1 (c), NFPA Model Code of Ethics and Professional Responsibility and Guidelines for Enforcement.*

You have an ethical commitment to meet deadlines. It is wise to maintain a personal tickler system in addition to any maintained by your firm. Such system may be in a notebook, on a computer, on loose cards or on a large calendar -- you will develop your own method. Using a six-week calendar rather than a monthly calendar will prevent a nasty surprise when a deadline appears on the first or second day of a month.

You must not accept assignments when you know you do not have time to fulfill the assignment in a competent manner. Use time management techniques to maintain an acceptable workflow, particularly if you receive assignments from more than one attorney. Learning to say "no" -- or, better, "I want to help, but adjustments must be made" -- is an ethical obligation as much as doing the work competently. Silently accepting too much work hampers your effectiveness and may harm the clients involved.

Be alert to assignments given without adequate instruction. Proceeding without proper instruction raises the possibility of violating the client's trust in a number of ways: erroneous work product, wasted time and billing wasted time to the client.

Contact with Parties and Witnesses

> A paralegal shall not communicate, or cause another to communicate, with a party the paralegal knows to be represented by a lawyer in a pending matter without the prior consent of the lawyer representing such other party.
>
> *EC-1.2 (b), NFPA Model Code of Ethics and Professional Responsibility and Guidelines for Enforcement.*

If counsel represents a party, you are obligated to deal with that counsel and must not contact or communicate with the party directly. If the party contacts you directly, you may not speak with him/her without clearing this with the party's attorney.

You must not mislead unrepresented parties. Not only are unrepresented parties acting without the advice of counsel, but they may be less sophisticated or less informed about the matter than represented parties. You should be certain that they understand that your employer does not represent them and that you cannot assist them.

Communications with the Court and Jurors

> A paralegal shall not engage in any *ex parte* communications involving the courts or any other adjudicatory body in an attempt to exert undue influence or to obtain advantage for the benefit of only one party.
>
> *EC-1.2 (a), NFPA Model Code of Ethics and Professional Responsibility and Guidelines for Enforcement.*
>
> A paralegal shall advise the proper authority of non-confidential knowledge of any dishonest or fraudulent acts by any person pertaining to the handling of the funds, securities or other assets of a client. The authority to which the report is made shall depend on the nature and circumstances of the possible misconduct, (*e.g.*, ethics committees of law firms, corporations and/or paralegal associations, local or state bar associations, local prosecutors, administrative agencies, etc.). Failure to report such knowledge is in itself misconduct and shall be treated as such under these rules.
>
> *EC-1.2 (f), NFPA Model Code of Ethics and Professional Responsibility and Guidelines for Enforcement.*
>
> A paralegal shall refrain from engaging in any conduct that offends the dignity and decorum of proceedings before a court or other adjudicatory body and shall be respectful of all rules and procedures.
>
> *EC-1.3 (a), NFPA Model Code of Ethics and Professional Responsibility and Guidelines for Enforcement.*

*Ex parte* denotes actions or communications conducted at the insistence and for the benefit of one party only, and without notice to, or contestation by, any person adversely interested. *Ex parte communications* with judges and jurors are prohibited.

<u>Candor and Honesty in Dealing with Binding and/or Relevant Authority</u>

A paralegal shall be aware of and abide by all legal authority governing confidential information in the jurisdiction in which the paralegal practices.

*EC-1.5 (a), NFPA Model Code of Ethics and Professional Responsibility and Guidelines for Enforcement.*

When you draft documents to be filed with the court, include all the relevant cases and not just cases favorable to your client. Binding and/or relevant authority must be included and, if it does not support your position, should be distinguished.

<u>Improving the Delivery of Legal Services</u>

A lawyer who employs a paralegal should facilitate the paralegal's participation in appropriate continuing education and *pro bono publico* activities.

*Guideline 10, ABA Model Guidelines for the Utilization of Paralegal Services.*

A paralegal shall serve the public interest by contributing to the improvement of the legal system and delivery of quality legal services, including *pro bono publico* services and community service.

*EC-1.4, NFPA Model Code of Ethics and Professional Responsibility and Guidelines for Enforcement.*

A paralegal shall be sensitive to the legal needs of the public and shall promote the development and implementation of programs that address those needs.

*EC-1.4 (a), NFPA Model Code of Ethics and Professional Responsibility and Guidelines for Enforcement.*

A paralegal shall support efforts to improve the legal system and access thereto and shall assist in making changes.

*EC-1.4 (b), NFPA Model Code of Ethics and Professional Responsibility and Guidelines for Enforcement.*

A paralegal shall support and participate in the delivery of *pro bono publico* services directed toward implementing and improving access to justice, the law, the legal system or the paralegal and legal professions.

*EC-1.4 (c), NFPA Model Code of Ethics and Professional Responsibility and Guidelines for Enforcement.*

A paralegal should aspire annually to contribute twenty-four (24) hours of *pro bono publico* services under the supervision of an attorney or as authorized by administrative, statutory or court authority to:

1. persons of limited means;

2. charitable, religious, civic, community, governmental and educational organizations in matters that are designed primarily to address the legal needs of persons with limited means; or

3. individuals, groups or organizations seeking to secure or protect civil rights, civil liberties or public rights.

The twenty-four (24) hours of *pro bono publico* services contributed annually by a paralegal may consist of such services as detailed in this EC-1.4 (d), and/or administrative matters designed to develop and implement the attainment of this aspiration as detailed above in EC-1.4 (a), (b), (c), or any combination of the three. EC-1.4 (d), NFPA Model Code of Ethics and Professional Responsibility and Guidelines for Enforcement.

A paralegal should aspire to contribute twenty-four (24) hours of Community Service on an annual basis. For purposes of this EC, "Community Service" shall be defined as: volunteer activities that have the effect of providing a valuable service or benefit to a local community, as distinguished from those services which fall within the traditional definition of *pro bono publico*. By way of example and not limitation, several examples of Community Service may include, working with Habitat for Humanity, volunteering with local women's shelters, volunteering for hurricane relief, serving meals at local soup kitchens or local homeless shelters. EC-1.4 (e), NFPA Model Code of Ethics and Professional Responsibility and Guidelines for Enforcement.

Staying Current in Your Area

A paralegal shall achieve and maintain a high level of competence.

*EC-1.1, NFPA Model Code of Ethics and Professional Responsibility and Guidelines for Enforcement.*

Ethics CLEs should be sought out and attended frequently as a pillar of paralegal competence. The paralegal is obligated to stay current in your field whether or not your efforts are funded by your employer. There are many ways to accomplish this. For example, take advantage of *advance sheet* services to which your employer subscribes. Read recent cases published in law-related periodicals. Subscribe to legal and paralegal periodicals, and utilize other sources of continuing legal education (CLE), such as:

- Meetings of and seminars offered by paralegal associations;
- Seminars offered by bar associations;
- Printed materials;
- Videotaped materials;
- Audiotaped materials;
- Internet or other computer-assisted materials; and
- In-house study with colleagues.

In addition, you should stay alert to developments in ethics through:

- Rules of professional conduct for lawyers in your jurisdiction;
- Your paralegal association's rules and codes;
- Any guidelines for utilization of paralegal services or ethics opinions adopted by a bar association or other entity in your jurisdiction;
- Ethics opinions of bar associations;
- Court cases dealing with paralegals; and
- Non-binding opinions offered by NFPA's Ethics Board.

***80.08 Billing and Compensation.***

*Ethics Issues Involving Financial Matters*

A lawyer may include a charge for the work performed by a paralegal in setting a charge and or billing for legal services.

*Guideline 8, ABA Model Guidelines for the Utilization of Paralegal Services.*

A paralegal shall ensure that all timekeeping and billing records prepared by the paralegal are thorough, accurate, honest and complete.

*EC-1.2 (c), NFPA Model Code of Ethics and Professional Responsibility and Guidelines for Enforcement.*

*Billing*

You must accurately account for your time. Best practices include: keeping daily time records, not relying on memory, inputting time as soon as you complete a task, using timers for each individual task, etc. Clients should not have to pay for unproductive time. Billing clients for work not performed is fraud. With heavy billable hour requirements in some firms, caution should be taken to resist any temptation to pad time.

If an employer bills a paralegal's time as an attorney's, the firm has committed fraud. If you become aware of such a practice, immediately bring the practice to the attention of management.

You may not bill your time for any tasks that only an attorney may perform. You may not bill for clerical tasks that do not require substantive legal knowledge, work experience or special training. You may not bill for any tasks not related to a client's matter.

You may encounter billing issues when working on two projects at one time. For example: you may be traveling for one client's case and working on another client's case. Or, you may be directed to monitor a document production. Instead of sitting idly, you work on another client's matter during that time. To bill in these situations, calculate the amount of time spent on the second client's matter and deduct it from the time spent traveling or in the document production. Do not double-bill for time.

<u>*Paralegal Time in Statutory Fee Awards*</u>

> A lawyer may include a charge for the work performed by a paralegal in setting a charge and/or billing for legal services.
>
> *Guideline 8, ABA Model Guidelines for the Utilization of Paralegal Services.*

Utilizing paralegals reduces the cost of legal services. *Missouri v. Jenkins*, 491 U.S. 274 (1989), held that: "[t]he effect of combining market rate charge for the services of lawyers and legal assistant should, in most instances, result in a lower total cost for the legal service than if the lawyer had performed the service alone."

This ruling allowed the paralegal's time to be billed at market rate rather than just the cost to the attorney. An attorney always has an ethical obligation to set a reasonable fee.

*Taylor v. Chubb*, 874 P.2d 806 (Okla. 1994) affirmed the *Missouri* decision and further clarified that paralegal time is included in the term "attorney's fees."

<u>*Compensation in the Form of Bonuses*</u>

> A lawyer may not split legal fees with a paralegal nor pay a paralegal for the referral of legal business. A lawyer may compensate a paralegal based on the quantity and quality of the paralegal's work and the value of that work to a law practice, but the paralegal's compensation may not be contingent, by advance agreement, upon the outcome of a particular case or class of cases.
>
> *Guideline 9, ABA Model Guidelines for the Utilization of Paralegal Services.*

Law firms may pay bonuses based on firm profitability, but may not tie compensation to a particular case. A paralegal must never be compensated for bringing in business to either their firm or any other.

*Handling Client Funds and Trust Accounts*

> A paralegal shall be scrupulous, thorough and honest in the identification and maintenance of all funds, securities and other assets of a client and shall provide accurate accounting as appropriate.
>
> *EC-1.2 (e), NFPA Model Code of Ethics and Professional Responsibility and Guidelines for Enforcement.*

> A paralegal shall advise the proper authority of non-confidential knowledge of any dishonest or fraudulent acts by any person pertaining to the handling of the funds, securities or other assets of a client. The authority to which the report is made shall depend on the nature and circumstances of the possible misconduct, (*e.g.*, ethics committees of law firms, corporations and/or paralegal associations, local or state bar associations, local prosecutors, administrative agencies, etc.). Failure to report such knowledge is in itself misconduct and shall be treated as such under these rules.
>
> *EC-1.2 (f), NFPA Model Code of Ethics and Professional Responsibility and Guidelines for Enforcement.*

Law firms must have at least two separate bank accounts. One is the operating account for the general expenses of the firm's business, such as payroll and utility bills. The other is a client trust account that is set up to hold funds that the law firm receives on behalf of clients from advanced fees, the settlement of a lawsuit, real estate sale or similar matter. Funds from these two accounts should remain entirely separate. Funds from the client trust account must not be used by the firm, nor may client trust funds be commingled with the firm's funds. Settlement funds that belong to clients must be disbursed to clients promptly. Only a lawyer can sign a client trust account check.

# 90.00 FAMILY LAW

## *90.01 Introduction.*

Although the practice of Family Law is state specific and the laws and procedures will vary from state to state, it is useful to be familiar with some basic concepts that are generally applicable. Additionally, the terms "family law" or "domestic relations" encompass more than divorce; they generally include such things as adoption, custody, visitation, spousal and child support and the division of marital assets and debts.

## *90.02 Divorce (Dissolution of Marriage).*

Issues in any of the areas mentioned above can be, and the majority is, resolved amicably between the parties either by themselves or with the help of an attorney. Sometimes parties will use the services of a trained mediator to assist them in reaching an agreement. The agreement is then presented to a court or appropriate jurisdiction for review and entry as an order. Approval by the court is almost automatic, so long as the agreement contains any statutorily required language and seems to meet minimal standards of fairness.

Each state will have its own requirements for residency or domicile; a few states have no residency requirement. Residency requirements in states that have them range from six weeks to one year; a period of six months is the most common time period. For a divorce to be granted in a state with a residency requirement, a party must have resided in the state for the requisite period of time.

The pleadings filed with the court must state the ground for divorce (or dissolution of marriage). A divorce may be based on no-fault or fault grounds. All states now provide for no-fault divorces; some 32 states also offer fault-based grounds as an option. The fault-based grounds available and proof required will be state specific. In a no-fault divorce, neither party blames the other nor is there any requirement to prove guilt or fault. Some common bases for a no-fault divorce are "irreconcilable differences, "irretrievable breakdown" or "incompatibility." Using these terms, it is clear the marriage is over; however, the court and the legal documents do not assign blame. Another basis for a no-fault divorce is the parties having lived separate and apart for a specified period of time and with the intent that the separation be permanent.

In our society today, "no-fault" has replaced "fault" as the dominant basis for obtaining a divorce. A no-fault divorce is considered by most to be a more humane and realistic way to end a marriage.

In the approximately 32 states that permit divorces based on fault, the grounds will vary but generally include:

- Adultery
- Physical cruelty
- Mental cruelty
- Desertion

- Habitual drunkenness
- Use of additive drug; and/or
- Insanity.

These are only a few. In those states permitting fault divorces, the division of property or an award of spousal support (alimony) and custody may be affected by a determination of fault.

A divorce decree which is valid in the jurisdiction where it is rendered is generally valid in every other jurisdiction. Following the *doctrine of comity*, divorces rendered in foreign countries will be recognized. The full faith and credit clause of the U.S. Constitution requires each state to give full faith and credit to the judgment of another state's decree. In situations involving determinations of child custody, visitation and support of minor children, jurisdictional issues may arise if later modifications to the initial orders become necessary. Fortunately, those issues have been resolved in large part by the Uniform Reciprocal Enforcement of Support Act (URESA), which most states follow. The Act is quite specific with regard to what courts have jurisdiction over matters concerning children of divorced parties.

Should one party move out of the state where the divorce was granted and thereafter wishes to modify the decree, they must first meet the residency requirements for the new state, and thereafter register the matter in the local court having jurisdiction over dissolution matters. This generally will require a fee payable to the Court for the clerical time involved in setting up the matter within their computer system.

***90.03 Custody.***

For many years, the courts followed what was known as the *tender year's doctrine.* Under this doctrine, the mother was presumed to be the best custodial parent for young children of "tender years" (usually children not yet in their teens). In order for a father to overcome this presumption, he would have to prove that the mother was unfit or significantly less able to care for the children. States are now recognizing that custody schedules for children under the age of 3 should contain a gradual increase in possession time to accommodate the emotional well-being of the child.

The *custody determination* of minor children is unfortunately one of the most litigated areas of family law. *Custody* is the term used to describe the care, control, and education of a minor child. It applies as long as the child is a minor or is still in high school and has not yet graduated. In some areas, the term "parental rights" may be used. The age at which a child is determined to have reached the age of majority will be based on the statute in the state where the child resides. A child's residence is determined by the child's permanent dwelling and is generally the state of residence of the primary custodial parent -- it is not necessarily where the child attends school or where the noncustodial parent may live.

In the past, it was virtually a given that the mother always received custody of minor children. Fortunately, that is no longer the case. The courts now must consider a number of factors to determine which parent is best able to care for the needs of the child assuming that the parties have not been able to reach an agreement in this area.

For many years, the courts followed what was known as the *tender year's doctrine*. Under this doctrine, the mother was presumed to be the best custodial parent for young children of "tender years" (usually children not yet in their teens). In order for a father to overcome this presumption, he would have to prove that the mother was unfit or significantly less able to care for the children.

As fathers have taken an ever increasing active role in the raising of their children, and many mothers now work outside the home, many courts have struck down the tender year's doctrine in favor of a case-by-case evaluation of who will best meet the interests and needs of the child. The standard is no longer a "one size fits all" approach.

Under this approach, it is not necessary for one parent to prove the other unfit; although, in some cases, the evidence may establish this. The courts look at what will be in the best interests of the child. As with any divorce, even those that are relatively amicable, it is extremely difficult for children of all ages, so the courts look at several areas that affect the child's life and their particular needs. The court then looks at the environment each parent will be able to offer the child. The environment that is most compatible with the child's needs is the one that is deemed to be in the child's best interests. Therefore, it is possible that both parents may offer a suitable environment, but the one that is *best* able to meet the needs of the child is the parent who will prevail. Some of the factors the court considers when making this determination may include, but are not necessarily limited to, the following:

- The ability of a parent to care for a child without extensive child-care services;
- The religion of the parent;
- The ability of a parent to attend to any special needs of the child due to the child's young age or any disability;
- Immoral conduct, such as drugs or alcohol problems, that would have a <u>direct</u> effect on the child (otherwise this is irrelevant);
- The ability to provide continuity to the child's current environment such as home, school and friends; and
- The ability to have continuing contact with members of the child's extended family.

None of these factors are individually controlling, and the court will consider factors unique to each situation when making their determination.

### *90.04 Property Division.*

Property settlement is dependent upon each individual state law. Marital property to be divided is either considered separate property or community property. Some states are separate property states, while others are community property states. You need to check with your own state's code to determine how marital property should be properly divided. For purposes of PACE, the following is a brief summary of separate property and community property.

In *separate property* states, the position is that all property individually owned prior to the marriage is individual property and not jointly owned marital property. Additionally, property acquired during the marriage through gift, inheritance or personal earnings, without contribution by the other spouse, is separate property. Divorcing parties are awarded their separate property respectively, and the court will determine how their marital property should be divided. In an absolute application of the separate property theory, a non-employed spouse might be entitled to virtually nothing at the conclusion of the divorce. As this outcome is not fair given each spouse's contribution to the marital relationship, many courts have modified the rule to result in a more equitable application. The courts have a duty to equitably distribute the marital property obtained during the marriage. Property may have been purchased solely with the earnings of one spouse, such as the marital home. However, if the other spouse cared for the home and otherwise supported and enabled the first spouse to earn the money to purchase the property, such property is considered the result of a joint effort and the court can fairly consider such property to be marital and divide it equally.

In *community property* states, a different approach is taken to the disposition of the property between spouses. Property acquired during the marriage through personal earnings is presumed to be community property. Also included is any property individually owned before the marriage that a party contributes to during the marriage, such as a bank account. If a spouse is able to establish that certain property was never commingled or otherwise shared with the other spouse as community property, then such property is not treated as community property in some states. However, in other states, even if the property is not commingled or otherwise shared, the court will consider any increase in value of the property during the marriage as a marital asset. Once a court has determined whether any separate property exists, it will then proceed to make a fairly equal division of the community property. For a court to make a significantly unbalanced distribution of the parties' assets, the circumstances must be rather compelling.

Another marital asset may be a pension or employee benefit program. If a spouse was employed and received an interest in a pension or benefit plan during the marriage, under either type of property state, the other spouse may have a claim to a portion of the amount to be received under the plan.

In order to distribute pension and retirement funds in a way that will be recognized by the Internal Revenue Service, a *Qualified Domestic Relations Order* (QDRO) must be issued, in addition to other documents such as a property settlement agreement and Final Decree of Divorce or Judgment of Dissolution of Marriage. The QDRO details the rights and obligations of the parties with respect to these matters. It should also be noted that many pension or benefit plans will gladly provide a template of their preferred language in order for the QDRO to be acceptable and implemented.

Parties who want to be divorced, but who cannot agree on the division of property, can still obtain a divorce in most jurisdictions. A petition must be filed to request a *bifurcation* of the divorce, whereby a divorce decree is entered, but the division of assets is tabled for an indefinite period of time. The doctrine of *divisible divorce* allows for a court in one jurisdiction to issue a decree while property located in another jurisdiction is divided there.

### *90.05 Division of Debt.*

The court may also be required to determine marital debt. The same tests used in determining the classification of property are also used to determine if debts are separate or community property. Likewise, the court will try to make an equitable distribution for responsibility of the parties' debt.

Marital debts, however, have an additional aspect that property generally does not -- the claims of third parties. While the divorcing parties may agree, or a court may determine, that certain debt belongs to an individual, problems with claims from third parties may arise. For example, when property is purchased with a joint credit card during the marriage, it is presumed that the property is jointly owned. If one spouse is assigned the debt in the property settlement agreement and fails to make payments on the debt, the third party can claim and collect the debt from the other spouse. While this may seem unfair, it should be remembered that the third party creditor is not bound by any court order as to who would bear the responsibility of the debt. Therefore, it is very important that all decrees contain a provision that entitles a spouse to collect reimbursement if he/she pays a debt that was the responsibility of the other spouse.

### *90.06 Spousal Support.*

For many reasons, the award of spousal support (formerly called alimony in some states – in others, there are separate awards for either spousal support or alimony) is becoming less of a guarantee. Previously, under a pure application of separate property, a wife often did not receive significant marital assets and needed support, at least for some period, in order to resume her life. All states now (whether they are community property or separate property states) attempt to provide a more equitable distribution. Women are more active in the work force than in the past. They have greater opportunities to become self-sufficient. The goal of the courts today is to give a spouse sufficient time and resources to prepare for financial independence. This means that the spouse required to pay support (and it's not always the husband) is not burdened with lifetime support of a former spouse. Likewise, the former spouse is not suddenly faced with lacking minimal resources to provide basic needs such as food and shelter.

The amount and duration of support are generally left to the discretion of the court. The court will consider such factors as the earning capacity and reasonable needs of the parties. If the age and educational level of a former spouse preclude their earning a sufficient income to support their basic needs, permanent support *may* be ordered. A modification of the support may be appropriate if significant changes in the circumstances of either party occur during the period of time for which support was ordered.

### *90.07 Child Support.*

While the obligation to provide support to a spouse may end when the divorce is finalized, the obligation for support of the children of a marriage continues for as long as the court determines is necessary. This is usually until the child reaches the age of majority as determined by the statutes in the child's state of residence or until high school graduation, or until the child is otherwise emancipated. The parties may reach an agreement as to the amount of support to be paid to the custodial parent. If they cannot agree, a hearing will be held to determine the financial needs of the child and the financial ability of the noncustodial parent to contribute to the needs of the child.

The court considers many independent factors that influence the amount of support it will ultimately order. Many states have established guidelines that provide formulas for calculating child support. Software has been developed to help the attorneys and courts determine the proper support figure. Some factors the court may consider include:

- The number of children from this marriage the parent is obligated to support;
- The number of children from other relationships the parent is obligated to support;
- Whether one of the parents provides health insurance for the child;
- The net income of each parent; and
- Any special medical or educational needs of the child.

While guidelines for child support have been adopted by most states, the courts are typically given leeway to override them in cases involving special considerations. For example, if a parent lives out of state, the court may consider costs of travel for visitation; or, may have one parent be financially responsible for the child's extracurricular activities, such as sports or dance.

Enforcing payment of child support when a noncustodial parent failed to pay the ordered support used to be particularly difficult when the noncustodial parent lived in another state. However, all states have now adopted the *Uniform Reciprocal Enforcement of Support Act* (URESA), which is a pact among the states to assist one another in enforcing support orders. An action may be filed in the state where the dependent resides. The Act provides that a public prosecutor in the state where the noncustodial parent resides may try the case there and enforce any orders of support or contempt. The noncustodial parent may no longer avoid support simply by moving beyond the jurisdictional and financial reach of the custodial parent.

### *90.08 Joint Custody.*

This is another area which has evolved over the years. Typically, in the past, one parent was awarded custody, which meant that parent had the primary responsibility for the care, control and education of the child. The noncustodial parent has visitation rights, but no *legal* right to take an active role in the decisions regarding the raising of the child.

Because this limitation was not acceptable to many parents and the evolving belief of the courts that children benefit from the active involvement of *both* parents, the concept of joint custody developed. It is a common misconception that joint custody involves only shared physical custody. While this can sometimes be the case in joint custody, it is not the primary purpose. Joint custody gives each parent the right to take an active, participative role in decision making regarding the raising of their child. Most states have enacted laws permitting the courts to award joint custody; leaving it to the discretion of the judges to determine on a case-by-case basis whether joint custody is appropriate or whether the best interests of the child would be best served by an award of individual custody to one parent.

With the increasing mobility of our society, the issue of court jurisdiction is becoming a more common issue. Parents now frequently live in different states. This means that enforcing a custody order can become a costly and time-consuming battle for parents who don't agree. To address this issue, the *Uniform Child Custody Jurisdiction Act* (UCCJA) was adopted. The UCCJA establishes guidelines for determining jurisdiction and provides for cooperation among the states in the enforcement of custody orders. While not a total cure, this uniform law has eliminated a great many of the potential problems parents face when they reside in separate jurisdictions.

### *90.09 Ethics Reminder.*

Legal Ethics are a very important aspect of the law in domestic relations. It is fairly common for only one of the parties to retain counsel. In those situations, the lawyer has an ethical obligation to make it clear to the other party that a lawyer cannot represent both sides of a legal issue. Even if the divorce is uncontested and the parties are basically in agreement, ethically, the attorney can represent only one of the parties. The other party who elects to agree to the terms may do so without the advice or counsel of the attorney. Although in some states, the court will not approve the settlement agreement unless there is specific language stating that the non-represented spouse had a chance to seek a review of the agreement from independent counsel and declines to retain an attorney. In addition, the agreement might need to be notarized if one party does not have counsel. This requirement varies according to both state and local rules.

It is wise to write a letter to the non-represented spouse suggesting that they seek the advice of an attorney regarding the settlement agreement, making it clear that the attorney represents the other spouse and therefore, cannot represent or give any advice to the non-represented spouse. Some attorneys ask the unrepresented spouse to countersign and return a copy of such a letter so there is no legal recourse down the line if the unrepresented spouse challenges something in the agreement based on their decision not to retain counsel.

In addition to the above, Family law practice may include legal representation that focuses on familial relationships requiring legal advice to help navigate the court procedures or complex forms that must be filled out. Some examples include: domestic relations (Dom Rel), adoptions (domestic or international), surrogacy, and prenuptial and antenuptial marital agreements. These are complex legal matters where clients are emotionally invested and need trusted advocates to help guide them.

## SAMPLE QUESTIONS FOR FAMILY LAW

1. The name of the document that divides the parties' community interest in a pension plan or defined benefit is known as:

    a. Qualified Domestic Relations Order.
    b. Joinder.
    c. Marital Settlement Agreement.
    d. Antenuptial Agreement.

2. The entry of termination of marital status only and reserving all other issues for later determination is known as:

    a. Adjunction.
    b. Bifurcation.
    c. Jurisdictional.
    d. Reformation.

3. A valid divorce granted in one state and property rights settled by a court in another state is known as:

    a. Documents fileable.
    b. Void marriage.
    c. Voidable marriage.
    d. Divisible divorce.

*Answers:*

1–a. A QDRO divides the pension plan without a tax consequence. Most plans will not divide the pension in a Decree of Divorce without a separate QDRO. A joinder is used to bring the pension plan into the action as a third party claimant. Though the pension could be disposed of in the Marital Settlement Agreement or the Antenuptial Agreement, again, most plans will not accept them without a separate order bearing a judge's signature. Therefore, answer (a) is the best possible answer.

2–b. Bifurcation is an option to separate the issues in a case so that one issue or set of issues can be tried and resolved before the others. If the property division is going to take some time to resolve, the parties may bifurcate that issue from the rest and petition the court to terminate their marital status. Adjunction is a permanent attachment; jurisdictional is having to do with jurisdiction; and reformation is a procedure in which the court will correct or reform a written agreement to conform to the original intent of the parties making the deal.

3–d. The doctrine of *divisible divorce* allows an ex parte divorce to be granted in one state while another state settles property rights because the state where the property is located has proper jurisdiction to dispose of it. A void marriage is one that is not legal in nature; for example, an incestuous relationship. A voidable marriage is where the marriage is valid except for one legal component, such as the failure to file the marriage license. Documents fileable are the required documents necessary to complete the action from start to finish, such as complaint, response, financial declarations and decree or judgment dissolving the marriage.

## 100.00 INTELLECTUAL PROPERTY

### *100.01 Intellectual Property History.*

The simplest explanation of intellectual property is that it is the product of a person's mind - an idea. Intellectual property comes in three forms: patents, trademarks and copyrights. Article I, Section 8 of the United States Constitution gives us the Patent-Copyright clause, making those rights constitutionally mandated. We can thank James Madison, one of the original signers of the Constitution and later President, for championing this clause in the constitutional debate. Citizens owe Mr. Madison a large debt of gratitude for having won this argument.

The first Patent Act was passed in 1790, which was very short. Under that Act, a patent could be granted by any two, acting together, of the Secretary of State, Secretary of War or the Attorney General. That act was repealed in 1793 and replaced by another act, primarily drafted by Thomas Jefferson, then Secretary of State. The definition contained in that Act states:

> [A]ny new and useful art, machine, manufacture or composition of matter and any new and useful improvement on any art, machine, manufacture or composition of matter.

When compared with criteria from 35 U.S.C. §101, it will be noted that the Act remains virtually identical, even today. Indeed, amendments since the time of the original Act have been infrequent. The most dynamic was the codification of the Patent Law into Title 35 of the United States Code in 1952. The laws pertaining to patents are contained in 35 U.S.C. § 100, et seq.

### *100.02 Patents.*

Webster defines the term "patent" as: "an official document conferring a right or privilege", *i.e.*, Letters Patent. Letters Patent are issued by the United States Patent and Trademark Office. The criteria for things that are patentable are set forth in 35 U.S.C. §101 as:

> Whoever invents or discovers any new and useful process, machine, manufacture, or composition of matter, or any new and useful improvements thereof, may obtain a patent therefor, subject to the conditions and requirements of this title.

There are three categories of patents: [1] UTILITY, which covers useful process, machine, article of manufacture and composition of matter; [2] DESIGN, which covers the ornamental characteristics; and [3] PLANT, which covers a new variety of asexually reproduced plant. In today's world of advertising, there is much talk about "provisional patents." There are NO provisional patents -- there are "provisional applications." A provisional application can NEVER mature into an issued patent UNLESS the provisional application is converted to a full application within one year of the filing date of the provisional application. It is not uncommon for applications pertaining to business methods to be designated as "process patents," even though they fall within the general category of "utility."

*Qualifying for Patent Protection*

Before an individual files a patent application, there are certain questions that must be answered in order to determine whether or not the inventor qualifies for patent protection:

1. Under §§102(g) and 115 of 35 U.S.C., the inventor must be the original and first to invent, or co-invent, the concept, or idea, for which you wish to have patent protection.

2. According to §101 of the 35 U.S.C., the invention must be new and useful.

Section 102 further states that if the invention was known or used by others in the United States, or patented or described in some other printed publication anywhere in the world BEFORE the applicant's invention, that applicant is not entitled to patent protection. § 102 also states that if the subject of the invention was patented or described in some other printed publication, in public use or on sale more than one year prior to the filing of an application, the inventor is barred from obtaining a patent.

*Utility Applications*

Once determined that the inventor qualifies to file an application, the next step in the process is an important question to consider. Whether the inventor wishes to attempt to file the application on their own or not, it is still wise to consult with a patent lawyer. It should be understood that only the inventor or someone specially licensed to practice before the Patent Office is allowed to file a patent application. Since there are numerous special rules pertaining to the content and format of applications, as well as drawings and terms used, it is oftentimes more economical for the inventor to work with a patent lawyer.

One of the requirements of a patent application is that the applicant discloses and discusses prior art patents. Because of that requirement, most patent practitioners perform a preliminary patentability search of the prior art at the Patent Office, in the various classes and subclasses, to determine what has been done previously in the particular field of endeavor. Once those patents are obtained, the patent lawyer will compare and analyze them in conjunction with the proposed invention and give the prospective applicant an opinion as to whether or not the lawyer thinks meaningful patent protection might be available. Upon authority from the client, an application is then written, submitted to the client for review and, once approved, filed with the Patent Office.

The Patent Office has an official guide which sets out the format for applications. The Manual of Patent Examining Procedure [MPEP] provides detailed instruction on the necessary formatting required in the application. The most common parts of an application include:

- the title of the invention

- background of the invention, including the field of the invention and a discussion of the prior art

- a brief summary of the invention and its objectives

- a brief description of the various views of the drawing
- a detailed description of the invention
- claims and the Abstract of the Disclosure.

The claims and Abstract of the Disclosure must start on new pages.

There are special rules pertaining to drawings such as, various elements of the invention must be numbered on the drawings. The reference numbers are shown on the drawings when those elements are described in the detailed description of the invention. The claims must particularly point out and distinctly claim the subject matter regarded as the invention. Claims are the metes and bounds of the protection provided by a patent. The scope of the claims can be a determining factor in the granting of patent protection.

Once these items are complete, then the application is ready to be filed. The filing must include an Oath and Declaration by the inventor confirming that he/she believes they are the original and first inventor and they believe the claim does not exist anywhere else in the world. If the inventor retains the services of a patent lawyer, a Power of Attorney must submitted authorizing the patent lawyer to act on behalf of the inventor in the prosecution of the application. Finally, the application fee must accompany the application. A fee schedule may be found on the United States Patent and Trademark Office (PTO) Web site at www.uspto.gov. Note that fees on the schedule are distinguished by "large entity" and "small entity." The differences are set out in the rules, but individuals and small companies usually qualify for the "small entity" payment.

If the inventor is an employee of a corporation or other entity, it may be that the application will be assigned to that entity. In that case, an Assignment of the invention should be executed and recorded with the PTO so that that information appears in the records. There is also a filing fee for the Assignment. An Assignment should be filed with the original application, if at all possible, but may be filed at a later date.

Once the application is filed, it is reviewed to make sure the application contains all the necessary documentation. If the reviewer deems the application complete, then they issue a "Filing Receipt" showing the date of filing and the serial number assigned to the application. This receipt should be reviewed for accuracy. If the receipt contains an error, a request should be made for a correction as soon as possible. The application is then assigned to a patent examiner in the particular field of the invention who is charged with examining the application as to "patentability."

The examination can take an extended period before it "issues as a patent" because a large backlog exists at the PTO wherein the time to receive a receipt of an "Office Action" (a potential reason for a denial) is approximately two years or more. A patent examiner performs his/her own search of the prior art and then issues the Office Action, which frequently includes a denial of patentability. It is seldom that an application "issues as a patent" from the examiner without an Office Action, which may contain a rejection of the claims of application which may be based on a variety of reasons.

It should also be noted that patent applications are automatically "published," or become public, after an 18 month-period passes. If the application issues as a patent, there is a $300 "publication" fee, which must be paid. This publication can be avoided by filing a form with the original application requesting non-publication.

There are numerous bases for the possible rejection of an application and its claims. One of the most common is that the invention is "anticipated" by a prior art patent. What this means is that the examiner believes that any person of ordinary skill in the particular field would look at the prior art patent cited and the subject of the application under review and deem it "obvious" to that person at the time of the invention.

Next, the patent application is argued before the examiner in an "amendment," which would explain why the prior art patent cited does not apply to the current application. Examiners are allowed to take elements from more than one patent, combine them and then state that on that combination, the claims of the current invention are "obvious." The patent application would be argued again in another amendment, stating the reasoning against the examiner's argument. In an amendment, changes may be made to the specification and the claims, all in an effort to overcome the substance of the rejections made by the examiner.

After the arguments have been reviewed, the examiner may agree with the applicant. If so, the examiner may also suggest changes to the language of the specification and/or claims that are deemed appropriate, prior to issuance. Once the examiner decides the matter at issue is entitled to patent protection, the applicant will receive a Notice of Allowance and Fee(s) Due. This is commonly referred to as the "issue fee." At the time the issue fee is paid, the applicant can request extra copies of the patent for a per copy fee. The Notice will include the date of payment. Failure to pay the required fees will result in the patent NOT issuing, so the sooner the fees are paid, the sooner the patent issues.

Prior to issuance, another notice, the "issuance notice", providing the date of the issuance of the patent and the patent number will be provided. Soon thereafter, the original patent and any extra copies ordered will be provided.

With the approval of a patent, the government has granted a limited monopoly from the date of filing with the Patent Office, which allows the patentee to exclude others from the manufacture, use and sale of the claimed invention. [35 U.S.C. 154] Utility patents filed after June 8, 1995 have a term of 20 years from the date of filing, subject to any statutory extension.

As noted on the inside cover of the original patent, maintenance fees are due at regular intervals during the term of the patent -- 3.5 years, 7.5 years and 11.5 years. If these fees go unpaid, the patent may be deemed abandoned and the subject of the patent forever dedicated to the public. In simple language, failure to pay the maintenance fees means the applicant loses all rights in the patent. It is possible to revive an abandoned patent, but the process is arduous and expensive.

Not every application issues as a patent. If the arguments are deemed "unpersuasive" by the examiner and the application is unable to overcome the reasons for rejection, the application process is, for the most part, terminated. There are provisions for continuing the prosecution of an application whereby a new matter may be added and the application substantially revised, but there is no guarantee of success. Choosing to revise the application means the process begins anew.

*Design Applications*

Design patents protect the way an article looks. Section 171 of 35 U.S.C. states that:

> Whoever invents any new, original and ornamental design for an article of manufacture may obtain a patent therefor, subject to the conditions and requirements of this title.

Part of the criteria for "qualifying" to file a patent application is set out in Section 102, which states that if the subject of the invention was patented or described in some other printed publication, in public use or on sale more than one year prior to the filing of an application, the inventor is barred from obtaining a patent. Section 172 of 35 U.S.C. modifies that time period for design patents to six (6) months for obtaining a patent. All other factors are the same.

An ornamental design may be embodied by the entire article, a portion of the article or some ornamentation applied to the article. If the application consists of only the ornamentation applied to an article, the drawings must show the ornamentation as applied to the article.

The content of a design application is significantly different from that of a utility application. The application starts with a preamble, which sets forth the name of the inventor, title of the invention and a brief description of the nature and intended use of the article. Following that is the description of the various figures of the drawing. A design application allows for only one claim. If your article has more than one feature for which you wish to have separate and distinct protection, then each of those design features must be the subject of a separate application.

Drawings are required and must be done in accordance with PTO rules. Unlike drawings for utility applications, there are no numbers on drawings for design applications. As in utility applications, the inventor must execute an Oath and Declaration. Again, if a patent lawyer prepares and files the application, the inventor must execute a Power of Attorney authorizing the lawyer to act on the inventor's behalf in prosecuting the application.

Once the application is complete, you are ready to file with the appropriate filing fee. Also, if the application is assigned, the procedure for recording an Assignment is the same as noted previously.

As is the case in a utility application, an official Filing Receipt is sent, which sets out the date of filing and the serial number assigned to the application. The application is then assigned to a patent examiner. Because a design application covers only the ornamental characteristics, the time for prosecution of a design application is much shorter than that for a utility application. It is possible that an office action will be sent requiring correction of certain "informal" matters, such as drawing descriptions. Once the application has been approved for passage to allowance, the applicant will receive the Notice of Allowance and Fee(s) Due, which must be paid by the due date on the Notice. Since design applications are not published, there is no publication fee. Extra copies may be ordered at the time of payment of the issue fee. Just like with a utility application, an issuance notice will be issued with the date of issuance of the patent and its patent number. Afterward, the applicant will receive the original and any extra copies ordered.

With the allowance of a design patent, the government has granted a limited monopoly of 17 years [35 U.S.C. 173] from the date of issuance, which allows the patentee to exclude others from the manufacture, use and sale of the claimed invention. [35 U.S.C. 154]

*Plant Patents*

Section 161, et seq. of 35 U.S.C. pertains to plant patents and states:

> Whoever invents or discovers and asexually reproduces any distinct and new variety of plant, including cultivated sports, mutants, hybrids, and newly found seedlings, other than a tuber propagated plant or a plant found in an uncultivated state, may obtain a patent therefor, subject to the conditions and requirements of this title.

Protection is limited to a plant in its ordinary meaning:

> A living plant organism which expresses a set of characteristics determined by its single genetic makeup or genotype, which can be duplicated through asexual reproduction, but which cannot otherwise be 'made' or 'manufactured.' [USPTO publication *General Information About 35 U.S.C. 161 Plant Patents*]

The general requirements for patentability also apply to plant patents. In addition, it is also required that: the plant be invented or discovered in a cultivated area; not a plant excluded by statute; and that the plant differs from known or related plants by at least one distinguishing characteristic, which difference is not caused simply by growing conditions or fertility levels.

In preparation for a plant patent application, the new plant should be observed through at least one growth cycle and careful notes made of the observations. Failure to make these observations during the growth cycle could conceivably result in an incomplete botanical description, rendering it impossible to overcome defects in the application interposed by an examiner. At the very least, it can prolong the prosecution of an application.

As is the case in a utility application, there is a title. Also included is a variety denomination for the plant. Also included are the background of the invention, including the field of the invention, a description and discussion of the relevant prior art, followed by a summary of the invention. The summary may present the novel characteristics which set the plant apart from others in its class. This is followed by a description of the drawings.

Drawings for plant patents should be photographic and in color when color is a distinguishing feature. If foliage, bark, flowers and/or fruit are part of the distinguishing characteristics, those plant parts should be included in one or more figures of drawing. There are no numbers on the photographs unless an examiner should require them at some point during the prosecution phase.

The detailed botanical description of the plant includes the genus, species and market class; also, the parents of the claimed plant may be specified. A description of the growth habit of the plant should be described, consisting of the shape of the plant at maturity and branching habit. Winter dormancy should be completely described, if appropriate, and a complete botanical description of bark, buds, blossoms, leaves and fruit should be included. Characteristics such as fragrance, taste, disease resistance, productivity and vigor, which are not readily shown in photographs, should be included. Even if depicted, the botanical characteristics must be substantively described.

A plant patent has only one claim. The application concludes with an Abstract of the Disclosure, which is a brief description of the plant and its novel and important characteristics.

As with all other patent applications, the inventor must execute an Oath and Declaration and if filed by a patent lawyer, a Power of Attorney and a filing fee. If the application is assigned, the applicant also pays the fee for recordation of the Assignment.

After filing, the process is basically the same as with other patents -- an official Filing Receipt will be sent showing the date of filing and the serial number assigned to the application. Check it for accuracy and request a correction if necessary. The application will then be assigned to a patent examiner for examination.

Office actions may be issued requesting further information with regard to the description of the plant and its characteristics. The applicant may receive a rejection based on a prior art plant patent. If the examiner determines that the applicant has a novel and unobvious plant, the application will be allowed and passed to issuance. The applicant will then receive the Notice of Allowance and Fee(s) Due. Once the issue fee is paid and order any extra copies, a notice containing the date of issuance and patent number will be sent.

Patent coverage for a plant patent runs for a term of 20 years from the date of filing, giving you the right to exclude others from "asexually reproducing the plant, and from using, offering for sale, or selling the plant so reproduced, or any of its parts, throughout the United States, or from importing the plant so reproduced, or any parts thereof, into the United States." [35 U.S.C. 163]

### *A Patent has been Issued – Now What?*

Because a patent is considered "personal property," it can be sold, licensed, bequeathed, given away in whole or in part and can even be lost. In addition to having the right to exclude others from the manufacture, use and sale, a patentee also has the right to license or sell all or a part of his/her rights. Typically, if rights in a patent are sold, an Assignment is drawn, wherein one's rights are transferred for whatever consideration, such as a sales price, a share of sales, or anything else of value agreed upon. That Assignment should be recorded in the Patent Office.

Alternatively, a patentee may execute a license conveying all or a portion of the rights in the patent. That license may be exclusive or nonexclusive. A patentee may grant an exclusive license to manufacture, but not sell or use, and may be limited to a specific territory. A royalty is usually paid to the patentee under the terms of a license.

Special care should be taken when inventors are employees who create an invention on the employer's time and with the employer's facilities. It is possible for the employer to acquire rights in the invention, known as a "shop right." Problems may also arise when research and development is conducted by contract through an educational institution or governmental agency, which research is either directly or indirectly financed by the government. The best way to determine if this is a problem is to consult with a patent lawyer to determine patent rights.

Inventors should also be aware that in the situation of joint inventors, all inventors have equal rights in and to the patent and each inventor may license or sell all, or a portion, of the patent rights. A co-inventor does not have to have the permission from other inventors, nor is it required that other inventors be notified of such action. An appropriate agreement by and between joint inventors is an essential part of this kind of relationship.

### *100.03 Trademarks.*

Of the three types of intellectual property, trademarks are probably the most recognized, as they are found in the newspapers and magazines, on television, on radio, on billboards and at sporting events, as well as many other venues

#### *Historical Perspective*

History tells us that the marking of items as a means of identifying the source of the goods goes back for centuries. In the Middle East, stone seals have been unearthed dating back as far as 3500 B.C. History also tells us that ancient cultures such as in Egypt, Greece, the Roman Empire and China used stampings and markings to indicate the creators of certain goods.

European trade guilds used markings in the Middle Ages to indicate the maker of specific products. Bell makers and paper manufacturers were among the first to adopt the practice of marking their goods. Silversmiths in the mid-14th century were required to mark their products and did so with a stamp, usually seen on the bottom of a piece. And everyone is familiar with a watermark on high quality papers.

Thomas Jefferson pushed for trademark laws in the late 1700's. Unfortunately, that legislation was not passed until 1870 and trademark law was not codified until Congress passed the Trademark Act of 1946, embodied in the Lanham Act.

Some early U.S. marks go back more than a hundred years and were issued to John Deere, RCA Victor and the Church & Dwight Company, makers of Arm & Hammer baking soda. These marks are still valid today.

#### *What is a Trademark or Service Mark?*

The definition of a trademark is contained in §1127 of Title 15 [the Lanham Act] of the United States Code and states:

> [a] trademark includes any word, name, symbol, or device, or any combination thereof – (1) used by a person, … in commerce … to identify and distinguish his or her goods, including a unique product, from those manufactured or sold by others and to indicate the source of the goods, even if that source is unknown. [Emphasis supplied]

A service mark is the same as a trademark except that it identifies and distinguishes the source of a service rather than a product. Since the process is the same for both, understand that this section applies equally to trademarks and service marks.

Service marks, as noted above, are the same as trademarks, the difference being that instead of providing a product under the mark, a service is provided. Again, under §1127 of 15 U.S.C., the definition is:

> [a] service mark means any word, name, symbol, or device, or any combination thereof –
>
> (1) used by a person, or
>
> (2) which its owner has a bona fide intention to use in commerce
>
> and applies to register on the principal register established by this Act, to identify and distinguish the services of one person, including a unique service, from the services of others to indicate the sources of the services, even if that source is unknown.

Service marks include UPS®, FEDEX® and banks.

Ideally, a trademark consists of a word or symbol by which a business becomes recognized for its product's characteristics, such as quality, size or price, or as the source of a particular product or service and, hopefully, both. A trademark in no way protects your product from being made by others. What it does do is identify the source of the product as coming from a particular company or individual.

If a mark is only used in intrastate commerce, an applicant is entitled only to file for registration in the home state. If the mark is used in interstate commerce, then the applicant is entitled to file an application for federal registration. That application is filed with the United States Patent and Trademark Office. Only marks that are federally registered are allowed to use the designation ® with their mark.

It is the use of a mark that builds recognition, and not its registration. It is not necessary to register a mark in order for it to be enforceable, but there are definite benefits. First, registration establishes the registrant's ownership of the mark and the registrant's prima facie right to exclusive use of the mark in commerce. Further, registration places the public on notice of such rights. For these reasons, the owner of a registered mark is better able to protect and enforce his/her rights because of the respect generally accorded trademark registrations. Because of the presumption of ownership and validity achieved through registration, courts are more willing to enjoin the use by others of confusingly similar marks and to award appropriate damages.

*Recognizing the Potential*

Many people remember being little and watching kids' shows on television and recognizing characters, companies and products before being able to read.. And most children can recognize McDonald's, Burger King, Shell Oil, Coke, Pepsi, Taco Bell when driving down the road. That is called name recognition, which makes it abundantly clear just how important a trademark becomes. A trademark sets an item apart from other things; it is unique.

*How do you get a Trademark?*

A trademark is just about the easiest of the proprietary rights available to acquire. A trademark is acquired by proper use of the mark in connection with the solicitation and sale of a product or service, without causing confusion in the minds of the consuming public as to other existing marks in the same channels of commerce.

Ideally, a trademark will consist of a word or symbol, or a combination of the two, which is distinctive and will lead the consuming public to, either consciously or subconsciously, connect the mark with the product. That recognition is the essence of a trademark and is known as secondary meaning.

At first blush, it might seem that the best mark would be one that describes the product or service, or what it does. Unfortunately, such marks are not always the best marks because such marks are almost impossible to register as the Trademark Office considers them to be merely descriptive. In the parlance of IP professionals, the best possible mark, both from the standpoint of recognition and registration, is one that is both arbitrary and fanciful. Examples of these marks would be the golden arches of McDonald's (a symbol), the MGM Lion and the WB for Warner Brothers, the elk for The Hartford Insurance Company.

In order to secure a particular word, or combination of words and symbols, it is essential that the proposed mark be used in a manner which will: [1] make it clear that its use is intended to be as a trademark; and [2] that the mark is either inherently distinctive, or at a minimum, is capable of acquiring a secondary meaning as it is used. Secondary meaning is a term of art which simply means that, in addition to its ordinary meaning, a trademark will also denote, or at a minimum, suggest, the source or origin of the product or service with which it is associated.

*Federal Registrations*

Title 15 of the United States Code, and the rules and regulations relating thereto, provide for the qualification of marks that are used in interstate commerce, or are intended to be used in interstate commerce, for federal registration in the following general terms:

> In order to be registered, a mark must be capable of distinguishing the applicant's goods from those of others. [§1052]

Marks are often classified in categories of generally increasing distinctiveness; following the formulation set out by Judge Friendly, they may be: (1) generic; (2) descriptive; (3) suggestive; (4) arbitrary; or (5) fanciful. See *Abercrombie & Fitch Co. v. Hunting World, Inc.*, 537 F.2d 4, 9 (189 U.S.P.Q. 759).

Keep in mind that trademark rights, unlike most forms of protectable intellectual property, are acquired and enhanced by usage. The more familiar the public becomes with your trademark, the stronger it becomes. As is the case with patents, it is possible that a trademark search may be in order. An online search can be made of the records at the Trademark Office to determine what may have been filed and/or registered previously. Note that the Trademark Office records contain only registered marks and applications for marks. It does not contain records for marks which may be in use, but which have not been registered. To obtain that information, it is necessary to have access to a search service. A qualified trademark lawyer can assist with searches.

The actual registration of a trademark is obtained from the United States Patent and Trademark Office by the filing of an application for registration. That application must state: the name and address of the applicant; whether the applicant is an individual or some business entity; when the mark was first used anywhere and when it was first used in interstate commerce; a description of the goods sold or services offered under the mark; and how the mark is applied to the goods, such as by stickers, or how it is used in connection with the services (*e.g.*, in brochures). A drawing is required which shows the mark as it is actually used; actual specimens of the mark must be included. Aa filing fee for each classification under which registration is sought is required.

Upon receipt by the Trademark Office, the application is reviewed to ensure it is complete and is then assigned to a trademark examiner. Quite often, the first action on an application will be a communication from the examiner noting that a search has been made of the Trademark Office records and no mark, or application for a mark, has been found which would preclude the registration of the requested mark.

It is also possible that the examiner will reject the application on the basis of a prior registration which the examiner believes to be "confusingly similar." The examiner may also require that the description of the goods be amended for clarification. If able to overcome the objections of the examiner, the mark may then be passed to publication. What that means is that the particulars of the mark are published in the *Official Gazette,* a weekly government publication. Once published anyone who believes they may be harmed by the registration of the mark must file an opposition to the registration within 30 days. If no such opposition is filed, the mark is then allowed and a registration is sent out.

Only a mark which has been federally registered may use the symbol ® in connection with the mark. The phrase "Registered in the U.S. Patent and Trademark Office" or "Reg. U.S. Pat. & TM. Off." may also be used. The term for a federal registration is ten years, and the mark may be renewed for additional ten-year terms so long as it remains in use.

In order to maintain the mark, the following steps must be completed. The first step is to file an affidavit of use -- which must be filed between the fifth and sixth anniversary of the registration date -- verifying to the Trademark Office that the mark is still in use and also supplying a specimen of the mark as used. Filing of this affidavit of use is only required during the first term of the registration. At the time of filing for a second renewal of a mark, the affidavits of use are combined with the application for renewal.

Another step is filing an intent-to-use application, which conveys to the Trademark Office that as the mark has not yet been used yet, but there is bona fide intention to use the mark. The only difference between this application and a regular application is that the mark has not as yet been used, but it gets the mark into the system. Once an intent-to-use application is allowed, the applicant has six months to file an Amendment to Allege Use [actual use] of the mark, which simply tells the Trademark Office the dates the mark was first used anywhere, the date of first use in interstate commerce and includes specimens of the mark actually used. It is possible to obtain an extension of time for filing the Statement of Use.

*Other Types of Marks*

Not so common in this group are certification marks [15 U.S.C. §1127] which:

> [m]eans any word, name, symbol, or device, or any combination thereof –
>
> (1) used by a person other than its owner, or
>
> (2) which its owner has a bona fide intention to permit a person other than the owner to use in commerce and files an application to register on the principal register established by this Act, to certify regional or other origin, material, mode of manufacture, quality, accuracy, or other characteristics of such person's goods or services or that the work or labor on the goods or services was performed by members of a union or other organization.

Examples are the GOOD HOUSEKEEPING SEAL OF APPROVAL®, The Underwriters Laboratory Seal of Approval (UL®) and various union names and marks. The marks RP® and PACE Registered Paralegal®, issued to the National Federation of Paralegal Associations, Inc. are also certification marks.

A collective mark means a trademark or service mark:

> (1) used by the members of a cooperative, an association, or other collective group or organization, or
>
> (2) which such cooperative, association or other collective group or organization has a bona fide intention to use in commerce and applies to register on the principal register established by this Act, and includes marks indicating membership in a union, an association, or other organization.

Examples are NFPA®, NFPA – The Leader of the Paralegal Profession®, PACE®, PACE Registered Paralegal®, *National Paralegal Reporter*®, RP®.

Finally, an unregistered trademark is designated with "TM" and is used for promotional purposes or brand goods. Examples are: NFPA – Your partner in your profession™, PACE – The Standard for Excellence™ and NFPA Tech Institute™; each is an unregistered trademark of NFPA.

*Appearance and Shapes*

In some instances, the appearance of a device, or a package, or a building [the Chrysler Building in NY] or a color scheme may serve the same purpose as a trademark, i.e., it will cause an association in the minds of the public between the appearance of a thing, and the source of the goods or services offered. The appearance must be distinctive; must be nonfunctional and, of course, must be capable of achieving secondary meaning. Marks in this area are sometimes referred to as nontraditional marks and the color scheme and shape of a building has been held to be trade dress; as has a scent; the ringing of the Liberty Bell; the audio and visual image of a coin spinning, or a pin dropping on a hard surface; the sound of a creaking door; and even the E-flat, G, C and F sounds electronically reproduced are all registered marks.

The shape of the Michelob beer bottle is another example of innovation regarding trademarks. And most children recognize the NIKE swoosh trademark.

You may recall that recently UPS made a push for the color brown - as in WHAT CAN BROWN DO FOR YOU? If you watch NASCAR, you will recall that Dale Jarrett's [now retired as a driver] car was brown with the UPS insignia prominently on the hood. In fact, NASCAR machines are dominated by trademarks of the various sponsors.

### *100.04 Copyrights – Historical Perspective.*

The first federal copyright law was enacted in May 1790 when the U.S. Constitution was adopted. James Madison submitted the proposition to the framers of the Constitution and the first bill (H.T. 10) was presented to Congress on June 23, 1789. Those provisions are contained in Article I, Section 8. That first law provided for a term of 14 years with the privilege of renewal for a second term of 14 years. Books, maps and charts were protected and application for Copyright registration was made in the U.S. District Court, where the author or proprietor was a resident. The first entry for Copyright was to John Barry for his publication *The Philadelphia Spelling Book*, which was registered in the U.S. District Court of Pennsylvania.

Over the years, protection was added for prints in 1802; music in 1831; dramatic compositions in 1856; and photographs and photographic negatives in 1865. In 1870, copyright activities became centralized in the Library of Congress and works of art were added. Many amendments have been made since then to afford protection to other forms of works. In 1998, the Sonny Bono Copyright Term Extension Act extended protection for most works to the life of the author, plus 70 years after the death of the author.

*What is a Copyright?*

In the world of copyrights, everyone is familiar with the notices contained in the inside of books, at the end of the credits on movies, on computer programs; and, if you are a musician, on sheet music or books containing a large number of compositions. Some may not be aware of the fact that works of authorship also include: motion pictures, sculptures, lamp designs, patterns for clothing items, handbags, shoes, theatrical performances and performances of various musical compositions, both vocal and orchestral, are also the subject of copyright.

Section 102 of Title 17 of the United States Code states that:

> (a) Copyright protection subsists, in accordance with this title, in original works of authorship fixed in any tangible medium of expression, now known or later developed, from which they can be perceived, reproduced, or otherwise communicated, either directly or with the aid of a machine or device…

Copyright protection is available on published, as well as unpublished works.

Works not protected are those that have not been fixed in a tangible medium of expression: titles, names, short phrases and slogans; familiar symbols or designs; mere variations of typographic ornamentation, lettering or coloring; mere listings of ingredients or contents; ideas, procedures, methods, systems, processes, concepts, principles, discoveries or devices, as distinguished from a description, explanation or illustration; and works consisting entirely of information that is common property and containing no original authorship.

Violation of the rights provided by copyright laws is illegal, but the rights are not unlimited in scope. In some cases, there are limitations and exemptions from liability. In order to claim the full measure of damages in a lawsuit, one must have a copyright registration prior to filing a complaint.

*Advantages of Registration*

As noted previously, there are certain advantages to securing a Copyright Registration. Among those are:

1. Registration establishes a public record of the copyright claim.

2. Registration of a work of U.S. origin is a requirement before filing an infringement action.

3. Registration establishes prima facie evidence of the validity of the copyright and of the facts stated on the certificate, if made before or within five years of publication.

4. A registration made within three months after publication or prior to infringement makes available statutory damages and attorneys' fees to the copyright owner. Otherwise, only awards of actual damages and profits are available. (There are two types of damages -- actual and statutory. Statutory damages are important where actual damages are hard or impossible to prove.)

5. A Copyright Registration may be recorded with the U.S. Customs Service to secure protection against importation of infringing copies. Further information on this is available through the U.S. Customs Service.

## SAMPLE QUESTIONS FOR INTELLECTUAL PROPERTY

1. A patent application may be filed by:

   a. The inventor.
   b. Any lawyer.
   c. A paralegal.
   d. An agent.

2. Which of the following patent applications has only one claim:

   a. Chemical patent.
   b. Utility patent.
   c. Plant patent.
   d. Formula patent.

3. Drawings for a plant patent must:

   a. Contain numbers.
   b. Be in color.
   c. Be in black and white.
   d. No drawings are required.

4. When a trademark application is published for opposition, it is published in the:

   a. *Trademark Reporter.*
   b. *Official Gazette.*
   c. *Federal Register.*
   d. *USPTO Reporter.*

5. An office action is a document prepared by a/n:

   a. examiner.
   b. lawyer.
   c. paralegal.
   d. applicant.

6. Plant patents pertain to plants:

   a. Growing wild.
   b. Asexually reproduced.
   c. Sport limbs.
   d. Grown from seeds.

7. Which of the following is an example of a service mark?

   a. GOOD HOUSEKEEPING SEAL OF APPROVAL®
   b. NFPA Tech Institute TM
   c. UL®
   d. *National Paralegal Reporter*®

8. Copyright protection is available to:

   a. Titles of works.
   b. Phrases and slogans.
   c. Published works.
   d. Designs.

9. Copyright protection ends:

   a. On the death of the author.
   b. 50 years after the death of the author.
   c. 70 years after the death of the author.
   d. 20 years after the death of the author.

*Answers:*

1–a. Under the provisions of 35 U.S.C., only the inventor, a lawyer licensed to practice before the USPTO or a licensed patent agent may file applications.

2–c. Under the Patent Office rules, a plant patent has only one claim, as does a design patent. All other patents normally have multiple claims, but it is a requirement that a plant patent have only one claim.

3–b. Because the description of the plant includes colors pertaining to the fruit and the plant itself, drawings must be in color. Color on a plant patent is normally an important part of the plant and its fruit since it differs from other varieties. Drawings for all other patents are black and white.

4–b. The official government publication is the *Official Gazette*, which contains information regarding trademarks, as well as patents. The *Federal Register* contains rules, proposed rules and notices from governmental agencies. The other choices are fictional.

5–a. An office action is a document issued to the person filing the patent application, stating reasons for rejection, requiring amendments, etc. An examiner is an employee of the USPTO.

6–b. Plant patent coverage is afforded only to those plants which have been asexually reproduced -- not grown from a seed.

7–d. A collective mark means a trademark or service mark: (1) used by the members of a cooperative, an association, or other collective group or organization, or (2) which such cooperative, association or other collective group or organization has a bona fide intention to use in commerce and applies to register on the principal register established by this Act, and includes marks indicating membership in a union, an association, or other organization. Examples are NFPA®, NFPA – The Leader of the Paralegal Profession®, PACE®, PACE Registered Paralegal®, *National Paralegal Reporter*®, RP®.

8–c. Published works are afforded copyright protection. The title of a work is not the actual work, nor is a design on a work. Phrases and slogans are not the subject of copyright protection, but rather, trademarks or service marks.

9–c. Under the Sonny Bono Copyright Term Extension, copyright protection ends 70 years after the death of the author. Works prepared before this amendment are subject to different terms and there are provisions for renewals.

# 110.00 PROBATE AND ESTATE PLANNING

## *110.01 Introduction.*

Societies, and particularly American culture, have created methods for distributing a person's property upon death based on common law. This concept is known as *testation.* From this word flows the common terminology used: *testator, testate* and *intestate*. In the United States today, the term of art used for providing instructions at death is also known as *estate planning.* Those individuals who do not provide instructions to and for their heirs, beneficiaries and assigns are referred to as having died *intestate* -- without a will. Thus, the Uniform Probate Code and subsequent, individual state probate codes, provide for the distribution of a decedent's estate through the laws of intestate succession.

A *consanguineous relationship* is one that is established through a blood or biological relationship. Children, siblings, parents, aunts, uncles and grandparents all have a consanguineous relationship to one another and to a decedent. The Uniform Probate Code and most states rely on the "Table of Consanguinity" to establish whether a person is a direct or lineal descendant, such as a "child," or is an ancestor, "parents or grandparents," or a collateral relative, "siblings, aunts, uncles, nieces, nephews and cousins" who are related, but not in a lineal or direct line.

State probate codes provide statutes that govern the requirements and construction of a valid will, the administration of wills, and intestate succession. Many states have also created statutes that enumerate the requirements and construction of valid trusts, trust administration, durable and general powers of attorney, anatomical gifts, health care instructions, estate tax apportionment and marital rights to property. These states also have codified various aspects concerning the manner in which estates may pass and the procedures for passing the real and personal property of a decedent. There are a few states, however, that continue to follow common law regarding these areas of estate planning. These statutes, where there is provision for passing property from a decedent to his or her heirs, also include references to the Internal Revenue Code, especially with respect to Estate (inheritance) taxes. A state may also have its own inheritance taxes which may need to be considered when a testator creates the necessary documents for testate succession.

One of the first things that must be determined when creating an estate plan or administering a decedent's estate are the laws of the state with respect to property ownership and marital rights. There are two types of marital property systems recognized in the United States: *common law* and *community property*. Each spouse owns his/her entire income and any property brought into the marriage or acquired during the marriage by gift in a *common law system.* Each spouse owns any property brought into the marriage or acquired during the marriage by gift, and one-half of his/her income, in a *community property system.* The other one-half of the income belongs to the other spouse. In most cases, married persons who have lived and/or acquired real property in multiple jurisdictions must determine the manner in which marital property is divided based on the domicile at the time the property was acquired. Thus, a married couple who acquires property in Nebraska (a common law state) and then moves to Washington (a community property state) may find that the property located in Nebraska must be divided as common law property and not community property, while the property they own in Washington will be subject to community property distribution if the property was acquired during the marriage in the names of both spouses and the decedent died in Washington. Personal property distribution, upon death, is determined by the domicile of the decedent regardless of the place it was acquired. The estate administration in the domiciled state is the *domiciled estate* or primary probate. Property distributed in the non-domiciled state is called an *ancillary estate* or probate.

Property, both real and personal, may be acquired through earnings, gifts, income and windfalls (found property, lottery winnings, etc.). Probate and non-probate transfers of property upon the death of the owner are considered gratuitous gifts because there is no monetary exchange made upon receipt of the property. The property is received by the beneficiary as a result of the appreciation and affection of the *giftor*.

### *110.02 Probate and Non-Probate Distributions.*

It must be determined upon the death of a decedent whether the person had a valid will. Secondly, it must be determined what, if any, real or personal property (assets) was owned by the decedent and whether the property is subject to probate or non-probate transfer. Some or all of the decedent's property may be considered non-probate property and will not be included in a probate; if it is determined one is required. *Non-probate property* is those assets that may be distributed at death subject to the terms of a contract or other property arrangement. Examples of non-probate assets are those where a beneficiary is named, such as life insurance and pay-on-death accounts. Property held in joint tenancy and assets held in a "living or revocable trust are also not subject to probate.

Assets subject to probate is property owned by the decedent that does not fall into the category of non-probate assets, regardless of whether the person did or did not have a will. A person who has created a valid will (*testator*) will have their property distributed as he/she has directed. A person who has not created a valid will is subject to their property being distributed as set forth in the laws of intestate succession in their state. Of note, however, is that the value of all property in the estate -- probate and non-probate -- needs to be included for federal estate tax and applicable state inheritance tax purposes, even though those assets are not subject to distribution in probate.

### *110.03 Community Property Jurisdictions.*

The surviving spouse retains one-half of all community property or, put more simply, the one-half that he/she already owns in a community property state. The surviving spouse typically has a right to inherit the one-half that was owned by the deceased spouse depending upon the terms of the will or the laws of intestate succession. Quasi-community property -- property that is owned by the married couple and located in the non-domiciled jurisdiction -- may or may not be subject to the community property distribution. The state laws of succession would need to be consulted for such ancillary property.

### *110.04 Descendants.*

Descendants may also be referred to as "issue" or "children." Most intestacy statutes provide that the descendants of the intestate decedent will receive his/her property, except for any portion that is to be distributed to the surviving spouse. If a person dies without a will and has no spouse, his/her estate will be distributed to his/her descendants. If there are no descendants, the estate passes to the ancestors and collateral relatives as set forth in the consanguineous relationship established in the Uniform Probate Code.

The first step in determining how the property should be distributed in an intestate estate is to identify the children of the decedent. Children who are born after the decedent's death, out of wedlock or who were adopted by the decedent must also be identified. Legally adopted children must also be identified and treated as heirs or beneficiaries. It must also be determined if any of the decedent's children predeceased him/her.

The division of the intestate decedent's estate is typically quite simple once it is determined if all of the decedent's children are alive. Each child will receive an *equal share*, which is called a *per capita* distribution. If any of the decedent's children have predeceased him/her, and there are children of the deceased child (grandchildren), the division becomes more complicated. There are three basic methods of dividing the decedent's property among descendants of different generations: *per capita*, *per stirpes* and *right of representation*. The individual states' statutes will determine the method of distributing property to multiple generations. Note that a will may also provide direction that heirs not specifically mentioned, or as a "catch all," may state that heirs should receive property *per stirpes* or *per capita* with right of representation.

The following is an overview of *per stirpes* and right of representation distribution of an intestate decedent's estate.

> *Per stirpes*, in Latin, means to take by the "roots or stocks." This means that younger generation descendants will divide the share the older generation (parent) would have received if they had survived. The estate is divided into shares, one share being created for each surviving and deceased child of the decedent. Each surviving child receives one share and the share created for a deceased child will be divided between his/her children in equal shares. For example, if the decedent had three children and one of them predeceased decedent leaving two children (grandchildren of decedent), the estate will be distributed 1/3 each to the surviving children and 1/6 each to the children of the predeceased child (grandchildren).
>
> *Per capita with representation* is similar to *per stirpes*, with one major exception. Rather than using the "root," the nearest "generation" is used. The division, when using the above example, under this type of distribution will be the same. However, if both the decedent's children predeceased him/her and there are differing numbers of children of each deceased child, their children (the decedent's grandchildren) will receive equal shares rather than disproportionate shares. For example, if the decedent had a son who had one child and a daughter who had three children and both children were deceased, the grandchildren would each receive 1/4 of the estate. In contrast, under *per stirpes*, the child of the deceased son would receive one-half and the children of the daughter would receive 1/6 each.

Most states prefer that the surviving spouse and the descendants (children, grandchildren and great-grandchildren) receive property before collateral relatives or ancestors. In the event none of the intestate decedents survives or the decedent was never married and had no children, the estate would pass to the ancestors and collaterals. Again, the Uniform Probate Code's Table of Consanguinity or statute will provide the information on the lineal descendants and how to determine whether a Mother, Father or sibling is entitled to inherit, and how far through the collateral lines one need to go to determine the rightful descendants of the intestate decedent.

In the event the intestate decedent died without leaving a spouse or children, the degree of relationship should be determined until the descendant's nearest ancestors on each side of the family are located. The estate will be divided in two halves (one for each side of the family) and will be distributed to the nearest ancestor or descendant of an ancestor. The following is an example of how the degree of relationship is determined and who would inherit the intestate decedent's property:

> The decedent's mother and father must first be identified. If both are living, then they will each inherit one-half of the estate. If either parent is deceased, then the decedent's siblings will inherit that parent's share in equal proportions. If any sibling has predeceased the intestate decedent, that sibling's share will be distributed to his/her children (the decedent's nieces and nephews). If there are no siblings, then the next collateral line is the grandparents of the intestate decedent. Should there be no grandparents, any aunts and uncles (siblings of the decedent's parent) would inherit.

You will find when you work in the area of probate law that it is best to refer to the Table of Consanguinity and then prepare a chart of the ancestors and collateral relatives to best determine the heirs of the intestate decedent. This will assist the client or executor in understanding who is entitled to inherit the intestate's property in the state where he/she was domiciled.

An estate that belonged to an intestate decedent who has no heirs is called *escheat*. In that event, any real property reverts to the state government where the intestate decedent was domiciled. Thus, if a decedent owned real property in another state, the state where the property is located would be able to claim the property through the escheat process. Personal, particularly intangible property -- such as bank accounts located in another state -- will usually be considered the escheat of the state where the decedent was domiciled.

***110.05 Wills.***

The most simple and common way that a person can avoid having their property pass under the laws of succession is by creating a will. Many people, particularly elderly individuals who do not "own" much property, will put a child's name as a "joint tenant" on property, which will avoid the probate process. Others may choose to create a revocable trust, which will, if properly prepared, also avoid intestate succession and probate. For more information regarding the advantages and disadvantage of holding property in joint tenancy, particularly with a person other than one's spouse, you should review real estate law.

All states provide their citizens with the opportunity to designate who will receive property upon death. The ability to execute a will is considered a privilege and will have no effect if the *testator* (person making the will) does not comply with the state's statutory requirements of a valid will. Most states have a statute that allows a will to be considered valid, if it is in substantial compliance with the requirements of the state. This is called a *savings statute*.

*Heirs and Beneficiaries*

Heirs and beneficiaries are differentiated, in most instances, by determining if the decedent had a will. Common law and most jurisdictions identify heirs as those people having a right to the decedent's estate. Thus, a person who dies intestate will have heirs to their estate. A person who dies having made a valid will has identified the beneficiaries of his/her estate. This method also allows a testator to identify his/her rightful heirs and determine whether or not those heirs should receive any portion of the estate. Thus, a person who makes a will may "disinherit" any beneficiary to whom they do not want their estate to pass.

*Validity of the Will*

The most common requirements are that the testator has the legal (and/or mental) capacity to execute a will and that he/she be of lawful age or considered emancipated. A testator must be able to understand the intent of the document and have executed same. If he/she intended to create or change a will, but did not execute the will prior to dying or becoming incapacitated, the intent cannot be proved.

A will must also be executed with certain formalities. The formalities assure that the testator acted deliberately and knowingly. Such formalities include language confirming that the testator knew what he/she was signing and that the will was not signed under coercion, duress or as the result of a contract with a named beneficiary. The testator will knowingly give property to certain individuals, as well as give the power to one or more individuals to carry out their wishes. The formality also provides the courts with the assurance that the testator did not commit perjury by signing the will and that the testator's wishes must be followed according to state statute and procedures. In addition, that the executor must follow and fulfill the testator's wishes, as well as has a fiduciary responsibility to the estate, the heirs and the court.

Of utmost importance is the manner in which the will is executed or signed. Most states provide that a will have two or more witnesses, unless it is a holographic will. A *holographic will* is one that has been handwritten, signed and dated by the testator. It does not have to be witnessed. All other types of wills must be witnessed. The witnesses do not need to have read or know the content of the will. Their signatures attest to the fact that they witnessed the testator sign the will and that the will was signed in the presence of the testator and each other. This is referred to as an *attestation* or *testimonium clause*. Some states require, and many attorneys prefer, that the will be signed by the testator and witnesses using a "self-proving affidavit." A number of states may also require that the signatures of the witnesses be notarized.

A person may choose to make a holographic will. Some states require that a holographic will be witnessed, while others do not. Note that a typed or computer-generated will is not considered a holographic will in any state. Most states do not mandate the requirements previously indicated for a formal will. As long as the testator signs and dates the will, they have satisfied the requirements in most states. It should also be noted that many of the states who recognize holographic wills, and particularly those who do not require that the will be witnessed, are more likely to require that several people testify as to the testator's handwriting. Some states limit the amount of property that can be disposed of by a holographic will or other types of requirements.

Soldiers' and Sailors' wills are permitted in most states even though they may not comply with that state's customary requirements. The Floyd D. Spence National Defense Authorization Act for Fiscal Year 2001, Section 551, provides that "military testamentary instruments" are exempt from state law formalities and should have the same effect as though the will were prepared and executed in the state of residence. This allows the Judge Advocate Generals (JAGs) and their assigned legal men to assist military personnel in the preparation of a will without having to know the laws of all fifty states.

Some states have passed laws that allow their residents to complete a statutory or "fill-in-the-blank" will. These forms vary tremendously, although they do, for the most part, follow the same format. Most of the forms contain warnings about the need for legal advice as well as explicit instructions about what information can be included on the will form. Any deviation may render the will void.

_Testamentary Gifts_

Gifts (estate property distributed) through a will can be classified based on the type of property the testator is distributing. Historically, at common law, a gift of real property was called a *devise*, while a gift of personal property was called a *bequest*. The practice continues today, and some state statutes will use the terms interchangeably.

_Specific Gifts_

A *specific gift* is one that is bestowed upon a beneficiary. An example of a specific gift or bequest is:

- "I give my pocket watch to my son Eric."

A specific gift may also be identified in more general terms; such as:

- "I give the funds held in any checking and savings accounts to my daughter Erica;" or
- "I give any vehicle I own at the time of my death to my granddaughter Stephanie."

This allows a testator not to have to revise their will if they should decide to move their checking and savings accounts from one bank to another, while still providing that the beneficiary will receive that property. When preparing a will, care should be taken to make sure that there is sufficient description of the property so that the court, the executor and others involved in probating the estate will not have to question the testator's intent. For example, if the testator has two pocket watches, there would need to be some additional information provided, such as the color (gold or silver), make, model or manufacturer and other descriptive information.

*General Gifts*

A *general gift* is defined as a testamentary gift not described in sufficient detail to be a specific gift. A legacy or gift of money is usually considered a general gift, although it seems specific in nature. An example of a general legacy gift is:

- "I give each of my grandchildren the sum of $1,000, provided each has turned 18 at the time of my death,"

Typically, the attorney will also include language that provides for the gift to lapse if the estate is not sufficient to make the gift or if the child is under 18, that a custodial account or some other "minor" transfer may be made to the child under the laws of state.

The testator may also want to give a general gift to a charity, church, or other organization. This bequest may fall under a specific, general or even a residuary gift, depending upon how the attorney words the client's will.

General gifts also typically include the testator's household goods, furniture and furnishings, clothing, jewelry, books and other general items of property that the testator is not likely to identify specifically. Another example of a general gift is:

- "I give all of my household goods, furniture, clothing, jewelry, books, heirlooms and other items of personal property not otherwise identified to my children in equal shares."

The testator may also create an account for the benefit of a beneficiary that is a Pay-on-Death account. The testator may create such an account for any person, adult or child and such account will avoid probate. Note, however, that a pay-on-death account created for a child may require that the a custodian be appointed to administer the account until the child reaches majority and can receive the property, pursuant to any state laws that have a minimum set amount. The UPA states that thc amount is $5,000. The same would be true for a person who died intestate.

*Residuary Gifts*

*Residuary gifts* are that property that remains after all specific and general property is identified. Residue can include items of great value and/or items of very little value. In some cases, a client will simply want their entire estate to be divided in equal shares among their children. If there are no specific or general gifts, as noted above, to be distributed to the specifically named beneficiaries, the general property is referred to as a common residuary gift. An example of a common residuary gift is:

- "I give all of my estate in equal shares to my children, Samuel, Donna and Charles, or the survivor(s) of them."

The will should also provide what is to happen if any of the testator's children predecease him/her. As indicated under the section on descendants, are the testator's grandchildren to receive the share their parent would have and at what allocation? The attorney may also wish to include a statement about what should happen to the residue if the testator has no beneficiaries at the time of his/her death. Does the property revert to being distributed to his/her heirs based on the consanguineous relationship or does the testator want his/her estate to be distributed to a charity, organization, friend or non-family member?

A will may also include provisions for property to be held in trust, either through a life estate or for a minor child, or by gift pursuant to The Uniform Transfer to Minors Act (UTMA). This federal statute provides, and many states follow or have parallel statutes, that a donor may make a gift to a minor (donee), over the amount of $5,000, and may retain the management as the custodian of the property or may name another individual to serve as custodian. The custodian will manage the property for the benefit of the minor until the minor reaches majority, at which time the property is distributed to the donee. The donor may state whether the donee will receive the property at another specific age, such as upon the 21st or 25th birthday. The testator who creates an account for a minor child prior to their death, naming the child as beneficiary, has created a *Totten Trust*. Typically, a will states the period of time under which a trust account must be held and administered. In the event the will is silent, the UTMA provides a 21-year period to allow for a child, even one who is not born at the time the will was executed, to become an adult.

*Will Construction and Interpretation*

The construction and interpretation of a will is very important. The more precise the will is in construction, the less error there will be with interpretation by the court. *Construction* is the attempt to assign a meaning to each provision of the will in the event the testator's actual intent cannot be ascertained. The court may be required to construe or make their best guess as to the testator's intent. As indicated above, if a testator states "I leave my pocket watch to my son Eric" and the testator has more than one pocket watch, the court will need to determine the testator's intent as to which pocket watch was meant for Eric.

Another concern of the court, and attorneys, in construction and interpretation is public policy. A testator who does not provide for his/her minor children in a will may have the court determine if the policy of the state requires that there is a need for property (or money) to be provided in lieu of support for minor children. If the decedent has minor children and has been paying child support up until his or her death, or owes back child support – the court is going to make sure that the children of the decedent have, at minimum, a share of the estate equal to the future support owed. To not provide for this support would be against public policy. Likewise, a testator who does not provide a mechanism for paying debts to creditors, taxes and expenses of last illness and/or burial will have the court make an interpretation, based on statute that requires the executor to pay such expenses out of the estate.

Ambiguity can lead to will contests, extend the amount of time required to complete the probate, and cost the estate (and ultimately the beneficiaries) a great deal of money. A paralegal can assist the attorney and aide the client in reducing problems with interpretation, construction and potential contests by knowing the required components of a will. Typically, a will must contain a statement as to the name of the testator, as well as any "also known as" names. For example, a woman who has recently remarried and who has children with a different last name may find it beneficial to state her previous married and/or maiden name(s). The will should state that this is their will and, as previously noted, that any previous wills and codicils are revoked. There will be numerous other types of "boilerplate" language that may be required in your state to have a valid will. In addition, as previously discussed, an attestation clause should be included for the witnesses, and the proper formalities in executing the will should be followed.

Boilerplate language will usually include, but is not limited to, the following subject areas:

- name;
- marital status;
- children;
- testator's domicile;
- incorporation by reference (existence of the testator's estate) specific gifts and/or general gifts;
- residue;
- identity of beneficiaries (may be the same and/or in addition to children);
- pour-over provisions (if there is a revocable trust);
- precatory language;
- payment of taxes, creditors, funeral and burial;
- no contest provision;
- guardianship (if there are minor children);
- disclaimer of property;
- nomination of personal representative; and
- bond requirements.

The following are some additional tips that will assist in assuring the continuity of the will and making it less likely for a will contest, especially as it relates to *how* the law firm prepared and maintained the integrity of the will. Each law firm may have its own requirements, which may or may not include some of these tips. Alternatively, check to see if there are any statutes or local rules that prohibit any of these tips. For example, some jurisdictions may require that "only blue ink" be used for signing a will. More are:

- The testator and witnesses initial each page;
- Sign the document with a blue pen so that the original is easily identifiable;
- Securely fasten/staple all pages of the original and do not take them apart, even for photocopying;
- Number the pages using current page and total page number footer;
- Use the same paper type, weight, color, etc. for all pages;
- Use the same font throughout the document. Some law firms use a specific font only for wills;
- Avoid blank spaces; if blanks are necessary, include the statement "intentionally left blank"; and
- Carry over sentences from one page to another rather than starting a new section to avoid being able to replace pages and/or sections.

<u>*Changing and Revoking a Will*</u>

A testator may wish to change or revoke his/her will at any time, for any reason. Since a will does not take effect until the testator's death, he/she has the ability to change or revoke a will as long as he/she has the mental capacity to do so. In many states, a will cannot be created where there is a contract with another that will affect the provisions of the will and/or under coercion or duress. Thus, a person cannot be forced execute a will, nor can they be forced to change or revoke a will.

The revocation of a will is typically covered by state statute. Most states provide for the revocation of a will either by executing a document that states the will is revoked, a violent act -- such as tearing up or shredding the will -- or by writing a new will or creating a codicil. A codicil is essentially an amendment that changes only certain portions of the will. The revocation, new will and/or codicil must be executed by the testator using the same formalities used in originally executing the will. As stated above, a will may be revoked by destroying it. However, it is not the best method, particularly if the testator provided copies to his/her executor and/or family members. In the event the original will is not located, a copy may be probated. If it was the testator's intent to revoke the will, destroying it, without the knowledge of anyone, may result in a copy of the will being submitted for probate. Destroying the will without formality may lead to will contests and litigation between the estate and beneficiaries.

A testator may wish to revoke or change a will for reasons, including, but not limited to, marriage or divorce, birth or adoption of child, death of a beneficiary, alienation or disinheritance. If the client decides to create a codicil rather than prepare a new will, the date of the previous will and any previous codicils should be noted within the document. The codicil should contain an attestation clause, be executed before witnesses and the witnesses should sign in each other's presence. In other words, the codicil should be executed using the same formalities as the will.

Depending upon the complexity of the changes required, the attorney might recommend that the client execute a new will and revoke the previous will. A client who has made several codicils, over a period of many years, will likely have an attorney recommend that a new will be created in order to avoid any confusion as to the testator's intent. Most law firms today retain wills and other estate planning documents on the firm's computer. It is simpler now, than in the past, to make changes that meet the needs of a client and simply print a new will. The new will should contain a "revocation clause," stating that any wills previously created are void upon the execution of the new will.

Because clients understand that changes can be more easily made, a paralegal may be asked directly by the client to make changes. The paralegal should never make changes without the attorney's knowledge or until the attorney has spoken with the client to confirm that the changes the client requests are appropriate. For example, the client may wish to make their child the executor. However, if the child is not eighteen, the will would be void as the executor must be an adult to act in that capacity. While an experienced paralegal may easily be able to draft a new will, it would be UPL to draft such a document without the attorney's supervision. The client should be reminded of that fact.

### *110.06 Estate Administration (Probate Process).*

In most cases, a probate must follow the same process whether the decedent had a will or died intestate. The primary difference in probating an intestate versus a testate estate is the steps that must be followed by the personal representative and his/her attorney in proceeding through the probate process. In most states, if there was a will, the decedent's estate will proceed more quickly through the probate process and the personal representative may not need to ask court permission of every step required, unless there is a contest. Note that a "pour-over" will -- one that is executed in conjunction with an *inter vivos* trust -- will not usually require probate. This issue will be addressed later under the Trust section.

The first steps the attorney and paralegal should take in assisting the client with the probate process are as follows:

- Request a copy of the death certificate;
- Determine whether the decedent had a will;
- Determine all of the decedent's potential heirs/beneficiaries; and
- Determine the property that was owned by the decedent at the time of death and the manner in which the property was held (title).

The death certificate will provide valuable information about the decedent. It will state his/her full (legal) name, social security number, date of birth and domicile at the time of death. The attorney will want to review the will to determine its validity. All wills, including holographic wills, must meet certain criteria as discussed above. The attorney will want to evaluate any potential problems, such as whether the original will can be located; whether the will may have been altered; if the will was revoked or a codicil prepared; whether the will met any specific requirements in the state and that the will was properly witnessed. In the event the decedent did not have a will, the attorney will need determine the proper procedure(s) and other considerations involved with an intestate estate.

The decedent's potential heirs and beneficiaries need to be determined. In the event the decedent had a will, those beneficiaries may be listed in the will. The paralegal can assist the attorney in determining the ages and addresses of each beneficiary. Additionally, if any beneficiary has predeceased the decedent, the issue of those beneficiaries will also need to be identified. The attorney will also want to identify any heirs who were omitted (disinherited) from the will to be prepared for a potential contest. If the decedent died intestate, all heirs, including collateral relatives, should be identified. Depending upon the jurisdiction, direct descendants and collateral relatives (the paralegal can help determine to what degree) may have to be notified of any pending probate matter.

The decedent's property should be located and identified. The paralegal will most likely work closely with the personal representative and the attorney to identify the decedent's property and to determine who has title of the property. This is very important, in that property that is held in joint tenancy with another, for example with a spouse, will not need to be included in the probate. Joint tenancy property passes by right of survivorship to the joint tenant and does not require inclusion in most probate proceedings. (Consult real estate law statutes for more information on this subject.) Joint tenancy property or property where there is a named beneficiary can be, in most cases, transferred to the joint tenant or the beneficiary. These are considered "non-probate" assets and transfers. Any property owned solely by the decedent or where there is any ambiguity as to the ownership will require a determination by the court as to who should receive the decedent's property. As discussed previously, even property held as community property by a spouse will likely require a determination by the court as to who owns what portion of the property and how it should pass. Property owned by an intestate decedent as community property with their spouse may have their one-half distributed to their children and/or their spouse rather than solely to the spouse, depending upon the state statutes governing intestate succession.

Property owned as a tenant-in-common with another individual, including a spouse, is property that is owned only in part by the decedent – usually one-half. For example, if Bill and his sister Jill inherit a family cabin from their parents, they may take title as tenants-in-common so that each person's share will go to their respective heirs or beneficiaries upon death. It will not automatically go to the survivor. It is, therefore, very important that a careful inventory be prepared, typically by the paralegal, at the onset of the probate procedure. It is important for the paralegal to have a clear understanding of the methods of holding title to property in order to help determine

One last aspect needs to be determined and that is who will be appointed by the court to act as the personal representative of the decedent and administer his/her estate. This person will be called by different names. If the decedent had a will, this person will usually be identified as executor. However, a person named as executor may decide that he/she does not want to serve in that capacity. Regardless, the court must either confirm the executor as the personal representative of the decedent or another person must be appointed to act. In the event the decedent died intestate, a person will need to be appointed by the court. This person can be a spouse, family member, friend or any other interested person.

The terms *of personal representative* and *administrator* are often used interchangeably. Note, however, that in most cases, the personal representative is the person nominated by a will –- the executor –- and appointed by the court. The *administrator* of an estate is typically the person appointed by the court when the decedent died intestate. If the person died intestate and has no known heirs, a "public" administrator may be appointed to serve in this capacity. Regardless, the court process of appointing this person is referred to as *Letters Testamentary* (Letters) in most jurisdictions. It will therefore be necessary for the attorney to make sure that the person who has presented his or herself as wishing to serve in this capacity is qualified to do so. It is possible that more than one person in an intestate estate may wish to be appointed as administrator.

*Probate Steps*

Note: For the purposes of this section, it will be assumed that the decedent died testate, unless otherwise noted.

The following is a summary of the probate process. While there is a specific sequence of events to follow for most probate procedures, there can be many variations. Just as no two people are exactly alike, no two probates are exactly alike. Because probate involves people and property, (money) tempers can flare and childhood issues can surface. The paralegal must take care to remain professional and neutral despite family disagreements that may arise. The law firm will represent the decedent's estate. Technically, the personal representative (administrator or executor) is not represented by the law firm, although it may appear so. The firm's primary responsibility is to follow the probate laws and procedures in the jurisdiction and to assure that the decedent's estate is distributed according to his/her wishes and intent, if he/she had a will, or according to the laws of intestate succession. It is the personal representative's (this term will be used generically whether or not the person had a will) responsibility to follow his/her fiduciary responsibility to the estate and not his/her personal feelings about the estate. As long as the personal representative maintains that fiduciary responsibility toward the decedent's estate, the law firm and the representative's responsibilities will be parallel. There is a potential conflict in the event the representative does not follow the statutes and maintain his/her fiduciary responsibility.

Once the attorney has determined whether there is any joint tenancy property or property that transfers to named beneficiaries, the firm can assist the executor in making said transfers. Depending upon the type of entity who "holds" the property, it will likely be the paralegal's responsibility to contact said entity to determine what document is needed to make the transfers. Real property laws should be reviewed to determine the appropriate method of transferring the property to the surviving joint tenant. In most cases, an Affidavit of Death of Joint Tenant, which contains a copy of the decedent's death certificate, will suffice in making the transfer. The paralegal should also be familiar with any local county or state regulations governing transfers of real property and assure that any collateral documents are prepared and submitted with any new deeds. The paralegal should also assist in tracking any transfers in the event the transfer is a taxable event.

In the case of assets, such as annuities, employee retirement plans, Individual Retirement Accounts (IRAs), insurance policies, Certificates of Deposit (CD), etc. where there is a named beneficiary, the paralegal will likely contact the entity or financial institution to determine what information is required for each entity. Often, these entities require that a specific form be completed and returned along with a copy of the death certificate and any other corresponding document. Additionally, the beneficiary may have to complete forms and information, such as a W-9 or, in some cases, background information required by the federal government under the Patriot Act or similar regulations. State and Federal rules and regulations that govern the transfer of assets after death should be consulted. For example, many jurisdictions require that an affidavit be prepared to transfer property after the death of the owner. The affidavit may require that a specific time period has lapsed and other supporting documentation be provided as to who has the right to receive the property.

The original will should be located if at all possible. In some cases, an order will need to be obtained from the court to drill a safe deposit box or to obtain the will if it is in the custody of another person or entity. The will should then be lodged (filed) with the court. In the event the original will cannot be located, most jurisdictions allow the will to be probated by lodging a copy. Local rules should be consulted to determine any specific procedures for lodging the original or copy of the decedent's will.

The Petition for Probate should be prepared and submitted to the court for filing along with the original will. Most jurisdictions also require that a copy of the will be attached to the Petition. Local rules should be consulted as to what information must be included in the Petition. Information such as the name and any aliases of the decedent, the named executor and whether that person is petitioning for appointment, the heirs entitled to notice of the probate proceeding and the property subject to the probate proceeding are usually required. Local rules should also be consulted as to any notice requirements of the probate proceeding.

The next step is for the person who wishes to act as the personal representative (executor or in the case of the decedent dying intestate, the administrator) to request that Letters Testamentary be issued and to request that the court "order" that a probate proceeding be initiated. The Letters will state who is entitled to act as the personal representative and will give the representative specific powers to act. The Letters and/or Order may also require that the personal representative be bonded. State statutes should be consulted to determine when a bond is required of a personal representative. If the decedent had a will, that will may state that the executor can serve without bond. However, if an appointment is made for someone other than the executor to be the personal representative or the personal representative lives out of state, the court may still require a bond. The size of the estate may also affect the court's ruling as to whether a bond is required. The firm should also provide information to the Executor as to the functions they will need to perform and about the fiduciary responsibility of the role they will play. Some states require the "notice" to be given, while in others this may be informal and up to the law firm to make sure the individual properly takes care of the decedent's estate with the assistance of the firm.

Once the personal representative has been officially appointed, he/she must (with the assistance of the law firm) notify all known creditors of the pending probate. Most states provide for a specific period of time in which the creditors must be notified after the Order and/or Letters have been issued. The creditors will also be given a specific period of time to respond and/or request that they be identified as a creditor. The personal representative must then pay the creditor out of the estate, unless the estate is insolvent. Most jurisdictions also prioritize the manner in which creditors and bills be paid out of the decedent's estate. Thus, if there are some estate assets, but they are not sufficient to pay all creditors in full, the personal representative (through his/her attorney) can determine the priority of those who must be paid. Also, the amounts due may be pro-rated.

During this time, the personal representative will be responsible for distributing any specific gifts made in the will. The representative may also need to sell property in order to make distributions pursuant to the testator's will or the laws of intestate succession. An inventory will need to be prepared listing all estate property. In most jurisdictions, an appraiser will be appointed by the court to determine the value of assets. Some assets will be quite simple to value. Financial institutions or even mutual fund accounts prepare regular statements as to the value of the asset. Assets such as vehicles, real property, jewelry, and other items of value will have to be appraised. The appraisal will need to be filed with the court. The personal representative (with the assistance of the law firm) will need to keep an accounting of all distributions of specific gifts, liquidation of property, payment of bills and creditors' claims, and any expenses he/she may have incurred while serving in their capacity as representative of the estate. The representative should also obtain receipts for all property distributed to any beneficiaries, as well as confirmation that the decedent's bills have been paid.

After the creditors' claim period has expired and the personal representative has performed his/her fiduciary responsibilities of distributing specific gifts, liquidating property and paying the decedent's bills, the estate is, in most cases, ready for final distribution and closing of the estate. The personal representative, with the assistance of the law firm, will prepare an accounting of all assets, including the sale and any gain or loss of the value, debts paid, and any other disbursements that affect the value and final distribution of the estate. Most states require that the inventory and accounting be provided to the decedent's heirs or beneficiaries. The account will also provide information on any expenses of the estate, attorney and executor fees (regular and extraordinary) and how the estate will be distributed to the beneficiaries as set forth in the decedent's will or pursuant to the laws of intestate succession.

For the purposes of this section, the information provided has been generic and overly simplified. As stated at the beginning of this section, each probate can be different depending upon the complexity of the will, the assets involved and the family dynamics involved in settling an estate. A paralegal who works in the area of probate and estate planning will need to further study the statutes, rules of procedure and local rules to determine any specific requirements. Additionally, wills may incorporate more complex distributions and, of course, an intestate decedent's estate may initially seem simple and straightforward, but will quickly become mired in personal issues as well as require additional court oversight that is not required of a person who prepared a will.

***110.07 Trusts.***

A *stand-alone trust* is a mechanism for probate avoidance, which has gained in popularity in recent years. While the concept of trusts -- those created for a life estate, for a child or other person after the decedent's death -- have been around since common law, the trust as a document created while a person is alive is a fairly new concept.

The *Inter Vivos Trust* -- *inter vivos,* meaning "between the living" -- is also referred to as the *Living Trust*, or a "revocable" trust This type of trust is created so that the person creating the trust -- the Settlor or Grantor -- gives his/her property to the trust during her lifetime. (For the purposes of this section, the preferred term will be settlor.) The settlor or settlors, if the trust is created by a married couple, appoint themselves as Trustee(s) of the trust and give themselves all the powers to act as though the property were not in the trust. One of the most crucial areas in creating a trust, and in which a paralegal is often involved, is making sure that *all* of the settlors' property is transferred into the trust once the trust is executed. The trust is also often referred to as a trust agreement because it is essentially an agreement between the settlor(s) and the trustee(s) to transfer the ownership of the property into the trust, that the trust property be treated with certain formalities to maintain the integrity of the trust, that the trustees uphold all fiduciary responsibilities and that they only perform the duties to which they are entitled. The trust is revocable because the settlor(s) can decide at any time to revoke the trust; they may also amend the trust as needed either during their lifetime(s) or after one of them has died, depending upon the provisions of the trust, which provide the ability to revoke and/or amend.

The primary reasons that people create trusts are to:

- Avoid the expense and time often associated with probate;
- Avoid or reduce attorney fees and executor fees;
- Maintain confidentiality of the settlor/trustee's assets;
- Reduce taxes; and
- Protection from creditors.

Provided that the settlor(s) assets are transferred – funded -- into the revocable trust, the trust assets do not require probate. A probate procedure may be required for any assets that are not transferred into the trust. When the settlor/trustee dies, an attorney should be consulted to determine if all assets were properly funded into the name of the trust created for the settlors. A paralegal is instrumental in assisting with asset transfers once the firm has created a revocable trust for the client. Thus, it is very important to gather as much information as possible at the beginning of the estate planning process to learn what assets the client owns. Real property, vehicles, retirement accounts, financial accounts and investments will require documentation to transfer the client's assets into the revocable trust once the trust agreement is executed. Items that do not have title associated with them (e.g., furniture, jewelry and personal belongings) may be "lumped together" into an assignment of property that states all of the settlor's personal assets are to be considered assets of the trust.

Since there is less likelihood that a probate will be required, the estate will not incur the executor fees associated with most probate actions. The attorney fees may also be less depending upon the complexity of the estate and the number of assets with which the client (successor trustee) will need assistance in transferring after the settlor's death. In many states, the attorney fees are statutorily mandated and therefore can be based on the value of the estate rather than on the actual work performed by the attorney in a trust administration.

Probate is subject to public knowledge. When a probate is filed with the court, as discussed above, the decedent's assets must be inventoried and that inventory must be filed with the court. Trust administration is private and therefore, in most cases, will not enter the judicial system where the public would have access to information regarding the client's assets and net worth.

A properly prepared and executed estate plan may reduce the settlor(s)' federal estate taxes provided certain formalities be maintained. The *declaration of trust* (trust agreement) should properly address the manner in which trust assets can be maintained and transferred after the settlor's death. This is particularly important with respect to married couples who have numerous choices of how their property can be maintained after the death of the first spouse. The attorney will work with the client to determine the best avenue for reducing the client's taxes and achieving the goal of transferring property to a spouse and ultimately to the couples' beneficiaries. The attorney will discuss with the client any of the following types of trust provisions that will achieve the clients' goals. Note that there are numerous "types" of trusts or trust provisions. The ones listed here are the most common types:

- Bypass Trust;
- Marital Deduction Trust;
- Disclaimer Trust;
- Survivor's Trust;
- Sprinkling Trust;
- Power of Appointment Trust;
- Special Needs Trust;
- Generation-Skipping Trust;
- Charitable Remainder Trust; and
- Revocable Life Insurance Trust.

A paralegal who works in the area of estate planning will quickly become familiar with the various types of trusts listed above, and others, along with the nuances of these trust provisions.

He/she will also quickly gain knowledge of the complex areas of estate tax and the role it plays in creating the trust for a client.

The area of "wealth management" in estate planning is very complex and involves numerous federal statutes and may involve state statutes in some jurisdictions. For the purposes of this section, the paralegal should be familiar with the Federal Estate Tax Return (Form 706) and know the Annual Exclusion and Unified Credit. The exclusions and credits vary year-to-year and pursuant to Acts of Congress. The current exclusions and credits were amended in 2009. Generally, the Unified Credit is the amount that a person can transfer to their spouse, if they are married, without incurring Federal Estate Taxes. The Annual Exclusion is the maximum amount a person can gift (give) to any individual each and every year. The gift does not have to be to a child of the giftor -- it can be to anyone the giftor chooses. The giftor must file a federal gift tax return each and every year that a gift is given in order to provide a paper trail with the IRS proving that the gifts were made, thus ultimately reducing the individual, or married couples', estate upon death.

One additional aspect of estate planning by using a trust is that it is still necessary for the person(s) to execute a will. This document is often referred to as a *pour-over* will. It is named such, because it "catches" any assets that were not funded into the trust. A common occurrence is that a person or married couple will create a trust and transfer real property into the trust. A deed will be required evidencing proper transfer. However, if the settlor/trustee wishes to refinance the property, the lender may require that the property be removed from the trust since the lender is unable to loan money to the trust. Money must be loaned to individuals, not the entity (trust). Once the loan process is complete, the person(s) forget to transfer the property back into the trust. If the settlor/trustee dies, it may be necessary to obtain a court order to treat the property as though it were intended to be in the trust. As previously discussed, a will can show the testator's intent. A pour-over will typically states that any property not transferred into the trust should be treated as though it was. Another example would be if the client won the lottery and had not decided how to invest or spend the money. While making that decision, he/she places the money in a basic savings account in their favorite financial institution, but that account is not held in the name of the trust. The attorney would have to petition the court, requesting that all assets held in that account should be considered trust assets and should be subject to trust administration rather than probate administration by virtue of the pour-over will.

*Irrevocable Trusts*

An *irrevocable trust* is similar in nature to the revocable trust; however, once the settlor transfers the assets into the revocable trust, he/she no longer may manage the trust property. A person other than the settlor must be named as trustee, and he/she is responsible for the management of the trust property. These types of trusts are often created so that a person or a married couple may reduce their estate by funding the revocable trust subject to the annual exclusion rate. They are similar to a Life Insurance Trust. This trust allows the settlor(s) to take the annual gift exclusion on their income taxes and also will not affect their taxable estate upon their death because the irrevocable trust names a beneficiary or beneficiaries who will receive the property upon the death of the settlor. Thus, federal estate taxes for the amount in the irrevocable trust are not taxable to the decedent's estate. The irrevocable trust will be funded, will accrue interest, cannot be touched by the settlor(s) or the beneficiary(ies), and all funds in the account --because they are liquid -- can be distributed to the beneficiaries upon the death of the settlor, or the second settlor, if for a married couple. The beneficiary(ies) may have to pay taxes on the amounts received pursuant to any federal (IRS) personal taxes and inheritance tax applicable in the state where the settlor(s) resided.

One of the most common types of irrevocable trusts is the *Crummey* trust, named as a result of the case *In re Crummey* (see the glossary), in which the Federal Court of Appeals ruled that the funds held by the irrevocable trust were not taxable under the federal estate tax laws (IRS). This type of irrevocable trust requires that the trustee notify the beneficiaries that he/she can individually elect to receive the share to which they are entitled in the trust. The beneficiary, if he/she has been properly informed of this right and the fact that any election to receive the share may have negative tax consequences, will elect <u>not</u> to receive his/her share. The beneficiary must execute a document (waiver) stating that they will not take the trust property. This is referred to as a *Crummey letter* and must be sent to each beneficiary every year until the death of the settlor or the second settlor if for a married couple.

Note: Anyone studying for the Paralegal Advanced Competency Exam should review the glossary carefully, particularly the words that relate to probate and estate planning. The author was unable to cover all of the aspects of estate planning and probate and the related terminology to give a full understanding of the relative statutes, processes and procedures in this area of law.

## SAMPLE QUESTIONS FOR PROBATE AND ESTATE PLANNING

1. Fred dies intestate. His wife predeceased him. He has three living children and one deceased child. His deceased child had two children (grandchildren). Under a *per stirpes* distribution, the grandchildren will each receive what share?

   a. One-quarter.

   b. One-sixteenth.

   c. One-eighth.

   d. One-fifth.

2. A client attends a meeting with your attorney. The client is the son of the decedent and has brought with him the decedent's holographic will. The attorney would ask the paralegal to initially do all of the following, except:

   a. Determine the names and addresses of the beneficiaries.

   b. Confirm that your jurisdiction will accept a holographic will.

   c. Determine the requirements for a holographic will.

   d. Confirm there are people who can identify the decedent's handwriting.

3. Which of the following is not an example of a beneficiary?

   a. Children named in the testator's will.

   b. Charitable organization named in the testator's will.

   c. Child of person who died intestate.

   d. Grandchild of a child who predeceased the testator.

*Answers:*

1–c. See glossary for *per stirpes* definition. *Per Stirpes* means that if there are two children of a deceased child, each grandchild receives one-half of the share their parent would have received. (Reference: Hanft & Beyer, Chapter 12)

2–a. The paralegal must do B, C, and D in order to determine if a holographic will meets the statutory requirements. (Reference: Hanft & Beyer, Chapter 5)

3–c. A beneficiary (see glossary) is defined as one named in a will to receive property. A person who dies intestate does not have a will. Any issue receiving property is called an heir rather than a beneficiary. (Reference: Hanft & Beyer, Chapter 19)

## 120.00 TECHNOLOGY IN THE LAW

### *120.01 Introduction.*

As technology in the law changes and expands to meet client demands, it is revolutionizing the daily practice of law. Technology is a critical part of a well-functioning law firm and is equally important in government and corporate in-house legal departments. More law firms and corporate legal departments are leveraging their technology as a key strategic asset. These changes and expansions have prompted legal professionals to become proficient at an ever-increasing assortment of communication, word processing, spreadsheet, database, presentation, and legal research applications.

The American Bar Association (ABA) has recommended that all attorneys stay current on the developments in technology, stating that "To maintain the requisite knowledge and skill, a lawyer should keep abreast of changes in the law and its practice, including the benefits and risks associated with relevant technology, engage in continuing study and education and comply with all continuing legal education requirements to which the lawyer is subject."[1]

As part of the legal team, all legal professionals should also stay current on technological changes, as they have had an impact on every aspect of the legal field, from law firm and corporate practice to courtroom procedures and document management. Having a basic understanding of what the different programs are used for, within the legal environment, is crucial. More importantly, one must understand and be able to communicate the concepts of a program with those who are experts.

### *120.02 Computers.*

Cloud Computing

Cloud computing[2] has become popular because it allows for team collaboration, as it allows its users to access systems using a web browser regardless of their location or what device used. An authorized member of the legal team can access the entire contents of the file from any computer with access to the internet or smartphone[3] in the world. It allows for collaboration by means of remote access to computer files. It also allows for the flexibility to share links and set permissions to who can access the files to users assigned the appropriate security permissions. Since, many cloud-based providers place security as a high priority, this level of access usually represents a safer way to access and share data and use applications. Google Drive™, Microsoft Office 365™, Dropbox™, or box.com™ are all cloud-based software services.

Case files can also be accessed via the law firm or corporate legal department's remote-access Virtual Private Network "VPN". A VPN is a network built to serve as a secure access point for a server or website. It connects to the Internet and essentially provides a secure two-way interface

[1] ABA Model Rules of Professional Conduct, Rule 1.1: Competence, Comment on Rule 1.1, Legal Knowledge and Skill, Maintaining Competence 8 *available at* https://www.americanbar.org/groups/professional_responsibility/publications/model_rules_of_professional_conduct/rule_1_1_competence/comment_on_rule_1_1.html (last visited Sept. 29, 2018).

[2] The practice of using a network of remote servers hosted on the Internet to store, manage, and process data, rather than a local server or a personal computer.

[3] A smartphone is a cellular telephone with an integrated computer and other features not originally associated with telephones, such as a camera, sending email, an operating system, web browsing, and the ability to run software applications.

between the information being accessed and the authorized user. When working remotely, having a safe way to access database resources is more important than ever in a world of increasing security threats. VPNs provide enhanced website security due to the data encryption that is transmitted between the authorized user and the network being accessed.

### *Case Management Systems*

Many law firms and corporate legal departments have adopted some form of a case management system. A case management system is simply a computer program that organizes different information for a particular case. It is essentially a computerized version of a traditional file. The benefits of such systems are far-reaching. For instance, case management systems can make the geographical location of the person or persons working on the file irrelevant with the use of telecommuting. The person could be at their desk in the office, using their laptop outside of the office, or in another state attending a deposition. The pertinent file materials are contained on a network that is connected to the Internet.

### *Data Security*

Cybersecurity is the internal protection against cyber hackers who use viruses, email phishing, spyware, or malware infections to cause serious data breaches, including compromise of confidentiality, loss of data, or unauthorized use of electronic data.

Data security is the responsibility of every legal team member, but security breaches are becoming so prevalent that the common thought in security today is that there are two kinds of legal departments: those that have been breached and know it, and those that have been breached but do not know it.

Data encryption is a strong data security measure that protects data stored on computers, laptops, smartphones, tablets, and portable devices. It is a basic safeguard that should be widely deployed and is increasingly being required by statutes for the protection of personal, health and financial information. Full drive encryption provides strong protection for all of the data. The data is then only readable when it is decrypted through use of the correct password or other access control.

Many organizations allow their employees to use their own personal devices to access, create, and manage company related information, a practice commonly referred to as "Bring your own device." Legal organizations usually mandate that software applications are loaded on the device that will remotely erase or block access to the device if it is lost or stolen.

Legal team members need multiple passwords for the varying array of devices, networks, services, and websites they use for work and personal use. But "the careless employee" plagues law firms and corporate legal departments of all sophistication levels when it comes to protecting information, whether it be by keeping a log of all of their passwords on a notepad by their computer or using the same password for all devices and websites. It is strongly recommended that users have a strong password different for each device, network, service, and website. Also, a simple privacy filter on a laptop screen can also aid in the protection of data by making the screen appear dark when looking at it from a specific angle. A filter should be used when using the laptop in public and high traffic areas.

Legal Organizations should regularly update their protocols or policies for handling data, as information security begins with an inventory and risk assessment to determine what needs to be protected and the threats that it faces. The inventory should include both technology and data and should be updated on a continual basis.

*Document Automation Programs*

In the early days of legal technology, the term "document automation" referred to the "mail merge" feature that is available in most word processing programs. This form of document automation is a sophisticated version of copying and pasting. More recent programs provide a new generation of document automation. These software programs are designed for document-intensive areas of the law; *i.e.*, probate law, contract work, corporate, etc. These programs essentially automate many of the functions that an attorney or paralegal would perform when working on a case. The user simply copies some standard information into the program (*e.g.*, caption, addresses of the parties and their respective counsel). Once that information is entered, the user will be directed to answer some quick, interview-like questions such as: who is the injured party or decedent, date of death of decedent, contact information of the parties involved, what type of case is it, etc. from a set of preprogrammed templates. The program will create a set of documents predetermined for it to assemble. Some examples are:

- The initial representation agreement;
- Letters to insurance carriers regarding representation;
- Initial discovery requests to opposing counsel;
- Fee petitions;
- Petitions For Distribution; and
- Marital Settlement Agreements.

The program fills in the correct names, dates, pronouns, singular and plural references and other details using a form of artificial intelligence. The entire process is automated and can essentially complete the work that would take an attorney, paralegal or legal secretary several hours to complete in a matter of minutes. However, document automation programs do have several downsides. For instance, a system described above takes time and money to build and set up correctly. Also, these systems are designed for project-based billing practices or flat-fee billing systems.

*Document Management Systems*

Document management systems have become a staple in most legal organizations. Document management systems are similar to case management systems, but are slightly more limited. Basically, a document management system is a complex database that enables users to associate the document with certain criteria; such as author, document type and file number. Users then have the ability to find certain documents with minimal search times. For instance, a user can search for all Motions for Summary Judgment created by Attorney X within the last two years.

The most important factor in aiding the success of document management systems (or any other database for that matter) is that the system is only as effective as the accuracy of the data entered. If users do not take the time to enter key information carefully and correctly when saving documents to the system, their search results will be degraded when searching for responsive documents.

*General Data Protection Regulation (GDPR)*

The GDPR applies to European Union (E.U.) residents' personal data, entrusted to businesses or individuals in connection with business activities. GDPR generally applies to businesses located anywhere in the world, that hold or processes the personal data of even one citizen of the E.U. The broad reach of this regulation, which took effect May 25, 2018, impacts law firms in the United States and Electronic Discovery service providers that take possession of protected data as a "processor" for litigation or investigations.

A few notable highlights of this regulation include:

- Both the data controller and processor are responsible for proper data protocols; and
- The GDPR includes breach notification obligations in every member state. In general, businesses that suffer a breach must report it to the relevant E.U. supervisory authority within 72 hours of detection, and, if the regulators instruct them to do so, to the affected individuals.

Monetary fines authorized under GDPR non-compliance, could total up to £20 million or 4% of the worldwide annual revenue of the company's prior financial year, whichever is higher.[15]

*Imaging Documents*

Many of the technological changes and expansions in the legal profession center around the transferring of paper documents into electronic documents. Although this process has different names, such as imaging, paper to PDF[16], digitizing, or scanning, the fundamentals of the process remain consistent. The process of imaging documents involves a scanner and a computer with some form of imaging software. The scanner can be as simple as a flatbed scanner connected to a single computer, or can be as complicated as a high-volume feed tray scanner connected to a computer network capable of sending the scanned images as email attachments to any email address. Certain scanners can even create cover sheets for scan jobs that will automatically route scanned images into certain document management systems or case management systems. The process scans the paper document(s) and creates an electronic document. The documents are

[15] European Commission, 2018 reform of EU data protection rules https://eur-lex.europa.eu/content/news/general-data-protection-regulation-GDPR-applies-from-25-May-2018.html (last visited August 10, 2025).

[16] Portable Document Format (PDF) is an electronic file format that provides an electronic image of text, fonts, or graphics that looks like a printed document. PDF/A ("A" stands for archive) differs from PDF by prohibiting features not suited for long-term archiving, such as font linking (as opposed to font embedding).

then referred to as "images" and are true and accurate copies of the electronic copies of paper documents.

Some people use the imaging process for disaster recovery/document retention purposes (*i.e.*, creating a backup copy stored on a computer, in the event that the original paper version is destroyed). Other people use the imaging process as replacement for the paper version, creating a virtual paperless office. Working with images has many benefits, including electronic searchability, the ability to highlight or flag documents, or print and email pages of a document.

Once the document has been imaged, software packages allow users to manipulate the electronic document that ultimately makes them superior to the static paper document. For instance, Adobe Acrobat Professional® has the ability to:

- Make the electronic document searchable by running an Optical Character Recognition "OCR" process on the document;
- Highlight sections of the document;
- Create and complete PDF fillable forms;
- Convert the PDF documents into other file types (Text, Spreadsheet, etc.) from file, save as menu;
- Securely redact information on the electronic document and, later, safely produce the document in electronic form;
- Read the document out loud, from the view menu;
- "Scrub" the electronic document to remove hidden metadata;
- Create electronic signatures;
- Combine multiple PDF documents;
- Use commenting features; and
- Add Bates-numbers to the electronic document.

***120.03 Office Productivity Resources.***

<u>*Archival Data Policies vs. Disaster Recovery Policies*</u>

In general, people and companies store information for archival purposes or disaster recovery purposes. Archival storage involves storing inactive information for possible later retrieval. Disaster recovery storage involves storing active information on a routine basis for potential system recovery in the face of disaster. Each type of storage has its own unique quirks and potential impact on ediscovery. For instance, archival storage can involve outdated media that is difficult to view, search and reproduce.

*Electronically Stored Information (ESI)*

Electronically Stored Information is the term specifically referenced in the amendments to Fed. R. Civ. P. 34. ESI refers to all digital information created or stored in computers. This includes any data found in email, voice mail, instant and text messages, databases, metadata, digital images and any other type of file.

*Artificial Intelligence (AI)*

AI has entered our everyday lives via smart speakers such as: Siri™, Echo™, Alexa™, or a simple internet search, with very few limitations. At least for the time being, one of the most significant limitations of AI as it relates to the law, is that it is not doing legal work for the legal team but is "pre-filtering" relevant content. AI's use in the legal setting has revolved around the computer's ability to perform a task or series of functions that had traditionally been the sole responsibility of a legal professional or team of professionals. This allows the legal team to narrow their focus on the issues that matter the most.

AI powered software can automate work and predict outcomes by analyzing words, classifying and searching for paragraphs, comparing documents and highlighting changes, which is also called "predictive coding", improving the efficiency of document analysis for legal use. AI software assists with data-driven decisions to improve efficiency and molding and shaping the future of almost every aspect of our lives, including the law. Though research on ways to use AI for legal work are ongoing, it looks as if AI may expand the work of lawyers by making them more efficient[17].

*Communication*

There are various options available to communicate with clients and within the legal environment, or that need to be preserved for potential production in litigation. The key is to select the appropriate communication tool to share information within a group meeting, a conversation with a peer, or with a client and be able to share that information securely. Though the list of resources is extensive, we offer a brief summary of some of the some of the more common below.

Blogs

Blogs[18] have evolved into sources for news and commentary about current events, politics and other subjects of interest. A blog typically works as follows:

(1) the author of the blog will post a short commentary on a subject of interest, *i.e.*, a Supreme Court decision; and

[17] *Automation in the Legal Industry: How Will it Affect if Affect Recent Law School Grads?* Pritkin, Martin, Smart Lawyer, 03/07/18

[18] http://www.abajournal.com/magazine/article/best_law_blogs_web_100?utm_campaign=sidebar Web 100: Best Law Blogs. (last visited August 10, 2025).

(2) the readers of the blog review the commentary and post their own comments and thoughts on the subject.

The posts and comments evolve into an online discussion.

In recent years, legal professionals have created legal blogs, also called *blawgs,* that exist on just about any subject imaginable and tend to be very specialized sources of information. For instance, there are entire blogs dedicated to discussing ediscovery or blogs designed especially for litigation paralegals.

Email

Email messaging is playing a huge role in most legal organizations as the main communication tool, as it is frequently used for routine correspondence, communication within the firm, and confirmation of court filings. Because emailing has become the most common way to communicate, it is imperative to protect both the sender of the email and the receiver from cyber threats.

Podcasts

Podcasts are audio files available for downloading over the Internet. The files are encoded in the .mp3 file format (a high-quality compressed audio file format) and incorporated into an RSS feed. RSS stands for Really Simple Syndication or Rich Site Summary. In its most basic form, it is a way to feed updates and/or headlines from websites to users both quickly and efficiently. The RSS feed enables a person to subscribe to a podcast and receive updated audio files with a few clicks of the mouse. Most media outlets have podcast subscriptions available on most major news shows. Since podcasts are disguised RSS feeds, the updated files are delivered to your computer, thus saving the need to search the Internet for new audio files. Podcasts are a great way for legal professionals to keep apprised of news and information relevant to their practice. Most legal educational companies and the ABA even offer CLE courses via podcast and some law schools and paralegal programs offer lectures via podcast.

Project Management Platforms

Skype™ is a telecommunications application that provides voice and video conference calls, between computers and portable devices via the Internet. Users are able to transmit and display digital documents and video. Skype™ also provides instant messaging services.

Slack™ is another chat and collaboration platform used by legal teams or between individuals to facilitate organized communication. It integrates with services on the web, like Dropbox and Google Docs.

Trello™ is a work flow and project management platform used by teams to facilitate collaboration and effective organization of project boards. It integrates with services such as Gmail™ and Slack™ and provides visual data on the status of work assignments, members assigned to specific tasks, and where a project is in a process.

Text Messaging/Instant Messaging

Based on client demands and the common usage of smartphones, communicating via text message has become common practice in the legal environment. Some conversations will always be better suited for an email, in person, or on the phone; however, using text messaging can save time when sharing:

- Office hours or directions;
- Meeting or court date notifications;
- Internal staff emergency communication; or
- Payment reminders.

Continue to maintain the same level of professionalism that other forms of communication have within the legal environment. While texting can save time and improve client communication, it is important to remember that it is an accompaniment and not a replacement for more formal communication. Also note, texting is discoverable because it is written information.

Instant messaging is a form of online chat that occurs in real-time through an intranet (through a LAN) or internet connection. These are usually short messages transmitted between two or more parties. Care should also be taken when using instant messaging to use the same care and professionalism as in other forms of written communications.

*Databases*

Databases allow users to organize large amounts of information in a systematic way that aids users in searching and retrieving the information at a later date. Databases are built to allow users to tag information with descriptions in "fields." The users can then retrieve information using search "queries." A query simply searches a specific field(s) in the data set for specific term(s). An example of a common database is to store information about people (*i.e.*, name, birth date, hair color, eye color, etc.). Someone wanting to search the database could customize their search by utilizing any information that was input into a field of the data set. For instance, the user could search for all persons whose last name begins with "S," who have a birth date in April and who have brown hair. More complex database queries can be built around "and/or" searches that either narrow or widen your search as appropriate. Databases can be built around people, documents, places, products or just about any other data set. Databases are often used by legal professionals to store information about people and are also used to store information about documents.

*Document Review*

Document review was traditionally done by trained members of the legal team who would examine static paper documents to determine whether the information should be turned over to an opposing party in response to a discovery request. ESI has increased the volume of digital information for review and a web-based platform like Relativity®[19] is used to locate information relevant to the pending litigation, for confidential, relevance, privilege, or work product content.

*Duty to Disclose; General Provisions Governing Discovery*

The amendments to Fed. R. Civ. P. 26 are closely intertwined with sections of Rule 16 requiring early discussion of ESI. Rule 26 expressly mandates that the parties discuss "any issues about preserving discoverable information." This amendment requires parties to have an understanding of their client's archive system, disaster recovery system and document retention policy. This obligation also encourages law firms and corporate legal departments to have plans for preserving discoverable information, such as litigation hold policies. Most businesses already have, or should have, a litigation hold policy that can be implemented in a short period of time to preserve discoverable information. This obligation is especially important in the digital era when ESI is moved, archived and/or deleted pursuant to preset or even the default system settings. Unlike traditional paper documents that take an affirmative act by a person when they are destroyed, ESI can be (and often is) destroyed without anyone doing anything. These amendments also require early discussion of "any issues about disclosure, discovery, or preservation of electronically stored information, including the form or forms in which it should be produced."

*Electronic Discovery*

Electronic discovery (ediscovery) refers to discovery of electronic or digital information. The most common discovery involves electronically stored information like email or text messages. The need for ediscovery has steadily increased while people and business move away from traditional paper files and correspondence to electronic files, email, and information stored in a digital form. The challenges of ediscovery and protecting the data involved in the process increase each year.

There are generally two schools of thought regarding the nature of ediscovery. Some believe that "discovery is discovery," regardless of the medium. Others believe that ediscovery is unique to traditional discovery models and is therefore entitled to special treatment, rules and guidelines. Regardless of which theory is closer to your own, everyone agrees that ediscovery has become a huge issue that is being thrust upon the legal profession with changes in technology. Simply put, if you are not actively and aggressively seeking information through carefully designed ediscovery practices, you are not getting all of the information that you should and you are not producing all of the information that you should.

The digital age has enabled people to produce, retain and store large amounts of information at a relatively modest cost. The sheer volume of information has grown exponentially and continues to do so. The practice of law, by its very nature, depends upon access to such information through the discovery process. The courts began to recognize this question during the years 2000 to 2003. Shortly thereafter, a list of proposed amendments to the Federal Rules of Civil Procedure (Fed. R. Civ. P.) was presented. The amendments include significant changes to Rules 16, 26, 33, 34, 37 and 45, as well as Form 35. During the years 2000 through 2003, the judiciary and affiliated bar organizations formed advisory committees and mini-conferences, and

[19] Relativity® Software Tutorial https://www.youtube.com/watch?v=TJnYPfRIHEw (last visited August 10, 2025).

established local rules to address the issues concerning electronic information. These groups also came together at The Sedona Conference®, an annual conference of attorneys, judges, business leaders, IT professionals and others. The conference was designed to help facilitate the exchange of ideas about technology issues confronting the legal profession. The conference formed a set of ediscovery guidelines known as "The Sedona Principles."[20]

In 2004, the Standing Committee on Federal Rules of Procedure presented a list of proposed amendments to the Federal Rules of Civil Procedure. These amendments were presented for public comment and proceeded through an amendment process. The amendments were finalized at a judicial conference in September 2005. The proposed amendments were then presented to the U.S. Supreme Court, which unanimously adopted the proposed amendments in April 2006. On December 1, 2006, the amendments went into effect for nearly all civil cases pending in United States District Courts.

The 2006 amendments included significant changes to the Federal Rules of Civil Procedure concerning discovery and also introduced several important terms into the legal lexicon of which paralegals should be aware.

*Electronic Filing*

Electronic Filing (e-filing) is the process of filing a court document either over the Internet through on an online system or through a scanning station located at a courthouse. The scanning station is designed to allow users walk-up access to scan a document and then route it to a certain court and cause number. This is usually accomplished through a touch screen interface. E-filing systems also work well with online dockets to allow users access to not only the docket, but also quick links to copies of the scanned images themselves. Allowing e-filing saves courts the trouble of imaging documents and preparing document descriptions for items being filed with the court.

Most e-filing systems work with a standard image format such as PDF or TIFF[21]. Once the image is uploaded and filed, the attorneys involved in the case receive an email from the filing system with a message about what was filed. The email usually contains a link to view the document itself. E-filing systems are extremely efficient because they save money on paper, printing and postage costs associated with filing a document and sending service copies. These systems also save money on imaging costs to the recipient since the document is already imaged when it is received. Finally, these systems save money on storage costs for all parties. Much like the online docket systems referenced above, e-filing systems are available at the federal court level. E-filing systems at the state court level are available in some states and counties. Most of the systems are funded by small surcharges billed to users either on a subscription fee basis or by the number of pages or documents filed.

---

[20] The Sedona Conference publishes annual writings on these issues referred to as *The Sedona Principles*. This set of 14 principles, while not binding on courts, have been cited in many of the major ESI court cases and provide a general framework for ESI in lieu of established practice and case law regarding same.

[21] Tagged Image File Format, abbreviated TIFF or TIF, is a computer file format. TIFF is widely supported by scanning, faxing, word processing, optical character recognition, image manipulation.

*Forensically-Sound Imaging*

The ediscovery process sometimes involves the need to preserve and reproduce exact copies or mirror images of hard disk drives, data found on devices like tablets, or smartphones. Reproducing a forensically-sound copy will often involve engaging the services of a computer forensics expert who will prepare a byte-for-byte copy of a hard drive or raw data from the computer, tablet or smartphone that will withstand judicial scrutiny. EnCase®[22] is one such web-based software tool that can assist with forensic data gathering.

*Hash Values*

*Hash values* are codes that are the digital equivalent to a fingerprint or DNA code. A hash value can be specific to a particular sentence, a file, a folder or an entire hard drive. The smallest change, *i.e.*, changing a period to a comma, will drastically alter the hash value. These codes are used to analyze sources of information and to examine their integrity.

*Horizontal and Vertical Deduplication*

The process of *deduplication* (also called de-duping) simply attempts to identify and separate files that are exact duplicates of each other prior to the review and production phases of ediscovery. De-duping may occur with a single user (*i.e.*, a party) or with several users (*i.e.*, key players or custodians). Vertical de-duping locates duplicates within the records and data of a single custodian. Horizontal de-duping applies globally across a set of custodians.

*Interrogatories to Parties*

The amendments to Fed. R. Civ. P. 33 simply incorporate ESI into the option to produce business records. In other words, if an answer to an interrogatory can be found by searching the ESI of a party, then a producing party can allow the option to access its electronic information systems to search for certain information or allow a party to simply produce certain ESI in response to particular interrogatories. A party who invokes Rule 33(d) may be required to provide direct access to its electronic information system. Such access would inevitably carry with it increased security and confidentiality concerns.

*Failure to Make Disclosures or to Cooperate in Discovery; Sanctions*

Fed. R. Civ. P. 37 states that, absent exceptional circumstances, a court may not impose sanctions under these rules on a party for failing to provide ESI lost as a result of the routine, good faith operation of an electronic information system. This "safe harbor provision" will rely heavily upon document retention policies and litigation hold policies to decide what is or is not "routine, good faith operation." There are also two important caveats to the safe harbor provision of Rule 37. First, the safe harbor provision *does not* apply to information which is lost after a preservation hold or litigation hold is initiated, or after litigation is initiated. Second, Rule 37 was also intentionally left limited in its scope with its reference to not being able to impose sanctions "under these rules." It does not affect other sources of authority to impose sanctions, violations of statutory responsibility or the rules of professional responsibility. Rule 37 is further

---

[22] EnCase® Software Tutorial https://www.youtube.com/watch?v=6S2hCDYTb2Y&t=91s (last visited August 10, 2025)

limited in that a judge is able to decide whether the facts of the case fit the "exceptional circumstances" exemption of this rule.

*Noisy Search Terms*

Search terms and search strings should be carefully designed to return the optimal number of responsive documents while avoiding irrelevant information. Noisy search terms are terms that return a high number of false negatives. Search terms should be concise, case-specific and general enough to capture relevant documents, but concise enough to avoid excessive results.

*Litigation Hold Policies*

Litigation hold policies have always been a part of litigation. They are essentially preset plans of action that are initiated when litigation is deemed "probable." These plans of action are designed to segregate potentially relevant information from inadvertent spoliation or destruction. Litigation hold policies in years past usually involved someone in management taking a file and locking it in a cabinet. However, when dealing with ediscovery, litigation hold policies have become more important and more complicated than ever. Ediscovery compliant litigation hold policies can involve segregating email accounts, copying computer hard drives, and disrupting automatic deletion protocols.

Many organizations allow their employees to use their own personal devices to access, create, and manage company related information, a practice commonly referred to as "Bring your own device" policy mentioned previously. These personal devices must be included in litigation hold requests.

A corporation may have to pay penalties if it does not comply with a litigation hold. The penalties include large monetary fines, reimbursement of the opponent's litigation costs, or inferences against the party failing to meet discovery obligations. Individuals who fail to comply with a litigation hold can also be sanctioned.

*Native vs. Converted Files*

Native file format is the original format of a particular file, for example, a Microsoft Word document (.doc or .docx). That same file can be converted to an image file, such as Adobe Acrobat® (PDF). One of the first questions that must be answered when addressing issues concerning ediscovery is whether the ESI is going to be produced in native file format or converted to a more user-friendly format such as PDF or TIFF. The best answer to the question will depend on very specific facts of a case. Native files generally have such benefits as intact metadata and search capability. At the same time, many databases are simply too large and cumbersome to handle native format and should be converted to PDF or TIFF.

*Online Docket Systems*

The entire Federal Court System is available online and accessible via the Internet through PACER (Public Access to Court Electronic Records). PACER is an electronic public access service that allows users to obtain case and docket information from federal appellate, district and bankruptcy courts and from the U.S. Party/Case Index. Online docket systems allow users to check the docket for most cases (most states restrict access to criminal case dockets) via the Internet. Some online dockets even allow users to view, save and print the documents listed. At the state court level, access to online court records is much more sporadic and varies from state-to-state, and from county-to-county. Some state courts have dockets available online for their upper-level courts as well as access to recent and archived court decisions. At the county level, some court systems have online docket systems while others are available through third-party vendors who charge a subscription or access fee to perform searches. Some county courts have no online docket systems available whatsoever, or online docket access available only to parties and counsel-of-record.

*Presentation Software*

Presentation software (*e.g.*, PowerPoint™ or Google Slide™) is used to create a complex slide show. The slide show can be a simple presentation to coworkers, a more complex presentation involving mediation, or presentation of a trial to a jury. Presentation software allows users to fully customize their presentation and integrate picture, videos, imaged documents and audio files into their presentation. The software also allows users to customize such things as the background of the slides, the color of text, the manner in which the text appears (animations) and the speed at which objects appear. Nearly every facet of the presentation is customizable.

*Pretrial Conferences; Scheduling; Management*

The amendments to Fed. R. Civ. P. 16 specifically require parties to discuss (within the 120 days of the filing of the complaint) "provisions for disclosure or discovery of electronically stored information." This amendment requires that each of the parties know either generally or precisely what ESI they are seeking and what ESI is in the possession of their respective clients. The parties will also need to know:

- How their clients archive or store information;
- What information is stored;
- For what duration is certain information stored;
- Where certain information is located;
- How information can be searched and/or indexed; and
- How ESI can/should be produced.

The parties are going to need to discuss practical limitations and sensible obligations regarding preservation and production of ESI.

These amendments also require the parties to discuss "claims of privilege or of protection as trial-preparation material after production." This concept is often referred to as "claw back," "take back" or "inadvertent disclosure" agreements. The courts clearly realized that the increase in the volume of ESI being requested and produced would inevitably lead to either: (1) more inadvertent disclosures of privileged information; or (2) a dramatic increase in litigation costs associated with pre-production attorney review of information. This amendment encourages the parties to reach an agreement regarding the consequences and handling of ESI or documents that are inadvertently produced during discovery.

Fortunately, the legitimacy of claw back agreements was clarified by way of amendment to Fed. R. Evid. 502 (Attorney-Client Privilege and Work Product; Limitations on Waiver), that took effect September 2008. It essentially sets to minimize the cost of ediscovery in litigation, while minimizing broad waivers of privilege in federal proceedings. The effect is that the inadvertent disclosure will not act as a waiver in the pending litigation and an agreement between the parties is binding only if it is incorporated into the Evidence Rule 502(d) order.

*Production of Documents, Electronically Stored Information, and Tangible Things, or Entering onto Land for Inspection and Other Purposes*

Fed. R. Civ. P. 34 has been amended to provide that any party may serve onto any other party a request to produce ESI. The rule would also permit the party making the request to inspect, copy, test or sample electronically-stored information stored in any storage medium from which information can be obtained. The responding party is also required to translate, if necessary, any ESI that it produces into a "reasonably usable form." A very important amendment to this rule also states that the request may specify the "form or forms" in which the ESI is to be produced. The three general forms of production are: native, quasi-native and converted. The producing party may object to the requested form or forms of production by stating the reason for the objection, *i.e.*, overly burdensome or cost prohibitive. If an objection is made to the form or forms of production, or if no specific form was requested, then the responding party would be required to state the form or forms that it intends to use for production purposes. If a request does not specify the form or forms for producing ESI, a responding party must produce the information in the form or forms in which it is ordinarily maintained, *or* in a form that is reasonably usable. A party need not produce the same ESI in more than one form. Although not required under the rules, the parties can stipulate to the production of ESI in more than one form for practical purposes. For example, Excel spreadsheets may be produced in native form so that cell formulas are visible, and also produced in a quasi-native format so that the spreadsheets can be Bates-numbered for use during depositions.

*Spreadsheets*

Spreadsheets allow users to collect and analyze data in many different ways. Spreadsheets are based on x-axis (rows) and y-axis (columns) models. Once data is collected in a spreadsheet, it can be analyzed and even exported to create charts, graphs and other graphics. Spreadsheets look and can act similar to tables that are available in word processing documents, but the main difference is that spreadsheets use formulas. Formulas can be as simple as an auto sum feature that will find the sum or average of a set of numbers, or as complex and advanced as Ph.D.-level physics and accounting formulas. Spreadsheets are a great tool for compiling lists of names, addresses and telephone numbers. They are also great for performing an analysis of damages.

Certain spreadsheets can also be web-based, which allows users to invite others to input data to the spreadsheet or perform an analysis of the data collection.

*Subpoena*

Fed. R. Civ. P. 45 has several important provisions that have serious impacts on both parties and non-parties alike. Rule 45 was amended to add that a subpoena shall command each person to whom it is directed to attend and give testimony or to produce and permit inspection, copying, testing or sampling of, among other things, ESI. In addition, a subpoena may specify the form or forms in which ESI is to be produced. Similar to Rule 34, if a subpoena does not specify the form or forms for producing ESI, a responding party would be required to produce the ESI in the form or forms that it is ordinarily maintained or in a form or forms that are reasonably usable. Rule 45 also incorporates the provisions of Fed. R. Civ. P. 26(b)(2)(B), stating that a party or non-party responding to a subpoena need not provide ESI from sources that the party identifies as not reasonably accessible due to undue burden or cost. However, motion practice on the issue places the burden on the responding party to show that the information is not reasonably accessible because of undue burden or cost. Even if such a showing is made, the court may order discovery from that party, or non-party, if the requesting party shows good cause considering the limitations that are set forth in Rule 26(b)(2)(C) (whether the discovery sought is unreasonable or the burden of expense outweighs the benefit). The court may also specify conditions for production of the requested ESI and in certain situations allow cost shifting.

Discovery historically has been characterized by collating collections of static paper documents, identifying such collections with Bates numbers, and creating some sort of organizational framework to utilize such documents in the litigation process. The digital age of discovery is making static paper documents obsolete. The idea of static paper documents is being replaced by dynamic databases that would dwarf even the largest paper files imaginable. The traditional discovery model is quickly being replaced by creative and adaptable systems to manage ESI. These changes to the established methods of discovery collection, production and organization will affect us all.

*Trial Presentation Software*

Trial presentation software (*e.g.*, PowerPoint™, TrialDirector 360™, and TrialPad™) provides legal professionals with the ability to present evidence in a digital format to juries. Jurors will oftentimes be provided with individual LCD screens to allow them view documents or videos. Trial presentation software also allows users to customize the effects of their presentation to create *box-out effects* (show a small view of a document and enlarge a particular sentence or section to show emphasis or importance). Users can also mix audio or video files to play alongside visual representations of prior testimony. This demonstrative effect can be a powerful method of pointing out inconsistent testimony from the witness' own words. A form of trial presentation software is to use virtual reality in the courtroom to allow jurors to visit the crime scene (virtually) or see a re-creation of an accident in a virtual environment. This gives computer programs the ability to re-create a virtual crime scene using pictures of a crime scene.

Jurors could move around and even watch re-creations of incidents through virtual reality headsets.

Another form of electronic trial presentation of importance is Video Evidence Presentation System (VEPS). Nearly all federal courts across the country have some level of a VEPS in place. VEPS are complex systems designed to encompass many different forms of evidence presentation technology into the courtroom. These systems include:

- Digital document cameras;
- VHS/DVD players;
- Touch screen monitors;
- Wireless touch screen remotes;
- LCD screens; and
- Wireless presentation controls.

Mixed visual and audio presentations can be made from the VEPS podium or from counsel's table via laptop connection.[23]

*Word Processing*

Word processing programs are primarily used to create text documents. However, there are many different types of word processing programs, each with their own unique characteristics. The most basic form of word processing program is a notepad program that simply allows users to type and save information as simple text files (.txt).

More advanced programs, such as Microsoft Word™ or Corel WordPerfect™, offer users much more complex formatting options with text documents. Options include:

- Highlighting text;
- Working with tracked changes; and
- Creating tables of contents and indices.

A third type of word processing program is web-based document creation. This type of system allows users to create and edit text documents from any Internet-ready computer, without any software other than a web browser. The key advantage to this type of system is that the documents are available to the person from any computer. The user simply goes to a certain website (*i.e.*, Google has a free web-based word processing program called Google Docs™), logs in and has instant access to their documents. The other unique advantage of this system is that it allows the document creator to invite certain people to be able to view and edit the document in

[23] The VEPS guide for legal professionals, *available at* http://www.insd.uscourts.gov/courtroom-technology and https://www.youtube.com/watch?v=V8aqOA0fZ5g . (last visited August 10, 2025).

real time, called file-sharing, which also allows for real time, multi-person editing of documents. The ability of real time editing is something that is unique to web-based word processing programs.

***120.04 Conclusion.***

Law firms and corporation legal departments must work more diligently than ever to protect the often highly sensitive electronic data entrusted to them, paying great attention to data security. The successful legal teams of the future will use technology to simplify workflows and update manual processes, as each legal professional should be dedicated to continually stay abreast of the changes in the law. Attorneys and their legal staff must also pay attention to changes in the technology that impact or have the potential to impact their clients so that they remain competent in defending the needs of their clients.

## BIBLIOGRAPHY FOR FURTHER RESEARCH AND STUDY

### Reference


*Abercrombie & Fitch Co. v. Hunting World, Inc.*, 537 F.2d 4, 9 (189 U.S.P.Q. 759)

*Age Discrimination in Employment Act* of 1967 (ADEA)

American Association for Paralegal Education, *Paralegal Core Competencies* (Revised 2002), available at: http://www.aafpe.org/p_about/core_comp.pdf., (last visited Dec. 30, 2010)

American Bar Association Informal Opinion 88-1526, *Imputed Disqualification Arising from Change in Employment by Nonlawyer Employee* (1988)

American Bar Association, *Divorce – Overview – ABA Family Legal Guide – Family Law*, available at: http://public.findlaw.com/abaflg/flg-3.html (last visited Dec. 30, 2010)

American Bar Association, Model Code of Judicial Conduct, 2011, available at: https://www.americanbar.org/groups/professional_responsibility/publications/model_code_of_judicial_conduct/ (last visited Feb. 10, 2019)

American Bar Association, *Model Guidelines for the Utilization of Paralegal Services*, 2018, *available at* https://www.americanbar.org/content/dam/aba/administrative/paralegals/ls_prlgs_modelguidelines.pdf (last visited Dec. 30, 2018)

American Bar Association, *Model Rules of Professional Conduct,* 2016, available at: https://www.americanbar.org/groups/professional_responsibility/publications/model_rules_of_professional_conduct/model_rules_of_professional_conduct_table_of_contents/ (last visited Feb. 10, 2019)

American Bar Association, *The Legal Assistant's Guide to Professional Responsibility* (2d ed. 2004)

*Americans with Disabilities Act* (ADA), 42 U.S.C. § 12101

*Barron's Law Dictionary* (Barrons 1996)

Block, Gertrude, *Effective Legal Writing* (3d ed. Foundation Press 1986)

Brown, Deanna Jean, "Time Management for Paralegals," as reprinted in *Fundamentals of Law Office Management Systems, Procedures and Ethics* by Pamela I. Everett, *infra.*

Bruno, Carole A., *Paralegal's Litigation Handbook* (2d ed. Delmar Thomson Learning 1993)

Burke, William J., *Accounting Systems for Law Offices* (Matthew Bender 1992)

Cannon, Therese A. and Aytch, Sybil Taylor, *Ethics and Professional Responsibility for Paralegals* (8th ed. Wolters Kluwer 2017)

*Civil Rights Acts of 1964 and 1991*

Cohn, Steven, "Beyond the 'Chinese Wall,'" *Legal Assistant Today*, November/December 1995, page 46

*Consumer Credit Protection Act,* 15 U.S.C. §§ 1601 *et seq.*

Eimermann, Thomas, *Fundamentals of Paralegalism* (4th ed. Aspen 1996)

Elwell, Celia C. & Smith, Robert Barr, *Practical Legal Writing for Legal Assistants* (West/Delmar 1996)

*Employee Retirement Income Security Act of 1974 (ERISA),* 29 U.S.C. §§ 1001 *et seq.*

*Equal Pay Act*, an amendment to the Fair Labor Standards Act, 42 U.S.C. § 201 *et seq.*

Everett, Pamela I., *Fundamentals of Law Office Management Systems, Procedures and Ethics* (West 1994)

*Fair Credit Reporting Act,* 15 U.S.C. § 1681 *et seq.*

*Family and Medical Leave Act of 1993*

*Federal Rules of Appellate Procedure* (West) (updated annually)

*Federal Rules of Civil Procedure* (West) (updated annually)

*Federal Rules of Evidence* (West) (updated annually)

Feldman, Robert A. & Nimmer, Raymond T., *Drafting Effective Contracts: A Practitioner's Guide* (2d ed. Aspen 2004), available at: http://www.aspenpublishers.com/Product.asp?catalog%5Fname=Aspen&category%5Fname=&product%5Fid=0735503761&Mode=SEARCH&ProductType=M

Fiske, Robert Hartwell, *Dictionary of Concise Writing* (Writer's Digest 1996)

Garner, Bryan A., *A Dictionary of Modern Legal Usage* (2d ed. Oxford 2001)

Garrett, Vena, *Introduction to Legal Assisting* (McGraw-Hill/Glencoe 1992)

Garwin, Arthur H., *The Paralegal's Practical Guide to Professional Responsibility* (4th ed., American Bar Association Center for Professional Responsibility, 2015

*General Information About 35 U.S.C. 161 Plant Patents,* available at: http://www.uspto.gov/web/offices/pac/plant/index.html (last visited Dec. 30, 2010)

Goode, C. Edward, *Mightier Than the Sword: Powerful Writing in the Legal Profession* (Blue Jeans Press 1989)

Hamilton, Robert W., *The Law of Corporations: In a Nutshell* (5th ed. West 2000)

Hanft, John K. & Beyer, Gerry W., *Wills, Trusts, and Estates for Legal Assistants* (3d ed. Wolters Kluwer 2009)

Harvard Law Review Association, *The Bluebook: A Uniform System of Citation* (19th ed. 2010)

Helewitz, Jeffrey A., *Basic Contract Law for Paralegals* (6th ed. Aspen 2010)

http://office.microsoft.com/en-us/default.aspx (last visited Sept. 29, 2018)

http://ww7.bankruptcycya.com/ (last visited Feb. 10, 2019)

http://www.adobe.com/products/acrobat/solutions/legal/ (last visited Sept. 29, 2018)

http://www.hotdocs.com/ (last visited Sept. 29, 2018)

http://www.justice.gov/ust/ (last visited Feb. 10, 2019)

http://www.pacer.gov/ (last visited Sept. 29, 2018)

http://www.paralegals.org/associations/2270/files/Model_Code_of_Ethics_09_06.pdf (last visited Dec. 30, 2010)

http://www.paralegals.org/associations/2270/files/Model_Code_of_Ethics_09_06.pdf (last visited Dec. 30, 2010)

http://www.paralegals.org/displaycommon.cfm?an=1&subarticlenbr=388 (last visited Dec. 30, 2010)

http://www.thebankruptcysite.org/bankruptcy-exemptions (exemptions for every state) (last visited May 20, 2016)

http://www.uscourts.gov/FederalCourts/Bankruptcy/BankruptcyResources/PovertyGuidelines.aspx (Poverty Guidelines 2019) (last visited Feb. 10, 2019)

https://biglawbusiness.com/client-communication-in-the-texting-era/ (last visited Sept. 29, 2018)

https://complexdiscovery.com/sedona-conference-updating-important-ediscovery-principles/ (last visited Sept. 29, 2018)

https://iprotech.com/ (last visited Sept. 29, 2018)

https://lawyerist.com/legal-competence-digital-age/ (last visited Sept. 29, 2018)

https://searchmobilecomputing.techtarget.com/definitions (last visited Sept. 29, 2018)

https://www.americanbar.org/groups/departments_offices/legal_technology_resources/resources.html (last visited Sept. 29, 2018)

https://www.paralegals.org/files/Model_Code_of_Ethics_09_06_rev12-9-14.pdf (last visited Aug. 30, 2018)

Hutzler, "How to Organize a Law Office Filing System," *Law Office Management* (American Law Institute and American Bar Association Manual No. 5 84, 1984)

*Immigration Reform and Control Act*, 8 U.S.C. §§1101 *et seq.*

Jakab, Peter, *Handling Federal Discovery* (James 1995)

*Jury System Improvement Act*, 28 U.S.C. § 1875

Kerley, Peggy N., *Computers and the Law* (National Federation of Paralegal Associations 1991)

Kolszynski, Phillip, *Preparing for Trial in Federal Court* (James 1996)

Kubasek, Nancy K., et al., *The Legal Environment of Business: A Critical Thinking Approach*, (5th ed. Prentice Hall 2008)

Larbalestrier, Deborah E., *Paralegal Practice and Procedure: A Practical Guide for the Legal Assistant* (3d ed. Prentice Hall 1994)

LeClercq, Terri, *Expert Legal Writing* (University of Texas Press 1995)

LeClercq, Terri, *Guide to Legal Writing Style* (4th ed. Aspen 2007)

Legal Assistant Management Association, Manager's Manual Series (LAMA 2000)

Legal Talk Network https://legaltalknetwork.com/podcasts/ (last visited Sept. 29, 2018)

*Manual of Patent Examining Procedure* [MPEP], available at: http://www.uspto.gov/web/offices/pac/mpep/mpep.htm (last visited Dec. 30, 2010)

Martindale-Hubbell, *Divorce Law Glossary*, available at: https://www.theattorneystore.com/legal/glossary/term/martindale-hubbell_law (last visited Dec. 30, 2010)

Murry, "Team Practice That Works: Putting an End to the Feeling of 'Us and Them' in the Law Office," 2 *Legal Assistant Today* (28, No. 3, Spring 1985)

National Association of Legal Assistants, *Code of Ethics and Professional Responsibility,* available at: https://www.nala.org/certification/nala-code-ethics-and-professional-responsibility (last visited Aug. 30, 2018)

National Federation of Paralegal Associations, *Model Code of Ethics and Professional Responsibility and Guidelines for Enforcement*, available at: https://www.paralegals.org/files/Model_Code_of_Ethics_09_06_rev12-9-14.pdf (last visited Feb. 15, 2019)

National Federation of Paralegal Associations, *Paralegals and Conflict of Interest*, 1995, available at: http://www.paralegals.org/displaycommon.cfm?an=1&subarticlenbr=390 (last visited Dec. 30, 2010)

National Federation of Paralegal Associations, *The Ethical Wall: Its Application to Paralegals*, Revised 2001, available at: https://www.paralegals.org/files/THE_ETHICAL_WALL.pdf (last visited Feb. 15, 2019)

Nesci, Vincent, "Case Management System Reduces Time Spent Handling Documents," *Legal Management*, May/June 1995, pages 104-106

Novachick, Deborah & Miller, Marjorie A., "Conflict Avoidance Strategies: An Update," *Law Practice Management*, September 1995, pages 32-37

Noyes, Dianna L., *The California Probate Paralegal* (Carolina Academic Press 2007)

*Occupational Safety and Health Act* (OSHA), 29 U.S.C. § 651 *et seq.*

*Older Workers Benefit Protection Act*, 29 U.S.C. §§ 623 and 626

Orlik, Deborah K., *Ethics for the Legal Professional* (8th ed. Pearson 2014)

Orlik, Deborah K., *Ethics: Top Ten Rules for the Paralegal* (Prentice Hall 2005)

Orlik, Deborah K., "The Chinese Wall: Fact or Fiction," *Legal Assistant Today*, September/October 1988, page 48

Ramo, Roberta Cooper, "How to Create a System for the Law Office," Section of Economics and Law Practice (American Bar Association 1975)

Revised Model Business Corporation Act, excerpts available at: http://academic.cengage.com/resource_uploads/downloads/0324595743_145749.pdf (last visited Feb. 10, 2019)

Schneeman, Angela, *Paralegals in American Law, Introduction to Paralegalism* (West/Delmar 1994)

Smith, Michael C., *O'Connor's Federal Rules, Civil Trials 2010* (Jones McClure 2010)

Sonny Bono Copyright Term Extension Act

Statsky, William P. & Wernet, John R., Jr., *Case Analysis and Fundamentals of Legal Writing* (4th ed. West 1994)

Statsky, William P., *Introduction to Paralegalism* (6th ed. West/Delmar 2003)

Statsky, William P., *Legal Research and Writing - Some Starting Points* (5th ed. West 1998)

Strunk, William & White, E.B., *The Elements of Style* (4th ed. Longman 1999)

Technology in the Law Office 4th ed., Thomas F. Goldman 2015.

Tepper, Pamela R., *Basic Legal Writing* (2d ed. Career Education 2006)

Tepper, Pamela R., *Basic Legal Writing for Paralegals* (2d ed. McGraw-Hill 2008)

*Texas Legal Assistant* Handbook (James 1995)

The 411 on Texting for Lawyers https://www.americanbar.org/content/dam/aba/events/law_practice_management/techshow/2018/The%20411%20on%20Texting%20For%20Lawyers.authcheckdam.pdf (last visited Sept. 29, 2018)

The HIPAA Privacy Rule https://www.hhs.gov/hipaa/for-professionals/privacy/index.html (Last accessed Feb. 10, 2019)

The Lanham Act [Title 15]

U.S. Constitution, Article I, Section 8 - Constitutional mandate for patents and trademarks

Uniform Commercial Code (model), available at: https://www.law.cornell.edu/ucc (last visited Feb. 10, 2019) *See* your specific state code for any revisions to the model version of the UCC

*United States Bankruptcy Code,* 11 U.S.C. §§ 25 *et seq.*

Walston-Dunham, Beth, *Introduction to Law* (5th ed. West/Delmar 2008)

Weinstein, Martin, *Summary of American Law* (2d ed. Lawyers Co-Operative 1989)

www.uspto.gov (last visited Dec. 30, 2010)

Wydick, Richard C., *Plain English for Lawyers* (4th ed. Carolina Academic Press 1998)

15 U.S.C. §1052

15 U.S.C. §1127

17 U.S.C. §102, et seq.

1976 Copyright Act, §106

35 U.S.C. §100, et seq.

## GLOSSARY

**Abatement -** the process of determining the distribution of bequests as directed by the decedent in his/her will when there are not assets sufficient to satisfy the bequests.

**Abstract of title -** a chronological summary of all official records and recorded documents affecting the title to a parcel of real property.

**Acceptance -** one of three requisites to a valid contract under common law (the other two being an offer and consideration). A contract is a legally binding agreement between two or more parties that starts with an offer from one person but does not become a contract until the other party signifies an unequivocal willingness to accept the terms of that offer. The moment of acceptance is the moment from which a contract is said to exist, not before. Acceptance need not always be direct and can, in certain circumstances, be implied by conduct.

**Accord and satisfaction -** a term of contract law by which one party, having complied with its obligation under a contract, accepts some type of compensation from the other party (usually money of a lesser amount) in lieu of enforcing the contract and holding the other party to its obligation. This discharges the contract.

**Acknowledgment -** a formal declaration before an authorized official by the person who executed an instrument that it is his/her free act and deed; the certificate of the official on such instrument attesting that it was so acknowledged.

**Acquittal** – the legal certification that an accused person is not guilty of the charged offense.

**Actual Notice** – direct knowledge a person has about the ownership and condition of title of real property.

***Actus Reus*** – Latin term: "guilty act." The wrongful deed that comprises the physical components of a crime and that generally must be coupled with mens rea to establish criminal liability.

***Ad hoc*** **-** Latin: for this purpose; for a specific purpose. An ad hoc committee, for example, is created with a unique and specific purpose or task. Once it has studied and reported on the matter, it stands disbanded.

**Adjudication -** giving or pronouncing a judgment or decree; also, the judgment given.

**Adjusted basis -** the basis of property used when computing gains for income tax purposes; the cost minus depreciation plus capital improvements.

***Ad Litem*** - person appointed to act, during the pendency of a matter, as guardian for a minor child. Person may also bring action on behalf of the child.

**Administration of Estate -** the management of a decedent's estate. An administrator is appointed to collect all assets and debts of the decedent so that administrative expenses and taxes are paid and the remaining assets are distributed to the heirs or beneficiaries.

**Administrative agencies -** agencies created by the legislative branch of government to administer laws pertaining to specific areas such as taxes, transportation and labor.

**Administrative authority -** the rules, regulations and decision created by federal, state and local agencies; the executive orders of the President and governors.

**Administrator (male)/Administratrix (female) -** a person who administers the estate of a person deceased. The administrator is appointed by a court and is the person who would then have power to deal with the debts and assets of a person who died intestate. A female administrator is called an "administratrix." An administrator is a personal representative.

**Advance Directive -** may also be referred to as a "living will." Document that expresses a person's wishes about his/her medical care in the event they are unable to communicate their desires or have a terminal illness.

**Advanced healthcare directive** – also known as living will, personal directive, advance directive, medical directive or advance decision, is a legal document in which a person specifies what actions should be taken for their health if they are no longer able to make decisions for themselves because of illness or incapacity. In the U.S. it has a legal status in itself, whereas in some countries it is legally persuasive without being a legal document.

**Advance sheets -** paperback pamphlets published by law book publishers weekly or monthly that contain reporter cases, including correct volume number and page number. When there are sufficient cases, they are replaced by a bound volume.

**Adverse Possession** – acquiring title through taking possession of land that belongs to another without the owner's consent and retaining possession for a statutory period time. Adverse possession must be: (i) hostile, meaning it must be without the owner's consent; (ii) actual, meaning there must be physical dominion and control exerted over the property; (iii) open and notorious, meaning anyone would be able to determine that possession was taking place through inspection of the property; (iv) continuous possession for the entire statutory period; and (v) exclusive, meaning that the adverse possessor cannot share use of the land in question with its title owner.

**Adversary proceeding -** one having opposing parties, such as a plaintiff and a defendant. Individual lawsuit(s) brought within a bankruptcy proceeding.

**Affidavit -** a statement that, before being signed, the person signing takes an oath that the contents are, to the best of his/her knowledge, true. It is also signed by a notary or some other judicial officer who can administer oaths, to the effect that the person signing the affidavit was under oath when doing so. These documents carry great weight in courts to the extent that judges frequently accept an affidavit instead of the testimony of the witness.

**Affirmative Defense (civil)** – a fact raised by the defendant that constitutes a defense to the complaint.

**Affirmative defense (criminal)** – a set of facts which tend to excuse the defendant from the crime with which they have been charged.

**Agency decisions -** opinions issued by federal and state administrative law judges as the result of disputes or controversies presented to the agency's administrative law judge or other person charged with hearing evidence and resolving issues involving matters under the agency's jurisdiction.

**Agency regulations -** rules written by federal and state administrative agencies.

**Agent -** a person who has received the power to act on behalf of another, binding that other person as if he/she were making the decisions personally. The person who is being represented by the agent is called the principal.

**Aid and abet -** to actively, knowingly or intentionally assist another person in the commission or attempted commission of a crime.

**Alien Corporation -** a corporation that was formed in another country, but is doing business in the United States or its territories.

**Alimony** – an award of money given from one spouse to the other. Duration of alimony can be for a very specific time period and will automatically terminate upon a specific date, or it may be unlimited, terminating only upon the death of the payor spouse or the payee spouse. Alimony is also known to as "Separate Maintenance" and/or "Spousal Support." It is important to note that, in some jurisdictions, spousal support and alimony are different. *See* Spousal Support.

**Alimony Pendente Lite (APL)** – an award of money given from one spouse to the other prior to entry of a final decree; more literally, pending the litigation.

**Allegation -** something to be proved or disproved through the introduction of evidence.

**Alternate Valuation Date** - the administrator may choose an alternative date to the date of death for the valuation of the decedent's estate for federal estate tax purposes.

**Alternative Dispute Resolution (ADR) -** methods by which legal conflicts and disputes are resolved privately, other than through litigation in the public courts, usually through one of two forms: mediation or arbitration. ADR typically involves a process much less formal than the traditional court process and includes the appointment of a third party to preside over a hearing between the parties. The advantages of ADR are speed and money: it costs less and is quicker than court litigation. ADR forums are also private. The disadvantage is that it often involves compromise.

***American Law Reports (ALRs)*** **-** a publication that reports cases from all United States jurisdictions by subject matter.

***Amicus curiae*** **-** Latin: friend of the court. Refers more specifically to a person asking for permission to intervene in a case where they are neither plaintiff nor defendant, usually to present their point of view (or that of its organization) in a case which has the potential of setting a legal precedent in their area of activity. This is common, for example, in civil rights cases. In some instances, this can only be filed with the permission of the parties or the court. Plural: *amici.*

**Ancestor** – relative of a previous generation.

**Ancillary administration** – estate administration established in a state where property is located outside of the domiciliary state.

**Ancillary probate** - a probate proceeding conducted in a different state from the one the deceased person resided in at the time of death. Usually, ancillary probate proceedings are necessary if the deceased person owned real estate in another state.

**Annual Exclusion** - the amount of money that a person can "gift" each year which is free from federal gift tax; requires the filing of a gift tax return. Currently, the allowable gift is $13,000 per person. A married couple may gift $26,000 per person and there is no limit to the number of persons who may receive a gift.

**Annuity** - similar to an insurance policy. A contract between the owner of the annuity provider and the purchaser (annuitant). The annuitant funds the account and interest accrues. The annuitant is then able to receive a yearly payment of a fixed amount for a specific period of time or for a specific amount until all of the value has been paid to the owner.

**Annulment** – the act of making something void and wiping it out completely.

**Anticipatory Repudiation** – occurs when one party positively states that they will not substantially perform a contract.

**Antitrust acts** - federal and state statutes to protect trade and commerce from unlawful restraints, price discriminations, price fixing and monopolies.

**Appeal** - to ask a more senior court or person to review a decision of a subordinate court or person.

**Appellate court** - a court having jurisdiction to hear appeals and review a trial court's procedure.

**Appellant** – the party who asks the higher court to review the lower/trial court's decision.

**Appellee** - the party against whom an appeal is taken (sometime the Respondent).

**Arbitration** - the hearing of a dispute by an impartial third person or persons (chosen by the parties), whose award the parties agree to accept.

**Arbitrator** - a private, disinterested person chosen by the parties in arbitration to hear evidence concerning the dispute and to make an award based on the evidence.

**Arraignment** - the hearing at which the accused is brought before the court to plead to the criminal charge in the indictment. The accused may plead "guilty," "not guilty," or, where permitted, "*nolo contendere*."

**Arrearages** - overdue alimony or child support payments. In recent years, state laws have made it difficult to impossible to get rid of arrearages; they can't be discharged in bankruptcy, and courts usually will not retroactively cancel them. A spouse or parent who falls on tough times and is unable to make payments should request a temporary modification of the payments before the arrearages build up.

**Arrears** - a debt that is not paid on the due date adds up and accumulates as "arrears." For example, if you do not pay your rent, the debt still exists and is referred to as "arrears." The same word is used to describe child or spousal maintenance or support that is not paid by the due date.

**Arrest** – the taking or keeping of a person in custody by legal authority in response to a criminal charge.

**Arson** - some countries define arson as the intentional setting of a fire to a building in which people live. Others include as arson the intentional setting of a fire to any building. In either case, arson is usually a felony and punishable by a long jail sentence.

**Articles of incorporation** - a document filed with state authorities (usually the secretary of state or corporations commissioner, depending on the state) to form a corporation. As required by the general corporation law of the state, the articles normally include the purpose of the corporation, its principal place of business, the names of its initial directors who will control it, and the amounts and types of stock it is authorized to issue.

**Articles of limited liability partnership** – public document that must be filed with the Secretary of State in order to form this type of partnership.

**Assault** - the touching of another person with an intent to harm, without that person's consent.

**Asset** - anything that has value which is owned by an individual, company or organization. Assets include real property, tangible and intangible property, including businesses, goodwill, promissory notes and accounts receivable.

**Assign** - to give or transfer responsibility to another. The assignee (sometimes also called "assigns") is the person who receives the right or property being given. The assignor is the person giving.

**Assumption of the Risk** – a defense used when it is alleged that the plaintiff assumed a risk knowingly and willingly of the possibility of harm.

**Attachment** - taking a person's property to satisfy a court-ordered debt.

**Attestation** – testimony or confirmation that something is true, genuine, or authentic.
An attestation is frequently in writing. For example, a witness attests a will by signing it; his or her signature may confirm, inter alia, that he or she witnessed the testator sign the will.

**Attorney-client privilege** - the client's right to refuse to disclose and to prevent any other person from disclosing confidential communications between the client and the attorney. Also termed lawyer-client privilege; client's privilege.

**Attorney General Opinion -** decision written by the chief legal officer of a state or of the federal government; this opinion is generally advisory in nature.

**Attractive nuisance -** something on a piece of property that attracts children but also endangers their safety. For example, unfenced swimming pools, open pits, farm equipment and abandoned refrigerators have all qualified as attractive nuisances.

**Bad Faith -** deceitful or devious intent which is motivated by self-interest, concealed purpose or ill will.

**Bail -** money or other security, such as a bail bond, provided to the court to allow a person's temporary release from jail and assure his/her appearance in court. "Bail" and "bond" are often used interchangeably. Applies mainly to state courts.

**Bailee -** the person who receives property through a contract of bailment, from the bailor, and who may be committed to certain duties of care towards the property while it remains in his/her possession.

**Bailment -** the transfer of possession of something (by the bailor) to another person (called the bailee) for some temporary purpose, such as storage, after which the property is either returned to the bailor or otherwise disposed of in accordance with the contract of bailment.

**Bailor -** the person who temporarily transfers possession of property to another, the bailee, under a contract of bailment.

**Bankruptcy -** the formal condition of an insolvent person being declared bankrupt under law. The legal effect is to divert most of the debtor's assets and debts to the administration of a third person, sometimes called a trustee in bankruptcy, from which outstanding debts are paid *pro rata*. Bankruptcy forces the debtor into a statutory period during which his/her commercial and financial affairs are administered under the strict supervision of the trustee. Commercial organizations usually add other non-legal burdens, such as the refusal of credit, upon bankrupts. The duration of bankruptcy status varies from state to state. It has the benefit of erasing most debts even if they were not satisfied by the sale of the debtor's assets.

**Bankruptcy Court** – a U.S. District court subunit comprised of bankruptcy judges within the district and exclusively concerned with administering bankruptcy proceedings.

**Bargain and Sale Deed** – a deed that conveys property to a buyer for valuable consideration but that lacks any guarantee from the seller about the validity of the title.

**Basis -** The basis of real property is the original purchase price; adjusted purchase price of property.

**Bates numbering** – a universal system for identifying documents in litigation.

**Battery -** a crime consisting of physical contact that is intended to harm someone. Unintentional harmful contact is not battery, no matter how careless the behavior or how severe the injury. A fist fight is a common battery; while being hit by a wild pitch in a baseball game is not.

**Bench trial (civil)** – a trial before a judge without a jury. The judge decides questions of fact as well as questions of law.

**Bench trial (criminal)** – a trial before a judge without a jury. The defendant must waive his/her right to a jury trial to allow the judge to decide all questions of fact as well as questions of law.

**Beneficiary** - a person who inherits or who is entitled to inherit under a will or trust or who is entitled to the proceeds of an insurance policy when the insured dies.

**Bequeath** - to give a gift to someone through a will.

**Bequest** - the legal term for personal property, meaning any property other than real estate, left through a will.

**Bequests** - testamentary gifts of personal property; Property left to a named individual by the decedent in his/her will.

**Bifurcate** - to separate the issues in a case so that one issue or set of issues can be tried and resolved before the others. For example, death penalty cases are always bifurcated. The court or jury first hears the evidence of guilt and reaches a verdict, then hears evidence about and decides upon which punishment to impose (death or life in prison without parole). Bifurcated trials are also common in product liability class action lawsuits in which many people claim that they were injured by the same defective product. The issue of liability is tried first, followed by the question of damages. Bifurcation is authorized by Rule 42(b) of the Federal Rules of Civil Procedure.

**Bifurcated trial** – the dividing of the proceeding into two phases; the guilt phase and the punishment phase.

**Bill** – a draft of a law presented to a legislature for enactment.

**Binding precedent** - the decisions of higher courts that set the legal standards for similar cases in lower courts within the same jurisdiction.

**Blockage Discount** - if the sale of an entire piece of property at the same time would decrease the value of the property, a discount in valuation may be allowed.

**Blocked Account** - a secure account that holds funds, usually proceeds from sales or other estate assets until distribution is to be made. Can also be a custodian account for a minor.

**Blog** – a website that contains an online personal journal with reflections and comments by the writer.

**Blue law** - a statute that forbids or regulates an activity, such as the sale of liquor on Sundays.

**Blue sky laws** - the laws that aim to protect people from investing in sham companies that consist of nothing but "blue sky." Blue sky laws require that companies seeking to sell stock to the public submit information to and obtain the approval of a state or federal official that oversees corporate activity.

**Board of directors** – individuals elected by the shareholders who are responsible for formulating policy and deciding the business activities in which the corporation should be engaged. The Board of Directors elects the officers of the corporation and also determines the capital structure, the sale of stock, payment of dividends and other business matters.

**Bond (civil)** – an interest-bearing document giving evidence of a debt issued by a government body or corporation that is sometimes secured by a lien on property and is often designed to take care of a particular financial need.

**Bond (criminal)** – money held by the court when given by a criminal defendant or by his/her surety to ensure compliance with the terms of bail and especially with the requirement that the defendant appears in court as scheduled.

**Boolean search** – search queries in online databases that allow the user to combine words and phrases with a series of operators to limit or define search parameters. Boolean operators are connector words like "and," "or" and "not."

**Breach -** a failure or violation of a legal obligation.

**Breach of contract -** a legal claim that one party failed to perform as required under a valid agreement with the other party. For example, "The roofer breached our contract by using substandard supplies when he repaired my roof."

**Brief -** a document used to submit a legal contention or argument to a court. A brief typically sets out the facts of the case and a party's argument as to why it should prevail. These arguments must be supported by legal authority and precedent such as statutes, regulations and previous court decisions. Although it is usually possible to submit a brief to a trial court (called a trial brief), briefs are most commonly used as a central part of the appeal process (an appellate brief). Don't be fooled by the name: briefs are usually anything but brief.

**Burden of proof** – the duty to prove a disputed assertion or charge.

**Burglary -** the crime of breaking into and entering a building with the intention to commit a felony. The breaking and entering need not be by force and the felony need not be theft. For instance, someone would be guilty of burglary if he/she entered a house through an unlocked door in order to commit a murder.

**Business judgment rule** – legal principle stating that corporate officers and directors are not liable for honest mistakes of business judgment when acting in good faith.

**Business records exception -** an exception to the hearsay rule. The exception allows a business document to be admitted into evidence if a proper foundation is laid to show it is reliable.

**Bylaws -** the rules that govern the internal affairs or actions of a corporation. Normally, bylaws are adopted by the shareholders of a profit-making business or the board of directors of a nonprofit corporation. Bylaws generally include procedures for holding meetings and electing the board of directors and officers. The bylaws also set out the duties and powers of a corporation's officers.

**Bypass Trust** - a trust which intends to save a "second tax" when the second spouse dies by "bypassing" his/her estate. This may also be called a credit shelter trust or B Trust.

**Canons of professional ethics** – standards promulgated by the ABA regulating the conduct of lawyers.

**Capacity** - having legal authority or mental ability; being of sound mind.

**Capital Gains Tax** - income tax upon financial gain resulting from the sale or exchange of capital assets.

**Case law** – the law to be found in a collection of reported cases that form all or part of the body of law within a given jurisdiction.

**Causation** – the act by which an effect is produced; one of four elements to be proven in a successful tort claim.

**Cause-In-Fact** – an action by the tortfeasor that resulted in an invasion of some legally protected interest of another to which the tortfeasor is held responsible for the harm caused.

***Caveat*** - Latin: let him beware; a formal warning. *Caveat emptor* means "let the buyer beware," a warning that buyers should examine and check for themselves things that they intend to purchase. They cannot later hold the vendor responsible for the condition of the thing bought.

**Certification** - 1) written attestation; 2) authorized declaration verifying that an instrument is a true and correct copy of the original; 3) a voluntary form of regulation.

Certifications available through NPFA:

CORE Registered Paralegal® – a designation used by a person who has successfully passed the PCCE®.

CRP® – a designation used by a person who has successfully passed the PCCE®.

PACE Registered Paralegal® – a designation used by a person who has successfully passed the PACE® exam; may be used interchangeably with RP®.

RP® – stands for Registered Paralegal; a designation used by a person who has successfully passed the PACE® exam; may be used interchangeably with PACE Registered Paralegal®.

***Certification marks*** - marks of a third-party (such as a consumer organization) which certify a quality or characteristic of a product or service. Certification marks are not established by the owner or manufacturer.

***Certiorari*** **-** a writ of superior court to call up the records of an inferior court or body acting in a quasi-judicial capacity. A *writ of certiorari* is a form of judicial review whereby a court is asked to consider a legal decision of an administrative tribunal, judicial office or organization such as a government to decide if the decision has been regular and complete or if there has been an error of law. For example, a *certiorari* may be used to wipe out an administrative tribunal's decision made in violation of a rule.

**Chain of title** – the succession of title ownership to real property from the present owner back to the original owner.

**Challenge for cause -** request from a party to a judge that a certain prospective juror not be allowed to be a member of a jury because of specified causes or reasons.

**Change of venue -** moving a lawsuit or criminal trial to another place for trial.

**Charging document** – a document in a criminal case that formally accuses a person of committing a crime, a/k/a indictment.

**Charitable Deduction -** a tax deduction allowed on federal income taxes for contributions or gifts made to tax-exempt charitable organizations which have been approved by the IRS.

**Charitable Remainder Trust -** a trust which benefits the settlor and/or his/her family for a specified period of time after which the remainder is distributed to charity.

**Charitable Trust -** also called a public trust. Trust created for charitable benefit.

**Chattel -** moveable items of property that are neither land nor permanently attached to land or a building, either directly or vicariously through attachment to real property. A piano is chattel but an apartment building, a tree or a concrete building foundation are not. The opposite of chattel is real property, which includes lands or buildings. All property that is not real property is said to be chattel. "Personal property" or "personalty" are other terms sometimes used to describe the concept of chattel. The word derives from the feudal period when cattle were the most valuable property other than land.

**Child support** – payment made by the non-custodial parent to the custodial parent for the necessities of life (shelter, food, clothing medical, etc.) for the benefit of the minor child(ren).

**Circumstantial evidence -** all evidence except eyewitness testimony. One example is physical evidence, such as fingerprints, from which an inference can be drawn.

**Citation** – (1) an official summons to appear in court; (2) reference to (citing) a statute, precedent-setting case or legal textbook; (3) section of a statute or name of the case, as well as the volume number, the report series and the page number of a case referred to in a brief, points and authorities, or other legal argument.

**Citators -** set of books that provide the subsequent history of reported decisions through a form of abbreviations or words.

**Cite-checking -** process to verify that the citations in a document are accurate and follow the format of the style manual that your organization is using.

**Civil law -** law inspired by old Roman law, the primary feature of which was that laws were written into a collection. Codified law, not determined, as is common law, by judges. The principle of civil law is to provide all citizens with an accessible and written collection of the laws that apply to them and that judges must follow.

**Claim -** a debt owing by a debtor to another person or business. In probate parlance, the term used for debts of the decedent and a procedure that must be followed by a creditor to obtain payment from the debtor's estate.

**Class action -** a lawsuit brought by one or more persons on behalf of a larger group.

**Class Gift -** a group of beneficiaries designated to receive a gift from the decedent by general reference rather than by their specific names, for example: "my children."

**Claw back** – a buffer for an attorney who realizes only after production that he/she has not adequately redacted the privileged or trial-preparation materials; the claw back provision of Fed. R. Civ. P. 26(b)(5) allows that attorney to request that the information be returned immediately, while Fed. R. Civ. P. 16(b) permits parties to create their own agreement for asserting claims of attorney-client privilege or protection of trial preparation materials after accidental production.

**Clean hands -** a maxim of the law to the effect that any person, individual or corporate, that wishes to ask or petition a court for judicial action must be in a position free of fraud or other unfair conduct.

**Clear and convincing evidence -** standard of proof commonly used in civil lawsuits and in regulatory agency cases; governs the amount of proof that must be offered in order for the plaintiff to win the case.

**Closing argument** – a prosecutor's/defense lawyer's final statement to the judge or jury before deliberation begins, at which time the prosecutor requests the judge or jury to consider the evidence and render a verdict of "guilty;" and, at which time the defense lawyer requests the judge or jury to consider the evidence and apply the law in his/her client's favor.

**Cloud on title** – a defect or potential defect in the owner's title to a piece of land arising from some claim or encumbrance, such as a lien, an easement or a court order.

**Closely held Corporation -** corporation held by a small group of individuals whose stock is not traded on the national securities exchanges.

**Code/Cone of silence -** another term for "ethical wall" (*see below*).

**Codicil -** an amendment to an existing will; does not mean that the will is totally changed, but changed only to the extent of the provisions in the codicil.

**Coding -** the review and extraction into a database of key pieces of information from a document.

**Collaborative law** – a form of alternative dispute resolution. The parties and attorneys work together in a determined spirit of cooperation to settle their dispute.

**Collateral -** property that has been committed to guarantee repayment of a loan.

**Collateral descendant -** a descendant who is not direct, such as a niece or a cousin.

**Collateral Relative -** person related to the decedent who is not his/her "issue." Siblings, aunts, uncles, cousins, nieces and nephews are collateral relatives. Descendants of the decedent's parents are "first-line" collateral relatives; descendants of the decedent's grandparents are "second-line" collateral relatives. See Table of Consanguinity.

**Collateral source rule -** a rule of tort law holding that the tortfeasor is not allowed to deduct any goods, services or money from the amount he/she is held to pay to the victim of the tort.

**Collective mark -** trademark or service mark used by members of a cooperative, an association or other collective group or organization.

**Commingling** – mixing of monies which should be separated.

**Common law** – a body of law that developed over time in England which resulted from judicial precedent and decisions. In America, common law refers to the body of case law developed by jurists through the history of the country.

**Community Property -** property acquired by either spouse during the marriage, except by gift, bequest or inheritance.

**Company -** a legal entity allowed by legislation that permits a group of people to create an organization that can focus on pursuing set objectives. The company structure provides the owners with a right to participate in the profits.

**Comparative fault -** a rule in admiralty law where each vessel involved in a collision is required to pay a share of the total damages in proportion to its percentage of fault.

**Comparative negligence -** the rule under which negligence is measured by percentage and damages are diminished in proportion to the amount of negligence attributable to the person seeking recovery.

**Compensatory damages** – money awarded to compensate the victim for the tortfeasor's negligence.

**Complaint** – a formal legal document that sets out the facts and legal reasons that the plaintiff believes support a claim against the defendant entitling the plaintiff to a legal remedy.

**Concurring Opinion -** one or more justices agree that the result reached by the majority or plurality opinion is correct, but wish to add their own thoughts on the reasons for the decision.

**Conditionally privileged communication -** a defamatory statement made in good faith by a person with an interest in a subject to someone who also has an interest in the subject, as an employer giving a poor but accurate job review of a former employee to a potential, future employer. The privilege may be lost on a showing of malice or bad faith.

**Confidential communication -** a communication made within a certain protected relationship -- such as husband-wife, attorney-client or priest-penitent -- and legally protected from forced disclosure.

**Confidentiality agreement -** an understanding between two or more parties, usually memorialized in writing, concerning certain matters that all parties to the agreement, and their employees or agents, understand are to be kept secret from those who are not parties to the agreement. Frequently used as an administrative tool in law practice between law firms and vendors to protect the confidentiality of documents the employees of the vendor will be handling for purposes of photocopying or enlarging for demonstrative evidence.

**Conflict check -** an administrative review of law firm's records performed before accepting a client for the purpose of ascertaining that the firm has not previously represented parties adverse to the potential client and that no other conflict, or appearance of conflict, exists that would prohibit the firm from accepting the client and vigorously advocating the client's interests.

**Conflict of interest -** 1) a real or seeming incompatibility between one's private interest and one's public or fiduciary duties; 2) a real or seeming incompatibility between the interests of two of a lawyer's clients, such that the lawyer is disqualified from representing both clients if the dual representation adversely affects either client or if the clients do not consent.

**Consanguineous Relationship** - a biological or blood relationship.

**Consent -** agreement, approval or permission as to some act or purpose, especially given voluntarily by a competent person. Consent is an affirmative defense to assault, battery and related torts, as well as such torts as defamation, invasion of privacy, conversion and trespass.

**Consequential damages** – a legal term referring to an injury or loss that is sustained by someone as an indirect result of another person's action.

**Conservator -** a person granted authority by the court to oversee the property of an incompetent person.

**Conservatorship -** legal right given to a person to manage the property and financial affairs of a person deemed incapable of doing that for himself/herself.

**Consideration -** under common law, there can be no binding contract without consideration, which was defined in an 1875 English decision as "some right, interest, profit or benefit accruing to the one party, or some forbearance, detriment, loss or responsibility given, suffered or undertaken by the other." Common law did not want to allow gratuitous offers, those made without anything offered in exchange, such as gifts, to be given the protection of contract law, so they added the criteria of consideration. Consideration is not required in contracts made in civil law systems and many common law states have adopted laws that remove consideration as a prerequisite of a valid contract.

**Consign -** to leave an item of property in the custody of another. An item can be consigned to a transportation company, for example, for the purpose of transporting it from one place to another. The consignee is the person to receive the property, and the consignor is the person who ships the property to the consignee.

**Constitution -** written for the United States of America and for each state individually, a constitution is the foundation document that established the authority for federal and state governments.

**Construction -** the legal process of interpreting a phrase or document; of trying to find its meaning. Whether it be found in a contract or a statute, a phrase may be unclear or open to several meanings. Then, lawyers or judges must attempt to interpret or "construct" the probable aim and purpose of the phrase by extrapolating from other parts of the document or, in the case of statutes, referring to an interpretation law that gives legal construction guidelines. Generally, there are two types of construction methods: literal (strict) or liberal.

**Construction lien** (or mechanic's lien) – allows certain persons and entities who provide labor or materials for the improvement of real property and who are not paid the statutory right to place a claim of lien on and ultimately foreclose on specific real property and any improvements thereon.

**Constructive Notice** – such notice as is implied or imputed by law, as in the case of notice documents that have been recorded in the appropriate registry of deeds.

**Constructive Trust** – implied trust used to right a wrong.

**Contingency fee -** attorney fee arrangement where a percentage of what the client is awarded as a result of the lawyer's work, is paid to the lawyer as his/her fee.

**Contract -** an agreement between persons that obliges each party to do or not to do a certain thing. Technically, a valid contract requires an offer and an acceptance of that offer, and, in common law countries, consideration.

**Contributory negligence** – a defense to negligence claiming the plaintiff's own actions contributed to the injuries.

**Conventional loan** – a loan made by a private lender in which the lender usually does not have any insurance or guarantee from a third party, such as a government agency backing the loan should the borrower fail to meet his/her loan obligations.

**Conversion** – stealing; unauthorized temporary use of an asset, such as trust account funds.

**Conveyance** - a written document that transfers property from one person to another. In real-estate law, the conveyance usually refers to the actual document that transfers ownership, between living persons (as opposed to transfer by the will of a deceased person) or that charges the land with another's interest, such as a mortgage.

**Cooperative** - a non-profit organization formed by individuals to market products.

**Corporate opportunity doctrine** – Principle established by case law that says corporate officers, directors and agents cannot take personal advantage of an opportunity that in all fairness should have belonged to the corporation.

**Copyright** - original works fixed in a tangible medium of expression, such as literary, musical and artistic works.

**Corporation** - a legal entity, allowed by legislation, which permits a group of people, as shareholders (for-profit corporations) or members (non-profit corporations) to create an organization that can focus on pursuing set objectives. A corporation is empowered with legal rights that are usually only reserved for individuals, such as to sue and be sued, own property, hire employees or loan and borrow money. The primary advantage of for-profit corporations is that it provides its shareholders with a right to participate in the profits (by dividends) without any personal liability because the corporation absorbs the entire liability of the organization.

***Corpus*** - Latin meaning "the body"; the capital of a trust or an estate; the principal and not the interest or income.

***Corpus Juris Secundum (CJS)*** - (Meaning, "Second Body of the Law") is an encyclopedia of United States law at the federal and state levels. It is arranged alphabetically, into over 430 topics, which in turn are arranged into subheadings.... CJS is published by West in print form and on Westlaw. Latin

**Corroborating evidence** - supplementary evidence that tends to strengthen or confirm the initial evidence.

**Counterclaim** - a claim made by the defendant in a civil lawsuit against the plaintiff. In essence, a counter-lawsuit within a lawsuit.

**Court of Appeals** – the court that hears the facts of a case by written argument, and possibly oral argument, which have already been argued at trial if that case on the district court level is not favorable to one party or the other.

**Court rules of procedure** - rules of the United States Supreme Court and state supreme courts that define the requirements for bringing civil and criminal cases to a trial court and appealing the cases to the next level. Court rules also define evidence and trial procedure.

**Covenant** - a written document in which signatories either commit themselves to do or not do a certain thing or in which they agree on a certain set of facts. Covenants are very common in real property dealings and are used to restrict land use, such as among shopping mall tenants, or for the purpose of preserving heritage property.

**Creditor's Claim -** creditors are required to file a "claim" in an estate requesting that they be paid from the assets of the estate within the course of the probate process.

**Cross-claim -** a pleading that asserts a claim arising out of the same subject action as the original complaint against a co-party. For example, one co-defendant cross claims against another co-defendant for contribution for any damages assessed against the first co-defendant.

**Cross-examination** – the examination of a witness who has already testified in order to check or discredit the witness's testimony, knowledge or credibility.

**Crummey Trust -** type of trust as set forth in *Crummey v. Commissioner*, 397 F.2d. 82 (1968); considered an Irrevocable Trust. Contributions made to the trust qualify for annual exclusions.

**Curtesy** – in common law, a husband's right, upon his wife's death, to a life estate in the land that his wife owned during their marriage, assuming that a child was born alive to the couple. The right has been largely abolished, although the term is still included in certain forms/agreements.

**Custody -** detaining a person by lawful process or authority to assure his/her appearance to any hearing; the jailing or imprisonment of a person convicted of a crime.

**Cyber legal ethics -** a term coined by the NFPA Ethics Board in 1996 to identify the emerging field of proper ethical conduct by legal professionals who use cyberspace devices such as the Internet, chat groups, or listservs.

**Cybersquatting -** buying a domain name that reflects the name of a business or famous person with the intent of selling the name back to the business or celebrity for a profit. The Anticybersquatting Consumer Protection Act of 1999 authorizes a cybersquatting victim to file a federal lawsuit to regain a domain name or sue for financial compensation. Under the Act, registering, selling or using a domain name with the intent to profit from someone else's good name is considered cybersquatting. Victims of cybersquatting can also use the provisions of the Uniform Domain Name Dispute Resolution Policy adopted by ICANN, an international tribunal administering domain names. This international policy results in arbitration of the dispute, not litigation.

**Damages -** a cash compensation ordered by a court to offset losses or suffering caused by another's fault or negligence. Damages are typically requested of a court when persons sue for breach of contract or tort.

**Database** – also referred to as "Computer database" is defined by 48 CFR 2.101 to mean a collection of recorded information in a form capable of, and for the purpose of, being stored in, processed, and operated on by a computer. The term does not include computer software.

***De novo* -** Latin: new. This term is used to refer to a trial that starts over, that wipes the slate clean and begins all over again, as if any previous partial or complete hearing had not occurred.

**Debenture -** a type of bond (an interest-bearing document that serves as evidence of a debt) that does not require security in the form of a mortgage or lien on a specific piece of property.

Repayment of a debenture is guaranteed only by the general credit of the issuer. For example, a corporation may issue a secured bond that gives the bondholder a lien on the corporation's factory. But if it issues a debenture, the loan is not secured by any property at all. When a corporation issues debentures, the holders are considered creditors of the corporation and are entitled to payment before shareholders if the business folds.

**Debtor -** person who owes money, goods or services to another referred to as the creditor.

**Decedent -** legal term for a person who has died.

**Declaration under penalty of perjury -** a signed statement, sworn to be true by the signer, that will make the signer guilty of the crime of perjury if the statement is shown to be materially false, that is, the lie is relevant and significant to the case.

**Declaration of Trust -** the creation of a trust by a settlor. The settlor declares himself/herself to be the trustee, gives themselves fiduciary powers and responsibilities and transfers the property to the trust which will convey the property to the trust's beneficiaries.

**Declaratory judgment -** a court decision in a civil case that tells the parties what their rights and responsibilities are without awarding damages or ordering them to do anything. Unlike most court cases where the plaintiff asks for damages or other court orders, the plaintiff in a declaratory judgment case simply wants the court to resolve an uncertainty so it can avoid serious legal trouble in the future.

**Deed** – a formal written instrument that conveys title to real property from one party to another.

**Deed of trust** – a deed conveying title to real property to a trustee as security until the grantor repays a loan.

**Defamation -** an attack on the good reputation of a person, by slander or libel.

**Default** – the failure to do something required by law.

**Default judgment** – a binding judgment in favor of either party based on some failure to take action by the other party. Most often, it is a judgment in favor of a plaintiff when the defendant has not responded to a summons or has failed to appear before a court of law.

**Defendant** – the party sued in a civil lawsuit or the party charged with a crime in a criminal prosecution.

**Degrees of separation** – number of generations a person is removed from the decedent.

**Deliberation** – the process by which jurors weigh the evidence and facts of the case in order to reach a verdict.

**Dependent -** one who derives existence and support from another.

**Deposition** – the taking of out-of-court oral testimony of a witness under oath before a court reporter that is typically transcribed into a written transcript for later use in court or for discovery purposes.

**Descendant** - those persons who are born of, or from children of, another are called that person's descendants. Grandchildren are descendants of their grandparents, as children are descendants of their natural parents. The law also distinguishes between collateral descendants and lineal descendants.

**Design Patents** - granted to a person who invents any new, original and ornamental design for an article of manufacture.

**Devise** - the transfer or conveyance of real property by will.

***Dicta* or *dictum*** - Latin: an observation by a judge on a matter not specifically before the court or not necessary in determining the issue before the court; a side opinion that does not form part of the judgment for the purposes of *stare decisis*. May also be called "*obiter dictum*."

**Digest** - an index or compilation of abstracts of reported cases into one, set forth under proper law topic headings or titles usually in alphabetical arrangement.

**Direct examination** – the first questioning of a witness in a trial or other proceeding, conducted by the party who called the witness to testify.

**Directed verdict** - in a case in which the plaintiff has failed to present on the facts of its case proper evidence for jury consideration, the trial judge may order the entry of a verdict without allowing the jury to deliberate.

**Directive to Physicians** - also called the Advance Directive or Living Will.

**Direct Skip** - transfer which skips a generation; used to calculate taxes imposed in the transfer.

**Disclaimer** - the right to refuse the acceptance of property.

**Discovery** – efforts of a party in a lawsuit through his/her/its attorneys to obtain information before trial through interrogatories, requests for production, requests for admission and depositions of parties and potential witnesses.

**Discretionary trust** - a trust in which the settlor has given the trustee full discretion to decide which (and when) members of a group of beneficiaries is to receive either the income or the capital of the trust.

**Dissenting Opinion** - an appellate court opinion setting forth the minority view and outlining the disagreement of one or more judges with the decision of the majority.

**Dissolution** - the act of ending, terminating or winding-up a company or state of affairs. For example, when the life of a company is ended by normal legal means, it is said to be "dissolved."

The same is said of marriage or partnerships that, by dissolution, ends the legal relationship between those persons formally joined by the marriage or partnership.

**Distributee** – intestate inheritor of personal property.

**Diversity jurisdiction** - the power of the federal courts to decide a dispute between citizens of different states, provided the amount the plaintiff seeks in damages exceeds $75,000.

**Dividend** - a portion of profits distributed by a corporation to its shareholders based on the type of stock and number of shares owned.

**Docket number** - the number the case is given when it is filed before a particular court.

**Doctrine** - a rule or principle, or the law established through the repeated application of legal precedents.

**Doctrine of Laches** – a legal right or claim may be barred from court if an unreasonable lapse of time in asserting that right or claim has prejudiced the adverse party, resulting in permanent damage to the adverse party's ability to defend him/herself.

**Domain name** - a combination of letters and numbers that identifies a specific computer or Web site on the Internet.

**Domestic Corporation** - a way to categorize a corporation as to where it was formed and where the Articles of Incorporation are filed.

**Domicile** - the permanent residence of a person; a place to which, even if he/she were temporarily absent, he/she intends to return. In law, it is said that a person may have many residences, but only one domicile.

**Donee** - another word to describe the beneficiary of a trust. Also used to describe the person who is the recipient of a power of attorney; the person who would have to exercise the power of attorney.

**Donor** - the person who donates property to the benefit of another, usually through the legal mechanism of a trust. The law books of some countries refer to the trust donor as a settlor. Also used to describe the person who signs a power of attorney.

**Dower** – in common law, the right of a wife, upon her husband's death, to a life estate in one-third of the land that he owned in fee.

**Due care** – proper and sufficient care as far as circumstances demand it; the absence of negligence.

***Duces tecum*** - Latin: bring with you. Used most frequently for a species of subpoena, as in "subpoena *duces tecum*," that seeks not so much the appearance of a person before a court of law, but the surrender of a thing -- a document or some other evidence -- by its holder to the court to serve as evidence in a trial.

**Due process -** a term of U.S. law that refers to fundamental, procedural, legal safeguards of which every citizen has an absolute right when a state or court purports to take a decision that could affect any right of that citizen. The most basic rights protected under the due process doctrine are the right to be given notice and an opportunity to be heard. The term is now used in other countries to refer to basic, fundamental legal rights such as the right to be heard.

**Durable Power of Attorney -** document that allows an agent to act on behalf of the principal; continues even if the principal is incapacitated.

**Duress -** where a person is prevented from acting (or not acting) according to his/her free will, by threats or force of another. Contracts signed under duress are voidable.

**Duty of Care** – the responsibility of corporate directors and officers to use care and diligence when acting on behalf of the corporation.

**Earned Income -** as defined by law, the income from personal services rather than real estate.

**Easement** – an interest in land owned by another person, consisting of the right to use or control the land, including the area above or below it, for a specific limited purpose.

**Electronic discovery** – aka e-discovery/eDiscovery; the compiling, storing and securing of digital information, such as email, text messages and other electronic files and data.

**Electronic signature (e-signature) -** a paperless method of entering into an electronic contract.

**Electronically Stored Information (ESI)** – information created, manipulated, communicated, stored and best utilized in digital form, requiring the use of computer hardware and software.

**Eminent domain -** the legal power to expropriate private land for the sake of public necessity.

***En Banc* -** all the judges of a court sitting together. Appellate courts can consist of a dozen or more judges, but often they hear cases in panels of three judges. If a case is heard or reheard by the full court, it is heard *en banc.*

**Encroachment** – an infringement of another's rights or intrusion on another's property.

**Endorsement -** something written on the back of a document. An alternate spelling, in some English jurisdictions, is "indorsement." In the laws of bills of exchange, an endorsement is a signature on the back of the bill of exchange by which the person to whom the note is payable transfers it by thus making the note payable to the bearer or to a specific person. An endorsement of claim means that if you want to ask a court to issue a writ against someone, you must "endorse" your writ with a concise summary of the facts supporting the claim, sometimes called a statement of claim.

**Endowment -** the transfer of money or property (usually as a gift) to a public organization for a specific purpose, such as medical research or scholarships.

**Entity -** a person or legally recognized organization.

**Entrapment -** the inducement, by law enforcement officers or their agents, of another person to commit a crime for the purposes of bringing charges for the commission of that artificially-provoked crime. This technique, because it involves abetting the commission of a crime, that is itself a crime, is severely curtailed under the constitutional law of many states.

**Equal protection of the law -** the guarantee in the Fourteenth Amendment to the U.S. Constitution that all persons be treated equally by the law; also referred to as the Equal Protection Clause.

**Equitable Distribution/Division** – marital property is distributed fairly and not necessarily as an equal division of property.

**Equitable title** – title giving the beneficiary the right to enjoy trust property subject to limitations imposed by the trustor.

**Equity of Redemption -** the right of a mortgagor, who is in default, to pay the debt on the mortgage in full, thus avoiding foreclosure.

**Equivalent Exemption -** the amount of property, including lifetime transfers, exempt from tax at death; equals the unified tax credit.

**Escheat -** the right of the state to take title to property after the death of a decedent who has not executed a will and who has no heirs.

**Escrow account** – a bank account held by a third party to be turned over only upon the fulfillment of some condition or by agreement of both parties.

**Estate** – interest in land; also, property of the decedent.

**Estate administration** – process of collecting assets, paying debts, and distribution of a person's property after his/her death.

**Estate law -** a term used by the law to describe that part of the law that regulates wills, probate and other subjects related to the distribution of a deceased person's estate.

**Estate Planning -** the protection of family assets through legal means.

**Estate Tax -** tax imposed by the federal government on estates.

**Estoppel -** a rule of law stating that when person A, by act or words, gives person B reason to believe a certain set of facts upon which person B takes action, person A cannot later, to A's benefit, deny those facts or say that his/her earlier act was improper.

**Ethics** – principles of conduct governing an individual or group.

**Ethical wall -** a screening mechanism that protects client confidences by preventing one or more lawyers within an organization from participating in any matter involving that client. This mechanism is designed to allow a lawyer to move to a new law firm without fear of vicariously disqualifying that firm from representing certain clients. Creating an ethical wall generally entails: (1) prohibiting certain lawyers and paralegals from having any connection with the matter; (2) banning discussions with or the transfer of documents to those individuals; (3) restricting access to files; and (4) educating all members of the firm, corporation or entity about the separation of the lawyers and paralegals (both organizationally and physically) from the pending matter.

**Evidence** – something that tends to prove or disprove the existence of an alleged fact. Evidence can be testimony, documents and tangible objects.

**Ex Parte** – Latin term: "without the party." Generally, communication made to the court by one party, in the absence of the other party, which is generally forbidden.

**Exculpatory clauses** – a contractual clause that releases one party from liability in case of wrongdoing by the other party involved.

**Exclusionary rule -** a rule of evidence that disallows the use of illegally obtained evidence in criminal trials. For example, the exclusionary rule would prevent a prosecutor from introducing at trial evidence seized during an illegal search.

**Exclusive license -** a valid contract in which a copyright owner authorizes another person or entity, called the licensee, to exclusively exercise one or more of the rights or portion of such rights that belong to the copyright owner under the copyright. The licensee is said to own the rights granted in the license and is referred to as a copyright owner.

**Executive order -** an order by the President or a state governor to direct the action of governmental agencies.

**Executor (male)/Executrix (female)** – personal representative named in a will.

**Exempt property -** all the property of a debtor that is not attachable under the Bankruptcy Code or the state statute.

**Exhibit -** an item of real evidence that is presented to the court.

**Express condition** – a condition that is clearly stated in the language of the contract that defines a particular circumstance that either creates or removes an obligation for one or more of the contracting parties.

**Express consent -** consent that is clearly and unmistakably stated.

**Expunge -** intentionally to destroy, obliterate or strike out records or information in files, computers and other depositories. For example, when the minor reaches the age of majority, state law may allow the criminal records of a juvenile offender to be expunged to allow the minor to begin his/her adult life with a clean record. Or, a company or government agency may routinely expunge out-of-date records to save storage space.

***Ex rel*** - Latin: an abbreviation of ex relatione, Latin for "on the relation of." Refers to information or action taken that is not based on first-hand experience, but is based on the statement or account of another person.

**Extortion** - forcing a person to give up property through the use of violence, fear or under pretense of authority.

**Extradition** - the arrest and delivery, usually under the terms of an extradition treaty, of a fugitive wanted for a crime committed in another country.

**Fact finder** – generally, another term for juror. Fact finders hear testimony and review evidence to issue a decision/render a verdict on the collective factual issues/ the defendant's guilt or innocence.

**Fact witness** – also known as a lay witness. Restricted to giving an opinion or making an inference that is based on first-hand knowledge and is helpful in clarifying the testimony or in determining the facts.

**Failure of consideration** - the refusal or inability of a contracting party to perform its side of a bargain.

**Fair market value** - the value for which a reasonable seller would sell an item of property and for which a reasonable buyer would buy it.

**Fair use rule** - a law that authorizes the use of copyrighted materials for certain purposes without the copyright owner's permission. Generally, uses intended to further scholarship, education or an informed public are considered fair use, but recent years have seen severe limits placed on the amount of a work that can be reproduced under the fair use rule.

**Federal courts** – a court having federal jurisdiction, including the U.S. Supreme Court, circuit courts of appeals, district courts, bankruptcy courts and tax courts.

***Federal Register*** - a daily publication that contains federal administrative rules and regulations.

***Federal Supplement*** - (F.Supp. and F.Supp.3d) A reporter that primarily publishes opinions of the United States District Courts.

***Federalism*** – the division of powers between the branches of federal and state governments.

**Fee simple** - the most extensive tenure allowed under the feudal system allowing the tenant to sell or convey by will or by transfer to an heir if the owner dies intestate. In modern law, almost all land is held in fee simple, which is as close as one can get to absolute ownership in common law.

**Fee Splitting** - 1) the division of an attorney's fees between the lawyer who handles a matter and the lawyer who referred the matter (some states consider this practice unethical); 2) the division of an attorney's fees between two or more lawyers who represent a client jointly but are not in the same firm. An attorney is prohibited from splitting a fee with a nonlawyer.

**Felony -** a serious criminal offense; under federal law, any offense punishable by death or imprisonment for a term exceeding one year.

**Fiduciary -** normally, the term is synonymous to a trustee, which is the classic form of a fiduciary relationship. A fiduciary has rights and powers that would normally belong to another person. The fiduciary holds those rights that he/she must exercise to the benefit of the beneficiary. A fiduciary must not allow any conflict of interest to infect his/her duties towards the beneficiary and must exercise a high standard of care in protecting or promoting the interests of the beneficiary.

**Fictitious name** – the operating name of a company, or the d/b/a (doing business as) name, as opposed to the legal name of the company. In the case of a corporation, a fictitious business name is any name other than the corporate name stated in the articles of incorporation.

**Fiduciary** – trustee; a person held to a standard of care higher than ordinary care.

**Fiscal year -** an accounting period; a different period may be chosen for an estate rather than a calendar year.

**Fixed fee -** attorney fee arrangement where an attorney is paid a specific amount for a particular service.

**Fixture** – personal property that is attached to land or a building, and that is regarded as an irremovable part of the real property, such as a built-in fireplace.

**Force majeure** – a common clause in contracts that essentially frees both parties from liability or obligation when an extraordinary event or circumstance beyond the control of the parties, such as a war, strike, riot, crime or an event described by the legal term "act of God" (such as flooding, an earthquake, or a volcanic eruption), preventing one or both parties from fulfilling their obligations under the contract.

**Foreclosure -** the forced sale of real estate to pay off a loan on which the owner of the property has defaulted.

**Foreign Corporation -** a corporation that is incorporated in one U.S. state, but which does business in another state.

**Foreperson** – the juror who chairs the jury during deliberations and speaks for the jury in court by announcing the verdict.

**Foreseeability** – the action by which, under particular circumstances, would produce an anticipated result such as an injury to someone.

**Form 706 -** Federal Estate Tax Return.

**Form 709 -** Federal Gift Tax Return.

***Forum nonconveniens*** **-** Latin: "an inconvenient court." Because strict written rules of jurisdiction and venue are now used to decide where a case can and cannot be properly filed, this term has largely lost any real meaning.

**Forum shopping -** the process by which a plaintiff chooses among two or more courts that have the power -- technically, the correct jurisdiction and venue -- to consider its case. This decision is based on which court is likely to consider the case most favorably. In some instances, a case can properly be filed in two or more federal district courts as well as in the trial courts of several states, which makes forum shopping a complicated business. It often involves weighing a number of factors, including proximity to the court, the reputation of the judge in the particular legal area, the likely type of available jurors and subtle differences in governing law and procedure.

**Franchise** – a party that owns a trade name or trademark (the franchisor) may contract with a party that wishes to sell, distribute or provide services and/or products using the trade name or mark (franchisee).

**Fraud -** deceitful conduct designed to manipulate another person to give something of value by: (1) lying, (2) by repeating something that is or ought to have been known by the fraudulent party as false or suspect, or (3) by concealing a fact from the other party that may have saved that party from being cheated. The existence of fraud will cause a court to void a contract and can give rise to criminal liability.

**Freehold -** an estate for life.

**Freelance Paralegal** – a paralegal who does contract work for lawyers.

**Full-text databases -** databases that contain the full text of documents.

**Funded Trust** - property that has been transferred to and is held by a "living" trust.

**Future Interest -** an estate or interest in land or personal property that is to come into existence in the future; may be real estate or personal property, including money.

**Garnishment -** the seizing of a person's property, credit or salary on the basis of a law that allows it for the purposes of paying a debt. The person who possesses the assets of the debtor and is the subject of the seizure is called a garnishee. This seizure is frequently used in the enforcement of child support where delinquent debtors will be subjected to salary garnishment. A percentage of wages is subtracted directly from the paycheck and directed to the person in need of support, with the employer acting as the garnishee.

**General Lien** – a lien that is not secured by any particular parcel of real property and, therefore, may affect all nonexempt property of a debtor. An example of a general lien is a lien for federal estate taxes. If these taxes are not paid, the United States government may go after any nonexempt property of the decedent's estate, as full or partial satisfaction of the debt.

**General partner -** a person who joins together with at least one other to own and operate a business for profit and who, unlike the owners of a corporation, is personally liable for all the business's debts. In addition to being responsible for all partnership debts and obligations, a general partner can take actions that legally bind the entire business. That means, for example, that if one partner signs a contract on behalf of the partnership, it will be fully enforceable against the partnership and each individual partner, even if the other partners were not consulted in advance and did not approve the contract. In contrast, a limited partner is liable only to the extent of the capital he/she has invested in the business. The term "general partner" may also apply to the managing partner of a limited partnership that is responsible for partnership debts over and above his, her, or its individual investment in the partnership.

**General Partnership -** a partnership in which the management responsibilities and profits and losses are divided equally among the partners.

**General Power of Appointment -** power under IRC§ 2014(b) which allows a future interest in Property; considered to be favorable to the decedent, his/her estate and/or creditors.

**General Power of Attorney -** power of attorney with broad powers that authorize the agent to take any action the principal would take.

**General warranty deed** – a type of deed by which the grantor states that he/she has valid title and will defend that title against any defect arising from the actions of the grantor or those of the grantor's predecessors. A general warranty deed provides the greatest degree of protection for the grantee.

**Generation-Skipping Transfer Tax (GST) -** estate tax imposed when decedent's interest in a trust passes to persons who are at least one generation younger than the donor.

**Gift -** transfer of property from one person to another without consideration or compensation.

**Gift Tax -** tax imposed on transfers of the donor's estate property during his/her lifetime. Estate tax is imposed upon death.

**Good Faith -** the honest and reasonable belief that one's conduct is performed without improper motive or negligent disregard.

**Goodwill -** an intangible business asset that includes a cultivated reputation and consequential attraction and confidence of repeat customers and connections.

**Grandparent clause -** a provision in a new law that limits its application to people who are new to the system; people already in the system are exempt from the new regulation. For example, when Washington, D.C. raised its drinking age from 18 to 21, people between those ages who could drink under the old law were allowed to retain the right to consume alcohol legally under a grandparent clause.

**Grand jury** – a body of people (usually 16 to 23) who are chosen to sit for extended periods of time and who, in ex parte proceedings, decide whether to issue indictments in criminal cases.

**Grantee** – the person to whom the real property is to be conveyed.

**Grantor -** the person who sets up a trust; also referred to as "settlor."

**Gross Estate** - all property in which the decedent had an interest at death.

**Gross negligence -** any action or omission in reckless disregard of the consequences to the safety or property of another. Sometimes referred to as "very great negligence," gross negligence is more than just neglect of ordinary care toward others or just inadvertence.

**Guarantor -** a person who pledges collateral for the contract of another, but separately, as part of an independent contract with the obligee of the original contract; compare with "surety."

**Guardian *ad litem*** - a person, not necessarily a lawyer, who is appointed by a court to represent and protect the interests of a child or an incapacitated adult during a lawsuit. For example, a guardian *ad litem* may be appointed to represent the interests of a child whose parents are locked in a contentious battle for custody or to protect a child's interests in a lawsuit where there are allegations of child abuse. The guardian *ad litem* may conduct interviews and investigations, make reports to the court and participate in court hearings or mediation sessions. Many guardians *ad litem* are trained by the national organization known as Court-Appointed Special Advocate (CASA).

**Guardian of the Estate** – person appointed and legally authorized to manage the property of an incapacitated person.

**Guardian of the Person** – person legally authorized to manage the personal, non-financial affairs of an incapacitated person.

**Guilty plea** – an accused person's formal admission in court of having committed the charged offense.

**Guilty verdict** – a jury's possible finding or decision on the factual issues of a case.

***Habeas corpus*** - Latin: a court petition ordering that a person being detained be produced before a judge for a hearing to decide whether the detention is lawful. Habeas corpus was one of the concessions the British monarch made in the Magna Carta and has stood as a basic individual right against arbitrary arrest and imprisonment.

**Harassment -** unsolicited words or conduct that tends to annoy, alarm or abuse another person. An excellent alternate definition can be found in Canadian human rights legislation: "a course of vexatious comment or conduct that is known or ought reasonably to be known to be unwelcome." Name-calling such as "dummy" is a common form of harassment.

**Headnote -** a brief summary of a legal rule or significant facts in a case that precedes the printed opinion in reports.

**Health Care Proxy** – legal document authorizing someone other than the principal to make health care decisions for the principal should the principal be unable to speak for him/herself.

**Hearsay** – testimony given by a witness who relates not what he/she knows, but what others have said.

**Heir** – intestate inheritor of real property.

**Hold harmless -** in a contract, a promise by one party not to hold the other party responsible if the other party carries out the contract in a way that causes damage to the first party. For example, many leases include a "hold harmless" clause in which the tenant agrees not to sue the landlord if the tenant is injured due to the landlord's failure to maintain the premises. In most states, these clauses are illegal in residential tenancies, but may be upheld in commercial settings.

**Holding** – the court's statement of how the case should be disposed.

**Holograph will -** a will written entirely in the testator's handwriting and not witnessed. Some states recognize holograph wills; others do not. Still other states will recognize a will as holographic if only part of it is in the testator's handwriting while the other part is typewritten.

**Homestead -** 1) the house in which a family lives, plus any adjoining land and other buildings on that land; 2) real estate that is not subject to the claims of creditors as long as it is occupied as a home by the head of the household. After the head of the family dies, homestead laws often allow the surviving spouse or minor children to live on the property for as long as they choose; 3) land acquired out of the public lands of the United States. The term "homesteaders" refers to people who got their land by settling it and making it productive rather than purchasing it outright.

**Homicide -** the killing of one human being by the act or omission of another. The term applies to all such killings, whether criminal or not. Homicide is considered noncriminal in a number of situations, including deaths as the result of war and putting someone to death by the valid sentence of a court. Killing may also be legally justified as excused, as in cases of self-defense or when someone is killed by another person who is attempting to prevent a violent felony. Criminal homicide occurs when a person purposely, knowingly, recklessly or negligently causes the death of another. Murder and manslaughter are both examples of criminal homicide.

**Hornbook** – often published as textbooks for law students; a primer for the student studying law in a particular area.

**Husband-wife privilege -** a special right that married persons have to keep communications between them secret and inaccessible even to a court of law. While this privilege may have been varied in some states, it has always been held to be lifted where one spouse commits a crime on the other.

***Id.*** – refers to the immediately preceding citation.

**Immunity -** an exemption that a person (individual or corporate) enjoys from the normal operation of the law such as a legal duty or liability, either criminal or civil. For example, diplomats enjoy diplomatic immunity, which means that they cannot be prosecuted for crimes committed during their tenure as diplomats. Another example of immunity is where a witness agrees to testify only if the testimony cannot be used at some later date during a hearing against the witness.

**Impeachment** - to call into question the veracity of a witness by means of evidence offered for that purpose or by showing the witness is unworthy of belief.

**Implied conditions** – those conditions that have not been expressly stated, but which the law presumes to be so inherently a part of the contract that it need not be set forth in clear and written terms. Implied conditions are to be understood by the parties.

**Implied consent** - consent inferred from one's conduct rather than from one's direct expression.

**Implied contract** - a contract not created or evidenced by the explicit agreement of the parties but one inferred by law; as the use of electric power in your home implies a contract with the light company.

**Implied trust** – trust created by operation of law.

**Imputed disqualification** or **vicarious disqualification** - disqualification of all the lawyers in a firm or in an office because one of the lawyers is ethically disqualified from representing the client at issue.

**Inadvertent disclosure** - the careless or accidental revelation of information that should be held confidential.

**Income Beneficiary** - person who is entitled to trust income.

**Incompetent** - one who lacks ability, legal qualification or fitness to manage his/her own affairs.

**Incorporeal** - intangible; some legal rights, such as copyrights or patents, are intangible.

**Indefeasible** - a right or title in property that cannot be made void, defeated or canceled by any past event, error or omission in the title. For example, certificates of title issued under a Torrens land titles system is said to be "indefeasible" because the government warrants that no interest burdens the title other than those on the certificate. This makes long and expensive title searches unnecessary.

**Indictment** - a formal accusation returned by a grand jury that charges a person with a serious crime. It is on the basis of an indictment that an accused person must stand trial.

***Infra*** - "below;" sends the reader to a section that will appear later in the document. This term is not used to refer to a source that will later be cited in full.

**Information** – a formal, criminal charge made by a prosecutor without a grand jury indictment.

**Inheritance Tax** - the tax imposed by state law on property inherited from decedent.

**Injunction** - a court order that prohibits a party from doing something (restrictive injunction) or compels them to do something (mandatory injunction).

**Injunctive relief -** a situation in which a court grants an order, called an injunction, telling a party to refrain from doing something or, in the case of a mandatory injunction, to carry out a particular action. Usually, injunctive relief is granted only after a hearing at which both sides have an opportunity to present testimony and legal arguments.

***In personam*** - Latin: a legal right that is a personal right attached to a specific person. All legal rights are either *in personam* or *in rem. In rem* rights are property rights and enforceable against the entire world.

***In rem*** - Latin: a legal right that is proprietary. All legal rights are either *in personam* or *in rem. In rem* rights are proprietary in nature; related to the ownership of property and not based on any personal relationship, as is the case with *in personam* rights.

**Insider trading** – use of material, non-public information received from a corporate source by someone who has a fiduciary obligation to shareholders and potential investors and who benefits from trading on such information.

**Intangible assets -** nonphysical items such as stock certificates, bonds, bank accounts and pension benefits that have value and must be taken into account in estate planning.

**Intellectual property** – property that has no intrinsic value in and of itself, but that represents something of value. Checks, stock certificates and patents are examples of intangible property.

**Intent** – the design, will or determination to act a certain way through a person's state of mind.

**Intentional tort -** a deliberate act that causes harm to another for which the victim may sue the wrongdoer for damages. Acts of domestic violence, such as assault and battery, are intentional torts as well as crimes.

**Intent-to-use application -** a type of application filed for registration of a trademark which has not been used in commerce.

***Inter alia* -** Latin: "among other things." Legal drafters use the term to precede a list of examples or samples covered by a more general descriptive statement.

**Interest on Lawyer's Trust Account (IOLTA)** – a mandatory trust account for depositing attorneys' fees not yet earned.

**Interlineation -** an addition of something to a document after it has been signed. Such additions are ignored unless they are initialed by the signatories and, if applicable, witnesses.

**Interlocutory appeal** – an appeal that occurs before the lower/trial court's ruling on the entire case.

**Interlocutory decree -** a court judgment that is not final until the judge decides other matters in the case or until enough time has passed to see if the interim decision is working.

**Internet service provider (ISP) -** a business that provides access to the Internet. An ISP may also offer services such as Web site hosting. An ISP can sometimes be held accountable for copyright violations for material posted by subscribers and users but is often protected by the Digital Millennium Copyright Act. The Communications Decency Act usually protects ISPs from charges stemming from subscribers or users posting obscenities or defamation.

**Interrogatories** – written questions served by an opposing party which the receiving party is required to answer under oath.

**Intervention -** an action by which a third person who may be affected by a lawsuit is permitted to become a party to the suit.

***Inter vivos*** **trust (a/k/a Living Trust) -** Latin name, favored by some lawyers, for a living trust. "*Inter vivos*" is Latin for "between the living."

**Intestate -** estate of a person who dies without leaving a valid will.

**Intestate Succession -** the manner in which property passes when the descendant died without a valid will.

**Inure -** to take effect, to result; to come into operation.

**Invitation to Treat** – an expression of willingness to negotiate. A person making an invitation to treat does not intend to be bound as soon as it is accepted by the person to whom the statement is addressed.

**Invitee -** a business guest, or someone who enters property held open to members of the public, such as a visitor to a museum. Property owners must protect invitees from dangers on the property.

**Involuntary bankruptcy -** a proceeding initiated by creditors requesting the bankruptcy court to place a debtor in liquidation.

**IRAC -** stands for Issue - Rule - Analysis - Conclusion; it is the process of applying case law to the problem you are researching.

**Irreconcilable differences** – grounds for divorce. Neither party is considered to be at fault.

**Irrevocable Trust -** trust created by the Settlor wherein he/she gives up control of the trust property. A trustee who is not the Settlor administers the trust.

**Issue -** 1) the questions explored in a legal research memorandum or in a court of law; 2) the persons who descend in a direct line from an ancestor: child, grandchild, great-grandchild and all lineal descendants.

**Jeopardy** – the danger that an accused person is subjected to when on trial for a criminal offense.

**Joint legal custody** – both parents share responsibility of providing for the health, education and welfare of the minor child(ren).

**Joint physical custody** – both parents will spend equal or substantially equal time with the minor child(ren).

**Joint and several liability -** liability of more than one person for which each person may be sued for the entire amount of damages done by all.

**Joint stock company** – partnership agreement in which members of the company own shares that are transferable, but all goods are held in the name of the members who assume partnership liability.

**Joint tenancy -** when two or more persons are equal owners of some property. The unique aspect of joint tenancy is that as a joint tenancy owner dies, his/her shares accrue to the surviving owner(s) so that, eventually, all shares are held by one person. A valid joint tenancy is said to require the "four unities": unity of interest (each joint tenant must have an equal interest including equality of duration and extent), unity of title (the interests must arise from the same document), unity of possession (each joint tenant must have an equal right to occupy the entire property) and unity of time (the interests of the joint tenants must arise at the same time).

**Joint venture -** relationship between two or more persons or corporations, or association between multinational and an agency of the host government national, set up for a specific business undertaking or for a limited period of time.

**Judgment -** the official and authentic decision of a court of justice upon the rights and claims of parties to an action or suit submitted to the court for determination.

**Judgment debtor -** one who owes money as a result of a judgment in favor of a creditor.

**Judgment lien** – a court-ordered lien placed against property when the homeowner fails to pay a debt.

**Judgment notwithstanding the verdict (JNOV) -** reversal of a jury's verdict by a judge when the judge believes that there were insufficient facts on which to base the jury's verdict, or that the verdict did not correctly apply the law. This procedure is similar to a situation in which a judge orders a jury to arrive at a particular verdict, called a directed verdict. In fact, a judgment notwithstanding the verdict is occasionally made when a jury refuses to follow a judge's instruction to arrive at a certain verdict.

**Judicial authority -** a court-made law known as case law.

**Judicial lien -** a lien obtained by judgment or other judicial process against a debtor.

**Judicial notice -** a rule of judicial convenience whereby the court takes note of certain facts that are capable of being known to a certainty, thereby relieving a party of the burden of producing evidence to prove these facts.

**Jukebox -** hold anywhere from six to hundreds of CDs, allowing network-based access to a single collection of images.

***Jurat*** - certificate of person and officer before whom a writing is sworn to.

**Jurisdiction** – the authority given by law to a court to try cases and rule on legal matters within a particular geographic area and/or over certain types of cases.

**In rem jurisdiction** – the power a court may exercise over real estate or personal property, i.e., large items of moveable property, such as a ship (to satisfy debts arising from the operation or use of the ship), located within the court's jurisdiction, or a "status" against a person over whom the court does not have personal jurisdiction. In rem jurisdiction assumes the property or status is the primary object of the action, rather than personal liabilities not associated with the property.

***Quasi in rem* jurisdiction** – refers to a legal action based on property rights of a person absent from the jurisdiction. Any judgment will affect only the property seized. In a *quasi in rem* case, the court may lack personal jurisdiction over the defendant, but it has jurisdiction over the defendant's property. The property could be seized to obtain a claim against the defendant.

**Personal jurisdiction** – the power of a court to hear and determine a lawsuit involving a defendant by virtue of the defendant's having some contact with the place where the court is located. This includes, but is not limited to, the defendant's residence within the state, out-of-state residents who have been in the state for a short period of time and corporations that were either incorporated in the state or do business within the state.

**Long-arm statute** – a state statute allowing for the assertion of personal jurisdiction over a nonresident defendant who has some connection (such as ownership or use of property, transaction of business or commission of a tort) within the state.

**Subject matter jurisdiction** – federal courts, under federal statutes, have subject matter jurisdiction over matters involving a treaty, bankruptcy, copyright, some discrimination matters, maritime, patent issues, federal constitutional issues, actions where the U.S. government is a party and cases involving diversity of citizenship.

**Jurisprudence** – the branch of philosophy concerned with the law and the principles that lead courts to make the decisions they do.

**Jury** – a body of persons selected and legally sworn to render a verdict according to the evidence presented.

**Jury selection -** the process by which a jury is seated in a jury trial or proceeding.

**Key Number** – Thomson West publications assign a specific key number to every topic and subtopic; West uses this same code and the key logo throughout its publications.

**Laches** - a legal doctrine whereby those who take too long to assert a legal right lose their entitlement to compensation. When you claim that a person's legal suit against you is not valid because of this, you would call your defense "estoppel by laches."

**Lapsed Gift** - gift intended for a beneficiary who predeceases the testator or donor.

**Larceny** - an old English criminal and common law offence covering the unlawful or fraudulent removal of another's property without the owner's consent. The offence of theft now covers most cases of larceny. However, larceny is wider than theft, as it includes the taking of property of another person by whatever means (by theft, overtly , by fraud, by trickery, etc.) if an intent exists to convert that property to one's own use against the wishes of the owner.

**Laws of Succession** – statutes indicating a person's intestate heirs.

**Leading questions** - those questions that suggest to the witness the answer. Leading questions are not proper on direct examination but may be used during cross-examination or the examination of a hostile witness.

**Lease** - a special kind of contract between a property owner and a person wanting temporary enjoyment and use of the property, in exchange for rent paid to the property owner. Where the property is land, a building or parts of either, the property owner is called a landlord and the person that contracts to receive the temporary enjoyment and use is called a tenant.

**Leasehold** - right under a lease to hold property for a specific term.

**Legal separation** – a proceeding in which the parties are granted a formal separation of their marital status, yet still remain legally married to each other.

**Legacy** - usually refers to cash left as a bequest in a will.

**Legatee** - the person who is the beneficiary of either real or personal property in a will.

**Legislative immunity** - legal doctrine that prevents legislators from being sued for actions performed and decisions made in the course of serving in government. This doctrine does not protect legislators from criminal prosecution, nor does it relieve them from responsibility for actions outside the scope of their office.

**Lessee** – one who has a possessory interest in real or personal property under a lease; a tenant.

**Lessor** – one who conveys real or personal property by lease; a landlord.

**Letter of deficiency** – informal letter issued by the SEC indicating what corrections need to be made in a registration statement in order for it to become effective.

**Letters of administration** - legal document issued by the court appointing a personal representative of a decedent who died intestate.

**Letters patent -** the official document sent to an inventor by the U.S. Patent and Trademark Office evidencing the issuance of the patent.

**Letters testamentary -** legal document issued by the court that appoints the executor or personal representative when the decedent had a valid will.

**Lexis/Nexis®** – an electronic, online, legal database of cases, statutes, secondary sources and other legal documents that can be searched using either natural language or Boolean searches.

**Liability -** any legal obligation, either due now or at some time in the future; could be a debt or a promise to do something. To say a person is liable for a debt or wrongful act is to indicate that he/she is the person responsible for paying the debt or compensating the wrongful act.

**Libel -** defamation by writing, such as in a newspaper or a letter.

**License -** a special permission to do something on, or with, somebody else's property that, were it not for the license, could be legally prevented or give rise to legal action in tort or trespass. A common example is permitting a person to walk across your lawn. If not for the license, such a walk would constitute trespass. Licenses are revocable at will.

**Licensing** – a mandatory form of regulation.

**Lien -** a property right that remains attached to an object that has been sold, but not totally paid for, until complete payment has been made; may involve possession of the object until the debt is paid, or may be registered against the object (especially if the object is real estate).

**Life estate -** a right to use and to enjoy land and/or structures on land only for the life of the tenant. The estate reverts back to the grantor (or to some other person) at the death of the person to whom it is given.

**Limited liability company (LLC)** – hybrid corporation-partnership, such as a Subchapter S corporation, but with fewer restrictions.

**Limited liability partnership (LLP)** – form of partnership in which all partners are limited and there are no general partners. This form of entity is often used by professionals as the partnership may continue even if one partner is sued; the partners are not jointly or severally liable.

**Limited partner -** a unique colleague in a partnership that has agreed to be liable only to the extent of his, her, or its investment. Limited partners, though, have no right to manage the partnership. Limited partners are often investors who seek the tax benefits of a partnership.

**Limited partnership (LP)** – a partnership that has one general partner responsible for managing the business, and one or more limited partners who invest in the partnership, but do not participate in its management and whose liability is limited to the amount of capital they contribute.

**Liquidated damages** – a stipulated contractual amount that the parties agree is a reasonable estimation of the damages owed to one party in the event of a breach by the other.

***Lis pendens*** - Latin: a dispute or matter that is the subject of ongoing or pending litigation.

**Litigation hold** – a/k/a stop destruction request; notice issued by either party to stop the destruction of pertinent electronic records such as email, calendar entries, contact and task lists because of anticipated or pending litigation.

**Living Trust -** trust created by the settlor(s) that takes effect will he, she, they are alive; Inter Vivos Trust.

**Living Will -** a document that sets out guidelines for dealing with life-sustaining medical procedures in the eventuality of the signatory's sudden debilitation. Living wills would, for example, inform medical staff not to provide extraordinary life-preserving procedures on their bodies if they are incapable of expressing themselves and suffering from an incurable and terminal condition.

**Load File** – a data file that defines the links between multiple records in a database and document images.

**Loan-to-Value Ratio** – the percentage of the property's value that is mortgage; divide the mortgage amount by the home's Fair Market Value to get the LTVR.

**Long arm statutes -** each court is bound to a territorial jurisdiction and does not normally have jurisdiction over persons that reside outside of that jurisdiction. A "long arm statute" is a statutory method of obtaining personal jurisdiction by substituted service of process over a nonresident defendant who has sufficient minimum contacts with a state.

**Magistrate judge** – conducts all proceedings in a jury or non-jury civil matter provided all parties consent and trials of persons accused of misdemeanors if the defendant consents.

***Magna Carta*** - charter subscribed to by King John of England on June 12, 1215 in which basic limits were set on the king's powers. King John had ruled tyrannically. His barons rebelled and committed themselves to war with the king unless he agreed to the Charter. Held to be the precursor of *habeas corpus*; Article 39 of the Magna Carta held that no man shall be "imprisoned, exiled or destroyed . . . except by lawful judgment of his peers or by the law of the land." The original document is on display at the National Archives in Washington, D.C.

**Maintenance -** refers to the obligation of one person to contribute, in part or in whole, to the cost of living of another person.

**Majority opinion -** one justice writes for himself/herself and for others, making up a majority of the judges hearing the case.

**Malice** – ill will or the intentional doing of a wrongful act or injury to someone without excuse.

**Mandamus -** a writ that commands an individual, organization (e.g., government), administrative tribunal or court to perform a certain action, usually to correct a prior illegal action or a failure to act in the first place.

**Mandatory authority -** primary authority in your jurisdiction.

**Marital deduction -** a deduction allowed by the federal estate tax laws for all property passed to a surviving spouse who is a U.S. citizen. This deduction, which really functions as an exemption, allows anyone, even a billionaire, to pass his/her entire estate to a surviving spouse without any tax.

**Marital Deduction Trust -** Trust created for a surviving spouse that will reduce federal income tax. The deceased spouse's estate is entitled to an unlimited marital deduction.

**Marital property -** most of the property accumulated by spouses during a marriage, called community property in some states. States differ as to exactly what is included in marital property; some states include all property and earnings during the marriage, while others exclude gifts and inheritances.

**Marital settlement agreement** – a legal and binding contract between the parties setting forth the division of marital assets, terms of spousal support, child support and custody and visitation; also known as Marital Separation Agreement or Postnuptial Agreement.

***Martindale-Hubbell Law Directory*** **-** a publication of several volumes that contains names, addresses, practice specialties and ratings of United States lawyers; also includes digests of state and foreign statutory law.

**Marshalling assets** – collecting and categorizing the estate of the decedent.

**Mechanic's lien** – see Construction Lien.

**Mediation** – a form of alternative dispute resolution where a neutral third party helps the parties resolve their differences.

***Mens Rea*** – Latin Term: "guilty mind, criminal mind or criminal intent."

**Metadata** – often described as "data about data." In the context of litigation, this term means information about electronic files, including author, time and date created, last revision, file size and a summary of the file.

**Military Justice Act of 2016** – see also Uniform Code of Military Justice. Legislative act amending the Uniform Code of Military Justice.

**Minimum contacts -** a requirement that must be satisfied before a defendant can be sued in a particular state. In order for the suit to go forward in the chosen state, the defendant must have some connections with that state.

**Miranda warning -** requirement that police tell a suspect in their custody of his/her constitutional rights before they question him/her. So named as a result of the *Miranda v. Arizona* ruling by the United States Supreme Court.

**Misappropriation** – unauthorized use of trust account funds.

**Misdemeanor -** a criminal offense lesser than a felony and generally punishable by fine or by imprisonment other than in a penitentiary.

**Mitigating circumstances -** these are facts that, while not negating an offense or wrongful action, tend to show that the defendant may have had some grounds for acting the way he/she did. For example, assault, though provoked, is still assault, but provocation may constitute mitigating circumstances and allow for a lesser sentence.

***Modus operandi*** - Latin: method of operation.

**Moot -** also called a "moot point": a side issue, problem or question that does not have to be decided to resolve the main issues in a dispute.

**Mortgage -** an interest given on a piece of land, in writing, to guarantee the payment of a debt or the execution of some action; automatically becomes void when the debt is paid or the action is executed. In some jurisdictions, it entails a conveyance of the land until the debt is paid in full.

**Mortgagee** – one to whom property is mortgaged; the mortgage creditor or lender.

**Mortgagor** – the person who has borrowed money and pledged his/her real property as security for the money provided by the lender (mortgagee).

**Motion -** an application to the court requesting an order or rule in favor of the applicant.

**Motion *in limine* -** a motion made by counsel requesting that information which might be prejudicial not be allowed to be heard in a case.

**Motion to quash -** an application to the court requesting to annul, overthrow or vacate by judicial decision. Typically, motions to quash involve quashing subpoenas or some form of discovery, such as depositions.

**Mutual Wills -** reciprocal wills.

**NFPA's Model Code of Ethics and Professional Responsibility** – standards of conduct for paralegals and guidelines for enforcement.

**National Stock Exchange** – entity for trading stocks of publicly held corporations. The two U.S. exchanges are the New York Stock Exchange (NYSE) and the National Association of Securities Dealers Automated Quotations (NASDAQ).

**Natural Heirs -** heirs of the body.

**Negligence** – the failure to use such care as a reasonably prudent and careful person would use under the same or similar circumstances.

**Negligence *Per Se*** – an action or omission where the evidence is clear and not controverted and was in violation of a statute.

**Negotiable instrument** - a written document that represents an unconditional promise to pay a specified amount of money upon the demand of its owner. Examples include checks and promissory notes. Negotiable instruments can be transferred from one person to another, as when you write "pay to the order of" on the back of a check and turn it over to someone else.

**Next of kin** - the nearest blood relative of the decedent.

**No-Contest Clause** - provision contained in the will that disinherits any person who contests the validity of the will; forfeiture clause.

***Nolo contendere plea*** - Latin for "I will not contest it." Used primarily in criminal proceedings whereby the defendant declines to refute the evidence of the prosecution.

**Nonlawyer** - man or woman who is not a lawyer; someone not authorized to practice law. Could include a paralegal or any person who is not an attorney.

**Nonlinear Descendant** - beneficiary who is not related to the decedent but is assigned to a generation based on his/her birthdate.

**Nonmarital children** – children born out of wedlock, or children from a former marriage or relationship.

**Non-probate Property** - property owned by the decedent, but that is distributed by other means rather than the decedent's will, such as life insurance, annuities, retirement accounts, property held in joint tenancy or that has a right of survivorship.

**Nonprofit corporation** - a legal structure authorized by state law allowing people to come together to benefit either members of an organization (a club or mutual benefit society) or for some public purpose (such as a hospital, environmental organization or literary society). Nonprofit corporations, despite the name, can make a profit, but the business cannot be designed primarily for profit-making purposes, and the profits must be used for the benefit of the organization or purpose the corporation was created to help. When a nonprofit corporation dissolves, any remaining assets must be distributed to another nonprofit corporation, not to board members.

**Nonprofit (Mutual Benefit) Corporation** - a non-profit corporation -- as defined by the IRS code -- is created to protect individual members of a board of directors from liability. This type of corporation is formed by groups which have such similar interests as travel, recreation, sports, the environment, etc.

**Nonresidential Alien** – a person who does not meet the IRS green card or substantial presence test to be declared as a "resident alien"; generally, a new arrival on a J-1 or F-1 visa. Nonresidential aliens are taxed differently than residential aliens.

**Notice to creditors** - 1) notice given by the bankruptcy court to all creditors of a meeting of creditors, sometimes called a "341 hearing" after that section of the Bankruptcy Code that provides for such a meeting; 2) notice given to all creditors of the decedent's death and that they must file their claim, if any, with the court.

**Notice statute** – a recording act providing that the person with the most recent valid claim, and who purchased without notice of an earlier, unrecorded claim, has priority.

**Novation** - the substitution of a new contract for an old one. A novation may change one of the parties to the contract or the duties that must be performed by the original parties.

**Nuisance** - excessive or unlawful use of one's property to the extent of unreasonable annoyance or inconvenience to a neighbor or to the public. Nuisance is a tort.

**Nuncupative Will** - An oral will made by the testator on his/her death bed, which is later transcribed by a person who was present.

**Obligee** - the person who is to receive the benefit of someone else's obligation; that "someone else" being the obligor. Also called a "promisee"; some countries refer to the recipient of family support as an "obligee."

**Obligor** - a person who is contractually or legally committed or obliged to providing something to another person; the recipient of the benefit being called the oblige; also known as the "promisor."

**Obscenity** - an elusive concept used in the context of criminal law to describe a presentation (such as a film or a publication) that is illegal because it is morally corruptive. The common law has struggled with this word as society has evolved toward greater tolerance of alternative sexual behavior.

**Offer** - an explicit proposal to contract that, if accepted, completes the contract and binds both the person that made the offer and the person accepting the offer to the terms of the contract.

**Offer of proof** - at trial, a party's explanation to a judge as to how a proposed line of questioning, or a certain item of physical evidence, would be relevant to its case and admissible under the rules of evidence. Offers of proof arise when a party begins a line of questioning that the other side objects to as calling for irrelevant or inadmissible information.

**Offeree** – a person or entity to whom an offer to enter into a contract is made by another (the offeror).

**Offeror** – a person or entity who makes a specific proposal to another (the offeree) to enter into a contract.

**Officers** – corporate employees who are appointed by the board of directors to manage the day-to-day operations of the corporation.

***Official Gazette*** - a weekly publication of the Patent & Trademark Office, listing trademark applications for objection purposes; information on newly issued patents and lists of patents for license or sale.

**Official reports** - the publication of cumulated court decisions of state or federal courts in advance sheets and bound volumes as provided by statutory authority.

**Opening statement -** the statement made by the attorney for each party after the jury has been selected and before any evidence has been presented. Opening statements outline what the party believes that the evidence will be and presents the party's theory of the case.

**Opinion** - a judge's written explanation of a decision of the court or of a majority of judges.

**Oral argument** – a spoken presentation before a court (especially an appellate court) supporting or opposing the legal relief at issue.

**Order to show cause -** an order from a judge that directs a party to come to court and convince the judge why he/she should not grant an action proposed by the other side or by the judge on his/her own (*sua sponte*).

**Ordinance -** an executive decision of a government that has not been subjected to a legislative assembly (contrary to a statute). It is often detailed and not, as would be a statute, of general wording or application. This term is in disuse in many jurisdictions; the words "regulations" or "bylaws" are preferred.

**Paralegal** – a person, qualified through education, training or work experience to perform substantive legal work that requires knowledge of legal concepts and is customarily, but not exclusively, performed by a lawyer.

**Paralegal Advanced Competency Exam [PACE®]** – an exam from NFPA, designed for experienced paralegals.

**Paralegal CORE Competency Exam [PCCE®]** – an exam from NFPA, designed for entry level paralegals.

**Parallel Citation** – a citation to two or more reporters for the same case decision.

**Parol evidence -** oral or verbal evidence; evidence given by word of mouth in court.

**Partition -** court proceeding that separates the interests of co-owners.

**Partnership -** a business organization in which two or more persons carry on a business together. Partners are each fully liable for all the debts of the enterprise, but they also share the profits (regulated by the Reformed Uniform Partnership Act -- RUPA).

**Patent -** a grant from the government for a limited monopoly, allowing the patentee to exclude others from the manufacture, use and sale of the claimed invention for a specific period of time.

**Patent and Trademark Office** (PTO) - a branch of the U.S. Department of Commerce responsible for examining and issuing all patents and trademarks in the United States.

**Patent claim -** a statement included in a patent application describing the structure of an invention in precise and exact terms.

**Paternity action** – a proceeding brought by either party, but often the mother, or a government agency to determine the father's identity.

**Payee** - the person to whom payment is addressed or given. In family law, the term usually refers to the person who receives or to whom support or maintenance is owed. In commercial law, the term refers to the person to whom a bill of exchange is made payable.

**Payor** - the person making the payment(s). Again, in the context of family law, the word would typically refer to the person paying to a support or maintenance debtor. In commercial law, "payor" refers to the person who makes the payment on a check or bill of exchange.

**Pendente Lite -** pending litigation.

***Per Capita* -** Latin meaning "by the head." Method for distributing an intestate estate; the decedent's estate where all persons are equally related. Each heir will receive an equal share of the decedent's estate.

**Percentage fee** - another form of billing in which the attorney takes a percentage of what is eventually received. This fee is common in collection practice.

**Per Curiam Opinion -** "*per curiam*" simply means "by the court." It is a decision, normally on a fairly routine matter, without a designated author. The term does not imply unanimity.

**Per Stirpes** – taking property by right of representation.

**Peremptory Challenge** – one of a party's limited number of challenges during voir dire that does not need to be supported by a reason unless the opposing party makes a case showing that the challenge was used to discriminate on the basis of race, ethnicity or sex.

**Perfect tender rule** – the legal right for a buyer of goods to insist upon "perfect tender" by the seller. In a contract for the sale of goods, if the goods fail to conform exactly to the description in the contract (whether as to quality, quantity or manner of delivery), the buyer may reject the goods.

**Performance** – the act of completing a transaction according to the terms given in the contract.

**Periodical** - published on a regular basis, the most frequently read periodicals include legal newspapers, publications by bar and paralegal associations, specialized publications and law reviews.

**Perjury -** an intentional lie given while under oath or in a sworn affidavit.

**Permanent injunction** - a court order requiring that some action be taken, or that some party refrain from taking action. It differs from forms of temporary relief, such as a temporary restraining order or preliminary injunction.

**Perpetuity** - forever; of unlimited duration. There is a strong bias in the law against things that are to last in perpetuity. Rights that are to last forever are said to hinder commerce as an impediment to the circulation of property. There is a rule against perpetuities.

**Personal property** – property that is movable; not real estate.

**Personal representative** - the person who administers an estate. If named in a will, that person's title is an executor. If there is no valid will, that person's title is an administrator.

**Persuasive authority** - primary authority in another state.

**Petition** – in the context of litigation, a petition is a formal, written request to a court for equitable relief.

**Piercing the Corporate Veil** – doctrine stating that if a shareholder dominates a corporation or misuses it for improper purposes, the corporate entity may be disregarded and the shareholder may be personally liable for the corporation's debts and obligations.

**Plaintiff** - the person who brings a case to court; the person who sues. May also be called "claimant," "petitioner" or "applicant."

**Plant patent** - covers any discovered and asexually reproduced distinct and new variety of plant.

**Plea** – an accused person's formal response of guilty, not guilty or no contest.

**Plea Agreement/Plea Bargain** – a negotiated agreement between a prosecutor and a criminal defendant whereby the defendant pleads guilty to a lesser offense in exchange for a more lenient sentence and/or a dismissal of the other charges.

**Pleading** - a document filed in court stating the position of one of the parties on the cause of action or on the defense. Forms of pleadings include the complaint, the counterclaim, the cross-claim and the third-party claim, as well as the answers or responses thereto.

**Plurality Opinion** - an opinion written for the greatest number of judges who can agree on a single opinion. It is less than a majority.

**Pocket part** - an insert in the back of a legal publication containing additions, revisions and deletions to the material in that publication.

**Police powers** – a state's Tenth Amendment right, subject to due process and other limitations, to establish and enforce laws protecting the public's health, safety and general welfare, or to delegate this right to local governments. Police powers include licensing, inspection and zoning, among others.

**P.O.D. Payee** - Pay on Death Account. The payee is the recipient of funds from the owner's account upon the death of the decedent. The owner has total control of the account during their lifetime.

**Posthumous -** that which is done after one's death.

**Post-Marital Agreement** - also called a postnuptial agreement. An agreement executed by a spouse after their marriage that sets forth the individual rights to property or transmutes property from separate to community.

**Pour-over will -** a will created at the same time as a trust to "catch" or "pour over" any assets which were not transferred to the trust.

**Power of Appointment** - the ability to appoint a new owner of the property or act for another, including an interest in the subject of the action.

**Power of attorney** - a document that gives a person the right to make binding decisions for another, such as an agent. A power of attorney may be specific to a certain kind of decision or general, in which the agent makes all major decisions for the person who is the subject of the power of attorney.

**Precedent** – a prior decision that can be used later as a standard in a similar case.

**Prenuptial/Antenuptial Agreement** – a written contract entered into prior to marriage that specifies how property will be divided upon divorce or death of a spouse; also known as Premarital Agreement.

**Preponderance of the evidence** – evidence which is of greater weight or more convincing than the evidence offered in opposition.

**Present Interest** - interest that is vested rather than a future interest.

**Pretermitted heir**- a child or other issue who is unintentionally omitted from the will.

***Prima facie*** - Latin: a legal presumption that means "on the face of it" or "at first sight." Lawmakers will often use this device to establish that if a certain set of facts are proven, then another fact is established *prima facie*. For example, proof of mailing a letter is *prima facie* proof that it was received by the person to whom it was addressed and will be accepted as such by a court unless proven otherwise.

**Primary legal authority** - publications that contain the law, such as judicial decisions, statutes and administrative rules.

**Primogeniture** - rule of descent used in the Middle Ages wherein the oldest male inherited the real property of decedent and excluded all other children.

**Principal -** the body (corpus) of a trust; or the person who creates a power of attorney.

**Private Mortgage Insurance (PMI)** – insurance from which the benefits are intended to insure the portion of the loan that exceeds the typical, conventional loan-to-value ratio.

**Privilege** – a right or immunity granted as a peculiar benefit.

Specific Privileges:

**Clergy-Penitent Privilege** – protects communications between a religious officiant and a penitent.

**Physician-Patient Privilege** – prevents release of medical records without permission from patient.

**Privilege Against Self-Incrimination** – the premise which prohibits a defendant from being required to testify against him/herself.

**Public Interest Privilege** – prevents compulsory disclosure of documents or information which is against the public interest.

**Spousal Privilege** – gives a husband and wife the right to refuse to testify about confidential statements made to one another.

**Without Prejudice Privilege** – the premise of one not losing or waiving any rights or privileges.

**Privileged communication** - communication that is protected by law from forced disclosure.

**Probable cause** – a reasonable ground to suspect that a person has committed, or is committing, a crime or that a place contained specific items connected with a crime. Probable cause is more than a bare suspicion but less than evidence than would justify a conviction must be shown before an arrest warrant or search warrant may be issued.

**Probate** - the judicial proceeding whereby a will is proven to be valid to the court; from that point on, the executor has the legal authority to execute the will.

***Pro bono*** - Latin: provided for free. *Pro bono publico* means "for the public good."

**Process server** – a person who delivers legal papers in lawsuits, either as a profession or as a government official (e.g., deputy sheriff, marshal or constable).

**Professional Corporation** - corporations formed, as allowed by state law, for the benefit of doctors, dentists, accountants and lawyers in order to take advantage tax deductions for health care and pension plans.

**Promisee** - a person who is to be the beneficiary of a promise, an obligation or a contract; synonymous to "obligee."

**Promisor** - the person who has become obliged through a promise (usually expressed in a contract) towards another, the intended beneficiary of the promise being referred to as the promise; sometimes referred to as an "obligor."

**Promissory estoppel** – a term used in contract law that applies where, although there may not otherwise be an enforceable contract because one party has relied on the promise of the other, it would be unfair not to enforce the agreement.

**Promissory note -** an unconditional, written and signed promise to pay a certain amount of money, on demand or at a certain, defined date in the future. Contrary to a bill of exchange, a promissory note is not drawn on any third party holding the payor's money; it is a direct promise from the payor to the payee.

***Pro per*** - a term derived from the Latin *in propria*, meaning "for one's self," used in some states to describe a person who handles his/her own case without a lawyer. In other states, the term "***pro se***" is used. When a non-lawyer files his/her own legal papers, he/she is expected to write "*in pro per*" at the bottom of the heading on the first page.

**Property** - property is commonly thought of as a thing that belongs to someone and over which that a person has total control. Legally, property is more properly defined as a collection of legal rights over a thing. These rights are usually total and fully enforceable by the state or the owner against others. It has been said that "property and law were born and die together. Before laws were made, there was no property. Take away laws, and property ceases." Before laws were written and enforced, property had no relevance.

**Proprietorship** - business that is owned by one person.

***Pro rata*** - Latin: to divide proportionate to a certain rate or interest.

***Pro se*** - Latin: in one's personal behalf.

**Prosecutor** – an attorney who conducts proceedings in court on behalf of the government.

**Protective order** - an order or decree of the court for the purpose of protecting a person or group from further harassment, service of process or discovery. See Fed. R. Civ. P. 26(c).

**Proximate cause** - the last negligent act that contributes to an injury. Generally, a person is liable only if an injury was proximately caused by his/her action or by his/her failure to act when he/she had a duty to act.

**Proxy** - a right that is signed-over to an agent.

**Public domain** - a creative work, invention or logo that is available for use without permission from its owner. This typically occurs after patent, trademark or copyright protection has expired.

**Public Access to Court Electronic Records (PACER)** – the federal courts' online database for retrieving and accessing court filings and court decisions.

**Publicly held Corporation** - corporation whose stock is traded on the national securities exchanges and is held by numerous shareholders (investors). The corporation is managed by officers and a board of directors.

**Punitive damages** - special and highly exceptional damages ordered by a court against a defendant where the act or omission that caused the suit was of a particularly heinous, malicious or highhanded nature. Where awarded, they are an exception to the rule that damages are to compensate, not to punish.

**Putative** - alleged; supposed; reputed.

**Putative spouse** – a person who believes in good faith, that his/her marriage was valid. Considered the innocent party in an annulment proceeding.

**Qualified Disclaimer** - property being disclaimed must satisfy the conditions of Internal Revenue Code §2518.

**Qualified Domestic Relations Order (QDRO)** - a court order that uses pension or retirement benefits to provide alimony or child support, or to divide marital property, at divorce. This special order is necessary to comply with federal law governing retirement pay.

**Qualified Terminable Interest Property (Q-TIP) -** the interest in property that ends with the death of the person who holds the interest. Ownership interest is not absolute.

**Qualified Terminable Interest Property Trust -** a (Q-TIP) trust that allows the surviving spouse with a life estate in order to qualify for the marital deduction. The surviving spouse will receive income and principal, if needed. May also provide an eventual gift to charity.

***Quantum meruit*** – Latin: "as much as is deserved." This is a legal principle under which a person should not be obliged to pay, nor should another be allowed to receive, more than the value of the goods or services exchanged.

**Quasi-community property** - a form of property owned by a married couple. If a couple moves to a community property state from a non-community property state, property they acquired together in the non-community property state may be considered quasi-community property. Quasi-community property is treated like community property when one spouse dies or if the couple divorces.

**Quasi-judicial -** refers to decisions made by administrative tribunals or government officials to which the rules of natural justice apply. In judicial decisions, the principles of natural justice always apply. However, between routine government policy decisions and the traditional court forums lies a hybrid, sometimes called a tribunal or administrative tribunal, not necessarily presided over by judges. These operate as a government policy-making body at times but also exercise a licensing, certifying, approval or other adjudication authority that is judicial because it directly affects the legal rights of a person.

***Quid pro quo*** - Latin: something for something.

**Quiet Enjoyment (Covenant of)** – a formal and binding agreement, usually inserted in leases and conveyances on the part of the grantor, promising that the tenant or grantee shall enjoy the possession of the premises in peace and without disturbance.

**Quitclaim deed** - a deed that transfers whatever ownership interest the transferor has in a particular property. The deed does not guarantee anything about what is being transferred.

**Race-notice statute** – a recording law providing that the person who records first, without notice of prior unrecorded claims, has priority.

**Race statute** – a recording act providing that the person who records first, regardless of notice, has priority.

**Real evidence -** an object relevant to the facts at issue and produced for inspection rather than described by a witness.

**Real property -** immoveable property such as land, a building or an object that, though at one time a chattel, has become permanently affixed to land or a building.

**Reasonable care** – a degree of care which a person of ordinary prudence would exercise in the same or similar circumstances.

**Reasonable doubt** – the highest degree of proof required to determine whether a criminal defendant is guilty.

**Reasonable person -** a phrase used to denote a hypothetical person who exercises qualities of attention, knowledge, intelligence and judgment that society requires of its members for the protection of their own interest and the interests of others. Thus, the test of negligence is based on either a failure to do something that a reasonable person, guided by considerations that ordinarily regulate conduct, would do, or on the doing of something that a reasonable and prudent (wise) person would not do.

**Reciprocal Wills** - wills that contain parallel dispositive provisions. Usually prepared by husband and wife or domestic partners; also called mutual wills.

**Recuse** - the process by which a judge is disqualified from hearing a case, on his/her own motion or upon the objection of either party.

**Redaction** - altering a document to cover words or other information, usually confidential, to suit a particular purpose. Commonly-used to delete confidential information in documents to be produced to opposing counsel.

**Redemption** - buying back. When a vendor later buys the property back, a right of redemption gives the vendor the right to buy back the property.

**Redress** - to set right; to remedy; to compensate; to remove the causes of a grievance.

**Registered mark** - trademark with the words "Registered in the U.S. Patent and Trademark Office" or the letter "R" enclosed within a circle (®).

**Relational databases -** also called flat file, summary, bibliographic, abstract or index databases. These databases store a summary of the document and are made up of files, fields and records.

**Remainder -** a right to future enjoyment or ownership of real property. The "leftover" after property has been conveyed first to another party. A remainder interest is what is leftover after a life estate has run its course. Contrary to a reversion, a remainder does not go to the grantor or his/her heirs.

**Remainderman** – person to whom legal and equitable titles merge.

**Remand – to return to the lower court, usually with instructions from the appellate court.**

**Replevin -** a legal action taken to reclaim goods that have been distrained.

**Reporters -** books that contain court decisions.

**Request for admissions** – written statements served on the opposing party requiring a response in which the opposing party must admit or deny the truthfulness of a fact or opinion and/or authenticate the genuineness of a document.

**Request for production (of documents)** – written requests served by an opposing party which seek the production of documents, correspondence, videos and/or any other tangible evidence relating to the action.

***Res* -** the principal property in a trust.

***Res Judicata*** – Latin: a thing decided.

***Res Ipsa Loquitor*** – Latin: the thing speaks for itself; a theory of negligence used when there is a rebuttable presumption or inference that defendant was negligent.

**Rescind -** to abrogate or cancel a contract putting the parties in the same position they would have been in had there been no contract. Rescission can occur in one of two ways: either a contract can be set aside (rescinded) because of some defect in its formation (such as misrepresentation, duress or undue influence) or it can be set aside by agreement by the parties (for example, if they reach a new agreement).

**Rescission** – terminates the contract, and the parties are placed in the position of never having entered into the contract.

**Residuary Clause -** a clause in a will or trust that provides for the distribution of any property which remains in the estate after the distribution of specific bequests.

**Residuary Devisee -** the beneficiary who will receive the remainder of the estate after distribution of specific bequests and all debts and expenses of the decedent are paid.

**Respondent -** the party that "responds to" a claim filed in court against him, her or it by a plaintiff. The more common term is "defendant."

**Respondeat Superior** – Latin: "let the master answer;" the master [employer] is liable in certain cases for the wrongful acts of his/her servant [employee].

**Restatement -** a publication that tells what the law is in a particular field, as compiled from statutes and decisions.

**Restitution** – a remedy designed to restore the injured party to the position occupied prior to the formation of the contract.

**Restrictive covenant** – a private agreement, usually in a deed or lease, which restricts the use or occupancy of real property, especially by specifying lot sizes, building lines, architectural styles and the uses to which the property may be put.

**Return of service -** the portion of the summons that specifies the signature of the person who served the summons, that the summons and petition were served, the name of the person to whom the summons was served, where it was served, how it was served, when it was served and when it was filed and returned.

**Reverse** – to overturn a judgment on appeal.

**Reversion -** a future interest left in a transferor or his/her heirs. A reservation in a real property conveyance that the property reverts back to the original owner upon the occurrence of a certain event.

**Revocable Trust -** trust created by the settlor (grantor) which he/she is able to revoke.

**Right of Representation -** inheritance received by right of representation is one that distributes the decedent's estate to the heirs by whatever share their predeceased parent would have taken if he/she had survived. May be used with terms such as *per capita* or *per stirpes*.

**Right of Survivorship -** a joint tenant automatically receives the other joint tenant's share upon death.

**Robbery -** felonious taking of another's property, from his/her person or immediate presence and against his/her will, by means of force or fear.

**Rule against perpetuities -** a common law rule that prevents suspending the transfer of property for more than 21 years or a lifetime plus 21 years. For example, if a will proposes the transfer of an estate to some future date, which is uncertain, for either more than 21 years after the death of the testator or for the life of a person identified in the will and 21 years, the transfer is void. Statute law exists in many jurisdictions that supersedes the common law rule.

**Running with the land -** a phrase used in property law to describe a right or duty that remains with a piece of property no matter who owns it.

**Salvage Value -** estimated value that would be obtained at the end of the asset's "useful" life. Used in tax law; may also be referred to as "garage sale" value.

**Sanction -** this is a very unusual word with two contradictory meanings. To "sanction" can mean to ratify or to approve, but it can also mean to punish. The sanction of a crime refers to the actual punishment, usually expressed as a fine or jail term.

**Sarbanes-Oxley Act** – SEC regulation that requires high-ranking corporate officials to validate and accurately report financial statements of the corporation. Failure to comply or falsification of financial records is corporate fraud and punishable under federal statutes.

**Satisfaction of judgment** – the complete discharge of obligations under a judgment; the document filed and entered on the record indicating that a judgment against a person or property has been paid.

**Savings Statute -** statute which allows an invalid will to stand even though it does not meet the state law requirements for a valid will.

**Scanning -** synonymous with both image capture and OCR. As used today, it typically means only capturing the bit-map of an image, perhaps with some limited indexing of batch type information about the document collection.

**Search engine** – software used to search data for specific information; programs, such as Google and Dogpile, that search documents for specified keywords and return a list of the documents where the keywords were found.

**Search warrant** – a judge's written order authorizing law enforcement to conduct a search of a specified place and to seize evidence.

**Secondary authority -** legal encyclopedias, treatises, legal texts, law review articles and citators. Writings that set forth the opinion of the writer as to the law.

**Securities and Exchange Commission (SEC)** – federal administrative agency charged with the regulation and administration of publicly-traded corporations.

**Security** – a stock or bond, or any other instrument of interest that represents an investment in a common enterprise with reasonable expectations of profit, derived solely from efforts other than those of the investor.

**Self-Dealing** – breach of fiduciary obligation in which trustee makes a benefit for him/herself instead of the trust.

**Self-incrimination (privilege against)** - the constitutional right of people to refuse to give testimony against themselves that could subject them to criminal prosecution. The right is guaranteed in the Fifth Amendment to the United States Constitution. Asserting the right is often referred to as "taking the Fifth."

**Self-Proving Will -** will that includes an attestation or affidavit by the testator and the witnesses as to the valid execution of the will.

**Seller's affidavit** – a sworn statement signed by the seller stating that there are no existing liens on the property that would encumber the purchaser's title.

**Separate maintenance** – another term for Alimony and Spousal Support. An award of money given from one spouse to the other. Duration can be for a very specific time period and will automatically terminate upon a specific date, or it may be unlimited, terminating only upon the death of the payor spouse or the payee spouse.

**Separate Property -** property that is acquired by a person before marriage; during marriage by gift, bequest or inheritance; or after the date of their separation. The property must be continued to be held separately during the marriage to be identified as such.

**Service mark -** a symbol, name, word or device indicating ownership, origin and quality of a service and distinguishes it from that of a competitor or others.

**Service of process -** the delivery of a formal notice to a defendant ordering him/her to appear in court in order to answer the plaintiff's allegations.

**Settlor -** the person who creates a trust, sets forth the duties and responsibilities of the trustee and who transfers the property into the trust. May also be called the Trustee, Grantor or Donor.

**Severability** – a provision in a contract which states that if parts of the contract are held to be illegal or otherwise unenforceable, the remainder of the contract should still apply.

**Sexual harassment -** a term used in human rights legislation and referring primarily to harassment in employment situations related to sex or gender that detrimentally affects the working environment. The most overt variation of sexual harassment is the *quid pro quo* offer of work-favor in exchange for sexual favor.

**Share -** abstract portion of a corporation bought by a transfer to the corporation of cash or other consideration of value, usually evidenced by a paper called a certificate.

**Shepardizing -** method for finding subsequent development of a legal theory by tracing status of a case as legal authority.

**Simultaneous representation -** a lawyer's effort to represent more than one client in connection with the same matter.

**Skip Person -** person who is at least two generations removed (younger) than the transferor.

**Slander -** verbal or spoken defamation.

**Slip law** – a law enacted by Congress but not yet published in a bound volume.

**Slip opinion** – a recently released court decision. These are bound into advance sheets and ultimately included in bound volumes of case law.

**Social media** – forms of electronic communication (as websites for social networking and microblogging) through which users create online communities to share information, ideas, personal messages and other content such as videos.

**Sole Legal Custody** – one parent has the sole responsibility for the health, education and welfare of the minor child(ren).

**Sole physical custody** – one parent has the sole responsibility for the day-to-day care and supervision of the minor child(ren).

**Sole Proprietorship** - a business owned by one person who has control over the operation, management, debts and assets of the business.

**Solicitation** - an attempt or effort to gain business.

**Sovereign immunity** - the doctrine that the government, state or federal, is immune to lawsuit unless it gives its consent.

**Special Administrator** - an administrator who is appointed by the court to administer some portion of the estate, or who is appointed as an interim administrator until the Letters Testamentary have been filed and the administrator officially appointed.

**Special Power of Appointment** - power of appointment wherein the donor specifies who may be appointees. The donor may not appoint a creditor or the donee's estate.

**Special warranty deed** – a deed in which the grantor covenants to defend the title against only those claims and demands of the grantor and those claiming by and under the grantor.

**Specific lien** – a lien that is secured by a particular parcel of real property (e.g., special assessment lien). The lienholder cannot go after other property of the debtor because the lien attaches to the real property itself and not to the debtor.

**Specific performance** - a remedy requiring a person who has breached a contract to perform specifically what he/she has agreed to do. Specific performance is ordered when damages would be inadequate compensation.

**Spendthrift Clause** - clause which prevents creditors from making claims on a trust beneficiary's interest and which also prevents bankruptcy.

**Spendthrift trust** - a trust set up for the benefit of someone who the grantor believes would be incapable of managing his/her own financial affairs.

**Splitting Fees** – a process where fees from a particular matter are shared.

**Spoliation of Evidence** – when a document or information that is required for discovery is destroyed or altered significantly.

**Spousal support** – another term for Alimony and Separate Maintenance. It is important to note that in some jurisdictions, the terms "spousal support" and "alimony" differ; e.g., alimony *pendente lite* cannot be sought if the parties are still residing in the same household, although spousal support can be awarded.

**Spousal Attribution Rule** - if the grantor's spouse is living with the grantor at the time the trust was created, the grantor may continue to hold the power or interest in the trust property.

**Springing Power of Attorney -** power of attorney created to become effective upon the person's disability and/or incapacity.

**Sprinkling Power -** trustee's power of distribution is limited to an ascertainable standard as set forth in the trust; conditions are placed on the distribution of income to the beneficiaries.

**Spurious** – lacking authenticity or validity in essence or origin; not genuine; false.

**Standard of proof -** indicates the degree to which the point must be proven. In a civil case, the burden of proof rests with the plaintiff, who must establish his/her case by such standards of proof as a "preponderance of evidence" or "clear and convincing evidence." (See burden of proof.)

**Standing -** the legal right to bring a lawsuit. Only a person with something at stake has standing to bring a lawsuit.

**Star pagination** – a system in case law that is the unofficial source to allow cross-reference to the pages in the official source and other parallel sources. Stars, asterisks or other special characters are inserted into the text of the unofficial reporter to show where the new pages begin in the official text.

***Stare decisis* -** Latin: a basic principle of the law whereby once a decision (a precedent) on a certain set of facts has been made, the courts will apply that decision in cases that subsequently come before it embodying the same set of facts. A precedent that is binding; must be followed.

**State courts** – a court of the state judicial system, as opposed to a federal court.

**Statement of Facts -** the section in a case brief or a legal research memorandum that summarizes the events connected with the case at hand.

**Statute of Limitation -** a statute that limits the right of a plaintiff to file an action unless it is done within a specified time period after the occurrence that gives rise to the right to sue.

**Statutes -** the written laws approved by legislatures, parliaments or houses of assembly.

**Statute of Frauds** – a statutory requirement that certain kinds of contracts must be in writing to be enforceable.

**Statute of limitations** – deadline for filing a legal action set forth in federal codes and state statutes, which can vary from state to state and by type of action.

**Statute of repose** – the time limit in which a victim can bring a lawsuit for injuries against a manufacturer or seller in a products liability case calculated from the time of sale of the product.

**Statutory law** – the body of law derived from statutes rather than from constitutions or judicial decisions.

**Stepped-Up Basis** - value of property which is inherited is "stepped up" to its fair market value as of the date of death rather than at the date of purchase.

***Stirpes*** - Latin: the offspring of a person; his/her descendants. For example, inheriting *per stirpes* means having a right to a deceased's estate because you happen to be a descendant of the deceased.

**Straight Life Annuity** - yearly payment of a fixed sum of money until the death of the annuitant.

**Stock** – capital raised by a corporation through the sale of shares that entitle shareholders to certain rights of ownership; the proprietorship element in a corporation usually divided into shares and represented by transferable certificates.

**Stock option** – warrant issued to employees, who cannot trade their options, but can sell them back to the corporation. (NOTE: this does not apply to the Chicago Board of Trade, which is the world's first and largest "options" exchange.)

**Stock (Purchase) warrant** – a certificate allowing the holder to purchase a specific amount of stock at a fixed price for a specified time.

**Strict liability** - tort liability that is set upon the defendant without need to prove intent, negligence or fault; as long as you can prove that it was the defendant's object that caused the damage.

***Sua sponte*** - Latin for "on its own will or motion." This term is most commonly used to describe a decision or act that a judge decides upon without having been asked by either party.

**Subchapter S Corporation** - a corporation that is formed and operated as a corporation, but is taxed as a partnership.

**Subpoena** - a procedural tool used in preparation for legal proceedings. A subpoena is a writ issued under the authority of a court to compel the appearance of a witness at a judicial proceeding.

**Subpoena *Duces Tecum*** - a court order commanding a witness to bring certain documents or records to court.

**Subrogation** - when you pay off someone's debt and then try to get the money from the debtor yourself.

**Summons** - the formal notice from the court ordering the defendant to appear and answer the plaintiff's allegations.

***Supra*** - "above"; sends the reader to a source that has previously been cited in full. "*Supra*" may not be used to refer to primary authorities.

**Surety bond -** a bond purchased at the expense of the estate to insure the executor's proper performance. Also referred to as "fidelity bond."

**Survey** – the measuring of a tract of land to confirm and verify its boundaries and contents; a map indicating the results of such measurements.

**Syndicate** – an investment group that privately agrees to come together for the purpose of financing a large, commercial project that none of the syndicate members could finance alone.

**Surety Company** - a company who engages in a business which promises to pay the debt or satisfy an obligation of another.

**Tangible Property** – personal property that is movable or touchable.

**Taxable Apportionment -** death taxes may be apportioned to individual gifts rather than charged against the estate or residuary gift.

**Taxable Distribution -** distribution from a trust to a skip person, other than a taxable termination or a direct skip.

**Taxable Termination -** termination to an interest in trust property which occurs upon death, lapse of time or release of power to a nonskip person. After such termination, a transfer may not be made to a skip person.

**Temporary restraining order (TRO) -** an order that tells one person to stop harassing or harming another, issued after the aggrieved party appears before a judge. Once the TRO is issued, the court holds a second hearing where the other party can tell his/her story and the court can decide whether to make the TRO permanent by issuing an injunction. Although a TRO will often not stop an enraged spouse from acting violently, police may be more willing to intervene if the abused spouse has a TRO.

**Tenancy by the Entirety -** form of joint tenancy between spouses.

**Tenancy in Common** – similar to joint tenancy. All tenants in common share equal property rights except that, upon the death of the tenant in common, that share does not go to the surviving tenant, but is transferred to the estate of the deceased tenant.

**Tenant -** a person to whom a landlord grants temporary and exclusive use of land or a part of a building, usually in exchange for rent. The contract for this type of legal arrangement is called a lease. The word "tenant" originated under the feudal system, referring to landowners who held their land on "tenure" granted by a lord.

**Tenants in common -** similar to joint tenants. All tenants in common share equal property rights except that, upon the death of a tenant in common, that share does not go to the surviving tenants but is transferred to the estate of the deceased tenant.

**Terabyte (TB)** – 1024 gigabytes; also, one trillion bytes.

**Terminable Interest -** interest in property that ends upon the death of the person who holds the interest or upon the occurrence of some event.

**Term Life Insurance -** life insurance purchased which is paid if the insured dies during the designated term.

**Testamentary capacity -** the legal ability to make a will.

**Testamentary Trust** – trust created by will.

**Testate -** person who dies leaving a valid will.

**Testate Succession -** the manner in which property passes under a valid will.

**Testator -** person (male) who makes a will (female: testatrix).

**Testimonium** – last clause in a will.

**The House [of Representatives] Open Multimedia Access System (THOMAS)** – the Internet site of the U.S. Congress which allows researchers to view legislation enacted by Congress.

**Throwback Rule -** trust income in a complex or accumulation trust may be "carried back" to the distribution year or the beneficiary may be taxed in the accumulated.

**Tickler System -** a calendaring system of things that must be done by certain dates.

**Title** – ownership of real property or personal property which stands against the right of anyone else to claim the property.

**Title insurance** – policy issued by an insurance company guaranteeing that the title to a parcel of real property is clear and properly in the name of the title owner and that the owner has the right to deed the property (convey or sell) to another.

**Title search** – the examination of county records for the property's title history by a title company, an abstractor, attorney or escrow officer to determine the "chain of title" and the current status of title, including owner, legal description, easements, property taxes due, encumbrances (mortgages or deeds of trust), long-term leases, judgments or other liens.

**Tort -** a private or civil wrong or injury for which the court provides a remedy through an action for damages.

**Tortfeasor** – one who commits a civil wrong; a wrongdoer.

**Totten Trust -** trust created by a person, using his/her own money and depositing it into a bank account, naming himself/herself as trustee for another person.

**Trademark -** any word, name, symbol or device, or any combination thereof, used by a person in commerce to identify the source of the goods.

**Trade name** - the name a manufacturer gives to a product or a range of products.

**Trade secret** - information including formula, pattern, compilation, program, device, method, technique or process that: 1) derives independent economic value, actual or potential, from not being generally known to and not being readily ascertainable by proper means by other persons who can obtain economic value from its disclosure or use; and 2) is the subject of efforts that are reasonable under the circumstances to maintain its secrecy.

**Treatise** - a formal and systematic book or writing containing a narrative statement on a field of law.

**Treaty** - a combination of an executive action, the decision of a foreign government and ratification of the United States Congress.

**Trial** – a formal judicial examination of evidence and determination of legal claims in an adversary proceeding.

**Trust** - a legal device used to manage real or personal property, established by one person (grantor or settlor) for the benefit of another (beneficiary).

**Trust account** - separate bank account maintained by a law firm exclusively for holding clients' funds in escrow as opposed to an operating bank account used to pay normal expenses in the course of business. Examples of funds that would be deposited in a trust account, as opposed to an operating account, are damages awarded in successful cases before they are disbursed to the client, "good faith" deposits to be disbursed on the occurrence of some anticipated event certain, and any funds that the attorney has consented to hold in escrow for others.

**Trustee** - the person or institution that manages the property put in trust.

**Trust Equivalent** - an arrangement which has substantially the same effect as a trust and which may include life estates, remainder estates, insurance and annuity accounts.

**Trustor** - person who creates a trust; the grantor.

**Unauthorized practice of law (UPL)** - the practice of law by a person, typically a nonlawyer, who has not been licensed or admitted to practice law in a given jurisdiction.

**Unclaimed Property** - property that has been abandoned may be distributed to the state through escheat.

**Unconscionability** - one party's taking advantage of a second party due to their unequal bargaining positions, perhaps because of the second party's recent trauma, physical infirmity, ignorance, inability to read or inability to understand the language. The unfairness must be so severe that it is shocking to the average person. It usually includes the absence of any meaningful choice on the part of the abused party and contract terms so one-sided that they unreasonably favor the party taking advantage. A contract will be terminated if the abused party can prove unconscionability.

**Uncontrolled discretion** - trustee is not held to a standard of reasonable discretion but to good faith.

**Undue influence** – unlawful control exercised by one person over another in order to substitute the first person's will for that of the other. Undue influence generally occurs in two types of situations. In the first, a person takes advantage of the psychological weakness of another to influence that person to agree to a contract to which, under normal circumstances, they would not consent. The second situation entails undue influence based on a fiduciary relationship that exists between the parties. This occurs where one party occupies a position of trust and confidence in relation to the other, as in familial or professional-client relationships.

**Unfair competition** - unfair competition is any number of wrongful business practices covered by both state and federal statutes, as well as the Lanham Act and regulations of the Federal Trade Commission (FTC). Unfair competition can take many forms.

**Unfunded Trust** - trust that was created but property was not put in.

**Uniform Child Custody Jurisdiction and Enforcement Act (UCCJEA)** (f/k/a UCCJA). – Designed to avoid competition and jurisdiction shopping in the matters related to child custody.

**Uniform Code of Military Justice** – see also **Military Justice Act of 2016**. Military justice legal system.

**Uniform Commercial Code (UCC)** - a uniform law governing commercial transactions.

**Unified Estate & Gift Tax** - IRS rules which became effective January 1, 1977 wherein estate and gift tax schedules were created to determine tax rates on lifetime gifts and estates.

**Uniform Gifts to Minors Act** - law which allows gifts of money to be transferred to a custodian rather than directly to the minor child.

**Uniform Interstate Family Support Act (UIFSA)** – a mechanism used in enforcing support orders made in the controlling state where the party resides or when a party moves away from the controlling state to a new state. UISFA is enforceable in all 50 states and US territories.

**Uniform laws** - a series of laws that each state can adopt in order to become uniform with one another, such as the Uniform Commercial Code.

**Uniform Probate Code** - federal act which was also adopted by several states, which seeks to simplify the probate process.

**Uniform Reciprocal Enforcement of Support Act (URESA)** – the forbearer of the Uniform Interstate Family Support Act.

**Uniform Transfers to Minors Act** - a statute, adopted by almost all states, that provides a method for transferring property to minors and arranging for an adult to manage it until the child is old enough to receive it.

**Unitary Transfer Taxes** - gift taxes transferred to a Clifford trust will be valued over a ten-year period.

**United States Patent And Trademark Office (PTO)** - governmental agency within the U.S. Department of Commerce which grants patents and registers trademarks.

***United States Reports*** - publication of court decisions of the United States Supreme Court.

**Universal Life Insurance** - whole life insurance which receives a competitive rate of return.

**Unjust enrichment** - a legal procedure whereby you can seek reimbursement from another who benefited from your action or property without legal justification. There are said to be three conditions that must be met before you can get a court to force reimbursement based on unjust enrichment: an actual enrichment or benefit to the defendant, a corresponding deprivation to the plaintiff and the absence of a legal reason for the defendant's enrichment.

**Unlawful detainer** - a detention of real estate without the consent of the owner or other person entitled to its possession.

**Unlimited Marital Deduction** - tax law that allows non-terminable interest gifts, in any amount, to the donor's spouse, that are generally deductible from gift and estate taxes

**Unliquidated debt** - remaining debt not determined; unassessed or unsettled; in dispute as to the proper amount.

**Unofficial source** – those sources that are not officially sanctioned as the "official" repository of codes or case law.

**UPL** - accepted abbreviation for "unauthorized practice of law" (*above*).

**Usury** - excessive or illegal interest rate. Most countries now prohibit interest rates above a certain level; rates that exceed these levels are called usurious.

**Utility patent** - covers a useful process, machine, article or manufacture and composition of matter.

**U.S. Courts of Appeal** – federal appellate courts having jurisdiction to hear cases in one of the 13 judicial circuits of the United States.

**U.S. District Court** – a federal trial court having jurisdiction to hear civil and criminal cases within its judicial district, also known as the court of original jurisdiction.

**U.S. Supreme Court** – the highest court in the U.S. legal system, also known as the court of last resort. The justices of the U.S. Supreme Court are appointed by the President and approved by the Senate.

**Variance** – an exception to a zoning ordinance, authorized by the appropriate governmental body, such as a planning commission, zoning board, county commissioner or city council.

**Vendor** - the seller; the person selling.

**Venue** - this word has the same meaning at law as it does in everyday English, except that in a legal context, it usually refers specifically to the location of a judicial hearing. For example, if a criminal case has a very high media profile in a particular city, the venue may change to another city to ensure objective jurors who would not have been tainted by media speculation on the crime.

**Verdict** - the decision of a jury. In criminal cases, this is usually expressed as "guilty" or "not guilty." In a civil case, the verdict would be a finding for the plaintiff or for the defendant.

**Vicarious liability** - when a person is held responsible for the tort of another even though the person held responsible may not have done anything wrong. This is often the case with employers who are held vicariously liable for the damages caused by their employees.

**Void or *void ab initio*** - not legally binding. A document that is void is useless and worthless; as if it did not exist. For example, in many countries, contracts for immoral purposes are said to be "void": unenforceable and not recognized by the courts. A good example is a contract to commit a serious crime such as murder.

**Void contract** – imposes no legal rights or obligations upon the parties and is not enforceable by a court. A void contract is, in effect, no contract at all.

**Voidable** - the law distinguishes between contracts that are void and those that are voidable. Some contracts have such a latent defect that they are said to be void (see definition of "void" above). Others have more minor defects to them and are voidable at the option of the party victimized by the defect. For example, contracts signed by a person when they are totally drunk are voidable by that person upon recovering sobriety.

***Voir dire*** - preliminary examination by the court and all parties' counsel of the prospective jurors or witnesses to inquire into their competence.

**Waiver** – 1) the voluntary relinquishment or abandonment -- express or implied -- of a legal right or advantage. The party alleged to have waived a right must have had both knowledge of the existing right and the intention of forgoing it; 2) the instrument by which a person relinquishes or abandons a legal right or advantage.

**Warranty** - a guarantee given on the performance of a product or the doing of a certain thing. For example, many consumer products come with warranties under which the manufacturer will repair or replace any product that fails during the warranty period; the commitment to repair or replace being the warranty.

**Warranty deed** – a deed containing one or more covenants of title, especially a deed that expressly guarantees the grantor's good, clear title and that contains covenants concerning the quality of title, including warranties of seisin, quiet enjoyment, right to convey, freedom from encumbrances and defense of title against all claims.

**Waste** - the abuse, destruction or permanent change to property by one who is merely in possession of it, as in the case of a tenant or a life tenant.

**Westlaw®** – an electronic, online, legal database of cases, statutes, secondary sources and other legal documents that can be searched using either natural language or Boolean searches and the West Key Number System.

**Whistleblower** – an employee who brings the wrongdoings of his/her employer or other employee(s) to the attention of a government or law enforcement agency.

**White Collar Crime** – a crime committed in a commercial context by a member of the professional-managerial class or an officer of a corporation or similar business entity.

**Whole Life Insurance** - life insurance policy wherein the proceeds are paid whenever the insured dies.

**Will** - a written and signed statement, made by an individual, which provides for the disposition of his/her property when he/she dies.

**Will contest** – legal challenge to the validity of a document presented as a will.

**Winding up** – process of completing all unfinished business and transactions, paying off outstanding debts, distributing assets and dividing remaining profits after a corporation or partnership has been terminated or dissolved.

**Window Minor's Trust** - trust created for minors that distributes the property upon the minor reaching the age of twenty-one. The trust gives the trustee the discretion to extend the trust beyond that time.

**With prejudice** - a declaration that dismisses all rights. A judgment barring the right to bring or maintain an action on the same claim or cause.

**Witness** - the regular definition of this word is a person who perceives an event (by seeing, hearing, smelling or other sensory perception). The legal definition refers to the court-supervised recital of that sensory experience, in writing (deposition) or verbally (testimony).

**Work product rule** - the rule providing for qualified immunity of an attorney's work product from discovery or other compelled disclosure. Fed. R. Civ. P. 26(b)(3).

**Writ of Attachment** – a court order directing a sheriff (or other law enforcement officer) to seize property of a defendant which would satisfy a judgment against that defendant.

**Writ of *certiorari*** - an order issued by the Supreme Court directing a lower court to transmit records for a case that the Supreme Court will hear on appeal.

**Writ of Execution** – a court order to a sheriff to enforce a judgment by levying on real or personal property of a judgment debtor to obtain funds to satisfy the judgment amount (pay the winning plaintiff).

**Younger Generation Beneficiary** - person of a younger generation than the person who created the trust.

**Zoning** - the laws dividing cities into different areas according to use, from single-family residences to industrial plants. Zoning ordinances control the size, location and use of buildings within these different areas.

# APPENDIX

## Appendix Form 1

***Lopez v. Superior Court (Friedman Brothers Investment Co.) 45 Cal.App.4th 705 , 52 Cal.Rptr.2d 821 (1996)***

[No. B095244. Second Dist., Div. Seven. May 14, 1996.]

FRANCES LOPEZ, Petitioner, v. THE SUPERIOR COURT OF LOS ANGELES COUNTY, Respondent; FRIEDMAN BROTHERS INVESTMENT COMPANY, Real Party in Interest.

(Superior Court of Los Angeles County, No. PC006059, William A. MacLaughlin, Judge.)

(Opinion by Lillie, P. J., with Johnson and Woods (Fred), JJ., concurring.)

### COUNSEL

Manuel H. Miller for Petitioner.

No appearance for Respondent.

Nouskajian & Cranert and Terrence L. Cranert for Real Party in Interest. **[45 Cal.App.4th 710]**

### OPINION

LILLIE, P. J.

We treat this appeal by Frances Lopez from a minute order granting summary judgment on her complaint in favor of defendant Friedman Brothers Investment Company (Friedman) as a petition for writ of mandate. fn. 1 The primary issue before us is whether Friedman, the owner and lessor of the commercial premises where Lopez allegedly fell, established it was entitled to judgment as a matter of law.

### Factual and Procedural Background

Lopez and Friedman agree that the following facts are undisputed. Friedman owned about 25 acres of farmland upon which stood a produce stand, Hubbard Farms, operated by Sam and Pina Scattaglia under a lease executed in 1977. The term of the lease was for one year, but the lease was renewed on an annual basis thereafter, up to and including the time of Lopez's slip and fall in 1991. Pursuant to the terms of the lease, the Scattaglias were entitled to farm the land and sell the harvested produce at the stand; the lease permitted the lessees, at their expense, to erect a small building for selling the produce, which improvement was to become part of the realty and belong to the lessor. The lease also provided that the lessor "shall have the absolute right to enter upon the premises at any time for the purpose of inspecting the same, or for the purpose of posting Notices of Non-Liability, or for any other reasonable purpose."

At least 10 years prior to Lopez's accident in May 1991, the Scattaglias erected a small market, which had a concrete floor. Although the Scattaglias were in possession of the premises on the day of the accident, they had in the prior 10 years subleased the market to Albert Dibb, Jr., for a 5-year period and had then subleased the market to a Korean couple for about a year; at the **[45 Cal.App.4th 711]** time of plaintiff's accident, the Scattaglias had taken the premises back from the Korean couple and Albert Dibb was working at the store as the Scattaglias' employee.

Three to four times per week prior to her accident, Lopez was a regular shopper at Hubbard Farms; according to her husband, neither he nor his wife had ever slipped and fallen at Hubbard Farms; on May 23, 1991, Mr. Lopez waited in their truck while Mrs. Lopez entered the market and walked back to find some lettuce; finding no lettuce, she picked up a bag of tortillas, went to the register, and paid for her items; as she was in the doorway leaving Hubbard Farms, she stepped on some grapes on the floor and slipped and fell; Lopez did not see the grapes before stepping on them; after her fall, she saw that her shoe was wet from the grapes which were smashed on the floor; her husband saw five or six smashed grapes on the floor.

According to the declaration of Albert Friedman, a partner of Friedman, Friedman made no improvements to the property for purposes of operation of Hubbard Farms and was not involved in any way in the operation of Hubbard Farms, or in the installation of the cement floor at Hubbard Farms; other than Lopez's accident, he was not aware of any other personal injury accident occurring at Hubbard Farms.

According to the deposition testimony of a witness, Bonifacio Gutierrez, in 1991, before the accident, he observed the floor of Hubbard Farms to be wet because the refrigerator was leaking water, which ran from underneath the refrigerator downhill towards the front door of the store and the parking lot; every time he went to the store, he saw grapes on the floor, but he could not remember specifically whether he saw any grapes on the floor on the day of Lopez's accident.

In January 1992, Lopez filed her complaint for personal injuries and damages against Friedman and Hubbard Farms, asserting theories of negligence and premises liability; she alleges that defendants "failed to repair, examine, investigate, inspect, make safe, clean or otherwise maintain or cause to be maintained a certain business premises commonly known as Hubbard Farms"; that defendants "negligently managed, owned, controlled, and operated the subject business premises in that the floors of the subject premises were slippery and littered with produce, glass, and other materials, refuse and debris, which defendants knew, or in the exercise of reasonable care should have known, constituted a dangerous condition and unreasonable risk of harm of which plaintiff was at all times mentioned unaware"; and that defendants "negligently failed to take steps to either make the condition safe or warn plaintiff of the dangerous condition." **[45 Cal.App.4th 712]**

Friedman filed a motion for summary judgment, supported primarily by the declaration of Albert Friedman and excerpts of the depositions of Lopez and her husband. Friedman contended that as a lessor out of possession, it was entitled to summary judgment because there was no evidence that Friedman had actual notice of the dangerous condition of the floor, the alleged dangerous condition was not created by any employee of Friedman, and there was no evidence of any prior slip and fall. Further, Friedman contended that "plaintiff has no evidence to support her claim that the alleged grape on the ground was on the floor a sufficient amount of time to trigger defendant's constructive notice of the dangerous condition," and "there is no reasonable inspection that landowner Friedman, as a lessor out of possession and without control over the produce stand, could have performed which would have revealed this particular dangerous condition."

In opposition to the motion, Lopez contended that the cement floor of the market was improperly constructed and finished so that when it was covered with leaking water or fruit, it became unreasonably dangerous; Friedman's lease permitted it to enter the premises at any time for inspection, or for any reasonable purpose; all construction, including the market, required the prior written consent of the landlord; the lease for one year was subject to annual renewal, and was annually renewed through the time of the accident. Lopez contended triable issues of fact remained as to whether Friedman was negligent in failing to inspect, or to conduct a reasonable inspection, to discover the dangerous condition of the floor, and as to the foreseeability of injuries to customers of its tenant from such condition.

After hearing on the motion, the trial court granted the motion. The minute order states in pertinent part: "Moving party has shown that it is the lessor of commercial property ..., that it did not conduct any operations on the property in question ..., that plaintiff allegedly slipped on grapes ..., and that plaintiff doesn't know how long the grapes had been there. This is sufficient to shift the burden to plaintiff to show that a factual issue exists. While plaintiff has contested some of the facts relied upon by moving party, there has been no showing that there is evidence to indicate that moving party had any actual or constructive notice of the condition that purportedly caused her accident. Rather, the gist of plaintiff's opposition is that a commercial lessor may be held liable for dangerous conditions on the premises and has a duty to inspect. The cases relied upon are inapplicable to this case, involving transient conditions as opposed to circumstances where the dangerous condition was of an unchanging and ongoing nature. There is no showing that any reasonable inspection required of a commercial lessor would have given notice of the condition complained of or that moving party in any way had actual notice." Lopez filed timely notice of appeal from "the **[45 Cal.App.4th 713]** Summary Judgment filed on or about June 22, 1995." We address the merits of the arguments raised in the parties' briefs by deeming the appeal to be a petition for writ of mandate. (Fn. 1, ante.)

### I. Standard of Review

[1a] "Summary judgment is granted when there is no triable issue as to any material fact and the moving party is entitled to judgment as a matter of law. (§ 437c, subd. (c).) We review the trial court's decision to grant [defendant] summary judgment de novo." (Hunter v. Pacific Mechanical Corp. (1995) 37 Cal.App.4th 1282, 1285 [44 Cal.Rptr.2d 335].) We are governed by the 1993 amendments to Code of Civil Procedure section 437c; Friedman's burden "could be met only by showing 'that one or more elements of the cause of action ... cannot be established, or that there is a complete defense to that cause of action.' (§ 437c, subd. (o)(2).) Once the defendant has met that burden, the burden shifts to the plaintiff to show 'that a triable issue of one or more material facts exists as to that cause of action ' " (37 Cal.App.4th at pp. 1285-1286, fn. omitted.)

[2] As noted by the court in Hunter v. Pacific Mechanical Corp., supra, 37 Cal.App.4th 1282, the 1992 and 1993 amendments to Code of Civil Procedure section 437c were intended to apply a particular burden-shifting characteristic of the federal procedure to California summary judgment motions: " 'Now, a moving defendant may rely on factually devoid discovery responses to shift the burden of proof pursuant to section 437c, subdivision (o)(2). Once the burden shifts as a result of the factually devoid discovery responses, the plaintiff must set forth the specific facts which prove the existence of a triable issue of material fact.' " (37 Cal.App.4th at p. 1287.) Under federal law, "the moving party always bears the initial burden of establishing the absence of a genuine issue of material fact. [Citation.] However, if the nonmoving party bears the burden of proof on an issue at trial, the moving party need not support its summary judgment motion with evidence negating an essential element of the nonmoving party's case to satisfy its burden. [Citation.] The moving party may simply point to the absence of evidence to support the nonmoving party's case. (Ibid.) The nonmoving party must then 'set forth specific facts showing that there is a genuine issue for trial.' [Citation.] This can be accomplished by producing 'specific evidence, through affidavits or admissible discovery material, to show that the dispute exists.' " (37 Cal.App.4th at p. 1286, italics in original.)

There is no claim by Friedman in this case that the 1992 and 1993 amendments to Code of Civil Procedure section 437c were intended to **[45 Cal.App.4th 714]** abrogate its burden on summary judgment to identify and respond to all theories of liability reflected in the complaint, "even if not separately pleaded." (§ 437c, subd. (o)(2).) [1b] Thus, "[w]hile a plaintiff who has pleaded several causes of action based on the same set of facts need sustain its burden of proof only on one of the theories in order to prevail at trial, a defendant who seeks a summary judgment must define all of the theories alleged in the complaint and challenge each factually." (Nazar v. Rodeffer (1986) 184 Cal.App.3d 546, 551 [229 Cal.Rptr. 209], abrogated on another point in Ornelas v. Randolph (1993) 4 Cal.4th 1095, 1103 [17 Cal.Rptr.2d 594, 847 P.2d 560].) "Nothing in the language of the 1992 adoption of section 437c, subdivision (n)(2), amendments abrogates this well-established summary judgment requirement that the initial burden rests with the moving party." (Villa v. McFerren (1995) 35 Cal.App.4th 733, 744 [41 Cal.Rptr.2d 719].) "[A]ll the 1993 amendments did in terms of the burden of proof of a moving defendant was move the language in section 437c, subdivision (n)(2) to subdivision (o)(2). No substantive change in the language occurred in the 1992 and 1993 amendments in terms of a moving defendant's burden of proof." (Id. at p. 746.)

We apply the foregoing principles to the theories of liability asserted against Friedman as the owner and landlord of the premises involving the alleged accident.

### II. Friedman's Liability as Landowner

[3] In premises liability cases, summary judgment properly may be granted where a defendant unequivocally establishes its lack of ownership, possession, or control of property alleged to be in a dangerous or defective condition. (Gray v. America West Airlines, Inc. (1989) 209 Cal.App.3d 76, 81 [256 Cal.Rptr. 877].) In the instant case, there is no dispute that Friedman is the owner of the premises leased to Scattaglia. Thus, to the extent the trial court may have concluded that Friedman had no duty to exercise due care to protect third persons, such as Lopez, who came onto the leased premises, the trial court erred. (Krongos v. Pacific Gas & Electric Co. (1992) 7 Cal.App.4th 387, 392 [9 Cal.Rptr.2d 124].)

Portillo v. Aiassa (1994) 27 Cal.App.4th 1128 [32 Cal.Rptr.2d 755], contains a good discussion of the duties owed by a commercial landlord. [4] "A landlord owes a duty of care to a tenant to provide and maintain safe conditions on the leased premises. [Citation.] This duty of care also extends to the general public. 'A lessor who leases property for a purpose **[45 Cal.App.4th 715]** involving the admission of the public is under a duty to see that it is safe for the purposes intended, and to exercise reasonable care to inspect and repair the premises before possession is transferred so as to prevent any unreasonable risk of harm to the public who may enter. [Citations.] An agreement to renew a lease or relet the premises ... cannot relieve the lessor of his duty to see that the premises are reasonably safe at that time.' [Citation.] [¶] Where there is a duty to exercise reasonable care in the inspection of premises for dangerous conditions, the lack of awareness of the dangerous condition does not generally preclude liability. [Citation.] 'Although liability might easily be found where the landowner has actual knowledge of the dangerous condition "[t]he landowner's lack of knowledge of the dangerous condition is not a defense. He has an affirmative duty to exercise ordinary care to keep the premises in a reasonably safe condition, and therefore must inspect them or take other proper means to ascertain their condition. And if, by the exercise of reasonable care, he would have discovered the dangerous condition, he is liable." ' [Citation.]" (27 Cal.App.4th at p. 1134, italics in original.)

[5] Thus, a commercial landowner "cannot totally abrogate its landowner responsibilities merely by signing a lease. As the owner of property, a lessor out of possession must exercise due care and must act reasonably toward the tenant as well as to unknown third persons. [Citations.] At the time the lease is executed and upon renewal a landlord has a right to reenter the property, has control of the property, and must inspect the premises to make the premises reasonably safe from dangerous conditions. [Citations.] Even if the commercial landlord executes a contract which requires the tenant to maintain the property in a certain condition, the landlord is obligated at the time the lease is executed to take reasonable precautions to avoid unnecessary danger." (Mora v. Baker Commodities, Inc. (1989) 210 Cal.App.3d 771, 781 [258 Cal.Rptr. 669].) "However, the landlord's responsibility to inspect is limited. Like a residential landlord, the duty to inspect charges the lessor 'only with those matters which would have been disclosed by a reasonable inspection.' [Citations.] The burden of reducing or avoiding the risk and the likelihood of injury will affect the determination of what constitutes a reasonable inspection." (Id. at p. 782.)

[6] It is apparent from the allegations of paragraph 24 of the premises liability cause of action of the complaint, as well as Lopez's opposition to the summary judgment motion (see, e.g., Pultz v. Holgerson (1986) 184 Cal.App.3d 1110, 1114-1117 [229 Cal.Rptr. 531]), that one theory of liability asserted by Lopez is that the floor of the market was inherently defective and dangerous because it was "improperly 'finished' " and became slippery when littered with produce, and that Friedman knew, or should have known, **[45 Cal.App.4th 716]** that the combination of produce litter with the type of cement floor "constituted a dangerous condition and unreasonable risk of harm of which plaintiff was at all times mentioned unaware." Lopez presented evidence from which it reasonably can be inferred that it was common for the floor of the market to be littered with grapes. Thus, it is clear that Lopez is asserting liability based upon a condition which was not "transient." Rather, given the ongoing use of the market to sell grapes and the allegedly defective finish of the floor, the dangerous condition was allegedly recurring or continuous. Thus, both Friedman and the trial court erroneously assumed that the

only defective condition at issue in this case was the "transient" existence on the floor of the particular grapes involved in Lopez's slip and fall. The trial court's minute order thus erroneously characterizes the dangerous condition in this case as "transient" and as involving only the presence of the grapes on the floor at the time of Lopez's fall.

[7a] Friedman's motion failed to address the theory of liability based on the claims that the floor was improperly finished and defective when littered with produce; that it was common for produce to be on the floor; that such a floor posed an unreasonable danger to customers; and the condition existed for a sufficient amount of time to be revealed by a reasonable inspection by the landlord. Friedman thus failed to present evidence addressed to the issues of whether it had actual knowledge of the type and condition of the floor in the market, or whether it can reasonably be charged with such knowledge due to its right to inspect the premises under the lease.

Moreover, without a further description of the nature of the cement floor where Lopez slipped, it cannot be determined whether or not the floor presented an obvious danger, or whether it posed a hidden or latent danger when littered with grapes. For example, we do not know the color of the grapes or the floor. Whether obvious or not, if Friedman had actual knowledge, or can reasonably be charged with knowledge due to its right to inspect the premises, that the floor in the market was dangerous when littered with produce, which was a common condition, then Friedman would have a duty to use due care to protect people coming onto its land from the danger. (See Krongos v. Pacific Gas & Electric Co., supra, 7 Cal.App.4th at p. 395.) [8] "Generally, if a danger is so obvious that a person could reasonably be expected to see it, the condition itself serves as a warning, and the landowner is under no further duty to remedy or warn of the condition. [Citation.] However, this is not true in all cases. '[I]t is foreseeable that even an obvious danger may cause injury, if the practical necessity of encountering the danger, when weighed against the apparent risk involved, is such that under the circumstances, a person might choose to encounter the danger. ' " **[45 Cal.App.4th 717]** (Id. at p. 393.) [7b] In this case, Friedman has not provided sufficient information about the nature and condition of the floor or the nature or scope of any of its inspections of the premises, for us to determine with any particularity what conduct or inspection by Friedman would have been sufficient to discharge its duty to Lopez. Thus, Friedman's motion did not establish that it had discharged its duty to Lopez.

As the party moving for summary judgment, Friedman had the burden to show that it was entitled to judgment with respect to all theories of liability asserted by Lopez. As in Mora v. Baker Commodities, Inc., supra, Friedman's showing was insufficient to meet its burden as it did not show that at the time the lease was executed and renewed there was an inspection, nor "were facts presented bearing upon the necessity for an inspection, nor facts which showed that any inspection conducted was reasonable under the circumstances. Respondent's failure to provide these facts indicates that granting the summary judgment motion as to the negligence cause of action was inappropriate." (210 Cal.App.3d at p. 782, fn. omitted.)

Because Friedman's summary judgment motion did not address the primary theory of premises liability asserted by Lopez, we find inapposite those cases cited by Friedman, including Union Bank v. Superior Court (1995) 31 Cal.App.4th 573 [37 Cal.Rptr.2d 653], and Hunter v. Pacific Mechanical Corp., supra, 37 Cal.App.4th 1282, where defendants were able to prevail on summary judgment motions by showing respectively, with plaintiff's factually vague interrogatory responses (Union Bank) and deposition testimony (Hunter), that the plaintiff could not establish a necessary element of his cause of action. In the instant case, Friedman fails properly to define and address all theories of liability, and its separate statement of disputed facts fails to deal with the issue of the allegedly defective floor of the market and the issue of how rare or common an occurrence it was for grapes or produce to be on the floor of the market. Thus, as Friedman failed to meet its initial burden on summary judgment, the Union Bank line of cases is inapplicable.

We conclude that on the instant record the trial court erred in granting the motion for summary judgment.

**Disposition**

Let a peremptory writ of mandate issue directing the superior court to vacate its order granting summary judgment and to enter a new order **[45 Cal.App.4th 718]** denying Friedman's motion for summary judgment. The parties are to bear their own costs in this proceeding. Johnson, J., and Woods (Fred), J., concurred.

FN 1. Although our record contains only a June 5, 1995, minute order granting summary judgment, Lopez's notice of appeal refers to a June 22, 1995, summary judgment. Our record contains a cross-complaint for indemnity and declaratory relief by Friedman against Sam Scattaglia, doing business as Hubbard Farms; Scattaglia was also sued by Lopez as a Doe defendant; both the main action and Friedman's cross-complaint appear to be pending as to Scattaglia. Thus, the pendency of Friedman's cross-complaint prevents the entry of a final appealable judgment as to Friedman. (Holt v. Booth (1991) 1 Cal.App.4th 1074, 1081 [2 Cal.Rptr.2d 727].)

At time of oral argument, counsel for Lopez conceded that no summary judgment had been signed by the judge, however both parties have submitted the matter on the merits of the motion for summary judgment. Accordingly, in the interests of justice and judicial economy, we elect to exercise our discretion to treat the notice of appeal as a petition for writ of mandate. (See Morehart v. County of Santa Barbara (1994) 7 Cal.4th 725, 746 [29 Cal.Rptr.2d 804, 872 P.2d 143].) Inasmuch as the action appears to be proceeding as to a codefendant, it would best serve the interests of justice that the matter of the summary judgment in favor of Friedman be reviewed now to obviate possible multiple trials in this case.

**Appendix Form 2**

## SHEPARD'S CITATIONS

### Abbreviations - Analysis

**History of Case**

| | | |
|---|---|---|
| a | (affirmed) | Same case affirmed on appeal. |
| cc | (connected case) | Different case from case cited but arising out of same subject matter or intimately connect therewith. |
| D | (dismissed) | Appeal from same case dismissed. |
| De | (denied) | Review or rehearing denied. |
| Dp | (dismissed in part) | Appeal from same case dismissed in part. |
| GP | (granted and citable) | Review granted and ordered published. |
| Gr | (granted) | Review or rehearing granted. |
| m | (modified) | Same case modified on appeal. |
| Np | (not published) | Reporter of Decisions directed not to publish this opinion. |
| Op | (original opinion) | Citation of original opinion. |
| r | (reversed) | Same case reversed on appeal. |
| RE | (republished) | Reporter of Decisions directed to publish opinion previously ordered not published. |
| s | (same case) | Same case as cited. |
| S | (superseded) | Substitution for former opinion. |
| v | (vacated) | Same case vacated. |
| US cert den in | | Certiorari denied by U.S. Supreme Court. |
| US cert dis in | | Certiorari dismissed by U. S. Supreme Court. |
| US reh den in | | Rehearing denied by U.S. Supreme Court. |
| US reh dis in | | Rehearing dismissed by U.S. Supreme Court. |

| | |
|---|---|
| US app pndg in | Appeal pending before the U. S. Supreme Court. |
| US cert gran in | Certiorari granted by the U. S. Supreme Court. |

**Treatment of Case**

| | | |
|---|---|---|
| C | (criticized) | Soundness of decision or reasoning in cited case criticized for reasons given. |
| d | (distinguished) | Case at bar different either in law or fact from case cited for reasons given. |
| e | (explained) | Statement of import of decision in cited case. Not merely a restatement of the facts. |
| f | (followed) | Cited as controlling. |
| h | (harmonized) | Apparent inconsistency explained and shown not to exist. |
| j | (dissenting opinion) | Citation in dissenting opinion. |
| L | (limited) | Refusal to extend decision of cited case beyond precise issues involved. |
| o | (overruled) | Ruling in cited case expressly overruled. |
| p | (parallel) | Citing case substantially alike or on all fours with cited case in its law or facts. |
| q | (questioned) | Soundness of decision or reasoning in cited case questioned. |

**Other**

| | |
|---|---|
| # | Citing references may be of questionable precedential value as review was granted by California Supreme Court or case was ordered not published. |

**Operation of Order**

| | | |
|---|---|---|
| A | (amended) | Order amended. |
| E | (extended) | Provisions of an existing order extended or amplified in scope. |
| L | (limited) | Provisions of an order declared not to be extended. |

| | | |
|---|---|---|
| m | (modified) | Order modified. |
| R | (revoked or rescinded) | Existing order abrogated. |
| Rein | (reinstated) | Order reinstated. |
| Rp | (revoked or rescinded in part) | Existing order abrogated in part. |
| Rs | (repealed and superseded) | Abrogation of existing order and substitution of a new order therefore. |
| Rv | (revised) | Order revised. |
| S | (superseded) | New order substituted for an existing one. |
| Sd | (suspended) | Order suspended. |
| Sdp | (suspended in part) | Order suspended in part. |
| Sg | (supplementing) | New matter added to an existing order. |
| Sp | (superseded in part) | New matter substituted for part of an existing order. |

**Appendix Form 3**

**SAMPLE BRIEF**

Case No. CRF-92-877W

IN THE DISTRICT COURT OF CLEVELAND COUNTY

STATE OF OKLAHOMA

THE STATE OF OKLAHOMA,

Plaintiff,

-vs.-

ROBERT THOMAS JONES,

Defendant.

TRIAL BRIEF OF DEFENDANT

ROBERT THOMAS JONES

Name of Attorney
Firm Name
Street Address
City, State, Zip Code
Telephone Number
[Fax Number - Optional]
Attorneys for Defendant Robert Thomas Jones

[Date of Filing]

The caption or style of the case is the first information the court will read -- it must be correct. Be sure that the parties' names are correctly spelled and listed. Always proofread the case number for accuracy. A transposed number could easily cause your brief to be misfiled by the court clerk.

Depending on court rules and local custom, the next section of the trial brief will often be an index of the headings and subheadings within the body of the brief called a Table of Contents.

**TABLE OF CONTENTS**

TABLE OF AUTHORITIES ii

INTRODUCTION 1

STATEMENT OF THE CASE 2

ARGUMENT AND AUTHORITIES 4

I. EVIDENCE OF THE DEAD MAN'S HISTORY OF CRIMINAL ACTS SHOWS A PATTERN OF VIOLENCE 4

II. EVIDENCE ON THE ISSUE OF WHO WAS THE AGGRESSOR SHOULD BE ADMISSIBLE AT TRIAL 7

CONCLUSION 9

-i-

www.ingramcontent.com/pod-product-compliance
Lightning Source LLC
LaVergne TN
LVHW060020210926
848481LV00013B/3749